MONKEY BUSINESS THEATRE

The Loafer and the Buzzard, 1977. Photo copyright © Macduff Everton

Monkey Business Theatre

BY ROBERT M. LAUGHLIN AND SNA JTZ'IBAJOM

University of Texas Press ◆ Austin

This series was made possible through the generosity of
WILLIAM C. NOWLIN, JR., AND BETTYE H. NOWLIN,
the National Endowment for the Humanities,
and various individual donors.

Requests for permission to reproduce material from this work should be sent to:
PERMISSIONS
University of Texas Press
P.O. Box 7819
Austin, TX 78713-7819
www.utexas.edu/utpress/about/bpermission.html

♾ The paper used in this book meets the minimum requirements of ANSI/NISO
Z39.48-1992 (R1997) (Permanence of Paper).

LIBRARY OF CONGRESS CATALOGING-IN-PUBLICATION DATA

Laughlin, Robert M.
Monkey Business Theatre / by Robert M. Laughlin and Sna Jtz'ibajom. — 1st ed.
    p. cm. — (The Linda Schele Series in Maya and pre-Columbian studies)
Includes bibliographical references and index.
    ISBN 978-0-292-71759-6 (cl. : alk. paper)
1. Tzotzil drama. 2. Tzeltal drama. 3. Puppet theater—Mexico. 4. Mexican drama.
5. Teatro Lo'il Maxil. I. Sna Jtz'ibajom. II. Teatro Lo'il Maxil. III. Title.
PM4466.Z77L38 2008
897'.428208—dc22

                                                            2007046963

DEDICATED
TO THE
PRESENT
AND
PAST
MEMBERS
OF
SNA JTZ'IBAJOM

CONTENTS

The Visitors' Question

CARTER WILSON

FOR FIFTEEN YEARS, most of my opportunities to see the plays of the Monkey Business Theatre, Teatro Lo'il Maxil, have come about through the happy coincidence of being where the company was performing at the right moment. As a friend of cofounder Robert M. Laughlin and several of the original actors, I have always kept an eye on the performance's effect on the spectators, whether the show is *Torches for a New Dawn* presented in the plaza of Zinacantán for Mayan schoolchildren or Rogelio Román Hernández Cruz's *The World Turned on Its Head* acted before a glittery overflow crowd in the Salón Manuel Ponce at Mexico City's Palace of Fine Arts.

At the Theatre's San Cristóbal de las Casas headquarters in 2000, one select audience was made up of eight or nine North American indigenous artists—actors, dancers, poets, and a director—traveling together through southern Mexico to better acquaint themselves with Mayan culture, ancient and present-day. The room was not large, barely space enough for the backdrop curtain, the stage action, and some hard wooden chairs for the guests. The show Monkey Business presented that afternoon was *When Corn Was Born,* which features the fearsome red-coated Earth Lord, a scorpion, and a scad of scurrying ants played by finger puppets, plus kibbitzing and a helping hand for the poor humans of the piece from two of the ancient Mayan gods, portrayed by actors' voices and huge puppet heads peering down from above the backdrop.

Several of the visitors had been trained in New York and were acquainted with the style of Ralph Lee, who had been coming annually to develop and stage a play with Monkey Business Theatre. In the discussion following the performance, the guests asked how much of what they had just seen was Ralph Lee and how much came out of the troupe's own indigenous traditions.

At first, the actors did not answer. The question seemed to have generated some tension, as though the guests had reservations about what they had just seen. Then company member Juan de la Torre made a short speech, pointing out that the Maya have preserved their languages and culture through the more than five hundred years since the arrival of the European invaders. And this they have done, he said, in the face of heavy opposition and disrespect, and with virtually no help from government agencies or other outside sources.

Juan's speech pleased the Native American artists. They began offering songs in their own languages as thanks to the Monkey Business actors, and then there was an exchange of handshakes and *abrazos* all around.

Most people in the outside world are aware that the ancient Maya had a fully functional writing system based on glyphs, and many may know that the modern descendants of the Maya maintain a rich oral story culture. But they know less about Mayan literacy, written literature, and dramatic traditions, either in the deep past or the present. The following brief sketch of this heritage provides a good introduction to the Monkey Business Theatre's first collection of plays, especially since, even though they usually perform in Spanish, Monkey Business is an important contributor to a vital movement to revive Mayan literacy and literature and to keep Mayan culture vital.

On a July day in 1562, less than fifty years into the Spanish occupation of the Yucatán Peninsula, Friar Diego de Landa, a Franciscan, had five thousand Mayan idols destroyed at the town of Maní and burned the twenty-seven Mayan books he could lay his hands on. Though Landa could not read the texts, he was convinced they must be full of lies perpetrated by the Devil. At the time, Landa's newly converted Indian flock "regretted" the destruction of their books "to an amazing degree," as Landa noted. It caused them, he said, "great affliction."

The Mayan glyphic writing system was a key accomplishment of a civilization that was nearly two thousand years old when the Spanish came along. No one really knows how many people in the Mayas' city-states could actually read and write, but archaeologists think maybe only 2 percent could write, most of them men, but some women as well. Nevertheless, the relatively small number who were literate were key contributors to social life and included not only ruling lords and ladies, but also the astronomers who interpreted the past in order to predict the future, prized artisans, the medical practitioners who could divine your illness and cast it from your body, the storytellers, and probably some of the professional entertainers. Friar Landa reported that those who could read and write did not always tout their skill in public, but they would have books buried with them, presumably so they could use them again in the next life.

From almost the beginning of their era, the Maya put writing everywhere: on brightly painted murals, on the carved stone pillars known as stelae, on the risers of magnificent flights of stairs, on the rims of ceramic pots, on carved seashell or polished bone jewelry, and even on the bodies of human figures in bas-relief sculpture. In scenes depicting court life, busy little supernatural writer rabbits scribble down the words of the powerful. When human scribes are pictured, they sometimes look harassed, with huge, messy clutches of pens stuck in their hair.

Even if only an educated elite knew how to produce the glyphs, ordinary people must have been able to comprehend much of what they saw on buildings and monuments. Public writing touted the accomplishments of rulers, thus functioning as billboards or character posters do in our times.

Reading and writing connected humanity to the divine. As poet Ámbar Past reminds us in *Incantations by Mayan Women,* the wife of the great god Itzamna was believed to have created the universe by writing it. The memory of writing's old power remains in modern Mayan beliefs and metaphors. In the Chiapas *municipio* of Zinacantán, the two unmarried scribes who keep the schedule for officials entering on religious obligations are known collectively as "the holy torch, the holy mirror."

The conceit that writing equals creating becomes even more resonant when we remember that in Mayan languages the acts of writing and painting are usually not distinguished from one another. The four rediscovered Mayan texts that the Spanish did not destroy bear little resemblance to modern mass-produced books. The pages, accordion-pleated like a road map, were covered in a white lime wash, then drawn upon and colored on both sides with a rich combination of writing, astronomical data, and intricate cartoon figures, most of them deities but often engaged in obviously human occupations such as digging holes and dropping in kernels of corn. No wonder the Maya who observed Landa's auto-da-fé at Maní were "greatly afflicted." It was their collective knowledge that the friar had consigned to the flames.

As colonizers, the Spanish found themselves with too few soldiers and priests to govern so large a native population effectively. Outlawing the old writing had symbolic force and was one aspect of a program to establish political and spiritual control through intimidation. During three centuries of colonial life and well into the modern period, limiting access to Spanish proved wise, as did the policy begun in the Invasion of emphasizing differences between Indian communities and keeping them pitted against one another. Without literacy, indigenous people faced enormous difficulties proving title to their land. Without "learning," Indians could not advance to the Catholic priesthood.

Despite the cleverness of the whites (or Ladinos, as they are called in Chiapas and Guatemala), there were still attempts to overthrow the Europeans, notably in Chiapas in 1712 and 1867, and in the Caste War of Yucatán, which began in 1848 and divided the peninsula into hostile nations, Maya and white, for more than sixty years. In each case, the whites noted disparate and usually antagonistic groups of Indians banded together and went to war when they discovered they shared a grievance (an onerous new tax, an increase in the cost of baptism, land grabs by Ladinos). The Maya, however, conceived of the problems as belonging to the spiritual realm. In their view, *they* were more true to the teachings of Jesus than the Ladinos.

Though 150 years apart, the Chiapas insurrections were alike in that both began with young women, girls really, announcing they had been asked by heavenly beings to found a new, Indian-only religion. The wisdom of keeping Indians illiterate was verified by the fact that in all three rebellions the male leaders turned out to have had some education in Spanish. At vast public meetings during the Caste War of Yucatán, the wooden "Speaking Crosses" venerated by the rebels addressed the faithful in tiny voices (probably ventriloquized by men or boys hidden below or behind an altar). The Crosses also dictated letters to encourage or threaten their allies in distant villages.

The ban on indigenous literacy had never been absolute. Soon after the Europeans' military control was secured in the 1520s, the priests began tutoring a select few, mostly sons of Mayan caciques, in Spanish. The intention was to build a loyal cadre of literate Indian vassals to assist in maintaining control. Among the religious were a few who also put great effort into learning Mayan culture from their students, desiring to know their new charges' hearts in order to save their souls. But they were sometimes also dangerously drawn to the gentility and artfulness of Mayan daily life (ironically, Diego de Landa himself was one of these; he set his findings down in a manuscript dated 1566 called *Relación de las cosas de Yucatan,* which became the first book-length ethnography of a Mayan people).

Teaching Spanish to an elite few while prohibiting the old writing system had an unexpected effect. These Maya began at once to employ the new alphabet to save the old knowledge before it was lost. The *Popol Vuh,* the epic of the K'iche' Maya of highland Guatemala, was probably set down first in K'iche' around 1555. Its authors spoke directly to the urgency of their task and the necessity for secrecy since the old order had apparently passed away and the K'iche' were forced to live in the shadow of the Christian cross. In the Yucatán, incantations and spells to drive out illness were rendered in alphabetic Mayan toward the end of the eighteenth century in the *El ritual de los Bacabes*

[The ritual of the Bacabes] (Arzápalo Marín 1987). Beautiful lyrics from before the Invasion, most likely originally sung in chorus, were preserved in *El libro de los cantares de Dzibalché* [The book of songs of Dzibalché] (Barrera Vasquez 1965). And throughout the colonial period, priests of the old religion continued under cover to write history in the preferred Mayan way. Since they conceived of time moving in great circles rather than in a line, events in what a European mind would conceive of as "the past" were often prophesied instead (the coming of the Spanish, for example, is "predicted" after the event). These works are found in *El libro de los libros de Chilam Balam* [The book of the books of Chilam Balam] (1963). Fourteen of them survive, and another five are known to have existed. Some of the *Chilams* were composed over several centuries, with a number of authors adding to each one.

Like the surviving painted books, many of the colonial Mayan texts were effectively "lost" for many years. Collected by antiquarians and European or North American travelers with little idea of what they had found, the works moldered away for centuries in libraries and manuscript collections. Their rediscovery and the new, better-informed readings of them in the second half of the twentieth century constitute the resurrection of a classic literature the outside world had little idea ever existed.

The rediscovery came during a critical period for the more than eight million modern Mayas of southern Mexico, Guatemala, and Belize. Along with other struggles, they now face the question of whether to continue living in traditional ways and speaking their own languages. The alternative would be to adopt Spanish (or, in parts of Belize, English) and the mindset of modernity. But when Mayan people make that choice, persistent racism almost inevitably forces them to enter mass society on the lowest rung of the ladder.

One reason that Mayan culture has endured in the Chiapas and Guatemalan highlands is that until very recently, indigenous people lived largely outside the national economies, called upon to link into them only as a part-time or seasonal workforce. In Chiapas, through the middle decades of the twentieth century, Indian men who could not make a living in the Highlands as corn farmers traveled down to "hot country" to pick coffee. In Guatemala, as Rigoberta Menchú (1984) recalls in her autobiography, whole families made the journey each year. In both countries, plantation conditions were barely human (the subject of Monkey Business Theatre's ironically titled *Let's Go to Paradise!*). Yet at least at the end of the contract the exhausted workers, often ill from hot-country diseases, went home to places where people spoke the same language and treated each other like human beings and not dogs. Today, for the million Maya who have gone to the United States in search of work, "home" is much farther away.

Though the plantation system is not dead, in the last thirty or so years it has been superseded by a more encompassing economic order. In the new vision of governmental and global planners, indigenous people should not be differentiated from others in the great pool of mobile job-seekers and active consumers. Mexico's former president Salinas de Gortari's putting an end to the *ejido* system, through which the poor might still obtain land of their own, stands as only the best example of the neoconservatives' push. Traditional life comes under attack from all sides—as inefficient, embarrassingly backward, or, most simply, boring.

Not surprisingly, attacks often focus on language. Deprived of their book-centered culture almost five hundred years ago, today's Maya are derided for their illiteracy and any hesitancy they have about learning Spanish. Otherwise well-informed journalists still describe indigenous languages as incomprehensible. As Robert Laughlin notes in this volume, a fashion persists for calling the languages *dialectos,* a way of making them appear less, somehow, than Spanish. In the 1960s, when I was first studying in Chiapas, a huge billboard beside the main road into the Tzotzil communities announced that 200,000 indigenous people lived in these hills, "95 percent of whom remain ignorant of Spanish." The sign was the work of INI, the Instituto Nacional Indigenista (National Indian Institute), whose primary purpose was to aid indigenous communities through educational, health, and agricultural programs. In INI schools, beginning students were taught the written forms of their own language, but only as a way of introducing the Spanish phonemic system. After the first two years, instruction in Mayan disappeared entirely. As a government agency, INI's responsibility was to integrate Mexico's remaining Indians into the national economy, not to support tradition.

Despite such efforts, absorption of the Maya into the mainstream did not proceed at the desired pace, largely because Mayan-speaking people began to attain a new sense of themselves, both as Maya and as political actors. A civil war broke out in Guatemala in the mid-1960s and continued at varying degrees of intensity for thirty years. The conflict made many Mayan people more critically aware that although they constitute a sizeable majority in the country, their share of national resources and citizens' rights is very small. When hundreds of thousands of them fled to the Mexican state of Chiapas to escape genocidal massacre at the hands of the Guatemalan Army in the early 1980s, the only people who housed and fed them at first were poor Mayan farmers like themselves.

In 1992, the state of Chiapas organized a grand congress of indigenous leaders from around the hemisphere to commemorate the 500th anniversary of the arrival of Columbus. The proceedings took place in the city of San Cristóbal de las Casas, a Ladino mountain bastion surrounded by indigenous *municipios*. During the congress, activists toppled a statue of Diego de Mazariegos, the conquistador responsible for subjugating the Highland Maya in the sixteenth century. The statue has not yet been put back on its pedestal.

Two years later, the armed Zapatistas appeared out of the Lacandón jungle and briefly occupied four Chiapas towns. Made up mostly of Mayas, the EZLN (Ejército Zapatista de Liberación Nacionál, or Zapatista Army of National Liberation) has since evolved into a political force with the aim of convincing the Mexican people to support autonomy and social justice for the country's indigenous citizens. Whatever else the EZLN may accomplish, it has galvanized consciousness among the Maya in Chiapas. For example, the five-day seizure of San Cristóbal encouraged Indians from the surrounding communities to treat the city as though it belonged to them even after the Zapatistas had melted back into the jungle. The change is much remarked locally, and by old-time San Cristóbal residents, with displeasure.

Approval of the Zapatistas in Highland Maya communities has been widespread but not universal. Generally, people in the poorer *municipios* have been more sympathetic. Those who are better off, like the Zinacantecs, or who have higher hopes for what the state or federal government might do for them, like the Chamulans, have been more circumspect.

Although the war in Guatemala and the Zapatista movement in Chiapas drew world attention, a less widely publicized effort to advance Mayan pride—or, better said, to restore it—has also been made. In both Guatemala and Mexico, cultural activists are focusing on Mayan literacy and the creation of a new literature by indigenous authors. They are committed to the idea that their traditions and the thirty-one Mayan languages still spoken are noble assets, not liabilities. They employ classes in schools, radio and television programs, and theatrical presentations to revive languages that appear to be on the wane. Most activists imagine a synergized future in which the stigma of indigenous illiteracy will be entirely wiped away, and the Mayas will function equally well in their home languages and in Spanish. (In language politics, ironically, preservation is most often the progressive, or even the radical, course of action.) In Guatemala, indigenous linguists at the Academia de las Lenguas Mayas (Academy of Mayan Languages) worked out a unified orthography to replace the confusing historical higgle-piggle of styles that different transcribers had employed over the centuries. The result is a writing system that emphasizes similarities across Guatemalan languages, which advances pan-Mayanism by making it easier for a native speaker of one Mayan language to understand or acquire others.

In its twenty-four years of existence, Sna Jtz'ibajom, Monkey Business Theatre's parent organization, has been heavily involved in offering adult education classes in Tzotzil and Tzeltal in the highland Chiapas communities. But since Spanish has become a lingua franca, especially for younger Mayas, Monkey Business decided on Spanish as the language for its plays in order to reach the widest possible audience. However, as Robert Laughlin points out in his chronicle of the Theatre's history, the actors themselves are so at home in various languages that at times they have agreed—in the van, say, on the way to give a show—to present that afternoon in Tzotzil, translating their own lines as they go along.

Though the plays may be performed in Spanish, the point of view is resolutely indigenous. It can be startling when Ladinos appear on the scene because of how completely Indian the world of the drama has been up to that moment. The indigenous characters are good and bad and struggle with moral issues, but the plays' Ladinos are stereotypes, comic windup toys who first appear menacing and then, usually, ludicrous in their unbridled greed or lust. The notable exception is the character of Erasto Urbina in *Let's Go to Paradise!* Urbina is a historical figure, considered a Ladino even though his mother was Mayan. In the 1930s, under a mandate from President Lázaro Cárdenas, Urbina worked to strengthen Indian communities as political entities and to get them out from under the thumb of conservative whites. A confrontational and apparently fearless individual, Urbina achieved the status of a hero among indigenous people for his advocacy in their favor.

The plays are presented here in the order they were created, between 1990 and 2003. This sequence allows readers to get a feeling for how the company responded to the changes taking place around them. The Zapatista offensive of January 1994 brought two-thirds of the Mexican Army into the state, as well as hundreds of journalists. Indian communities were forced to declare themselves "pro-Zapatista" or "loyal" to the Mexican government, a difficult and in some ways false set of alternatives. As Robert Laughlin points out, the Monkey Business troupe responded to the situation with plays that were more critical of the existing order. But they resisted the either/or of pro- or anti-Zapatista, understanding how that choice would polarize their home communities and work against a growing collective Mayan spirit. In works like *From All for All* they turned instead to traditional solutions, especially to the idea of restoring human concord through intelligence and compromise, and living in harmony with nature—all methods the old Mayan deities would heartily approve of.

As literary creators, Monkey Business members are in step with other authors who invoke the ancient Mayas' literary achievements and cyclical view of time to characterize their own movement as the *rebirth* of a writing tradition rather than as a cultural development imitative of European forms. Monkey Business's *Jaguar Dynasty* attempts to revitalize the legends of the old Mayas for their living descendants. *Torches for a New Dawn* undertakes a revisionist version of colonial history that features, among other things, Landa's burning of the books and the role of enforced illiteracy in the long oppression of Mayan people.

In his own introductory remarks, Monkey Business's Robert Laughlin recalls the early struggles that the troupe had in projecting their voices and gesturing "large," not at all the "proper," self-effacing behavior dictated by their upbringing. Laughlin also mentions how little experience of Western-style theatre the actors had to draw on at first. But if the definition of theatre is enlarged to include fiesta performances and some of the dramatic rituals of daily life, then today's Mayas are the inheritors of a long and, in some cases, uninterrupted tradition of drama and spectacle.

What is surprising about Mayan public celebration is how much the Europeans allowed it to remain as it had been before the Invasion. Again, a principal reason was the colonizers' inability to put an end to the natives' fiestas, together with their failure to understand how much of the old theology was embodied in the rituals. The events must have been grand in the old days—in his *Relación*, Diego de Landa describes occasions in the Yucatán in the 1540s and 1550s when eight hundred men danced together in step to music.

One surviving verse and dance drama, *Rabinal Achí: A Mayan Drama of War and Sacrifice* (Tedlock 2003), takes place in an entirely pre-Christian world of heroes, royal captives, slaves, and Mayan gods. It is still performed today in K'iche' in the Guatemalan town of Rabinal. Dennis Tedlock, the play's English translator, says that for almost two hundred years during the colonial period, Ladino authorities repeatedly banned works like *Rabinal Achí* on the grounds that they contained references to the barbaric practice of human sacrifice. Such seditious plays remained popular, however, and Tedlock believes this is because they kept alive the memory of the time when the Mayas controlled their own society.

Diego de Landa commends the mimetic skills of native actors in his *Relación*. They would "hire themselves to the Spaniards for nothing other than to observe the jests the Spaniards pass with their servants, their wives, and on themselves" and would later imitate (or burlesque) their masters "with as much art as attentive Spaniards could" (36).

Mayan murals and ceramic vases are populated with antic dancers, musicians, and comic actors in elaborate costumes. Archaeologist Karl Taube argues that many figures once thought to be part-animal/part-anthropomorphic gods are actually actors or dancers dressed as deities, with their human hands and feet visible under their fancy garments or their faces peering out from behind their masks. The distinction is subtle but valuable. If the paintings depict performances, they tell us more about which mythic themes got acted out in the old days.

Major characters found in the paintings have survived into the twenty-first century. The jaguar god, widely depicted, still prances through many modern Mayan festivities. Continuity from the time before the Europeans can also be traced in the ongoing observance of the old calendar's five-day evil or danger-filled month called the *uayeb,* which marked the end of one year and the beginning of another. Mockery was apparently as potent a force in earlier Mayan society as it is today, and the *uayeb* was the period when ridicule could make its palpable sting in the context of laughter and buffoonery, with no harm done.

The ancient Mayas idealized their lords when they were young, portraying them in paint or stone as paragons of beauty and heroic character. But while respect for older people was a widely held value, as the "tired" old year was winding down, ageing rulers were subject to being made fun of. The *uayeb* fell usually in the month of February in the Gregorian calendar, near the Europeans' Carnival (*Carnavál* in Spanish, *Mardi Gras* in French). In Mayan-speaking towns in the Yucatán today, the pre-Lenten holiday is ruled over by a scamp named Juan Carnavál. In Tecoh, he plays scurrilous tricks to mock the authorities, such as leaving his bicycle outside the mayor's wife's window, implying that he is in her bed. In Hocobá, as Mayanist Victoria Bricker reports, when Juan and his cohorts are finally brought to trial for their misdeeds, their lewd responses to accusations about their drinking, stealing, and happily prostituting themselves to homosexuals make it obvious they are unrepentant. Whether Juan Carnavál is a European character or a Mayan one makes no difference since he so clearly represents a melding of Old and New World traditions.

On feast days in Europe the Church sponsored religious dramas performed for huge crowds, usually in the courtyard or on the steps of a cathedral or other great church. In Mesoamerica the priests imagined theatre as a way of converting the natives in large numbers and providing them with moral instruction. Often they wrote the plays themselves and then had them translated and performed by "their" Indians. In Momostenango, in the Guatemalan highlands, they still perform dance dramas that sixteenth-century Spanish Dominicans collaborated on with indigenous members of the old elite highly versed in classic

Mayan cosmology. As a result, the nominal subject of an Easter week play may be the Passion of Jesus Christ, but according to anthropologist Garret W. Cook, the theme that comes out most strongly is the renewal of the Mayan year.

Less is known about how the pageantry of the highland Chiapas fiestas evolved. On the surface they resemble Spanish celebrations of Christian saints' days. Volunteer "religious" officials engage in long sessions of prayer, drinking, sharing meals, changing the vestments of the figures of saints, and bearing them from the church in public parades through the town. Other official groups organized on military models run clutches of huge, colorful cloth banners to and fro across the plaza. Music plays all day and into the night: ancient flute and drum; Spanish-descended harp, guitar, and violin; a hired brass oompah band—or all three at once, competing with the Mexican ranchera or hip-hop music emanating from the bars and the stalls of hucksters in the market. Skyrockets whistle into the air and explode, and hand-held "bombs" go off like cannons everywhere. The Catholic church and the plaza before it are the focal point, and the people of the *municipio* the audience. But as in a multi-ring circus, several dramas may play out at once, some in the homes or courtyards of the officials, and others along the streets, up at springs or crosses in the surrounding hills, or down by the river. At peak moments, the whole town can be transformed into the locus of the action, which is fitting since the big fiestas are complex pastiches or collages of historical events and Mayan and Christian legends, not so much reenacted as recalled by allusion. Fiestas play out in "real" days and hours, of course, but they are also occasions when time (at least in the Western sense) comes unglued and everything happens at once.

As in Guatemala, fiestas in Chiapas are populated with many characters from Mayan rather than Catholic traditions. Figures such as the *j'ik'aletik,* or black men, and the *max,* or monkeys, are especially prominent in year-change or year-renewal festivities. Both *j'ik'aletik* and *max* have pre-Hispanic ancestry and disruptive duties: they frighten the children, make fun of authority, and feed the chaos, work which is also considered special and holy. Other characters—such as Nana María Cocorina in Chamula, a relentlessly lusty woman played by a man—come from regional history. "She" attempts to distract officials from their serious business by sitting on their laps and making lewd propositions. Anthropologists have accounted for the male transvestite actors as reinforcing conservative indigenous sexual norms by parodying Ladino women as wantons. A character like the bumptious, rude blonde secretary Socorro in Monkey Business's *From All for All,* who is played by a man and always gets big laughs, thus stands in a theatrical tradition well over five hundred years old of rude burlesquing of those in power.

Just forty years ago, "entertainment" for indigenous people in highland Chiapas still consisted almost entirely of the spectacle of the fiesta and storytelling in the home. Today the range of choices is much broader. An adolescent boy at a fiesta can spend a few pesos to sit in a darkened room with his pals and watch *Rambo* movie videos. The soundtrack is broadcast outside to advertise the show, adding the voice of Hollywood schlock to the festive hubbub. With electrification, Mexican radio and television shows reach the *municipios,* and young people listen to their Walkmans as they hike the familiar paths home.

There are some promising uses for the newly available technologies. Local radio broadcasting in Mayan languages, for instance, contributes to communication between the communities and thus to Mayan solidarity. And traditional life may not be affected as much as we might imagine by the onslaught of mass media since indigenous people rarely find themselves reflected there. When an indigenous female "type" is called for in a TV advertisement, she is usually played by a light-skinned, blue-eyed young woman in pigtails—the pigtails being the chief clue to her being an Indian. The cliché about the Zapatistas is that they have been more effective as media specialists than as armed insurgents. Though their leader, Subcomandante Marcos, is not Maya, since 1994 the EZLN has provided the only voice widely heard for the 12 percent of Mexican people who are indigenous and for the country's great number of other disenfranchised poor as well.

In its own way, the Monkey Business Theatre also confronts the relative absence of a principled indigenous viewpoint in the larger popular culture. That their plays would each have a clear moral was a goal that emerged in the beginning of the group's creative process. A play, of course, will not reach an audience of the size the mass media can command. However, I am not thinking here of numbers, but of the experience of seeing the stories you grew up with dramatized, or the world you inhabit at last represented. This, I believe, is a principal reason Monkey Business plays are so enthusiastically received when they are staged in the *municipios* or for migrant workers living in bad conditions in rural Florida. Historical authenticity can be proven by tracing the antecedents of a creative endeavor, but another sort of authenticity is present when the work connects at once with what matters to its core audience. That is what the Monkey Business Theatre's plays have done now for more than a decade and a half.

Recollections of a Ghost

RALPH LEE

ONE JANUARY MORNING IN 1989, I found myself in a clearing surrounded by scrubby woods on the outskirts of the old provincial capital of Chiapas, San Cristóbal de las Casas. I was guiding a group of somewhat bewildered Mayan Indians through a series of physical and vocal warm-ups designed for actor training. The situation was probably as unlikely for them as it was for me. They responded dutifully but with little display of enthusiasm. Most of them were in their twenties, with the exception of one sedate older man who withdrew from active participation. Some were quite stiff and found it difficult to move their limbs independently from other parts of their bodies. Others had a more comfortable rapport with their physicality. One woman was frozen with a mix of terror and determination. Also present was a Mexican writer, an associate of the group who acted as my interpreter. He made it clear that he had some experience with theatre and counted himself my ally. Robert Laughlin, who had invited me to run this workshop, joined in the exercises vigorously. Prior to my coming to Mexico, he had expressed concern as to whether the participants would take to the notion of doing theatre, since it meant assuming the role of another person, a character in a play. In doing so, one ran the risk of losing one's soul in the process. Also present was Peter Canby, a writer doing research for a book on Chiapas. I had met Peter a year earlier at a Christmas party in New York City; I had described my search for folk material from Mexico for a play with my theatre company. Peter had said, "I know exactly who you should talk to." It was Bob Laughlin. And that's how it all began. That, plus a nod from the Librarian of Meso-American Studies at Princeton, Alfred Bush, who had seen a production of mine based on Yup'ik Eskimo material in New York and thought I might be good for the job.

After the warm-ups I had the group embark on some standard improvisations: one of them would get up and engage in an activity: planting seeds in a garden, reading a newspaper, making tortillas. One by one, others joined. Situations developed. Conflicts erupted. The characters and their relationships became clear. We observers were dumbfounded. These folks had obviously been acting, playing roles their whole lives; they knew what this was all about. It was second nature to them. If the improvisation they were performing took place in the market in San Cristóbal, they would speak Spanish. If it were located in their home, Tzotzil was spoken. As they continued, we felt we were privy to events and behavior that outsiders would otherwise never have an opportunity to witness. There was no self-consciousness; they would easily engage in each theatrical moment as it evolved. They would burst into uproarious laughter at their own jokes, puns, and double entendres. Much of the humor sailed right over my head, and past Bob's as well, despite his fluency in Tzotzil.

Some members of the group displayed more promise than others, but the possibility of them coming up with a theatrical production was not out of the question. We moved forward, continuing the improvisations and exercises, but beginning to focus on a play. We had three weeks. Before I came to Chiapas, I had read many stories collected by Bob from the Highland Maya. There were several on the theme of the lazy man and the *zopilote* (the buzzard). We agreed that they would make a good short play. Palas, our translator, was given the task of writing the script. Maryan (see appendix 1 for full names), a leader in his community who later became mayor of Chamula, seemed a likely candidate for the *zopilote*. He was tall and confident, with a zany sense of humor, and he could move with freedom. Manvel had a good head on his shoulders and was alert and responsible—a little stiff, but that could be used for comic effect. He would be the lazy husband who trades places with the *zopilote* in his search for the easy life. The central character in the play, around whom the action revolves, is the wife. Chavela, who had recently joined the group, would play the part. As time went on, I learned her story. She had left her village at an early age to become a maid in San Cristóbal. Her boss, an American woman, had undertaken her education. She had witnessed her husband's death in a car accident, and she was raising a son, then around ten years old. When she first came to Sna Jtz'ibajom, she fell into the traditional woman's role: mopping the floor, tidying up, waiting on the men. But that was not why she was there; she wanted to act, create theatre.

As rehearsals proceeded, I tried to give the actors specific tasks to do in the scenes to help anchor them in the reality of the play. It was not all easy going. Maryan was great at improvising scenes but had a hard time remembering lines. He could move with ease but could not remember from which side of the scene to enter. Manvel had a clear idea of what to do, though often after he had rehearsed a scene, he would no longer engage as fully in it as he had when it was fresh. Chavela slowly took her place at the center of the piece, but she was very guarded. It took a lot of coaxing and persuasion to woo her out of her shell. The discomfort of taking a risk can be hard to bear. The other three actors in the show, who functioned as a sort of chorus of nosey neighbors, shuffled a bit and stared at the ground, but they became a forceful presence. Tziak, one of this group, had energy to spare but often arrived late to rehearsal from playing basketball. As time went on, his participation in forward-thinking politics increased, and he was often a strong voice for Sna Jtz'ibajom at presentations and conferences.

The day of the first performance arrived. I had spearheaded the fabrication of a many-colored curtain on a freestanding frame for a backdrop, a big beaked mask and wings for the *zopilote,* and other props. Traditional Zinacantec clothing had been found for the actors. Although we were scheduled for a rehearsal that morning, Maryan did not appear. He had no phone and lived in a distant Chamulan hamlet. We waited until it was decided that someone would have to take his part. Xun was the obvious choice. He and his brother Antun were the sons of Romin Teratol, Bob's teacher in his earlier research in Zinacantán. They both emerged as fine actors and prime movers in the company. Xun had been an efficient prompter in rehearsals and miraculously knew all the *zopilote*'s lines as well as the blocking. What a sweet surprise, straight out of show business!

We set up our stage in the courtyard of Na Bolom, since 1950 the home of Frans and Gertrude Blom, pioneers in research among the Maya and Lacandón, and now a haven for Mayan studies. An audience, primarily anthropologists and other scholars, assembled. At that time the group was reluctant to perform in their own villages for fear of being laughed at and compromised. Antzelmo, the elder in the group, a shaman, welcomed the audience. I said a few words with the help of Palas's translation, which somehow sounded more flowery than the statements I was making. The show went on without a hitch: much laughter and applause. Xun was so confident in his role that we all forgot he had not been rehearsing it for weeks. The big surprise for everyone was Chavela. That afternoon she battled away her fear and came out loud and strong.

I went to Chiapas to work with Sna Jtz'ibajom for twelve years, one month each year. Each time we put together a new theatre piece. Early on, Chip Morris, who had spent years helping the native women revive traditional weaving methods and start a weavers' collective, had warned me not to become too attached, too indispensable; otherwise, the group would not grow on its own. I was also concerned that my notions might put too much of a stamp on their work, but as time went on, I worried less. If I proposed something they thought inappropriate, they would reject it. It was clear that they were making choices. It was also clear that the form of theatre I had been developing with the company I directed in New York shared many of the same requirements as Sna Jtz'ibajom: to be compact, portable, spare, yet highly visual and colorful. Both were involved with storytelling, bringing alive myths and traditions. The exception was that here I was working with the people who were the direct inheritors of these stories. This was a rare privilege for me.

Our second play was based on stories of the *Cimarrón* (Spook), an unsavory, black-faced, bat-like bogeyman who waylays travelers out too late and women alone by the hearth. I wanted to get a clearer sense of this individual's character and his physical traits. At our first rehearsal I asked the group to tell me about him. Much colorful and revealing information came forth, some contrasting and contradictory. Finally Antzelmo spoke up, "The time I saw one . . . ," and continued to describe a time when he was walking home at night. A *cimarrón* had appeared and barred his path. A knock-down fight ensued, which Antzelmo barely survived. In our play we were not dealing with a picturesque notion from times gone by but a tangible force to be reckoned with. At one performance of this play a whole passel of little girls spent the entire time trembling underneath a big blanket. Occasionally one would peek out to see if the way was clear, then withdraw to safety in a flash.

I saw the group become a working company with all the familiar rhythms of touring productions: packing, schlepping, and setting up. Some of my fondest memories are of performances that took place in remote hamlets, where the primary language was Tzotzil, and they would instantaneously translate their lines from Spanish into their mother tongue. They seemed to add all kinds of jokes—the shows lasted much longer—and the colorful musicality and lilt in the speaking of the dialogue made it a magical experience.

After a few years the group took over the playwriting. They wanted the dialogue to reflect their particular thought processes and turns of phrase more accurately. This was a rather arduous and drawn out process. The whole company was usually present, though only a few individuals were active contributors. Unless I objected, discussions were in Tzotzil, which left me out of the process. For years I begged them to write the play before I got there, but that never happened. Often not even the theme of the new production had been determined in advance of my arrival. For many days they would sit and quibble over a turn of phrase. Sometimes I supplied a plot line. For *¡Vámonos al paraíso!* (*Let's Go to Paradise!*)—the play based on the conscription of Mayan workers for the German-run coffee plantations in the lowlands—they were moving toward a heavy melodrama about servitude and the tragic separation of family members. I suggested that the central character might be a trickster, a kind of buffoon who made fun of and played jokes on the bullying foremen and bosses often responsible for exacting cruel, punishing labor from the Mayan workers. The group seized on this idea, and the show became a rollicking slapstick comedy that still described the harrowing conditions on the fincas in vivid colors.

One of their most popular plays *De todos para todos* (*From All for All*), written when the Zapatista uprising was in full swing, was the result of a compromise. The Chamulans and Tziak from Tenejapa wanted a play that dealt with the political and economic conflicts then on everyone's minds. The Zinacantecs, customarily more conservative, proposed a play based on folk ecology. The two elements were combined, and the resulting play showed in an exciting way how traditional values and the present crisis affect each other, and that the individual cannot afford to lose sight of either one.

Most of the people in the group had tough, compact bodies. They appeared to have done more than their share of hard, physical work. Their spirits seemed to need lifting. If I could loosen up their bodies, it would loosen up their minds and get their creative juices flowing. One exercise, in particular, involving movement phrases and nonverbal sound came from my time with the Open Theater in New York. In this exercise it is important to jump right in without thinking, to go with your first impulse. It can be very freeing and also very revealing. Particular moves showed up time and again, such as clutching the lower leg, limping and making sounds of pain, or flying like an airplane, arms outspread, with the sound of the engine and bombs dropping, or repeatedly grabbing at imaginary food and gulping it down in a frenzy. Were these gestures chosen simply because they were easy choices when one was on the spot, or did they express something about the shared inner anxieties and preoccupations of these people? It was often harder for the women than the men. Their lives had been more guarded, more sheltered: they were not used to letting loose, especially around the men. But as time went on, they achieved a strong, energized group dynamic that found its way into performance.

The group initially had a poorly developed sense of rhythm. If a dance step was involved, or a unison group movement, a lot of drilling was required. But that also changed over the years. There were occasions—some in rehearsal, some of them social—when we all danced together. Those were particularly joyous times.

In a country where there is such a rich tradition of masks, the Highland Maya of Chiapas are an exception. I taught them simple ways to make papier-mâché masks. Old crones, poisonous toads, ceremonial jaguars, Earth Lords, jungle animals, German gentry, and don Tomate took on vivid visual representation. The mask of the *Cimarrón* migrated from Sna Jtz'ibajom back to Zinacantán, where he is now a regular feature in the traditional carnival.

Members of the company came and went. Chavela and Petu', another very strong performer, left to create a theatre for women, FOMMA (Fortaleza de la Mujer Maya [The Strength of Mayan Women]), which has received a lot of attention and has made a valuable contribution to redefining the role of women in indigenous society. Both of them are published playwrights. Many other promising performers and contributing members of the group have moved on. While they were with Sna Jtz'ibajom, they brought exuberant, infectious life to their performances. It's difficult for me, the theatre die-hard, to imagine why they would want to be anywhere else. Their commitment to the work and the life of the company was total.

I regret that my command of Spanish remained rudimentary, and I never got to know many of the group on a personal level. In rehearsal, communication was seldom a problem. When words failed, body language, gesture, and tone of voice would get through, although the strangest looks would wash over their faces when I used the wrong word in Spanish.

During one rehearsal when everything was unraveling and drifting apart, Bob leaned over and said, "To them we are only ghosts." Yes, we are outsiders, from another world, looked at with curiosity and bewilderment. But the body of work we managed to create together is extensive, and this would not have occurred if we had not shared a vision of theatre. I'm not aware of there being much abstract discussion about the direction we were taking: the work defined itself through the process of creation. Through this activity the members of the group found their voices and inspired others in their communities.

It's hard to know if any of this would have happened without Bob Laughlin. He once revealed to me that he had been a champion coxswain for the lightweight Princeton crew as an undergraduate. Whatever skills Bob may have developed in that role have matured and flourished in his work with Sna Jtz'ibajom. He has rallied and cajoled, confronted and cheered, and kept the group on course all these years with good humor, a dash of irony, and unflinching faith and determination.

ACKNOWLEDGMENTS

A great host of people, many known and many more unknown, have given life and substance to the Monkey Business Theatre, Teatro Lo'il Maxil, projecting it to the world outside.

The first word of thanks should go to Karen Bassie, who reformatted this text and undid in the play scripts Word's magical trick of turning all italics into regular print and all regular print into italics!

Amy Trompetter was the midwife for the birth of the theatre, reassuring the members of the Tzotzil-Tzeltal writers' cooperative, Sna Jtz'ibajom, that puppeteering could be fun both for them and for the unsuspecting audience. Later, at Antioch College, she astonished us by presenting her "Punch:Judy Show" from beneath the folds of her voluminous skirt.

Amy was followed by Ralph Lee, who spent every February for a decade of his life creating a live stage where the actors learned to find their place, raise their voices, and speedily propel themselves into the next scene. While San

Amy Trompetter's Punch:Judy Show, 1982.
Photo courtesy Miriam W. Laughlin

Ralph Lee, 2006.
Photo courtesy Casey Compton

Francisco Álvarez Quiñones, 1992.
Photo courtesy Sna Jtz'ibajom

Michael John Garcés, 2006.
Photo courtesy Clara NiitSki

Cristóbal food was not kind to Ralph, he persisted in his goal to make this a first-rate theatre whose simplicity would appeal to Mayas, Ladinos, and all others. The lively response of Indian audiences and the standing ovations by those abroad are a measure of Ralph's achievement. His presence enlivened us all, sparking a desire to judge wisely every detail of a performance. He taught us that *febrero loco,* his month with the group, though rigorous, could be a delight.

Francisco Álvarez Quiñones dedicated endless hours to creating Spanish versions of many of our plays and directing our earliest ventures. When everything went wrong, you could count on Palas (as he is known in Tzotzil) to be optimistic, to toast us with a flurry of possibilities—even impossible ones. His humor lightened every day.

Michael John Garcés directed *Mexico with Us Forever.* When the actors tired of our exercises, he tossed them a ball, then another and another and another until the exercise became a game. In addition, he achieved the impossible, training the actors to jump in unison.

Diego Méndez Guzmán took a course for body movement directed by Margie Bermejo in Mexico City. More recently, with the support of CONACULTA (Consejo Nacional para la Cultura y las Artes) and INBA (Instituto Nacional para las Bellas Artes), he received training by Luís de Tavira. Following this he was our first actor to become a director. His production of *The World Turned on Its Head,* performed at the Palacio de Bellas Artes in Mexico City, called up a crescendo of laughs from the audience of five hundred.

The entire group received exercises by the Chilean director Carlos Barón and by Consuelo Anderson.

Reynaldo Pacheco, a student at Wabash College, joined us for the past two summers to bring a young voice to several of our plays.

Antonio Coello revived puppetry for us and created our first bilingual video, *El rey de Zinacantán,* starring Juan de la Torre's son, Maryan, as the Indian king.

Christine Weber, director of National Geographic's *Lost Kingdoms of the Maya,* and John Sayles, director of the movie *Men with Guns,* with full appreciation of Mayan culture, lifted a number of our actors up to worldwide visibility.

Mexico's first two Indian women playwrights, Isabel Juárez Espinosa and Petrona de la Cruz Cruz, initially members of the House of the Writer, have, by their establishment of a women's cultural center and theatre, FOMMA (Fortaleza de la Mujer Maya [The Strength of Mayan Women]), expanded the demands for a new world, which Petrona's son and fellow playwright, Rogelio Hernández Cruz, turned on its head.

Jeffrey Jay Foxx documented the beginning of our theatre with sensitive photographs. Patrick Breslin, Siena Craig, and Teague Channing have, in their illustrated articles, championed our cause in the United States, and Janet Schwartz on the Web, while Brenda Currin's thesis brought it to academia. Carlos Montemayor's *Renacimiento del teatro maya en Chiapas* gave the Mexican public a bilingual presentation of five of our plays.

Cynthia Steele's and Donald Frischmann's articles, beginning in 1992, have explored thoughtfully and intensively the literary and social values of our theatre. Donald's association over the years with the House of the Writer has been deeply appreciated by all.

Newspaper reporters in Mexico and the United States, too many to mention by name, have introduced us into the media.

Carlota Duarte, director of the Chiapas Photography Project, trained many of our members in black and white photography and the use of a darkroom and a photo archives. Her first student, Maruch Sántiz Gómez, is Mexico's first recognized Indian woman photographer. The tradition is being carried on by Rosenda de la Cruz Vázquez and Juan de la Torre.

Francisco Álvarez and Diego Méndez Guzmán have been in charge of video photography. Bright color photos by Macduff Everton and George O.

Jackson highlight our actors and our plays. Marcia Bakry, illustrator of the Smithsonian Institution's Department of Anthropology, created the two maps and aided me countless times in mastering my computer. James Di Loreto and John Steiner of the Center for Scientific Imaging and Photography of the National Museum of Natural History prepared for publication all but one of the photographs in this book.

Carlos Martínez Suárez created our first commercial videos, filming three of our early plays in a natural setting. David Pentecost, together with me and the members of the cooperative, created a quadrilingual Smithsonian Institution virtual exhibit, *Unmasking the Maya: The Story of Sna Jtz'ibajom*.

Performances in San Cristóbal have been hosted by FOMMA, la Casa de las Imágenes, la Universidad Nacional Autónoma de Chiapas, Na Bolom, for Wabash College by Nancy and David Orr, and for the Experiment in International Living Elder Hostel by Barbara Gomez. In Palenque we performed repeatedly at the Mesa Redonda, arranged by Merle Greene Robertson, and for the National Endowment for the Humanities Summer Institute, arranged by William Scheper. Elsewhere in Chiapas we have performed for Margaritas Radio and for the Maya-Zoque Festival, first under Jacinto Árias and then under Enrique Pérez López, director of CELALI (the Centro Estatal de Literaturas y Artes Indígenas). With the support of CONECULTA (Consejo Estatal para la Cultura y las Artes) and CELALI, we have been sent on many theatre trips throughout the state of Chiapas. Andrés Fábregas Puig, rector of the Universidad Nacional Autónoma de Chiapas, urged us to create a play about *Zapatismo*, resulting in *From All for All*.

Jack Warner, director of Teatro la Faragua in Progreso, Honduras, invited us twice to his remarkable theatre.

On our first trip to the United States we were hosted at SUNY Albany by Robert Carmack and Gary Gossen, at Harvard University by David Maybury-Lewis, at Cornell University by Frank Cancian, and at Princeton University by Alfred Bush. Then Donald Frischmann invited us for two trips to Texas Christian University. We were hosted at the University of Texas at Austin by Frances Karttunen, and at the Guadalupe Theater of San Antonio by Juan Tejeda.

In the Midwest, Laura Martin invited us twice to Cleveland State University. Esmeralda Martínez-Tapia welcomed us to Oberlin College. We performed at the Mexican Fine Arts Center Museum in Chicago under Encarnación Teruel. With the aid of Richard Lange and Elizabeth Perrin we performed in Milwaukee at the Indian Summer Festival, the Catholic Archdiocese, and the University of Wisconsin, as well as at St. Norbert's College and at the Oneida Nation of Wisconsin hosted by Richard Ackley.

Traveling south, Will Hoffman, together with Kate Dwyer, Brigid Burns, and their companions of Sister Cities in Asheville, arranged for venues at the University of North Carolina and Western Carolina University, guided by Philip E. Coyle, and A-B Tech, followed by the Highlander Center, where James Sessions and Candie and Guy Carawan made us feel at home. Then on to the Laurel Theatre in Knoxville and to Emory and Henry College with Anita Coulthard and Frederick Kellogg.

At the University of Georgia in Athens, Brent and Elois Ann Berlin invited us to perform for the National Society of Ethnobiology and later for the International Society of Ethnobiology. Allan Burns brought us to the University of Florida and arranged for performances in Indiantown, Fort Worth, and Immokalee in the Everglades, where the members of the Coalition of Immokalee Workers—via Laura Germino, Greg Absted, and its director, Lucas Benítez—arranged for two subsequent visits.

In New York City Elizabeth Weatherford arranged for sessions at the National Museum of the American Indian, and the Reverend James Morton, director of the Interfaith Center of New York, found a place for us at La Tea Theatre.

My colleagues Daniel Rogers and Jane Walsh of Anthropology in the National Museum of Natural History in Washington, D.C., hosted our theatre. In addition we were welcomed at the Mexican Institute of Culture by Salvador Nava and its director, Ignacio Durán, and at the Gala Hispanic Theater by Hugo Medrano.

Very little of our cooperative's efforts and very few of these visits would have been possible without the financial aid of various institutions. First, many of my trips to Chiapas were made possible by the Research Opportunities Fund of the National Museum of Natural History. The Theatre's trip to Washington was supported by the Latino Initiatives Fund under Refugio Rochin.

In the early years we were supported by the Inter-American Foundation and CEBEMO of the Netherlands, by Lynne Wasser of the Steiner Foundation, and Josie Merck of the Merck Family Fund. Our very first grant was bestowed to us by Cultural Survival, Inc., whose director, David Maybury-Lewis, and his wife Pia, as well as Theodore MacDonald, Mark Camp, and Sofia Flynn, with great generosity and warmth gave us an economic home. Our new home at the Maya Educational Foundation, directed by Christopher Lutz, and aided by Armando Alfonso and Susan Feinberg, has extended that generosity and warmth. For many years Flavia de Rossi Robinson, director of the Daniele Agostino Foundation, has aided us in our everyday activities and in times of emergency. For five years, the Ford Foundation's representative in Mexico,

Norman Collins, let us breathe easy. The foundation's support was continued for a year by Pablo Farías. Samuel Ruiz, bishop of San Cristóbal de las Casas, aided us in securing funds in the Netherlands. Such friendships with our supporters have been a great boon.

Every year I send an appeal to a veteran group of donors, and more recently to the purchasers of my *Mayan Hearts*. Their generous contributions have meant that even under the most anxious times the members of Sna Jtz'ibajom have believed that *sk'an kajvaltik*, God willing, we would survive and flourish.

In addition to those whose names have appeared above, some barely known, and some lifelong friends, there follows a parade of people who have enriched our lives and made us all feel worthy of their friendship and respect: Mariclaire Acosta and John Burstein, Thor Anderson, Wicky Bridgeforth and the late John Rinnell, Francesca Cancian, George and Jane Collier, Lourdes de León, Jan DeVos, Susanna Ekholm, Kees Groetenboer and María Elena Fernández Galán, John Haviland, Kippi and Ron Nigh, Joan and Barry Norris, Ámbar Past, Jan and Diane Rus, Suzanne Ruta, Celia Serrano Rodríguez, the late Henning Siverts, Kari Siverts, the late Evon Z. (Vogtie) Vogt, Catherine (Nan) Vogt, Carter Wilson, Percy Wood, and the late Nancy Wood.

Theresa J. May, editor-in-chief of the University of Texas Press, warned me that it would be "a rocky road" for my manuscript to reach Texas, but after Carter Wilson paved the way so comfortably, there has been smooth riding for Monkey Business Theatre. Theresa and sponsoring editor Allison Faust have given me great encouragement. My copyeditor, Alexis Mills, was extraordinarily sharp-eyed in discovering my literal and numerical inconsistencies. Her rephrasing of all three writers' prose was admirable.

For these many years the love and imagination of my wife, Mimi, gave me strength when confronted with the impossible. She, too, celebrated with me our achievement of the impossible. My children, Liana and Reese, gave me youth, and my grandchildren, Adrian, Walker, and Elena, were witnesses to *The World Turned on Its Head*.

Robert M. Laughlin, 1998. Photo courtesy Sna Jtz'ibajom

PRONUNCIATION AND TRANSLATION

Tzotzil and Tzeltal vowels are as in Spanish, as is the *j*. *X* is as *sh*. An apostrophe between vowels is a glottal stop as in the modern pronunciation of "uh-oh," Jewish Brooklynese "bottle," and "Hawaii." Consonants followed by an apostrophe are glottalized, giving them an explosive quality.

A word on the translations: I had suggested that a good first play could be based on "The Buzzard Man" tales (T42, T43, T48, and T69) I had translated from Tzotzil into English and published in *Of Cabbages and Kings: Tales from Zinacantán*. Francisco Álvarez reviewed them and wrote a first translation in Spanish. *Jaguar Dynasty* was designed by Francisco and written in Spanish. *Christ, I Never Knew You! The Story of Our Roots* was written by me in English following a tale I had recorded in Tzotzil. Francisco also translated this into Spanish. Rogelio Hernández Cruz wrote *The World on Its Head* in Spanish. Each of these plays was greatly reduced in length as the actors (principally Juan de la Torre and Diego Méndez) and I, conversing in Tzotzil, created a new draft that was reviewed and changed by the other actors.

The creation of the remaining plays began with discussions in Tzotzil by the above triumvirate, except for *Mexico with Us Forever,* for which I was absent.

MONKEY BUSINESS THEATRE

1

Looking Back, Looking Forward

IN THE BEGINNING

WHEN I FIRST LANDED in the colonial city of San Cristóbal de las Casas, Chiapas, in 1957 as a graduate student in anthropology at the Escuela Nacional de Antropología e Historia in Mexico City, I never dreamt I would spend the rest of my life exploring Tzotzil Mayan culture. Transferring to Harvard University, I began my fieldwork in Zinacantán, accompanied by my wife, Mimi. The first task was to learn Tzotzil. We became the house guests of a young man, Domingo de la Torre (Romin Teratol in Tzotzil), a puppeteer whom I had met the year before at the National Indian Institute. He agreed to be my teacher, enabling me to collect myths and tales, and a year later, dreams (Laughlin 1977, 1976). In 1963 Domingo and his next door neighbor, Anselmo Pérez Pérez (Antzelmo Péres Péres), were my chief collaborators in compiling an English-Tzotzil, Tzotzil-English dictionary. As part of this project, they accompanied me on two visits to the United States in 1963 and 1967. In that capacity, they produced the first Mayan descriptions of the United States, appearing in *Of Shoes and Ships and Sealing Wax* (1980). The publication of *The Great Tzotzil Dictionary of San Lorenzo Zinacantán* (1975), with its 30,000 entries, was then the most comprehensive dictionary of a New World language. This gave me particular satisfaction because ever since I had entered Mexico, I had heard all Indian languages referred to as *dialectos*—mere dialects.

In 1982 my life took a new turn. I became, to my surprise, an advocacy anthropologist. It happened that I was codirector of a conference in San Cristóbal, "Forty Years of Anthropological Research in Chiapas." Earlier, three ex-members of the Harvard Chiapas Project—Antzelmo; Romin's son, Xun, of Zinacantán; and Maryan Kalixto of Chamula—had asked for my help in creating a Tzotzil-Tzeltal Mayan cultural association. I urged them to speak to the participants of this meeting to plead their cause.

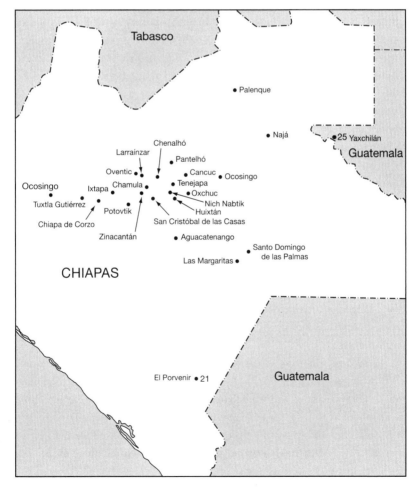

The complaint was one often heard by foreign researchers: that they extract their data like miners extract ore, cart it away for processing elsewhere and leave nothing behind. "You have awakened our interest in our culture," the informants told the scientists. "You have published many studies, but always in other countries where we never see the results.... We would like at least to put on paper our customs for the sake of our children and grandchildren." (Breslin 1994, 80)

Cultural Survival responded with a grant of $3,000 seed money, and so was born Sna Jtz'ibajom, as it is called in Tzotzil and Tzeltal: The House of the Writer.

With the title of literary coordinator of the cooperative, I have served as a sort of impresario, seeking funds outside of Mexico, arranging international theatre tours, and serving as introducer and moderator on tours to the United States. Being a cofounder of Sna Jtz'ibajom, and its oldest member, when in Chiapas I participate in the association's meetings, offer advice, and make corrections in the spelling of the Tzotzil texts. Previously, together with Ralph Lee, I was intimately involved in the creation of the plays regarding the script, casting, costuming, and so on.

In 1985 the members had been writing and publishing bilingual booklets for three years. The booklets were designed so that each Tzotzil or Tzeltal paragraph was matched on the facing page with the Spanish translation. But we soon learned that if the books were read at all, it was only in Spanish. The school system, not bothering to teach literacy in the native languages, had encouraged an ignorance and disdain of them that was difficult to surmount. Spanish was the language of civilized people; why bother with the other?

It occurred to me that perhaps we could gain a readership if we had puppets to project the folktales in the booklets. It was a vain thought (we added no readers), but our puppet theatre gave Sna a new face. I made this decision knowing that twenty-five years before, the Instituto Nacional Indigenista (the National Indian Institute), with the aid of the novelist Rosario Castellanos, had introduced puppet theatre to "civilize" the Indians. Despite its popularity, it conferred no prestige on the Indian puppeteers, whose communities had no history of staged performance. All that we would call "theatre" occurred in religious celebrations of saints' days and Carnival in which the performers were religious officials whose scripts had been handed down orally for generations. Although many of these performances traced the histories of the towns, there were no Mayan dramas of war and sacrifice, such as the *Rabinal Achí* (also known as the Dance of the Trumpets), which has survived for hundreds of years in Guatemala (Tedlock 2003).

To initiate this experiment, we hired Amy Trompetter of the Bread and Puppet Theatre to give us a two-week workshop. For Amy it was a frustrating affair. The actors did not want to parade around with giant puppets. They did not want to be seen. Amy persevered, showing them how to make papier-mâché hand puppets, how to put them in motion, and how to make a portable theatre.

To her distress, the first skit they chose to perform was a folktale that tells of a newlywed whose wife's head mysteriously disappears at night to eat corpses. But Amy succeeded. In two weeks they were on the road, after naming the theatre Teatro Lo'il Maxil, literally Monkey Talk Theatre, but which I have named in English the Monkey Business Theatre. Now, performing for the first time, the actors cowered behind the curtain. They were so nervous, cramped in the enclosed space, that their bodies became soaked with sweat. They chugalugged cane liquor to give them the courage to open their mouths, to sweep away their embarrassment. Chavela recalls, "I had no idea of how to move my hands, my voice, all that! They tried to teach me, but my hands grew stiff" (Laughlin 1991/1992, 45). Antzelmo, a highly respected shaman, not only did not wish to be seen in his community in the role of a puppeteer, but he did not even want his voice to be heard and recognized. The members limited their participation to showings in towns where they were not known.

However, Manvel remembers of the puppet theatre, "While you are acting with the puppets you feel as if that puppet were you yourself, you have fun; if

Puppet newlyweds, 1985. Photo courtesy Robert M. Laughlin

Puppet theatre, 1993. Photo copyright © George O. Jackson Jr.

the public responds to you and you give them some advice or you make them laugh or scare them you feel at ease, very pleased, just like the people" (Pérez Hérnandez 1992).

But the personalities of the puppets became an integral part of our society. When a representative of the Inter-American Foundation came to inspect our project, the troupe provided her with "an unorthodox profile" of its members, drawing on the characters of a tale in which Zinacantec merchants are castrated by the Guatemalans and then saved by a team of animals and natural forces:

MARYAN: Thunderbolt, who makes so much noise, but is, indeed, the strongest leader

ANTZELMO: Whirlwind, who rushes around to make sure that everything is in order

XUN: Fog, who approaches each problem from every conceivable angle until we are so befogged that we always accept his solution as being the best

XAP: Hawk, who dives down, knocking us aside to do what he knows is right

MATYO: Blowfly, who eagerly tackles all the dirty jobs, washes his hands clean, and cheerfully begins again

TZIAK: Butterfly, who glides about silently, observing everything, and then keeps us well-informed

The puppeteers write the dialogue in Tzotzil, Tzeltal, and Spanish and learn the lines by heart, but there is tremendous liberty, creative invention, and improvisation when the puppets are in action. Some of the puppeteers are adept at including the public by having the puppet direct questions to them. And at the end of the performance, a puppet demands that the public clap hands.

In the beginning, presentations of the Theatre in the communities required the approval of the civil officials and cooperation from the schoolteachers, who often provided benches for the audience and announced the Theatre's arrival over their loudspeaker. Before long, the troupe had gained such popularity that it was receiving fifteen to twenty invitations a month. Generally, the stage is set up at the courthouse door or what in many communities is the social center of the town: the cement basketball court. The children sit or stand in front, behind them the men, and in the rear, the women, sometimes on school benches. For a time, the puppet theatre became a basic ingredient of school holidays. The children's "folk dances" and the daylong basketball tournament would be followed by the puppet theatre, often in very remote hamlets that could only be reached on foot (Laughlin 1999, 495–496).

The puppet theatre had its first performance in San Andrés Larraínzar, then in four other Tzotzil towns, three Tzeltal towns, and San Cristóbal. That same year Xun and Antzelmo traveled to the United States to perform as puppeteers at Princeton, Harvard, Cornell, the State University of New York (SUNY) at Albany, and in a Newark ghetto garage. At SUNY, where all the students were lying around in their bathing suits on the first warm day of the year, we all saw our first ATM. Antzelmo wondered how the man could fit in such a confined space to be pushing out the dollars to us.

The year 1987 was a prosperous one for Mexico. Accordingly, we performed not only at traditional fiestas and graduations, but also at the inauguration of new schools, clinics, and town water systems. The Theatre's repertory expanded beyond folktales to include didactic spoofs of alcoholism and Western versus herbal medicine. Performances in Jalapa and Mexico City followed three productions at the K'inal Winik festival at Cleveland State University, where the mythic *Long-Haired Devil* skit accompanied the historical *Battle of Chamula,* and the didactic exposure of the disaster of bilingual education.

A popular puppet piece was *The Devil Priest,*

> based on a timeless folktale from Zinacantán which recounts how a village priest made use of numerous tricks to seduce local women. The priest is presented not as a mere human gone astray, but rather as an incarnation of the devil, thus providing insight into Indian attitudes regarding the ministers of the Roman Catholic Church; those who have committed moral transgressions have therefore earned the dubious distinction of having passed into the oral tradition. Laughlin observes that "the Zinacantec does not bear fools or priests lightly. ... Here the vagaries of priests, their amorous adventures, are the subject not of humor (as in similar Spanish stories), but outrage." (Frischmann 1991, 122)

By 1989 the puppeteers had become so skilled that in Austin, Texas, in a skit involving a Tojolabal shaman, Antun invented his version of the Tojolabal language with no American in the audience realizing it was pure gibberish. In addition to the skits mentioned above, they now wanted to address social issues comprehensively, so they dealt with (1) family planning, (2) deforestation and wildlife depredation, (3) racism, (4) indentured labor, and (5) land rights, especially of women.

The future of the Monkey Business Theatre was decided by an unexpected event in 1987 at the ninth Taller de Lingüística Maya in Antigua, Guatemala, where the members of Sna, together with Guatemalan Mayas, decided upon a standard alphabet for all the Mayan languages.

After our puppetry was roundly applauded, Nicholas Hopkins and Kathryn Josserand shoved a stack of papers at us, saying that this was a Ch'ol folktale and that the puppeteers had performed so well they should act out the tale the next day. The Indians' response was "How dare they?" As we ate our lunch in the market, our one mestizo member [Palas] enthusiastically read with determination a synopsis of the folktale, but no one would listen, as they called for basket after basket of the tiny Guatemalan tortillas. Retiring to the hotel room, he began to read the story. Soon the puppeteers were sitting up, listening to the dialogue, and when he got on the floor and demonstrated the paddling of a canoe, everyone became a paddler. They learned the lines, acted out their parts, giving the role of Thunderbolt to the senior member, who threatened to act his part naked unless he were given some cane liquor first. Lacking a woman performer, Matyo was chosen to be Frog, wearing a green dress. They decided I should be the Crocodile and rolled me up in blue plastic sheeting, instructing me to take a bite out of Antzelmo, the Thunderbolt's leg. It was the memory of this performance that a year later bolstered the puppeteers' confidence enough that they considered becoming actors in live theatre. (Laughlin 1999, 496)

2

Febrero Loco

A LIVE THEATRE IN THE MAKING

IN 1989, WE BROUGHT Ralph Lee from New York City to Chiapas. "… [A]s artistic director of the Mettawee River Company, which performs as an itinerant troupe in rural upstate New York and New England during the summer, [Ralph] had for years peopled the stage with spirits, gods, and demons from around the Greenwich Village's famous Halloween parade, he had filled the streets with giant masks and puppets. What magical figures would he bring to life now?" (Laughlin 1995, 528). Every *febrero loco* (Crazy February), as the month is known locally, he would direct the creation of a new play based on local material. Ralph arrived with his craggy face, bushy beard, penetrating brown eyes, and just a couple of words of Spanish on his tongue—enough to put fear in the hearts of any Maya! But Ralph, who had studied mime in his youth in Paris, was not to be stopped. First he had them improvise out in the woods. They dreamt up a scene of Indians visiting a "talking saint." This was witnessed by Peter Canby of the *New Yorker,* who later exclaimed, "I've just seen a short story created before my eyes!" (Laughlin to McAlpin 1989, 3, 10).

Then Ralph introduced "Exercises." What was not considered outlandish in Greenwich Village was thought by the Mayas to be crazy, horrible, every person mocking each other. Patrick Breslin described some of these exercises:

Lee led Lo'il Maxil's actors through a series of loosening-up exercises. The actors, five men and three women, were bent at the waist, their arms sweeping the floor, looking like elephants snuffling after peanuts. Soon, they moved on to voice exercises, opening their mouths wide, sticking their tongues out. Lee began to make sounds—grunts, whinnies, snorts, wheezes, vibratos. The actors imitated him. Then they started doing improvisations. One man imitated a monkey loping along with its hands touching the ground.

Two of the women, Chave [Chavela] and Petu' Krus Krus, threw hysterical fits. (Breslin 1994, 84) (See appendix 1 for a list of both the Mayan and Spanish names of individuals referred to in this and other chapters.)

For Mayas who are trained to keep their voices low and their gestures measured, this was a difficult introduction to the theatre. Next, one member was to choose an improvisation, enact it in the center, then pass it on to another who would mirror it and create his or her own to be passed on again.

Particularly for the women, at first, the exercises were an embarrassing, fearsome experience that sometimes was enacted in the privacy of the rehearsal room, but often in a green meadow where Indian passersby would stop and gape. But "Gradually, their inhibitions and the personal preoccupations they brought with them each morning receded. Physical awkwardness was replaced by ease of movement, and they projected their voices strongly. There was also a growing camaraderie, uniting everyone" (Laughlin 1999, 496). No longer did they need shots of cane liquor to give them confidence, to quell their embarrassment. Before this, Xun recalled, "We had no idea how to move around on the stage" (Frischmann 1994a, 221).

Together we created each play, following Ralph's direction to make scenery, dialogue, and action as simple as possible. Surveying the subjects, half are based on folktales and myths, while half deal with the economic, social, and political problems that have confronted the Mayas since pre-Columbian times and continue today. Whether performed in Spanish or Tzotzil, these plays represent not only the magical and supernatural elements of their lives, but also the pleasures and sufferings of Mayan daily life. Even the darkest scenes are infused with humor. This is how the Mayas have learned to endure their marginalization.

Prior to Ralph's arrival a subject was chosen, and Francisco Álvarez Quiñones (Palas), our one non-Indian member, presented us with a script. Although the Tzeltal members had learned Tzotzil, which was the group's lingua franca, the Tzotzil had not learned Tzeltal. Nor have they ever learned the closely related language, even though during post-performance celebrations, fortified with plenty of cane liquor, they swear to do so.

Consequently, we began with a Spanish script. I served as translator of Spanish for Ralph and translator of Tzotzil for Palas, who at first would present us with an impossibly long operatic script that needed extensive cutting. Later, the veteran actors and I would create the script, some parts in Tzotzil and others in Spanish. This was then converted entirely into Spanish and fine-tuned by Ralph and the group as a whole. The older actors, previously illiterate, became so sophisticated that when revising the text, they would say, "A comma is needed here!" to permit a pause.

Unlike commercial theatre in the United States, where unions control activities, here everyone was free to collaborate in every way. Ralph assigned the roles and taught the cast the appropriate stage movements and blocking of scenes. A major reordering of scenes occurred collaboratively, but this could be exceedingly frustrating for Ralph when veteran actors disagreed and an hour, or hours, of heated discussion in Tzotzil ensued until solidarity was achieved. Work was interrupted only for a mid-morning fruit break and lunch together at a local restaurant.

Ralph designed and made the masks, but after training the actors, he had them make the masks and half-masks. The decision about which character was to wear a mask was decided collaboratively, and frequently an actor would say, "I will make it this way," with the group concurring. Originally, Ralph, too, fashioned the sets, insisting that they be as simple as possible, a tradition that continued when the actors took charge.

The first seven plays were written and performed in both Spanish and Tzotzil. These I have translated from Tzotzil. The following five were written and performed only in Spanish, though *Christ I Never Knew You* was based on a Tzotzil tale that I had translated into English and rewritten as a play. My play was converted by Palas into Spanish and shortened by the group.

Ralph's visits, at first only two weeks, extended to three weeks or a month as the years passed. Eventually we added the technique of video filming our performances so that we could study them and devise improvements. This multicultural venture seemed to all of us to be a miracle, particularly in light of the following strictures:

1 These are Indians from particular towns who worked on an equal basis with Indians from another town.
2 These are towns where the sexual division of labor is very strict, and where no respectable woman would act in the theatre.
3 These are towns where great attention is paid to age difference, where no shaman or ex-*presidente* would act on the stage.
4 These are Indians who have been dominated for centuries by Ladinos and who have the greatest suspicion of foreigners.
5 Our intellectual Ladino, who has a Romantic vision of the Mayas, is working together with Indians and Americans—Americans who represent the domination of Mexicans by Americans.

6 We, Americans, who refuse to recognize our position as dominators of Mexicans.

7 We, Americans, some from the East Coast, some from the West, some rural, some urban, everyone of us very sensitive to our own perceptions of the right way. (Laughlin to Breslin 1992)

The people of Zinacantán consider themselves, and are considered by both Indians and Ladinos, to be the highest class of Indian. According to Zinacantecs, their patron saint, San Lorenzo, watches over them when they travel, but San Juan, who has so many children in Chamula, cannot cope, and many poor Chamulans are left to die on the roadside. Both Zinacantecs and Chamulans consider themselves to be superior to the Tzeltal-speaking Tenejapans. However, after a performance, "they all danced with each other; the ex-*presidente* of Chamula with a Tenejapan, the chief shaman of Zinacantán with the barefoot Chamulan woman. Revolutionary!" (Laughlin to Adams 1990).

During the lifetime of the cooperative there have been fifty-five members (thirty-three Tzotzil, eighteen Tzeltal, and four Spanish speakers) from eight different communities:

Chamula, 18
Zinacantán, 14
Tenejapa, 13
Cancuc, 2
Aguacatenango, 1
Huixtán, 1
Oxchuc, 1
Pantelhó, 1

The actors are not chosen by audition; rather, they are the members of Sna Jtz'ibajom, the House of the Writer, who must be literate in their native language to enter the cooperative. Every writer is expected to be a member of the Theatre. None have had previous acting experience.

The length of service of the individuals who have been Theatre members follows:

10–21 years, 8
3–9 years, 14
1–2 years, 17
6–11 months, 6

2–6 months, 7
1 month or less, 5

Great resilience is required of members. Frequently men choose or are drafted by their community to become civil or religious officials. Their duties often require night-long sessions, which for the religious officials involves considerable drinking and dancing. Another problem is that husbands can be jealous and unwilling to have their wives participate in national and international theatre tours: in one week three women quit to be married. Some members have also been fired by the group for inappropriate romances and thievery. One actor, Ermenejildo, falsely accused by a local politician of kidnapping, was jailed for six years. After the Zapatista Rebellion the *coletos auténticos*—the conservative, racist families of San Cristóbal—included Sna in a list of "subversive" organizations that they denounced to the Mexican State Department, but no action was taken.

A less serious problem is the weather. When performances are given outside, the wind can blow the curtains about wildly. Unequipped with microphones, the actors' words are blown away. And then there is the sun: presenting *Jaguar Dynasty* in Palenque, "in the blistering noonday sun our actors said they never noticed the heat during the play, but unlike their ancestors, after the performance, with their sopping faces nearly purple, they gulped down gallons of ice water!" (Laughlin to Jaffé 1993).

Rain is another frequent challenge. Again in Palenque we were the victims of the first summer thunderstorm, when rain poured through the hotel roof. Later, we waited in the town auditorium for our audience, which had been reduced to a sopping wet Mexican tourist, an equally wet German, and a sleeping custodian. But at Palas's insistence we performed the play. One storm descended on us at a school graduation in a remote Indian hamlet down a muddy road.

> . . . [the actors] replaced the basketball players on their cement court. At first it was a slow, but steady rain, but then as dogs and kids dashed for cover, it came down in sheets. The audience with their backs pressed against the school walls, seeking the cover of a few inches of projecting roof tiles, filled the air with their laughter and boisterous comments, as the actors and actresses, soaked to the skin, and the turkey buzzard with water streaming from its wings, undauntedly proceeded through the last act. Warmed at the end with a bit of cane liquor and laced punch, they felt like cultural heroes. (Laughlin to Jaffé)

In Mérida "the [theatre] festival director at the last minute opted to send forty busloads of people to watch the spring equinox in Chichén Itzá, leaving us to perform before row after row of empty seats. It was quite a disappointment after winning first place for the festival and enduring the fifteen-hour bus ride. The splendid performance was appreciated by a handful of American and Mexican writers" (Laughlin to Negroponte 1992). As it rained in Chichén, our prospective audience saw nothing—no magical serpent descending the pyramid.

Staging could be difficult in the Indian communities. Our puppet theatre kept threatening to collapse until we redesigned it to stand more securely. With live theatre the actors changed their clothes behind the curtain, often watched by a bevy of young boys who, when the play began, would rush around to the front of the curtain and leave no room for the actors to perform. A rope would be brought out to cordon off the public, but usually only policing by local officials would keep the staging area clear. Throughout the play boys would dart around the curtain to see what was happening next, and at the end, as the actors removed their masks, the boys would grab them, put them on their heads, and prance around. Unlike theatre audiences in the United States, where no sound is made, Mayan audiences often shout out suggestions, laugh loudly, and whistle. In the open air and in large theatres, the actors' lack of individual microphones has been a problem. The women, especially, have found it difficult to project their voices.

With the puppet theatre we learned that performances in a community are not given in a vacuum. Knowing that we would have a big crowd at a major fiesta, we set up our theatre, equipped for the first time with small speakers, in Zinacantán at the Fiesta of San Sebastián. Because the town was divided into two long-standing economic and political factions—the *camioneros,* or Truckers, and the *campesinos,* or Farmers—and because our Zinacantec members were Farmers, we asked the Trucker mayor to see that his constables would protect the theatre in case a problem arose. Just as we were starting to perform, a bunch of Truckers shouted to their kids to set fire to the theatre. As they came rushing forward, no constables were in sight. In a jiffy we pulled down the speakers and dismantled everything. From then on we never tried to perform at a fiesta, aware that with many people coming in from the various hamlets, there is usually a heightened tension.

Quite different was a problem in Santo Domingo de las Palmas, a community of Tzeltal fundamentalist Christians who, many years ago, had moved down from the Highlands to the Lacandón jungle. Just before our theatre was to go into action, a group of Oxchuc Tzeltals that had accompanied Sna on the tour, seeing a row of three crosses, lighted a handful of incense. As the clouds of incense rose up, the Fundamentalists, who had totally forgotten the use of incense, thought it must be something like a ballistic missile and ordered the troupe to depart immediately. Only when the harmlessness of incense was explained to them did they calm down sufficiently to allow our play to proceed.

As we gained prominence in theatre circles, new acting opportunities arose. In 1991 Cambridge PBS asked us to perform a sample curing ceremony "for posterity." After considerable deliberation, Antzelmo agreed, on condition that the prayers be short so that the gods would not be tricked and would realize that it was just "theatre, a token."

The following year I met Xun, Manvel, and Petu' at the Mexico City airport Holiday Inn on their return from Copán, where they had taken part in the filming of National Geographic's *Lost Kingdoms of the Maya*.

So in they came, wearing their Z[inacantec] clothes and each sporting a National Geographic baseball cap. Manvel had been assigned the part of a priest letting blood from his penis! At first he felt his simulation was a sham, a slap at Mayan religion, but the photographer spotted his distress, and after sensitive explanations and reassurances, Manvel was able to play the part with gusto.

Petu' and Xun were Classic Mayan peasants. Petu' was handed a Honduran baby who had won the prize for calmness. She was told to strip to her waist, was handed the baby, and told to nurse it. Xun was advised to speak to her in Tzotzil, anything he wanted. So he decided to try some lines from one of our plays. And in typically authoritative Zinacantec male style he said, 'Are you there, woman, I'm hungry! So then, seeing Petu' half-naked for the first time in his life, he tossed out some provocative lines about where she was going to put the baby so they could sleep together. Petu' said it was amazing, she was so into her role that she never even heard Xun, never laughed.

They said they had never worked harder: filmed until four in the morning, in clouds of mosquitoes, aching in every joint of their body, but exuberant. (Laughlin to Laughlin 1992)

In 1997 five of the actors—Tziak, Antun, Kristobal, Tumin, and Ermenejildo—traveled to San José Babilonia, a Ch'ol colony of Palenque, where John Sayles enlisted them to act as Indian rebels in his film *Men with Guns*. Originally, Sayles was fearful that the government would not authorize production of the film because much had been photographed in 1994 during the Zapatista

Rebellion. In an effort to avoid problems, he gave his movie the working title *Cerca del cielo* [Near Heaven]—a title that was praised for its beauty over the local radio station.

Our team created the Tzotzil script for the scene, teaching the Ladino lead actor his few Tzotzil words. Then they were ushered into a trailer where a bullet hole was painted on the foreheads of the three doomed men. Responding to the soldiers and to each other in Tzotzil, they were led to the cemetery, where Tziak became the executioner, and they were laid to rest in their graves. Afterwards many Americans told me they thought this was the most dramatic scene of the whole movie. Despite John Sayles's warmth and praise, they returned home feeling quite ill, not only due to the psychological stress, but also because they had swollen up from the mosquito bites and the stings of so many ants that had been disturbed by the digging of the graves.

In 2002–2003 we created a quadrilingual virtual exhibit, *Unmasking the Maya: The Story of Sna Jtz'ibajom,* at www.mnh.si/anthro/maya/. Here can be seen in color a review of the Monkey Business Theatre.

Finally, in 2003, under the direction of Antonio Coello, a DVD was crafted of *El rey de Zinacantán/Jk'ulej ta Sots'leb* [The king of Zinacantán], a folktale presented in Tzotzil with Spanish subtitles in which Xun's son, Maryan 2, took the part of the Indian king. Puppetry, which had been abandoned for many years, had been reinstated.

Life has been given to the Monkey Business Theatre for seventeen years by the Mayan men and women who have created and presented their plays and puppet skits to the local, national, and international public. Both Chiapas state and Mexican federal government departments are showing a growing interest in, and support for, the Monkey Business Theatre.

3

The Theatre on the Road

THE GREAT ADVENTURE

WHEN THE ACTORS OF the Teatro Lo'il Maxil puppet theatre first ventured to distant hamlets, carrying the wooden curtain frame on their backs or on muleback, it seemed a great adventure. It was less so when they graduated to buses, and the bus drivers refused to transport the boards without a hefty tip. Shifting to light metal poles solved the problem.

The theatre tours sometimes had an extraordinary mix of good and bad. In 1987, invited to a national Indian/campesino theatre festival in Coxquihui in the Totonac region of Veracruz, the group set off very preoccupied because their lead actress informed them at the last minute that she could not go because her child was sick. Although they had figured out how to improvise the play, they were unhappy when they arrived in Tuxtla, but to their amazement their actress boarded the bus there, saying only, "I thought I could catch up with you." At the festival they watched more than fifty theatre and dance groups, including the Voladores, who with their feet tied by a rope, swing down from the top of a tall pole.

On the basis of their own performance they were chosen to be the Chiapas coordinators of the Teatro Comunidad de la República. Then, returning to Veracruz on a government bus, everyone conversing happily and singing, a passenger shouted that something was on fire. When the driver stopped, he discovered that our loudspeakers were burning, perhaps because someone had tossed a cigarette butt behind them. Even so, they were able to perform at a historic tower, but the bus never returned to take them to the hotel. "Asking everywhere, with all our baggage on the street, with night approaching, and dying of hunger, we had the town authorities send us an ambulance, which finally took us to the hotel, blowing its siren. We laughed and joked, saying, 'The poor drivers must be thinking that it's a wounded person. If only they knew the ambulance was full of puppeteers!'" (Pérez Hernández 1992, 97).

Once, traveling in a government vehicle down the mountain road to Tuxtla, the driver turned to me and said, "I have no brakes!" But as he pumped the brake pedal continuously, we arrived safely. In 1990 we were invited to Oxchuc by a group, Tres Nudos (Three Knots), formed to oppose the mayor's political party, Partido Revolucionario Institucional (PRI). As their driver gunned our pickup up the hill beyond Huixtán, he swerved into the wrong lane on a curve, and we were struck by a Lacandonia bus. The passengers poured out of the bus to grab ahold of our truck as it teetered on the edge of a steep drop. Tziak's and Antun's faces were covered with blood, Petu' had a broken wrist, and I had two broken ribs. A bus passenger applied cane liquor to Tziak's and Antun's wounds before the two were taken first to a clinic in Huixtán and then to one in San Cristóbal, but in Tziak's words, "We didn't lose our fear until we had drunk some shots of cane liquor!" The passenger who came to our aid, a man from Abasolo, became a friend of Tziak and of Sna, and together they made a video record of Abasolo's religious ceremonies.

In 1996, returning from a performance in Margaritas, our government truck broke down in the middle of nowhere, and we waited for hours as dusk fell while the driver did his best to repair the vehicle. In 2003, on the Guatemalan border in El Porvenir (The Future), the car assigned to the group burst into flames, forcing the actors to jump for their lives. They scrambled for something to put the fire out with, and finally Coca-Cola did the trick, but the car was a ruin.

On a bus trip to Mexico City in 1996 to perform at the Centro Cultural San Ángel, the bus was stopped by the army twenty times and took twenty hours. In 2003, soldiers and immigration officials again stopped the bus to search for firearms and undocumented Central Americans heading north. Arriving in Puebla, they were told that they could not proceed to the capital because the license plate numbers did not conform to the restrictions imposed to reduce pollution from vehicle exhaust. The group was forced to buy tickets for the last lap while the bus waited until after midnight to reach the city. In addition, a member of Taller Leñateros (the Woodlanders' Workshop), who accompanied them and was supposed to provide funds for a meal, told them they had to pay for it with their own money.

On her first trip to Mexico City María's *rebozo* caught in the escalator. She watched helplessly, twisting, as the metal steps pulled her shawl underground.

That was not the only surprise Mexico City had for us. Once, while waiting for a cab to take us to the American Embassy to get visas, a car pulled up and two men flashed badges, asked why we were in Mexico City, and ordered us into their car. Fearful of having their money stolen if they left it in the hotel, my companions had decided to bring it along with them. They passively surrendered a million pesos and their papers to our kidnappers, who drove us around for half an hour before returning our papers and delivering us to the embassy. Fortunately, Antun had hidden some bills in his sock, just enough to buy the photos needed for the visas. Afterwards they exclaimed, "Thank God we had money or they would have killed us!"

Crossing from Guatemala into Honduras in a bus of the Instituto Chiapaneco de Cultura of the state government, we were delayed for hours at the immigration office after the men in uniform told us, "The way you Mexicans treat us, now we'll give you a lesson!" Eventually, after receiving a large bribe, they let us continue but stationed an armed guard in the front of our bus. As he snored away, we considered disarming him!

On another trip, as we counted our numerous bags in the Mexico City airport, Xun realized to his horror that his suitcase and all his clothes were gone. He had left it in the taxi. Borrowing money from his companions, he bought a set of clothes in the United States. Several years later, entrusting himself with everyone's passports, Xun left the folder under his seat when we changed planes. Only in Washington, our final destination, could new passports be issued.

In 1994, arriving from Chiapas at the Mexico City airport, we were singled out for luggage inspection as if we had come from another land. A caustic remark by one of us (which I didn't hear) nearly brought us down—"*¡Vamos a la comandancia!*" (We're going to headquarters!)—a threat retracted only after a display of international letters of invitation. We worried about the rest of the group coming the next day, fortified with a box of Zapatista dolls. It was only as we were about to board the plane for Florida that our wooden guns, props for *From All for All,* were discovered. "We'll have to advise the pilot!" exclaimed the Delta stewardess. "Why didn't you check them?" Fortunately, a last-minute approval by the pilot permitted us to board the plane. Those were innocent days!

Two years later, Umberto was refused a visa, and Antun and Kristobal, traveling to Florida at the invitation of Laura Germino of the Coalition of Immokalee Workers, arrived in Miami to be told that their visas were good for only one trip and were no longer valid. After a three-hour interrogation they were told they could pay a two-hundred-dollar fine or return to Mexico, but after calling Laura, she drove to Miami to rescue them.

Traveling itself was not always easy either. Tumin recalls, "Looking out the plane window everything below seemed so tiny. I realized it was because we were up so high. It made me dizzy. I didn't look anymore." On a trip to Washington, D.C., I agreed to chauffeur the group to a guesthouse, but when I stopped the van in front, I shifted the gear to neutral instead of parking. As I was standing next to the van, it began to roll backwards, and the door knocked me to the ground. The van continued across the road until it banged into a stone wall. Everyone thought I was dead. Just lucky!

There were also water perils. In April 1984 I was taking Xap and Maryan out on the Potomac River in my canoe when a high wind suddenly kicked up and we capsized. A carpenter working on a neighboring house called the Fairfax County Fire Department. Maryan, next to me in the less than 40-degree water, tried frantically to climb back into the canoe, where Xap was sitting with freezing water up to the gunwales. Neither knew how to swim. Finally Maryan "saw" his patron saint, Saint John, and knowing he would survive, quieted down. We clung to the sides for thirty minutes before a fire truck approached and the rescue squad cut the chain to release a neighbor's canoe. To my horror I saw them capsize as well. They righted the canoe and tried to reach us, paddling with just a fire shovel until two of the firefighters, who, like us, lacked life vests, jumped into the frigid water and pulled the rescue canoe towards us against the strong current. The fire chief, on land, kept shouting to us to make sure it was worth risking his men's lives. At last we were pulled to shore. Xap and I were whisked by county ambulance to the hospital, while Maryan was rushed there in a police helicopter. The doctor was amazed we were still alive—"Another five minutes and ..." Horrified at first that for hypothermia he had to receive a transfusion of gringo blood, Maryan, once home, believed it gave him special strength that would perhaps last for the rest of his life.

Land, however, was not that much safer for Xap. Walking in Greenwich Village, he spotted in a store window a green plaster mermaid whose facial features were just suggested. It was love at first sight. He was transfixed. Nothing would break his entrancement. For twenty minutes Mimi's pleas were unheard, until with great sorrow he abandoned his *sirena*. Back in Chiapas, he turned away from our work to poetry and tie-dye, until drink and drugs took him from us.

Although the group nearly always traveled in good spirits, in 1990, at the first Maya-Zoque Festival, in Motozintla, the Theatre performed two plays that were well received. That night the various groups of Indian musicians and dancers invited the troupe to join them while they played traditional music and celebrated with glasses of liquor. The next morning, after Sna had been asked to repeat their plays that night, Palas, Tziak, Xun, and a new member went to town to alleviate the heat with some beers. But Antzelmo, Manvel, and Chavela—who had not shared in the drinking and had complained about the food they were given—angrily slipped empty liquor bottles in their companions' bedding, abandoned their fellow actors, and returned to San Cristóbal. The remaining actors were obliged that evening to improvise the two plays with a drastically reduced cast—a feat they claim they carried out with great success.

Remembering their trips to the United States, everyone commented on how friendly people were to them, but they all had one complaint: "They starved us!" The food was different. There were no tortillas, no chiles. In San Antonio, Texas, it was freezing cold, so Kristobal asked for tea to warm himself. They brought him ice tea! Worse were the "plastic tortillas," and most horrifying of all, pizza, that stretched and stretched. But now pizza is common in San Cristóbal. "We've learned to eat it."

It was hardest when the actors were put up in private houses. Antun recalls one such experience: "'Eat, get what you want!' she said, but there wasn't anything. They just gave us one apple. We're not used to that!" Kristobal says, "I think we had bad luck since they didn't feed us. They just gave us half a glass of water and some fruit in the morning and at night. Nothing. We suffered from hunger almost every day. When we joined the others, we just ate a little bread. But when the time came to present our play, I almost fainted from lack of energy or strength. I couldn't act and I couldn't concentrate either, but that was an unforgettable occasion." Another actor recalls that during a visit to the University of Georgia, "We were given glasses of water and cookies, just two or three meals!"

Also unforgettable was eating in the commons at Antioch College, bursting with noise and blazing with color, including one young man's bright red mohawk hair. Two quiet Asian women students came over to join the Chiapas women, bringing them a little peace. But after Rosa, from Cancuc, whom we all thought of as being rather coarse, was invited to join a group of women, she could not resist questioning them about the fashionable boy with the mohawk, a philosophy major who later was our chauffeur. "Is it red down there, too?" she asked.

Rosenta commented that "You don't see people walking in the street. They just go by car. The university students have cars. It seems as if we walk on the streets like ants." And Xpet complained that "Sometimes we want to talk with someone, [but] we can't. They just smile at us."

But there were also pleasant surprises. In 1995 in Chicago with my Zinacantec companions in their red tunics, "while we were walking the streets of the Mexican barrio, cars passed by, their drivers honking their horns and giving a solidarity fist. A street vendor asked, '¿Cómo está Marcos?' [How is Marcos (leader of the Zapatistas)?] One of our guys answered with a laugh, '¡Muy bien, muy bien!' Afterwards, laughing about it, as we chatted, another of my Zinacantec companions commented, 'But you should have said, '¡*Estoy muy bien!*' [I am very well!]" (Laughlin to Warner 1995).

One experience, however, was particularly sad. María returned to her mother's home in the Chamula hamlet of Nichnabtik one evening to find her sister's baby crying on her bed. When María asked her mother where her sister was, she said she didn't know, nor where her brother-in-law was. She went to her brother's house, but he had no idea either. Finally she learned they had abandoned their baby and gone to the States, looking for jobs. They had gone to Immokalee, Florida. When we arrived there in 1994, she asked for her sister and was told, "*¡Batem ta Tenesi!*" (Gone to Tennessee!).

During a later trip to Knoxville, in high spirits after our performance, we were eating supper together at a restaurant when María began to cry. We learned for the first time about the baby and how María had hoped to see her sister, not realizing that Shelbyville was far off, halfway across the state. Before they returned to Chiapas, she handed me an envelope with a letter written in Tzotzil. As one of our Tzotzil literacy teachers, María had taught her sister to read and write in their mother tongue. She showed me the photographs she had taken of the little boy, of his lavender plastic scooter in front of their home, of the family lined up in front of the church of Chamula. She asked me to please send it to her sister, but afterwards I discovered there was no address on the envelope. I decided to open the letter and read it, and found a most moving message urging her sister and brother-in-law, lacking the family around them, not to quarrel, but to live happily, knowing that her family back in Nichnabtik was rooting for them and taking good care of their baby. María later bought a cell phone so they could speak to each other. The boy's father came back to Chiapas, hoping to take his son to Tennessee, but lacking the necessary papers, he was told it was an impossible task, so he returned to the States alone.

Unfortunately, with the continuing economic situation in Mexico being so critical for Mayan farmers, the temptation for them to risk all to reach *el Norte* is on the increase.

4

Personal and Social Impacts

IN 1992 THE STATE OF CHIAPAS gave scholarships to two young men to join the cast and learn from us. From faraway Cancuc, they were considered by Zinacantecs to be "forest animals." The first day the men watched our bizarre exercises intently. Then, the second day, they added their own playfulness with an abandon no one could believe. Although unrelated, Petul and Xun 2 looked almost identical, and soon we were calling both of them Petulxun.

The lack of self-consciousness among new actors has always surprised me, but I wonder if it isn't that everyday Mayan life in Chiapas is itself so theatrical. Visits to other people's houses are staged with considerable formality. A person walking or talking in public knows that he or she is being closely watched.

Clothing is an important aspect of a person's position. The members of Sna were, and still are, encouraged to wear traditional clothes in the office and on theatre tours, but this has diminished greatly, especially among the men. Albina, from Huixtán, wore a different *ladina* dress every day. "Where does she get the money?" they wondered.

The exercises forced women to adopt new footwear and pants (though these were often changed after the rehearsal). The wearing of pants by women is a personal decision that changes now from day to day.

Then there is the question of costuming. Rosenta was embarrassed in her role as a U.S. waitress because she had to wear a red skirt that showed her knees. Matyo (a man) wore a green dress as a frog, and Antun was unhappy being the buxom daughter of the German *finquero* and afraid of being laughed at in his town. In *Jaguar Dynasty,* "dressed in loincloths and feathers, they parade about the stage—an activity and a sight as strange for them as it would be for a down-Mainer. They can't believe their daring. Their off-stage smiles are dazzling" (Laughlin to Lewis 1992). Maryan, the former *presidente* of Chamula who acted with the troupe between 1983 and 1994, exclaimed, "I'll never be afraid again!"

Another challenge was speech. First was the difficulty of learning the lines and having to take the script home at night to memorize. Regarding his role in *Jaguar Dynasty*, Maryan explained, "I accepted the role of Matahuil, the prophet . . . but I found it difficult to learn my lines, the words seemed very ancient" (Craig 1993, 65). When plays were performed in Tzotzil, the Tzeltal actors had to brush up on the neighboring language, as different, say, as Spanish and Italian.

Petu' complained, "We have only performed our plays in Spanish, because the men knew that with every town divided by political factions, their enemies would have great sport with them enacting the roles of spooks and buzzards. Then our playwright exclaimed, 'Don't you think I've heard every kind of black gossip for working with seven men? Has it hurt me? Get some courage and let's perform in our communities!'" (Laughlin to Sandrock 1990). So the first two plays were translated into Tzotzil; for *The Loafer and the Buzzard* it took five days.

"On the way [to Romerillo], several of the actors said, "'Let's do it in Tzotzil!' Margarita protested. 'I've never done it in Tzotzil!' 'Oh, you can do it!' And she did, as if she had always done it in Tzotzil—except when she was bawling out her husband she used the word *'puta,'* that brought down the house" (Laughlin to Lee 1993).

The roles themselves could be a problem. After Maryan was removed from the presidency of Chamula, we made the mistake of converting him into the Buzzard—a situation so unbearable that he quit the cooperative for a year. He was not much happier as the constable in *Deadly Inheritance*, but was well satisfied when instead he became the *presidente*. Shortly before the performance of *Jaguar Dynasty* Maryan had a dream.

> He was walking through a beautiful valley when he saw feathers from a quetzal lying on the ground. This bird's plumage had been prized by the ancient Mayan nobility. One long and iridescent feather caught Maryan's attention and he wanted to take it, but he was afraid of being caught with something so exquisite without permission. Suddenly, the owner of the property appeared and asked Maryan what he was doing.
>
> "It's nighttime and I'm an actor who's dreaming," replied Maryan.
> "Ah, so what is your role?" the man asked.
> "Matahuil, the prophet," answered Maryan.
> "That's a very important role. You should take a feather."

But Maryan demurred and began walking again. He came to railroad tracks. A train rumbled straight at him and he couldn't get out of the way.

"I started to get more and more strength, like Hercules on television. It was incredible!" he exclaimed to me while waving his arms, his voice straining and fluctuating in octaves. "I just grew stronger and stronger until I was able to pick up the train with my bare hands." The soft-spoken man with eyes like puddles of moist adobe after a rain was completely awed by his own power.

Maryan was about to toss the train over a cliff when suddenly it spoke to him.

"Don't push me, please, We are friends."

The train had turned into a Mexican man. (Craig 1993, 60–61)

While in Tzotzil dreams it is not unusual for a powerful figure, like a bull, to become a man, this transformation is quite inventive!

Other challenging roles were those that involved religion. "For men it has been difficult performing the role of a saint, or of Christ, as they fear that the Mayan audience will accuse them of perverting their Mayan Catholicism or of using it for personal gain.... Xun was deeply disturbed by a scene in a play recreating the Spanish Conquest where the friar orders the general to burn the Indian leader. 'But I am a Catholic, too!'" (Laughlin 1999, 496).

For women, there are other issues as well. Analyzing the gender situation, Petu' explains:

In the indigenous communities of Chiapas, women have many problems: tradition demands that women stay in their houses, because people think that only men can and should work in the fields or in other non-domestic activities. People believe that a woman's duty is to clean the house, cook, have and take care of the children, fetch water and firewood, and constantly weave, because the family should wear new clothes at each religious festival, and since there are many festivals, women have to be forever at the loom, weaving new clothes for each celebration.

But that's not all. Distrust is also common, and many husbands are jealous; they don't like women to talk to other men, unless it is absolutely necessary. This is how male children are also brought up, so not even single women have the freedom to speak or express their ideas or feelings, since the whole family is watching to see that the girls don't talk to or smile at the boys. For these reasons, most indigenous women grow up to be very shy; they are embarrassed to say what they think, they can't openly express their emotions, their needs, their suffering or happiness, because there is so much criticism. Any conduct that isn't in keeping with tradition makes people have a low opinion of women and criticize them. (Steele 1994, 254)

Because of this traditional upbringing, the women were initially uncomfortable acting, especially with men.

For a Mayan woman to agree to work with a group of males and to present herself to the public on stage takes tremendous courage. Petu's father asked her, "Why don't you get a decent job and be a maid?" This, even though it is common knowledge that Indian maids frequently are sexually abused by their mestizo employers. The first time a woman acted in one of the plays, an Indian spectator exclaimed, "You must have bought her!" (Ibid.)

Markarita, a trained secretary with a high school education, remarked, "Some of our male colleagues mock us women. They think that acting is not for us. They think we should stay at home" (Rojas 1993, 55). Chavela confessed, "It's not just the men who gossip. The women are jealous, and they talk among themselves about me" (Laughlin 1991/1992, 45).

When two Chamulan women joined the group, one who just whispered and the other who trembled all day, my wife Mimi became "their grandmother" and made them feel more at home, an experience she found rewarding: "It has been very exciting to watch a barefoot Chamulan woman gain her voice" (Laughlin to Mora 1990).

Rosenta, especially, found acting difficult.

I gambled on including Rosenta on our trip to accompany María even though for two years she has seemed to have zero acting ability. We gave her a part with no script, but she returned to Chiapas with a whole store of confidence. We have been reviving one of our old plays that has a scene between two women [*Deadly Inheritance*] and Rosenta is speaking up with good intonation and considerable strength. Our newest female member, Leti from Tenejapa, who is so shy that she can barely open her mouth, reminds us of how much patience is required. (Laughlin to Collins 1997)

Leti eventually overcame her shyness. In 2001 she became Sna's first female president, and she was reelected in 2002.

The personal impact of being involved with Sna can extend to family relations. Maruch spoke of the power of the theatre: "I used to be very timid, very fearful. But as an actress, I learned how to use my voice better. When I spoke with my father, it wasn't with anger, but yes, he listened" (Underiner 1998, 369).

When asked to describe what theatre meant to them, the actors responded:

Chavela (regarding FOMMA): "It's the force of the group that gives energy!"
Petu': "Theatre is my life!"
Sokoro: "Theatre was my dream; now it is my reality."
Chep: "Theatre is a way to express my culture."
Xun: "Theatre gives me great liberty."

This sense of liberty even extended to me when we were performing *From All for All* in Mérida at the Casa de Cultura. "As the shots rang out I stood up and fell at the feet of the judges, to their great surprise, rising to scream, '*¡Viva Chiapas!*' Tziak was very pleased to have me become a corpse before his eyes" (Laughlin to Lee 1996).

With new confidence the actors suddenly began to flourish in many endeavors: writing, photography, radio, weaving, community affairs. Pleased to hear both Indians' and Ladinos' compliments, they felt smarter. Although they recognized the importance of acting as kings and gods, when asked which roles they most enjoyed, those that brought the laughs are the ones remembered most fondly.

One major surprise occurred when Petu', whom we thought had been out sick, returned to work saying, "Here is my play, I haven't figured out yet how the ending should be" (Laughlin to Sandrock 1990). This play, *Una mujer desesperada* (*A Desperate Woman*), is now available in English (Costantinto and Taylor 2003, 293–310). Soon Chavela took to writing a play, and Mimi noted that "her play improves on every reworking ... she's as sophisticated as a Radcliffe student" (Laughlin to Merck 1991).

Both Chavela and Petu' were invited in 1991 to the Second International Women Playwrights' Conference in Toronto, becoming Mexico's first Indian women playwrights. The next year, after penning a play, *La desconfiada* [The distrustful woman], on the airplane, they participated in the Smithsonian Institution's Quincentenary Conference, "Images: Women in the Americas."

"Flanked by women from Spain, Portugal, North, Central, South America, all women with PhDs or noted novelists, etc., these two high school graduates captured the hearts of the whole audience with their simplicity, their direct, dramatic enactment of the personal importance of communication" (ibid.).

In 2002–2003, both Tziak and Petu' were trained in theatre direction and pedagogy by the renowned Mexican director Luis de Tavira.

Currently both Tziak and Petu' are actively involved with Sna and FOMMA in the direction of new plays. Tziak has radically redesigned *Danza para la vida,* which Michael Garcés helped create in 2001.

In 1990, at the request of the Fundación Mexicana de Planificación Familiar (Mexfam), Palas created two family planning plays: *El burro y la mariposa* [The donkey and the butterfly] and *Cuando menos burros, más elotes* [With fewer donkeys, more corn on the cob]. These were performed in twenty-five towns in Chiapas. Under the Theatre's contract with Mexfam, Petu' became a member of Sna.

In 1993, believing they were the targets of male discrimination within the association, Chavela and Petu' established their own all-female cooperative, La Fortaleza de la Mujer Maya (FOMMA) (The Strength of Mayan Women), providing a unique service for urban Indian women and children. In FOMMA's theatre the women took the male roles and addressed women's problems with their own voices.

The members of Sna believe that every play, besides being entertaining, should have a message. Following a performance they welcome questions and comments by the audience. They cannot recall a single play that was not appreciated. This is especially so in the hundreds of hamlets in Chiapas. In the autonomous Zapatista communities, which have set up their own governments in opposition to the national political party system, the audience is surprised by the Theatre's focus on the injustices suffered by Mayas. Again and again we have been told, "This is the truth!" Manvel speaks of the congratulations:

> It's so good you are doing this: Aside from [the puppet shows] being pretty, they're very interesting. This way we can remember the legends that our ancestors told, and for the children it is something new. After seeing them they begin with questions, and we tell them what our fathers told us. If this continues they will never be lost. It will always be in our memory, and we will tell them to the new gener-

ations. They will remember our grandfathers with respect. They will love our language, because that is the most important thing, since you present [the shows] in our language without it being hard to understand, not like Spanish which we don't know how to speak, and much less understand what is said. (Pérez Hernández 1992, 94)

In these communities where there is little if any television or other entertainment, children receive messages from the plays and imitate the actions in their games, while adults have taken our messages as a model to transform social life. Many plays have also been presented on local TV channels, now accessible in the Indian hamlets.

Play performance in San Juan Chamula, 2004. Photo courtesy Sna Jtz'ibajom

Our audience in Chiapas has ranged from the governor's wife and the wife of President Salinas, Cecilia Occelli de Salinas, from whom we received a letter of praise, to Zoque refugees from the Chichonal eruption, to Tzotzil orphans of the Acteal massacre, to inmates of the San Cristóbal jail who sat in the courtyard while the guards on the roof clutched their semiautomatics and laughed together uproariously. After the show an Indian convict stood up to thank the group, repeating over and over, "Don't forget us!" In 1989 our theatre was invited by the San Cristóbal authorities to perform at the spring fair, the first time that an Indian group had participated in the event.

In 1990 at the XI Muestra Nacional de Teatro in Monterrey we were the only Indian theatre among the fifty-one contenders, and we won sixth place.

In 1991, when we performed for the Sociedad Mexicana de Antropología in San Cristóbal, I commented, "It will be strange to see Indians mixed in with all those Marxist anthropologists who haven't given a damn about them."

Through the years the Monkey Business Theatre has performed at many theatre festivals in southeastern Mexico and Mexico City. As Petu' says, "The theater has also been a great help for the mestizo public, which has disparaged our language and our culture for so long, that [now] they may know our way of living and thinking, and we notice that they consider us with more respect, and in many cases even admiration" (Laughlin 1991/1992, 47). In addition to its participation at several Mesa Redondas in Palenque, the group has presented plays for the Experiment in International Living and the National Endowment for the Humanities Summer Institute.

In the United States the Theatre has performed at fifteen universities; at museums in Austin, Chicago, Cleveland, New York City, and Washington, D.C.; and at the Laurel Theater in Knoxville, La Tea in New York City, the Guadalupe Theater in San Antonio, and the Gala Hispanic Theater in Washington, D.C.

Our multicultural outreach is impressive. In Milwaukee we acted in the Indian Summer Festival and for the Oneida Nation at St. Norbert's College. On Labor Day in Milwaukee we rode on a flatbed truck to protest NAFTA, which had meant the loss of 80,000 jobs in the city. In Cleveland we acted in an inner city African American school, an Italian/Polish blue-collar family school, and at the Laurel School for girls in Shaker Heights, from where they sent us the children's drawings. At the Duval School in Lake Worth

the actors, with their animal masks, cavorted among elementary school students, finally asking them if they wanted to wear the masks. Every hand shot up. In one school, 700! As they departed single file, the white and black students joined the Latinos in shaking the actors' hands, saying, "¡Adiós amigo!" while many stopped to touch with one finger a toad mask. Though one teacher reportedly complained that the actors were just stirring up trouble, looking for help for the rebels, others wrote to say it had been a "social catharsis" for the black kids to see "people of color" acting with pride and assurance. Reviewing their role, the actors concluded, "We entertain. There is always a bit of joking, but it's the truth. We see great hardship. It isn't just entertainment." (Laughlin 1995, 531)

As Donald Frischmann (1991, 122–123) notes, "Such projects manifest an active consciousness of the different self, or of otherness, which may also be identified with the concept of nativism and a contemporary indianist philosophy."

5

The Immokalee Special

IN 1994 ALLAN BURNS, a professor of anthropology at the University of Florida, arranged with Laura Germino of Guadalupe Social Services and with Greg Absted and Lucas Benítez of the Coalition of Immokalee Workers a trip to Immokalee in the Everglades, where five thousand Mayan and Haitian workers pick tomatoes, chile peppers, and oranges. The recently formed coalition was confronting the abuses inflicted on these immigrant laborers.

They commented that our theater would be an effective way of dealing with social problems among the field hands. "What would you do?" they asked. "We would improvise." That meant nothing to them, so the actors stood up and enacted the return of a Mayan immigrant "who had not been careful," and who, after fruitless visits to a shaman and a doctor, finally died, not of SIDA (AIDS), but of *cidra*—cider.

Immokalee was a town of 15,000 in the non-picking season that grew to 45,000 when the pickers poured in. As it was March, we were met with cries of "Here are the Zapatistas!" In fact, one of our group was stopped and questioned by an immigration official. We were put up for the night in the ramshackle trailers where the pickers were housed. Conversing there and the next day we learned a bit of the local Spanish vocabulary, *"el agua del dich,"* the ditch water the workers were told they could drink! We added *"El Pelón,"* "Baldy," the nickname for one of the notorious foremen. Then there was *"la troca,"* the truck, *"el dompeador,"* the man who dumped the tomatoes in the truck, *"día y daime,"* day and dime, a unique system of economic exploitation.

As dark fell, 300 Indians formed a semicircle [to watch *From All for All*]. I asked if any were from Chiapas and ten hands went up.

Watching in rapt attention, quite predictably they laughed uproari-ously as the campesino couple stretched out under their blanket. They cheered when the campesina upbraided the men with, *"¿No son hombres?"* (Laughlin 1995, 531)

Next we improvised a play later entitled *El largo camino a $5.25* [The long road to $5.25]. In our play, using the vocabulary we had learned, we showed the hard lives of the pickers and the many abuses they endured. The play ended with the creation of the Coalition. One member of the Coalition, believing we were Zapatistas, exclaimed, "In just two days these Zapatistas learned all about us!" Afterward a Chamulan addressed us in Tzotzil:

"That's the way it is in my country." He thanked us, wished us "strong hearts," and exclaimed, "Don't let this be the last time you come. God willing we will see each other again!" Other immigrants there asked, "Is it true what you were showing or did you just think it up in your heads? Years and years pass and the government does not attend to our demands. This is not the same as the newspaper, which does not speak clearly! We must see about this because there are many people working here illegally. We must do the same thing. We are going to know what our rights are, too."

The immigrants said "they wanted to prepare themselves in the same way, to do the same thing so that their problems would be seen, would be recognized."

In the words of the Haitian social worker, "It was a magical night." (Ibid.)

In January 1997 the Coalition and Florida Legal Services invited us, with Ralph, to dream up a new play that would build on our previous improvisation. Ralph molded a wonderful, enormous red tomato head for *Don Tomate y sus coyotes* [Mr. Tomato and his smugglers]. This we performed near the Coalition headquarters. We were all to depart at six the following morning. Ralph and I shared a room. Not until years later did I hear that the Coalition had received word that the foremen, accusing the actors of being Zapatistas, were going to attack them, and so Lucas spirited them out at 2 a.m. to drive them to the air-port. Our visit made the front page of the *Naples News* on January 23 with the headline, "Mexican Troupe Dramatizes Farmworkers' Plight."

Despite the threat of violence, the Coalition was anxious for us to return in March to give a workshop to teach the pickers to create their own theatre, to make masks, and to act. We went to a retreat to work with the pickers, but it was very frustrating because often they were unable to attend our sessions. Finally, we incorporated several pickers in our cast. We held a dress rehearsal where Lucas Benítez, president of the Coalition, stood on the stage and spouted long speeches about the injustices. We told Lucas he must act, not just talk, and waited worriedly for the evening's performance. But he filled his role with amazingly quiet dexterity at La Belle and Immokalee.

The Coalition had a flatbed truck for *Don Tomate,* and we spent hours trying to figure out how we could present the play on such a narrow stage, and how to arrange the lighting, finally secured with the headlights of a car. This was for our second performance, when a big crowd gathered on the dirt. Partway through the play a bottle sailed over the heads of the audience and struck one of our actors, but we persisted. Then rain came down in sheets. The only place we could continue was in the cramped office of the Coalition, which immediately was chock full. With their bodies crammed together under the roof overhang, and their noses pressed against the wet window panes, others watched us perform, a scene reminiscent of Luis Valdez's Teatro Campesino in California in the 1960s.

Again we made the front page of the *Naples News* (March 24, 1997), with "Act 1 for New Farmworker Theater Troupe in Immokalee: The New Group Hopes to Share Problems and Find Solutions through Artistic Expression." On a later trip that year Kristobal, Tumin, and Leti returned for a short trip to Immokalee to provide a theatre workshop.

According to Lucas, "Our relationship with Sna Jtz'ibajom was instrumental in organizing our community of farm workers here in Immokalee, because their plays helped us to see our reality. They gave us the chance to examine the lives we are living and in that way seek solutions to our problems. Their theatre is a theatre of analysis and a major part of our program of popular education, which is designed to create in our members what we call 'Conscience + Compromise = Change,' a change from the grassroots up."

Although it was not possible for the Coalition to form their own theatre, our presentation, which insisted on the necessity to respond to the unfairness of workers' salaries, inspired their first hunger strike in the United States which, with Jimmy Carter's intervention, achieved their salary hike to $5.25. For their demonstrations they hired Ralph to craft a number of masks and made their own, too, later paraded in the streets in support of their successful Taco Bell boycott. Lucas and his Coalition have won many prizes, including the Robert Kennedy Prize, for bringing to light the fact that Immokalee workers, having moved to other jobs farther north, were subjected to slavery by armed

Chicano contractors. Individuals who were able to escape came to Immokalee to report firsthand to the Coalition—testimonies that led to having the slavers arrested and jailed.

Recognizing the fast-growing number of Highland Mayas seeking jobs across the border, Sna returned to Chiapas and created *Trabajadores en el otro mundo* (*Workers in the Other World*).

The visits to Immokalee had a strong impact on our actors. They became anthropologists, even recording in memory the voices of the undocumented workers. Tziak told me, "We go not to teach, but to learn."

In our virtual exhibit, *Unmasking the Maya: The Story of Sna Jtz'ibajom* (Laughlin 2002–2003), they report on their experience and give their analysis of what they saw and heard. Xun speaks:

> Parts of Mexico have industry, technology, and other signs of progress, but Chiapas remains a poor agricultural state, the poorest in the country, and one of the poorest regions in the world. People are destitute. There are few opportunities for finding work and, since the North American Free Trade Agreement, our native corn is being displaced by hybrid corn imported from the United States. Industrial corn is only good for feeding pigs. It has no soul, like our corn that was a gift from the gods. Their corn is cheaper, and now we can't count on a local market where we can sell our harvest. Because of this, many of our countrymen have to emigrate to the U.S. in search of jobs. They think that migrant work will be better than starving or suffering under the military oppression that has followed the Zapatista Rebellion.
>
> As soon as we arrived in Immokalee, the workers surrounded us, and we asked them about the problems facing them. Many were poor Mayas who either had no work or were paid starvation wages in their own countries. They told us of their suffering, which was almost as bad as the abuses they have experienced here.
>
> One member of our group was caught and interrogated: "Where are you from and what are you doing here?" But since he had the proper papers, nothing bad happened. The directors of the Coalition of Immokalee Workers went to talk to the *migra* and freed him, and later the story appeared in the local newspaper.
>
> In Immokalee they live in trailers. Each trailer has a kitchenette, a bathroom, and three or four small rooms. Three or four people live in one room. Each one pays $500 a month for a little place to sleep.

Those with the good fortune to reach Immokalee have no guarantee of work. Every morning at 6 a.m. thousands line up in the town plaza to wait for the trucks that will carry them to the fields. When the trucks are filled, many men are left by the side of the road. Some get work only two or three days a week.

Some save a lot of money. Even though they only work three days a week they can live and send money home to their families. Those who have been here a few years can buy a small used car. Those who don't know how to save their money spend it on beer. They go to the cantinas, to night spots where there are prostitutes, of which there are many in this small town. They spend all the money they've earned.

The ranchers own the beer stores, grocery stores, and clothing stores. The stores sell used clothes that are infested with fleas.

The contractors are all Chicanos who know how to speak English. They are the ones who deal with the ranch owners. The workers have no idea who the owner is. The workers are badly treated by the contractors. The contractors are vicious. They only paid the workers $4.00 an hour.

Our play would reinforce their demand for a raise in pay, from $4.00 to $5.25 an hour, the basic minimum wage. That was the idea and that is what happened. The workers told us that after one day of not working the ranch owners lost thousands of dollars. The following day the contractors offered $5.25 an hour. We changed the title of the play to $5.25.

The plays were a kind of catharsis. The migrants said they wanted to prepare themselves in the same way, to do the same thing, so that their problems would be seen, would be recognized. We returned the following year, and again in 1998, to give classes in body movement, voice projection, improvisation, playwriting, and theatre production.

Undocumented worker speaks:

We suffer a lot to get here, because we came as wetbacks. We have to cross deserts, hide in sewer drains, because if the immigration officers see us, they send us back where we came from. They look for us on horseback, on motorcycles, with airplanes, with dogs. When a plane passes over, we cut down a tree and hide under it or we use the tree as an umbrella.

Kristobal speaks:

After we presented *De todos para todos,* the audience asked us why the Zapatistas took up arms. "Because there is so much corruption, and that's no lie," we told them. The EZLN represents the best values and the hope for justice with dignity for native people, not only in Chiapas but in all of Mexico. They have no other way to be heard with respect than to follow the armed path.

Rosenta speaks:

On their days off they can't leave to go into town, like in our country, because if they go out, the *migras,* or immigration officers, grab them. They have to go out secretly, because the *migras* will see they're illegal. The immigration officers know immediately because the illegal guys can't speak English.

Undocumented worker speaks:

When we go to cut tomatoes, they give us each a bucket. For every bucket they give us a chip. If the bucket's not full, they scold us, they hit us, and won't give us the chip. They treat us like dogs. When we go to work, they growl at us if we don't work fast enough. When we're thirsty, they say, "Drink the water from the ditch!" Then they kick us.

Maryan 3 speaks:

Our hope is that the seed we planted there will grow. That the group and its art will reproduce and be robust.

Tziak speaks:

When we mounted *De todos para todos* (*From All for All*) in 1994, we dedicated it to the memory of our countrymen who fell in ancient and recent wars in Chiapas, struggling against the same social, economic, political, and cultural conditions that we have endured for over 508 years. The play reflects our beliefs and convictions about the causes of the Zapatista movement, which surprised the entire world with its armed uprising.

They learn to be invisible, but many return in a coffin. Others lose their lives without anyone knowing their names or who they are.

The coyotes, or smugglers, entice men and women to cross into the United States on the pretext that a more beautiful life exists in this country and they can earn a lot of money. They say that the gringos wipe their behinds with dollar bills. They say that all you have to do is enter the bathrooms, take the bills from the wastebaskets, wash them off, and you can return with a pile of green dollars.

After they cross the border they endure mistreatment by the bosses, bad pay, sickness, sleeping with cockroaches and rats. Many sleep in the streets because they can't afford to rent a room for $100 a week.

The Coalition of Immokalee Workers adopted the slogan, "From the People, for the People." They teach the undocumented workers about their human rights. We lived with them and slept in their trailers. Only in this way could we understand their story. We thought we were on the coffee plantations in Chiapas, but much worse.

"March in the streets to attract the public!" the members of the Coalition told us. It was a great surprise for people to see Indians from Tenejapa, Chamula, and Zinacantán marching in their native costumes through the streets. The onlookers shouted, "¡Viva los Zapatistas!"

At our second meeting a man appeared who had been beaten. His shirt was covered with blood. He had asked for a drink of water and they beat him savagely. Then they told him to drink the water from the ditch, which was contaminated with pesticides used to fumigate tomatoes.

We went to the authorities, along with reporters from the local newspaper and television channel. They presented the bloody shirt as evidence of maltreatment by the bosses. But the result was negative. As undocumented workers, they have no right to ask for justice.

We presented *De todos para todos* in the patio of a church where many people gathered. Some of the ranchers came to watch. They said that the play was about *Zapatismo*. They turned around, put on their dark glasses, and told the workers to appear for work at 4 a.m. the next morning.

Because of the impact caused by our play, the workers were changed in attitude, and this bothered the bosses. "Let's capture the Zapatistas before they cause more problems and the workers rebel against us!" they said. Immediately the workers ran to advise us, and we left at two in the morning so they wouldn't grab us and throw us as food to the crocodiles, which are abundant in the lakes and swamps of Florida.

For my part, it was an historical experience but a drastic one, to know that places exist in the world where there is still racism, intolerance, and no recognition of human rights. The rich only think of money and not of the well-being of humanity. For many a life with justice and dignity is still a utopia.

Turning from the actors' assessments of the world to the world's judgment of them, it is instructive to note the newspaper headlines in Mexico and the United States (see bibliography). Again and again they are championed as presenting their "ethnicity in action" by reinforcing their tradition, stimulating their literary and dramatic creativity, offering their history and their understanding of the world and their problems, protesting their marginalization, finding solutions, and sharing all the above with fellow and other Indians as well as with foreigners. As Frischmann documents, these actors, like the Zapatistas, are demanding that they be treated as *subjects* and not *objects* (Frischmann 2001, 116).

6

The Future

FOR THE MAYAS time is thought to be cyclical. The future repeats and develops from the past. Just so, Mayan myths repeat old truths, but adapt them constantly to the present situation. The same is true of the Monkey Business Theatre. Currently, the major support for the cooperative is from the State of Chiapas and Oxfam International. We were concerned that government involvement might threaten the cooperative's autonomy, but the Chiapas officials have given us total freedom. However, support from Oxfam is now conditional, requiring that the Monkey Business Theatre attend to poverty and the search for peace. The actors were upbraided for ignoring a crisis in Zinacantán during which the Partido Revolucionario Democrático (PRD) members of the civil government and their supporters in several hamlets were cutting off all water to the Zapatista members of those hamlets, arguing that the Zapatistas were refusing to enter the religious hierarchy or to perform community activities. The Zapatistas' promise to do so was ignored. After increased harassment, more than a hundred families fled their homes. Then, two hundred masked Zapatistas from their highland headquarters in Oventic offered to escort those families back to their hamlets. The march was overseen by five hundred police with a helicopter overhead. Despite the government's insistence that tranquility has been restored, nothing has been resolved, and tension remains high.

Indeed, the Zapatista leader, Subcomandante Marcos, focused on this act to show that the supposedly "leftist" PRD party was no such thing. Seeing that no political party would support the Indians, he called on people to ignore the 2006 presidential election and to unite in a broad campaign for change.

Despite Oxfam's admonishments, the Zinacantec members of Sna Jtz'ibajom, as well as those from Chamula and Tenejapa, were unwilling to become embroiled in this dangerous political upheaval. Consequently, they came up with a trick to keep surviving. There now is a new version of *De todo para todos* (*From All for All*) that focuses on the necessity of sharing water in the Indian communities. Last year, puppeteering was revived by Antonio Coello, who directed *El General Grillo* [General Cricket], which was presented by the Theatre to Lacandóns at Naja. The Monkey Business Theatre will repeat the moral lessons of the past in the future, but "for women as well as for men, the discipline of the theatre itself can work for change within a culture as well as in the larger world in which it presents itself" (Underiner 2004, 76).

On December 15, 2006, the cooperative received from President Fox the Premio Nacional de Ciencia y Artes; Arte Tradicional y Popular. "This prize is the highest recognition that the Mexican Government bestows on those who have followed such a special course and have carried out endeavors that contribute to enlarging the cultural, scientific and technological patrimony of our country." More specifically, *"arte tradicional y popular"* refers to Indian cultural achievement.

Upon receipt of the prize, our president, Xun, urged President Fox to create an Instituto de Ciencia y Artes Maya at a university level. The president stated that "Tomorrow I will set the first stone." Currently, in the role of untitled academic adviser, I am a member of the commission, led by Sna Jtz'ibajom, to create this institute as a project of the new Universidad Intercultural de Chiapas, based in San Cristóbal. Since the founding of Sna Jtz'ibajom, its members had dreamt of creating an Indian-directed autonomous cultural unit of high prestige. They hope that such an institute will stimulate greater respect for and wider presentation of their plays, as well as permit them to train the younger generation to become actors and playwrights, ensuring a long life for Mayan theatre.

THE PLAYS

The Loafer and the Buzzard

(1989)

FOR OUR FIRST PLAY I suggested a folktale I had collected (Laughlin 1977) that was widely known in Mexico and Guatemala. Versions of what I call here *The Loafer and the Buzzard* (*El haragán y el zopilote*) had been recorded among the Yaqui of Sonora; Tlapanec of Guerrero; Mixtec of Oaxaca; Tzotzil of Chamula, Chenalhó, and Zinacantán; and among the Awakatek, Kaqchikel, Mam, and Tz'utujil in Guatemala. In the role-switching motif of this version, the Loafer, dressed as a Zinacantec, learns to his distress, including eventual death, that the Buzzard's life is not so easy as it appears. On the other hand, the Buzzard, by his hard work, convinces the Loafer's wife that despite his foul odor, he is a worthy husband.

In the Mayan world, man struggles to raise corn, dependent on the good will of our Lord, the Sun. The Loafer addresses the Buzzard, named here "Juan," with great respect, lest with his supernatural power the Buzzard cause him harm. The Buzzard, too, must seek permission from our Lord. This tale was familiar to all the members of the group. It required few actors, a limited script, and with the dramatic mask crafted by Ralph Lee, it would surely captivate the public.

At a time when we were sorely in need of funds to continue in operation, we sent a proposal to a Catholic foundation in the Netherlands. A letter of recommendation from Bishop Samuel Ruiz, who later became the chief mediator between the Zapatistas and the Mexican government, seemed in order, so I instructed our Buzzard to accompany me to the bishop's office next to the Cathedral of San Cristóbal. A *madrecita,* with some consternation, ushered us into Tatik Sam's room, where he looked up, surprised, from his desk. When we explained our mission, he readily agreed and, indeed, attended our first performance that afternoon in the house of Diego de Mazariegos, the sixteenth-century Spanish conquistador.

Residents of the Indian towns in highland Chiapas customarily wore, or still wear, clothing distinctive of their towns. This informs the costume choices of this and all the other plays.

This play became an early favorite, especially among children, and was filmed in a natural setting by Carlos Martínez (Martínez 1993). His video was shown repeatedly on Chiapas television. See Montemayor 1996a for the Tzotzil and Spanish versions.

LOAFER'S WIFE: Zinacantec clothing, with shawl
NEIGHBOR 1: Zinacantec clothing
NEIGHBOR 2: Zinacantec clothing
NEIGHBOR 3: Zinacantec clothing
LOAFER: Zinacantec clothing
BUZZARD: mask, short pants, black cloak, huaraches
BUZZARD MAN: same as Loafer
BUZZARD MAN'S WIFE: same as Loafer's Wife
LOAFER BUZZARD: same as Buzzard

Act I

SCENE 1

(A field near Zinacantán. A Zinacantec woman appears carrying a heavy load of laundry. Walking along, she addresses the public as if she were talking with her friends who accompany her to the river.)

LOAFER'S WIFE: Oh, I don't know what to do! Since we got married my husband never wants to work. He gets up very late and doesn't even talk. It seems as if he is really tired. I make his coffee, I make his breakfast. He just eats. He doesn't even look up. It seems as if he's ashamed. Maybe it's because he didn't get a good crop of corn last year. This year we've had to get loans. I'm ashamed to ask for more from our neighbors. But what can we do? The hunger's too much. I don't want to talk to them anymore, because I know they'll say he never works, he never does anything, that he just goes to sleep in his cornfield. I hope that isn't so or how in the world are we going to be able to eat! When I finish washing the clothes, I'm going to pray to our Lord so my husband will come to his senses! *(She exits.)*

SCENE 2

(A Zinacantec man enters, wearing his work clothes, looking from side to side as if someone were chasing him. When he is about to flee, several men come in from the other side. They shout as he flees.)

NEIGHBOR 1: You bastard, don't you hide! When are you going to pay me for the ten pounds of corn I gave you?

NEIGHBOR 2: You said you'd pay me at Christmastime. How can you pay me when you haven't even cleared your cornfield?

NEIGHBOR 3: Don't you run away, you bastard! Loafer! You're so free and easy.

(They exit angrily, chasing after him.)

SCENE 3

(The man being pursued returns exhausted. He looks about him to see if anyone is chasing him. He seems to be really tired when he walks. He spreads out his woolen poncho. He lies down. He uses his tortilla bag as a pillow. Then a buzzard glides by. It circles around without moving its wings.)

LOAFER: Oh, holy Buzzard, how do you manage to go about doing nothing? You just glide along without even moving your wings. You never work. As for me, I suffer so much, I'm in a bad way. Look at my hands, all blistered! My hands are being ruined. They hurt so much that now I can't work. No, I'll die if my hands get worse. If only I'd been given a chance to be a buzzard!

(It thunders and then a buzzard arrives next to the man.)

BUZZARD: Okay, okay, what do you want of me? That's enough whining. Our Lord sent me. What do you want?

LOAFER: (*Scared*) Nothing, nothing at all, Sir John, it's because you soar in the sky wonderfully. You never move your wings. But me? I suffer so much. Work makes me so tired, and my corn never turns out well. My wife is scolding me now, since I don't have any corn. So I borrow it. When I ask for corn, when I ask for beans, when I return home, "Wife, now we have corn and beans," I tell her. It's just lies. Afterwards I have to go into hiding because I'm asked to give it back. How can I pay for it?

BUZZARD: (*Looking up into the sky*) My Lord, see the Loafer! (*Addressing the Loafer*) Get to work, you haven't even cleared your cornfield! All you do is keep repeating, "Oh god, the work is so hard! I'll see about it tomorrow." Then you take a nap. That's the way it is every day. What you need to do is work.

LOAFER: Oh no, I can't bear it. I've never figured out what other people do. My work never ends.

BUZZARD: Now me, I've seen that whoever works, wins out. Before dawn they've already gone to work—clearing, planting, weeding, hoeing. When the corn is ready, they come home exhausted for sure, but they're happy. They bring a lot of corn, a lot of beans. Who do you think wouldn't be happy with that? Those who know how to work have full stomachs.

LOAFER: That's what you say, since you don't get blisters on your hands. We sweat so much, we stink. Well, pardon me, Father Buzzard, Sir John, pardon me, is it true that you want to become a man?

BUZZARD: Well, that certainly wouldn't be a bad thing! It's true I sure don't like my food. What I see is that your wife tastes wonderful ... I mean she prepares really good food. I can't get my food in a jiffy. Sometimes we find it, sometimes we go to sleep hungry. If we can't find any the next day, we have to eat shit.

LOAFER: See here, Father Buzzard, if you'd like ... we could change ourselves. You would become a man and eat good things, and I would turn into a buzzard and soar in the sky. You would pay my debts. We'd both be happy, while I go off and you stay here. What do you say? Give me your feathers, your wings, 'cause they look so good to me! And I'll give you my clothes, too. Please, Father John!

BUZZARD: Well ... I don't know, I'll have to think it over. Oh, and besides I can't decide about it by myself. First I have to ask permission. We'll see. I'll let you know what I've been told.

LOAFER: Okay.

BUZZARD: Wait for me on Tuesday ... no, it's better on Thursday.

(The Buzzard flies off. The man stays behind happily, pretending to fly like a buzzard.)

LOAFER: How do buzzards fly? Ooh, it's probably great! Whoosh, crauuk!

(Several neighbors appear and look at him as if he were crazy.)

NEIGHBOR 1: What in the world are you doing?

NEIGHBOR 2: Has your hunger driven you mad?

LOAFER: No, I'm practicing to ... to ... So I won't find the work too hard, because now I'm preparing a big cornfield. That's why I'm exercising.

NEIGHBOR 1: Ha, ha, ha! Look at him! God!

NEIGHBOR 2: That's what people do who don't want to work!

NEIGHBOR 3: It looks to me as if he wants to turn into a buzzard.

(The neighbors exit on one side while the man bends over to pick up his things and exits on the other side.)

SCENE 4

(The inside of a Zinacantec house; a couple of chairs, a table, a hearth on the floor. A woman appears, preparing corn gruel. The man appears and walks over to the woman.)

LOAFER'S WIFE: How is your work going? Have you finished clearing away the brush?

LOAFER: Ah, it's nearly over. I've just cut off the branches from everything I cut down.

LOAFER'S WIFE: Oh, that's really good! If it's true you're working, then we can probably return the corn that we borrowed. May our Lord give you a good crop!

(The neighbors arrive and look around inside the house to see if there is any corn, if there are any beans. The Loafer hides behind his wife.)

NEIGHBOR 1: Well, things are going well with you now. When have you decided you'll pay me back for everything I loaned you?

NEIGHBOR 2: Your lazy husband never works.

NEIGHBOR 3: We went to see if he'd cleared his land. He hasn't even started it!

NEIGHBOR 1: When he isn't sleeping, he's just muttering to himself like a crazy guy. Maybe he thinks he's seeing us face to face!

LOAFER'S WIFE: No, forgive us, because he was sick. Now he's well, now he's working. Don't you worry. When the corn is ready, we'll give it to you, because you've been so kind.

NEIGHBOR 1: Oh, ma'am, you don't realize you've been tricked too!

NEIGHBOR 2: What's it to me? The two of you can figure out what to do when you're dying of starvation.

(The neighbors exit, muttering. The husband steps out from where he was hiding and gets a scolding.)

LOAFER'S WIFE: So I was right! That's why we haven't anything. Oh, my mother always told me, "Don't you marry that loafer!" As for you, you tell me you're working. Why did I ever believe you? Get out! Get to work! You'd better hurry up!

LOAFER: You're right, wife, but how can I work on an empty stomach? Give me a little corn gruel then! It's true that I worked hard. God, it's so hard. See here, give me a couple of tortillas so I can work!

LOAFER'S WIFE: Hmm, well, I'll give them to you, but if I hear it's true that you're loafing about, I don't know what I'll do!

(She gives him his tortillas, and then they exit. The man reenters on the other side. He looks up into the sky. He doesn't see anything. He sits down unhappily.)

LOAFER: Oh, I'm hungry again! And the Buzzard hasn't come. It's so hot! I'll mix myself a little corn gruel. Oh, it's so hard! Now I can't return my loans. The stinking Buzzard just tricked me. It told me it would come back on Tuesday. Who knows if it isn't Thursday today. Three days have passed. Damn it! That awful Buzzard is just a liar! Let it keep eating its stinking food!

(It thunders, and then the Buzzard glides in.)

BUZZARD: Rauuc! What! What are you doing, talking to yourself? Tell me, tell me! What do you keep repeating?

LOAFER: *(Scared)* Nothing, nothing, Father Buzzard! I was just wondering if you were given permission for us to change into one another.

BUZZARD: Ah, so then you still want us to make the change!

LOAFER: It's because I just can't do the work. How about it? Can we still make the change?

BUZZARD: He says we can. Our Lord has given his word. If it's with all your heart, we can change into each other if you no longer want to be a man. You fly off! I'll be your replacement. That's what I was told.

LOAFER: That's terrific! Oh, it feels like I can already fly.... But what if my wife realizes it's not me anymore?

BUZZARD: No, she won't realize it. Don't you see, it's our Lord's command. It's not me who gives the orders!

LOAFER: Well, let's change, then! Give me your clothes!

(The Loafer and the Buzzard change clothes.)

BUZZARD: Well, it's fine! Fly off now! Fly!

LOAFER: Now I'm happy! What do I do when I'm hungry? How do you look for your food?

BUZZARD: See here, don't make a mistake! When you see smoke puffing up from the woods, it's because there's something dead there. If you see a little bit of smoke, then it's only something small that died, like a sheep, a pig, or a chicken. If there's a lot of smoke, then it's surely a big meal, like a horse or a cow. When you see their smoke coming out, you go down. Then you eat!

LOAFER: Is that just what I do then? So when we're buzzards, we find food right away.

BUZZARD: Yes, in just a minute. Fly off now. Go have a good time! Come and see me the day after tomorrow or the next day, and we'll see how things are going with you. Fly off! Fly off!

LOAFER: (*He flies away.*) Oh, oh, oh, this is great. Now even an eagle can't keep up with me!

BUZZARD MAN: (*Transformed now into a man, he picks up his axe, thinking it looks very strange.*) Well, what am I supposed to do with this? (*He tries it out for a minute. He learns what it's for. Quickly he cuts down all the trees.*) Now my wife will be pleased! (*He exits.*)

Act II

SCENE 1

(*Inside the one-room house the Buzzard Man's Wife is fixing a meal when the Buzzard arrives.*)

BUZZARD MAN: Are you there, wife? Is my food ready, because I'm hungry.

BUZZARD MAN'S WIFE: Already? It's the first time I've seen you sweating when you come home. Now it seems you've been working.

BUZZARD MAN: Yes, wife, today I finished chopping down all the trees!

BUZZARD MAN'S WIFE: Are you telling the truth?

BUZZARD MAN: Yes. If you don't believe me, go take a look tomorrow, because I want you to help me with the burning so it won't run wild.

BUZZARD MAN'S WIFE: Oh, that's probably right. Well, here it is, eat up! (*She sniffs.*) What is it that smells so bad? Haven't you noticed it's like a dead dog? (*She goes and looks out the door.*) Where can that smell be coming from?

BUZZARD MAN: (*He is eating happily.*) I don't know. I don't smell anything bad.

BUZZARD MAN'S WIFE: (*Disgusted*) Oh, it's a terrible stink! Maybe somebody took a shit near here! Come on, we'll look for whatever it is that stinks. If we find it, we'll toss it off far away.

BUZZARD MAN: Okay, but I don't smell anything bad.

(*They both exit.*)

SCENE 2

(*They are there in the brush where the trees have fallen. The Buzzard Man had done a lot of work. Then the Loafer who turned into a buzzard glides in from the right.*)

LOAFER BUZZARD: Oh, oh, oh, I'm having such a good time! There's nothing like this, me, soaring in the sky. I don't even move my wings. How about you?

BUZZARD MAN: I'm just fine, working here.

LOAFER BUZZARD: Oh, it's true I wasn't good for anything. All the work you've done in such a short time. You've probably cleared five hectares in three days! I'll bet my wife really liked you. How was it, when you arrived? Didn't she tell you that I was good for nothing?

BUZZARD MAN: No, she didn't say much to me. She just asked me why I smelt so. "You really stink!" she told me.

LOAFER BUZZARD: Well, what did you say to her?

BUZZARD MAN: Oh, I told her, "Well, it's true I smell. It's because now I have been working. Before all I did was sleep. Now, go take a look, help me with the burning so the fire doesn't run wild!" I told her.

LOAFER BUZZARD: So you're coming with her?

BUZZARD MAN: That's what we decided.

LOAFER BUZZARD: Well, well, I'm going then. I'll see if I can find a little food, because I've flown a long time. I'm dying of hunger.

(Both exit.)

SCENE 3

(The Loafer Buzzard glides in and lands next to the house.)

BUZZARD MAN: Are you ready now, wife?

BUZZARD MAN'S WIFE: Let's go now, let's go now! I'll just put away my yarn. Change your clothes first! You really stink! It seems as if you'd eaten a buzzard!

BUZZARD MAN: Oh, wife, you know it's because I work so hard. (*He sniffs his armpit.*) Do you think I smell bad?

(He changes his shirt. When his wife is putting away her yarn, the Loafer Buzzard gets behind her.)

LOAFER BUZZARD: Crauuk! Wife, give me my meal!

BUZZARD MAN'S WIFE: Oh, how horrible, you scared me! Oh, it's you who stinks so bad. I blamed my husband for it!

LOAFER BUZZARD: Please give me one of your tortillas! I'm dying now of hunger!

BUZZARD MAN'S WIFE: What's this son of a devil saying? Get out you horrible, stinking thing! Whoosh, whoosh! Get out, you smelly devil!

The Loafer Buzzard hoping for a meal, 1987. Photo courtesy Sna Jtz'ibajom

LOAFER BUZZARD: Don't be like that, Mary! 'Cause I'm your husband. Give me some coffee, give me one of your tortillas, give me something, even if it's just a turd!

BUZZARD MAN'S WIFE: Why isn't that spiky-beaked bird scared of me? Get out, you stinker! (*She whacks it with a stick.*) Get out! Get out, you horrible thing! I don't want to look at your face anymore. Phew, phew, what a stink! (*While she is hitting it, her husband is laughing. She addresses him.*) Well, let's go now! I'll make sure if it's true that you've done a lot of work. Don't laugh! You seem like a crazy man. I blamed you for the horrible smell of that spiky-beaked bird!

SCENE 4

(*The man and the woman arrive in the brush, where there are lots of felled trees to be burned to clear the field for planting.*)

BUZZARD MAN'S WIFE: Look at all the work you've done! Oh god, if you get a good crop, we can pay back all the corn and beans we borrowed!

BUZZARD MAN: So you sit down here while I go and light the fire.

BUZZARD MAN'S WIFE: Okay.

> (*She sits and fixes her husband's meal while he's working. When he comes back, they eat. Smoke puffs up from the trees, and the Buzzard appears.*)

LOAFER BUZZARD: Crauuk! When a dog dies, when a pig dies, the smoke comes out of its head. If you want something to eat, first you look to see if there's any smoke. There's smoke here and I'm hungry! Now I can get my meal here! Whooosh! (*The Loafer Buzzard jumps into the fire.*)

BUZZARD MAN'S WIFE: Oh god, that horrible buzzard has come back again! What could it be doing? Oh!

BUZZARD MAN: (*He pulls his wife aside as the Buzzard catches on fire.*) Get out of the way! Get out of the way!

BUZZARD MAN'S WIFE: Oh, I'm right, the buzzard's so stupid. What could've gotten into the head of that awful spiky-beaked bird that it would come and land in the fire! It seems like it's the stinky buzzard I chased out of the house. That's what it is!

BUZZARD MAN: That seems to be the truth! He got what he deserved! He was warned about it. "If you want to be a buzzard so badly, then fly off!" he was told. That was the story.

The Loafer Buzzard lands in the fire, 2006. Photo courtesy Sna Jtz'ibajom

BUZZARD MAN'S WIFE: What's that? What are you saying? Who told him that?

BUZZARD MAN: It's just a saying, wife. Don't you pay any attention to it. Well, today we've burned up a lot of the trees. And besides, let's go throw away the smelly buzzard so it won't ruin the flavor of our meal.

SCENE 5

(The woman is at home, putting fruits and ears of corn on the table.)

BUZZARD MAN'S WIFE: At last, now we have some of our own corn! I'm so happy. Look how good the fruit is!

NEIGHBOR 1: That's not half bad! So things are getting better!

NEIGHBOR 2: Now you have a lot of corn and beans. Look how big your ears of corn are!

NEIGHBOR 3: And look at the size of the pears! And the size of the peaches, too!

BUZZARD MAN'S WIFE: Ah yes, I'm so happy. Take some fruits, whatever you want! I can't forget how good you were to us. Now we can pay you back!

NEIGHBOR 2: Now it's fine. If it were still because of your late husband, we'd have had to forget your loans. Yes indeed, he had such a hard time. The poor guy was so lazy!

BUZZARD MAN'S WIFE: How come my late husband? So I have two husbands or what? Don't you scare me! What did you all do to my husband?

NEIGHBOR 1: No, ma'am, we're not talking about your new husband.

NEIGHBOR 2: We're talking about your late husband!

BUZZARD MAN'S WIFE: Who, indeed, is the dead one? Please don't drive me crazy! Didn't I have just one husband shouting about?

NEIGHBOR 3: Now why don't you admit it, ma'am?

NEIGHBOR 1: Admit you had another husband. We saw him!

BUZZARD MAN'S WIFE: Oh, if my husband heard this, he would be furious. He'd surely kill us all! Get out of my house! When my husband returns, you can come and ask for our debts. I don't want to hear anything more. Where is my other husband that you're talking about?

NEIGHBOR 2: You claim you don't know. You claim you don't know!

NEIGHBOR 3: Isn't he the one who changed places with the buzzard?

BUZZARD MAN'S WIFE: What? A buzzard? Don't come and trick me! You decided you wanted me and my husband to split up.

NEIGHBOR 1: Don't tell us you didn't know!

NEIGHBOR 2: I don't believe you're so stupid that you didn't realize it!

NEIGHBOR 3: Now you're telling us you didn't know!

BUZZARD MAN'S WIFE: What didn't I know?

NEIGHBOR 1: What do you mean, ma'am? Your lazy husband changed places with a buzzard, the one who's your husband now.

BUZZARD MAN'S WIFE: My husband . . . a buzzard! You're just tormenting me!

NEIGHBOR 1: No, ma'am, because we saw him. It was the buzzard that died in your field.

BUZZARD MAN'S WIFE: What? What? How could I imagine it? Oh . . . my husband . . . my husband now used to be a buzzard!

NEIGHBOR 1: We certainly didn't want to tell you!

BUZZARD MAN'S WIFE: He really did a good job lying to me. Now I understand . . . his smell, his stink, because he changed with my late husband, who deserved what he got because he was always so lazy. And now this is the way it is!

NEIGHBOR 3: It's Sir John, the Buzzard!

NEIGHBOR 1: He surely is a good worker!

NEIGHBOR 2: What I'm saying is right, isn't it, Diego?

NEIGHBOR 3: For sure! He doesn't drink and he doesn't smoke.

BUZZARD MAN'S WIFE: (*She is recovering from this now.*) Well, okay, it certainly is an improvement. You couldn't stand his odor.

NEIGHBOR 1: Ha, ha, ha! Now you can, ma'am! Stick a piece of corncob up your nose! Ha, ha, ha! Well, we'll talk again some time.

NEIGHBOR 2: We'll come when Sir John is here. Give him my best!

(They exit laughing. The woman is left alone.)

BUZZARD MAN'S WIFE: So he really was a buzzard! He sure fooled me. So that's why he smelt so bad.

BUZZARD MAN: Are you there, wife? I'm hungry!

BUZZARD MAN'S WIFE: Why don't you go look for some smoke!

BUZZARD MAN: What happened to you to make you angry? What did the neighbors come and tell you? Why are you mad?

BUZZARD MAN'S WIFE: Why did you fool me? Why didn't you ever tell me that you had changed places with my husband, since you were a buzzard! That's why you stink so.

BUZZARD MAN: Me? Hell! What the people won't say so we'll return our debts! Me a buzzard!

BUZZARD MAN'S WIFE: You see, I'm right, it's true! I could always tell you smelt like a buzzard!

BUZZARD MAN: I never thought I was a buzzard. It's just that when I work, I sweat a lot. So what's it to us? I don't like you telling me I smell like a buzzard. Who was it spreading such gossip? You never used to get mad at me.

BUZZARD MAN'S WIFE: Just as I said! So you're still lying to me? When … when it was the Loafer, I certainly did get angry because I had nothing to eat.

BUZZARD MAN: Well, that's true. You're certainly right that you used to get angry.

BUZZARD MAN'S WIFE: I just don't want you telling me lies. So what's the difference? Okay, the lazy buzzard got what it deserved.

BUZZARD MAN: So then you aren't mad at me?

BUZZARD MAN'S WIFE: No, not at all. There are probably lots of women who'd want to have a husband like you, since you work so hard. Look at all the corn we have now, and the fruit! We're happy when our stomachs are full! Let's go to bed. You're probably *really* tired!

(She takes his hand and they exit, embracing each other.)

Who Believes in Spooks?

(1990)

WHO BELIEVES IN SPOOKS? (*¿A poco hay cimarrones?*) was created by the group to dramatize a local belief among the Tzotzil and Tzeltal Maya. Mothers warn their children to come inside at dusk lest they be carried off by a bat-like boogeyman, a spook. When the corn boils over and makes the fire hiss, it is thought to be a sign that a spook is about to pay a visit. In addition, spooks are considered to be in league with the civil engineers, providing victims for them to inter in the foundations of bridges.

For this play we collected all the lurid spook details known to our members, as well as many scenes I had published in *Of Cabbages and Kings: Tales from Zinacantán* (Laughlin 1977). This demon, this black bat creature, boasts a long pedigree and is probably the amalgam of cultural beliefs and historical events spanning thousands of years. In the ancient K'iche' Maya book, the *Popol Vuh,* the heroes, Hunahpu and Xbalanque, "were put inside Bat House, which had only bats inside. It was a house of death bats. These were great beasts with snouts like blades that they used as murderous weapons" (Christianson 2000, 112).

In the sixteenth century, when the Dominican friars arrived in Zinacantán (known as "Bat Place"), they found that the people "called themselves Zotcil Vinic which is the same as saying batman.... Their ancestors ... discovered a stone bat and considered it God and worshipped it" (Ximénes 1929, 360). *The Great Tzotzil Dictionary of Santo Domingo Zinacantán,* compiled in the sixteenth century, gives as the Tzotzil name for Zinacantán "Ik'al Ojov," or Black Lord (Laughlin and Haviland 1988, I:145). This term is remembered by no one today. In modern Acala, however, both Zinacantecs and vampire bats are called *chinacos*. And two legends from Chiapa de Corzo describe how the town of Ostuta was destroyed by thousands of huge black bats. Perhaps this refers to a historical incursion of Zinacantecs (Laughlin 1977, 65).

Another early report is given by Bishop Nuñez de la Vega:

In many towns … of this bishopric seven Blacks, corresponding to the seven days of the week, are painted on the repertories or calendars for making divinations and predictions.… The Indians are greatly afraid of negroes because they preserve the memory of one of their original forefathers having the color of Ethiopia[ns], who was a great warrior and extremely cruel according to a very ancient historical notebook in our possession that is written in their language. Those of Oxchuc and other towns of the lowlands hold in deep veneration [a god] called Yalahau [Ical-Ahau] which means Chief Black or, Lord of the Blacks. (Ordoñez y Aguiar 1907, 13)

According to Alan Payne (1932, 63), "A representation of this deity was carved on a beam of the church in Oxchuc in the form of a ferocious negro, like a piece of sculpture or a painted bust, with human limbs." It was destroyed by Bishop Nuñez de la Vega in 1687. It is possible that Ical-Ahau is kin to Ek Chua, the principal god of Yucatec merchants, who was always portrayed in black paint. This same god is also a warrior god.

Drawing upon a multitude of parallels in Mayan literature from Yucatán and Guatemala, Sarah Blaffer concludes that the Spook is the ancient bat demon associated with sexuality, blood, sacrifice and death (Blaffer, 1972, 57–67; see also Laughlin 1977, 348).

In *The Great Tzotzil Dictionary of Santo Domingo Zinacantán*, "*j'ik'al*" is given as "*negro de guinea*" (Laughlin and Haviland 1988, III:725).

The Spook's negroid features may derive from a memory of the African slaves. Although negroes are no longer native to the region, as late as 1778 there were 733 living in San Cristóbal. They were treated more as confidants than as slaves, for they were permitted to wear daggers and to dress in European clothing. As such, they served the role of majordomos and foremen who most likely were entrusted with the task of inflicting physical punishment on their master's Indian serfs. (Favre 1971, 81–82)

It is not farfetched to assume that the Spaniards increased their authority by spreading stories of the Africans' former cannibalistic appetites. In 1813, when the captain general declared that "here, even the stones are insurgents," he set out to recruit "ferocious Negroes" in the surrounding fincas to serve as a paramilitary force (Aubry 2004, 145). The Spook's cave-dwelling habits may possibly be traced to a memory of African slaves who escaped from the lowlands and sought temporary refuge in the wildest mountain areas. This is supported by the Spanish name for the Spook, *Negro Cimarrón,* Black Runaway Slave (Laughlin 1977, 348). While the term *spook* today is often used pejoratively to refer to African Americans, its traditional meaning is "specter": "(1) an apparition, (2) any object of fear or dread" (*Webster's* 1955, 1400). This is the sense in which I use it.

Today African Americans inspire great fear among Mayas traveling across the border. Realizing that this play would be performed in the United States with African Americans possibly in the audience, the actors emphasized the bat-like feature of the Spook in his mask. In Zinacantán, for Carnival the men dressed in Ladino clothes to impersonate spooks, but in recent years, with many Zinacantecs wearing Ladino clothes, they changed to rubber-masked clowns. When Antun performed in our play, he appeared in Carnival wearing his bat mask and his black cloak. His outfit was so popular that some people today, having learned from him how to make these masks in the Casa de Cultura, don the black cloaks and carry on the traditional ideas in a new custom.

When we were rehearsing the scene where a young woman is discovered hiding in a rolled up *petate,* or straw mat, Viktoria refused to act. Finally she explained that in her town of Chamula it used to be that the dead were rolled up in *petates* for burial. (To our astonishment, this highly conservative woman later went to Cancún, where she became a singer!) Confronted with this problem for the Theatre, Petu' agreed to be rolled up in the straw mat in her stead.

When this play was performed, the actors believed that it would be presumptuous to take the roles of God, the Virgin Mary, or the saints. But in *Who Believes in Spooks?* they converted the saints—San Juan, San Sebastian, and San Lorenzo—into three old men: Xun (Johnny), Xap (Sebby), and Lol (Larry). Brave women and men become the saints' soldiers, dealing deadly blows to the fearsome predator.

In 1992 I reported,

We have just witnessed the rebirth of the Mayan theatre in Chiapas, in Milpoleta, Chamula! After a dispirited performance of "Who Believes in Spooks" for Mexican cultural politicians in the Casa de las Imágenes, that they hadn't produced for six months, and which won them a harsh scolding by Ralph Lee, they ventured to Milpoleta. Xun asked me, as we stood on the basketball court, if Ralph would mind if they spoke Tzotzil for a part of it. "Not all in Tzotzil because the

Spook speaks Spanish!" I assured him that, no, he would be pleased. Without a pause, without a lapse, they flew into Tzotzil, double entendres galore. Maryan, ex-president of Chamula [enacting the role of their patron saint, Saint John], pointed to a pine tree where a bunch of women were sitting, too shy to approach the ball court, and said to the Spook, "Oh there, beneath that pine tree is sitting a complaining old hag who I'll give to you gladly!" (Laughlin to Vogt 1992)

When we came to the scene where the Spook carried the old woman into a real cave, only Petu' agreed to take the part, for caves are such a fearful element in Mayan culture, being the entrance to the underworld.

While the Spook is assumed to be a lecherous cannibal, it appears here as a rather pathetic creature—lonely, gullible, and wondering about its own identity.

Potovtik is a tiny Zinacantec hamlet, far removed from the center, virtually unknown to most other Zinacantecs.

Carlos Martínez videotaped this play in the natural setting (Martínez 1990). For the versions in Tzotzil and Spanish, see Montemayor 1996a.

CAST OF CHARACTERS

FIRST WOMAN: wearing Zinacantec clothing, including the blue skirt

COMADRE (SECOND WOMAN): wearing Zinacantec clothing

SPOOK: wearing black mask and black hat, white shirt, black pants and cloak

FIRST AND SECOND MEN: wearing Zinacantec clothing, hats, and short pants

WOMAN FROM POTOVTIK: wearing Zinacantec clothing

THIRD AND FOURTH WOMAN: wearing Zinacantec clothing

XAP (SAN SEBASTIÁN): wearing Zinacantec clothing with white mask and white cap

LOL (SAN LORENZO): wearing Zinacantec clothing with white mask and Zinacantec hat

XUN (SAN JUAN): wearing sombrero, white mask, Chamulan white clothing, with long white pants

MULE: wearing mask and Zinacantec woman's clothing

OLD MAN: wearing Chamulan clothing

OLD WOMAN: with mask, wearing black Chamulan clothing

GRANDMOTHER: with mask with long white hair, wearing black Chamulan clothing, with walking stick

FIRST AND SECOND BATHING GIRLS: wearing Chamulan clothing

Act I

SCENE 1

*(A woman appears, her Indian clothes covered by an overcoat.
She looks at the audience.)*

FIRST WOMAN: There aren't any spooks anymore. We don't hear of them anymore. Now there are many fewer. They say only where roads are being made or bridges. We hear there are some people who still see them, but we hardly see them. It's not like it used to be when there were lots of them. There were many spooks in the olden days. Loads of them. And besides, there weren't many people. We couldn't go out of our houses at nighttime. The people hid. That's how they survived long ago. When they killed them, it was by sticking a pole up them until it came out of their mouths. That's how they got rid of the spooks.

*(The woman exits and takes off her overcoat. She appears wearing her
Zinacantec clothes. Then her* comadre *peers in and speaks to her.)*

COMADRE: I'm going to bed now, *kumale!* Oh, tell me if my corn boils over! Please, *kumale!* I may not hear because I'm going to sleep next to the fire.

FIRST WOMAN: Okay, *kumale!* I'll probably hear it. I'll be listening.

(She sits on the ground and falls asleep. In a minute she seems to hear the water hissing as it spills on the fire.)

SPOOK: *(It peers in.)* Whooshtale, *kumaaale!* Your corn spilt!

FIRST WOMAN: *(She wakes up.)* It spilt, *kumale!* It spilt!

SPOOK: *(It peers at the woman.)* Whooshtale *kumaaale!*

FIRST WOMAN: *(Then she hides. She gets up scared and shouts when it peers at her.)* Ohh! It's my *kumale's* blood! The Spook killed her. *(She flees.)*

SCENE 2

(Two Zinacantec men appear, carrying their nets. They put them down and rest. One sits down.)

FIRST MAN: Well, *kumpare,* let's take a rest here for a little while.

SECOND MAN: Okay, why don't you give me a shot of cane liquor?

FIRST MAN: Ey, not yet, *kumpa.* They say my grandfather's brother-in-law saw the Spook come out here. Oh my god, I said its name! I should have called it "trunk" or "stubble." I guess we'll see if it appears and does the same thing to us that it did to the other guy. Do you know what happened to him?

SECOND MAN: Oh, wasn't it that he got completely soaked?

FIRST MAN: Yes, indeed. Because they got drunk right here. I'm told they passed out. They fell down here. Then he felt that he was being shaken. He probably thought it was my grandfather waking him up. Then he heard, "Brudder-in-law, brudder-in-law!" instead of "Brother-in-law, brother-in-law!" and then he saw it was a spook … like a … like a tree trunk. Since he was drunk, the Spook thought he was on fire because it could see the vapors from the cane liquor coming out. It thought it was a wildfire. It poured water on his mouth, on his hands, until it left his whole body wet.

SECOND MAN: Oh, so it was here! I was told that there was a Chamulan who got a lot of money from the Spook. It gave him loads of money so he wouldn't kill it. But when he received the money, he killed it anyway. He wasn't scared of it. He shot it and then he cut off its wings. They say since he buried the money, it didn't turn into potsherds. Those Chamulans are right smart!

FIRST MAN: Well, *kumpare,* I'm getting scared. It's better if we go to sleep. *(They sleep for a while, but then this man wakes up and speaks.)* Hell, it's so cold! I don't know why I'm shivering like this! Is something about to happen to me?

(The second man wakes up.)

SECOND MAN: What's the matter with you? I thought you were brave. What was it that scared you so much? Haven't you got any balls? Did you put on a blue skirt?

FIRST MAN: Oh hell, I don't know. It's a good thing if you can be the brave one.

SECOND MAN: No, I'm brave, just put a lot of wood on the fire! Now you won't have anything to be afraid of. These days there aren't any more spooks. *(The first man, who's still scared, puts on the firewood.)*

FIRST MAN: Well, let's go to sleep then, *kumpare*.

(They cover themselves with their blankets and fall asleep. Then the Spook swooshes in. They wake up, terrified.)

SPOOK: How are things, friend? What are you doing?

FIRST MAN: *(Shaking with fear)* Nothing, nothing. I'm not doing anything, sir!

SPOOK: Oh, okay! I'm going to warm myself here for a minute.

FIRST MAN: Okay, you do that, sir!

SPOOK: Oh, would you like a smoke?

FIRST MAN: Okay, if you please. *(He takes the cigarette and out of fright crumples it.)*

SPOOK: You bastard! What are you doing to my cigarette? As if I gave it to you so you could crumble it up! I hadn't even lit it!

FIRST MAN: Well, that's what I always do when I take a smoke, sir. It'd be good if you gave me another one. *(He's given it, and just the same way, he crumples it before lighting it.)*

SPOOK: You crumbled it again! What are you doing? Are you scared?

FIRST MAN: Me, scared? No, sir. That's the way I always smoke. Why don't you give me another one?

SPOOK: It looks to me as if you're scared. Then smoke this one! We'll see about the third one.

FIRST MAN: *(He takes the third one and ruins it the same way.)* Damn it! I dropped it. So why don't you give me another one.

SPOOK: I've given you three, you bastard! So you want to have a fight?

FIRST MAN: Well, if you know how to pick a fight, that's okay, but me, I don't. I'm just warming myself by the fire. Why are you calling me a bastard? Is it because you have such kinky hair? Nobody's going to call me a bastard!

SPOOK: Well, I'll draw a line here. *(Then it draws a line with its sword and sticks the sword in the ground. The man grabs a stick and whacks the Spook three times.)* Ow, what are you doing to me? *(It runs off. There is a straw mat where the Spook was squatting. Then the two men talk together.)*

SECOND MAN: (*He gets up, shaking and shaking.*) Oh god, I got scared. I pissed in my pants from fright. What'll I do? I was really scared.

FIRST MAN: You talk big, saying you're so brave! You had me think you were brave! And you pissed in your pants out of fear! You coward! (*He grabs a stick and the other guy runs past the straw mat.*)

SECOND MAN: Wait, wait! I was about to fall over this! It wasn't here before! It's a straw mat! Come on over and we'll unfold it to see what's inside!

(*They untie the mat.*)

FIRST MAN: The Spook left it behind! What? Who are you? Are you a Spook, woman?

WOMAN FROM POTOVTIK: No, it's me, sir! Don't kill me! Untie me! Please, I'm from Potovtik. The Spook grabbed me when I went out to toss away my lime water. It was the Spook that grabbed me.

FIRST MAN: Okay, you're free now. I saved you. Shall we shack up together?

WOMAN FROM POTOVTIK: Okay, that's fine!

FIRST MAN: So then let's go on to Zinacantán! (*The first man and the woman exit.*)

SECOND MAN: That woman may be bad since she lived with a spook. Or maybe she'll die. (*He exits.*)

SCENE 3

(*Three Zinacantec women are cooking their meals. They are very worried.*)

SECOND WOMAN: Oh my lord, what'll we do? We can't go outside early in the morning! Not until nine o'clock when the sun's up. And just nearby, because it's still dark in the woods. We don't have any more firewood. We'll have to go out together so the Spook won't do anything to us. They say it goes as far as Chiapa de Corzo to steal chickens and turkeys and eggs, even bread baskets.

THIRD WOMAN: Haven't you heard the talk about the girl from Potovtik? They say she got sick, that her pee was like lime water. They say that every day she ate chicken. What probably made her sick was giving birth to six babies. The poor woman had a child a week. They went to get a medicine man, but she died, poor thing.

SECOND WOMAN: There was another woman, too, whom the Spook took off. She was pulled out of a cave with a rope. The night before, she gave birth to a child who was already talking the next day, saying, "Nanny, nanny!" That was just one day after it was born! When I saw it come out of the cave, it was hanging on to her skirt, shouting "Nanny, nanny!" She held on to the rope with one hand, and with the other she pulled it off so it would fall. Right away she swelled up, the way we do after we drown. The poor thing died.

THIRD WOMAN: When spooks come to the house, and they do still come, you can't sleep. They scratch at the door. They get in under the eaves, like cats. Sometimes they're very big. Sometimes they wear a hat. Their hands are horribly cold! My little boy nearly died when he was touched by a spook!

SECOND WOMAN: Oh my god, what's that that's getting in?

(The Spook enters.)

SPOOK: Nanny, nanny, will you fix me my meal? I'm hungry now.

SECOND WOMAN: Come on in, sit here next to the fire! Drink some soup, drink lots of soup, while there's still enough!

(The Spook takes the bowl, and while it's drinking, the women toss the rest at his face. The Spook screams with pain.)

EVERYONE: Drink lots of soup, you bastard! Don't you like the soup? (*The Spook, spinning around, drags itself out.*) We won, we won! The bastard got burnt!

(The women exit, all laughing heartily.)

SCENE 4

(Two gentlemen appear, walking on what seems to be a narrow trail. They are well-dressed. They are busy, holding candles, gathering flowers. Each one enters his own door. Then the Spook arrives, suffering from the burns on its face.)

SPOOK: Damn it, the way those women burnt me! I thought they'd like me. They sure messed me up! I'm always looking for somebody to fix me a meal. A pretty girl who'd know how to chat with me. Who wants to help me? (*It knocks on the first door.*) Lol, Lol, see how your damned daughters burnt me! Give me at least one or two young girls so I can take them home, so I'll have a little bit of company. Oh, I'm so lonely. I have to have somebody to talk to.

LOL: I don't know, I don't know. I'm busy. Who knows what my older brother, Xap, will say? Why don't you ask him? If Xap says, "Take her!"—if he tells you that, what can I say? Nothing! So you better talk to him!

SPOOK: (*It goes to the house of the other gentleman.*) Please, sir Xap! Won't you give me one or two of your girls? I see you have lots! You'd never notice they'd gone if you gave me a few.

The Spook lamenting his burns, 1988. Photo courtesy Sna Jtz'ibajom

XAP: Are you crazy or what? So I'm supposed to give away my children? I won't give them to you. D'you hear? And you, what have you given me? You're just pestering me. Get out of here! You scare down my chickens from the peach tree, and you steal them too. You steal everything from pigs to dogs. You go and steal lots of girls from their homes, and then you abandon your kids. They can't even be killed. I'll never give you one! Get out! It's better if you ask my younger brother, Lol. I'll never give you one!

SPOOK: (*It knocks on Lol's door again.*) Oh, Lol, don't get mad at me! Give me one of your daughters! I see you have a lot of them.

LOL: Okay, and what have you given me? You just knock here, bothering me every day. (*He gestures with his hand.*)

SPOOK: Oh, Lol, even if you give me one who's thirteen years old that would be all right !

LOL: I'll never give you one! Did you hear me? Stop pestering me!

SPOOK: (*It goes to the other door.*) Xap, Xap, don't do this to me! Lol never gave me one. Just give me one of your daughters, because it's true that I need a friend to talk to.

XAP: Spook, you're telling lies! Supposedly you only want to be happy. Supposedly you want to chat. Who knows why you want to hole up in a cave or in the jungle? I'll give you a good whack with a stick if you keep coming to pester me! Do you think I'm so crazy I'd give you one of my kids? Your pestering makes me sick!

SPOOK: Don't be like that! I want one to cook my meals.

XAP: Oh, is that the truth? Well, if you want, I'll give you one, so you'll stop bothering us. See, come over here! There's one on the path. I'll give her to you. Go grab her! You hide here! When she passes by, I'll shout to you to grab her.

SPOOK: Will you really give her to me? I always said, Xap, that you were a good guy! (*It speaks to the audience.*) Ha, ha, ha! I finally softened him up!

(*It quickly hides. A woman wearing the mask of a mule appears, covering her nose with her shawl.*)

XAP AND LOL: (*They talk together in secret and then address the Spook.*) Are you ready, Spook? There comes the girl!

SPOOK: Oh, nanny, nanny, you're so beautiful, nanny! (*The mule whinnies angrily.*) Don't be mad, nanny!

(*It wants to hug her, but the mule draws back.*)

XAP AND LOL: Hug her, Spook! Can't you see she wants to be hugged?

(*The Spook rushes over and stops the mule on the path. Whinnying, the mule kicks the Spook twice and exits, leaving the Spook lying unhappily on the ground. The gentlemen are laughing.*)

SPOOK: Ow, ow, ow! Why did you do that to me? Didn't you agree to give me a fifteen-year-old girl? The last time, because of you, I hugged a hawthorn. It hurt a lot.

XAP: (*They are laughing.*) It's because you can't see anymore, Spook! Now you've got to be blind. The girl was walking along behind the mule. She laughed a bit when she saw you being kicked by the mule.

SPOOK: Oh, you're just telling me lies! Where can I find a woman? Ow, that kick hurts badly.

XAP: Wouldn't it be good if you stretched your legs? Go and look in Chamula! My younger brother, Xun, is there. He has lots of kids. He might give you one.

LOL: Yes, that's right. He has lots of girls. It'd be good if you went to Chamula.

SPOOK: Okay, okay. I'll go. I guess I'll see if Xun gives me one, but you guys are just so angry. (*It exits.*)

XAP: Well, thanks to God the pest has gone. It's worth it if it doesn't come back to Zinacantán.

LOL: Thanks to God, brother! (*They go into their houses.*)

Act II

SCENE 1

SPOOK: Well, here I am in Chamula. Now what'll I do? Uh-oh, I can't seem to think what. What can I do? Would it be a good idea to steal a candle from over there in the church? Would it please him if I gave him a candle? Might he think I was drunk? And if he chases me away? Does he like to drink? But if he doesn't? No, let's skip it. It's probably okay to give him a candle. (*It hurries out. When it returns, the Spook has a candle, which it stands up by the door. The Spook stands impatiently, silently.*) Why doesn't he come out? Xun, are you there? I've brought you your candle, *kumpare*! No ... he doesn't come out. Maybe it would be a good idea to ring the church bell. Right at midnight. (*It pretends to be climbing a ladder and rings the bell.*) Dong, dong, dong.

LOTS OF PEOPLE: Hey, who climbed up to ring the bell at midnight? A robber! Shoot him down with a bullet! Get lots of people! (*They blow their bullhorns as if it were Carnival.*) Catch the thief! He stole a candle from the church! Don't let him get away! Kill him!

(*The Spook flees, chased by all the people. It reappears from the other side, exhausted, carrying the big candle it had stolen.*)

SCENE 2

SPOOK: All the Chamulans came! If only I could find a church where they don't chase you. They're so angry! Well, I guess I'll go and talk to him another time. I'll see if he gives her to me. (*Xun comes out, accompanied by an old man and an old woman. When the Spook sees them, it comes over to entreat Xun.*) Look, Xun, at the present I brought you. It's a big candle for you!

XUN: Didn't you steal it? So now, Spook, you know what kind of a present to bring!

SPOOK: Oh, I've always done this!

XUN: Well, you've been thinking up something. What did you come to ask me for?

SPOOK: Don't be like that! Give me one of your girls! I see you have lots of them. You probably aren't happy to be giving them fish and june bug grubs and maggots. Don't do that to them. Give me just one. I won't eat her. I just want her to join me.

XUN: Hell, you're so awful! I can't stand you anymore. Just 'cause I don't want to see your face anymore ... just because you gave me my candle ... take her! You can, take her away! I don't ever want you to come back again!

(The Spook is given the old woman, wraps her in its cape, and appears to fly off with her.)

The Spook and his consort, 1990. Photo courtesy Sna Jtz'ibajom

SPOOK: Hooray! Now I won! He gave her to me, he gave her to me. She's got flesh on her bones, and she's got a long neck!

OLD WOMAN: (*She talks like a very old woman.*) What? Where are you taking me, son? Where is the service going to be?

SPOOK: Wait, nanny, wait, nanny, wait, nanny!

OLD WOMAN: In Xunka's house. Which Xunka' is it, son?

SPOOK: No, girl, I'm taking you to the Spook's house!

OLD WOMAN: Oh, then my house is far behind.

SPOOK: Well, now we've arrived! (*The Spook takes its cape off her.*) If you're hungry, here's some good bread. Fix your meal! Eat up! There's no need to worry. Don't be sad!

OLD WOMAN: Oh, I feel so dizzy. What's happening to me?

SPOOK: Nanny, Mary . . . now night's fallen, sweetie. I'll kiss you. And then we'll sleep together. Did you hear me? Answer me, you lazy woman! Wake up! Who do you think you are? So I bring you here and all you do is sleep? Answer me, lazy woman, or I'll get you up with a beating! (*The Spook shakes her. Then it sees that she's dead.*) Oh, she's dead! She's dead! It was the Spook that killed her! (*The Spook turns her over a couple of times. It's as if the Spook had been chased. It has a hard time breathing. Then it rests for a minute.*) Is it the Spook? Aren't I the Spook? He'll be punished for this, scaring people like this. Poor gentleman! He'll be punished for not looking after his kids. I'm going to bawl him out. (*The Spook pulls the old woman off stage.*)

SCENE 3

(*Xun appears, feeling at ease. The Spook appears, too.*)

SPOOK: And you, Xun, why did you do that to me? Why are you scaring everybody? The poor old woman died of fright. She just asked me, "Where are you taking me? Where are you taking me?" and then she died. It's because she was so old. You sure played a dirty trick on me. Why did you give me that old lady? If you'd given me a woman who was a little younger, she certainly would have been brave enough. You don't know anymore how to take care of your kids, Xun. It's better if you give me a girl.

XUN: No, not me, I'll never give you anyone anymore. Why don't you go ask a grandmother for one? She's right there next to the sweat bath. It's true. You'll find her nearby.

SPOOK: Over there? Oh, now I see her! Okay, then I'll go! Ha, ha, ha! You'll still have to deal with a devil! Ha, ha! (*The Spook exits.*)

XUN: Watch out, the way you're treating me! You're a nuisance, begging and begging. I'm sick of it, you liar, you thief! It's you who's going to run into trouble, you bastard!

(Xun exits angrily. Then two women bring out a sweat bath. They converse. One of the women is carrying firewood that she piles up next to the sweat bath.)

GRANDMOTHER: All right, girls, now you can take your bath while I go and bring more water so there'll be enough.

BATHING GIRLS: Thanks, grandmother!

(They talk together and enter the sweat bath. They toss out their skirts and blouses. Then the Spook appears.)

SPOOK: So here I am, the devil himself! This time I won't fail! But why can't I seem to be able to see well? Maybe it'd be better to sniff her out! So they won't bother me. What, what . . . do I smell here? The devil knows! These are women's skirts! (*It sniffs them and that drives it crazy.*) Oh, that smells wonderful, really wonderful! Could the women be in there? What could they be doing? Are they bathing? I guess I'll see. What's this? It's devil's play! What could they be doing?

GRANDMOTHER: What are you doing peeking at us with your droopy eyes? Wouldn't it be better if you went back to your stinky cave? Get out of here, unless you want me to give you a whack on the head with a stick!

SPOOK: Oh, don't be angry, ma'am. I only came to ask if you wouldn't give me one of your little girls, since I'm all alone. Because my wife died recently. There's no one to make me my meals. There isn't even anyone to talk to. Don't be like that! Give me one of your girls!

GRANDMOTHER: Which girl, which girl? And afterwards you'll . . . you'll eat her! Where do you come from? Do you think you're a mestizo, do you think you're the boss? Later you'll take off more of my girls. Get out of here! Awful spook, have you no shame? The best thing to do is to beat you off!

SPOOK: (*It lies down by the clothes and entreats her.*) Oh, don't behave like that to me, grandmother! Let me rest a minute here. You see, I just got a beating even though it was Xun's fault. He tricked me. He told me you'd give me one of your little girls.

GRANDMOTHER: As if I'd give you one of my girls! Do you think I'm crazy? Okay, rest a while and pull yourself together. You hear? I don't want you staring at me anymore.

SPOOK: No, why do you think that? As soon as I recover, I'll leave!

GRANDMOTHER: Well, I tell you frankly that if you don't leave pretty soon, I'll knock you over the head! (*She exits reproachfully.*)

SPOOK: Oh, that old woman is so angry! She doesn't want to give me one of her girls. It smells so good! (*The Spook madly sniffs the skirts again.*) Oh, so sweet! I certainly won't go unless I can get her! If I hurry up, I'll win out! I'll take her away! I'll take her away! (*It sniffs the skirts once again.*) Oh, it's so wonderful! Now I'll steal her away! (*The Spook does its best to enter into the sweat bath. Then the grandmother appears. She sticks a pole up its ass until the pole comes out of its mouth. Blood everywhere. The Spook is screaming now.*) Ow, now you've killed me! Why did you do that to me? Ow, nanny, naanny!

(*It dies. The old woman exits happily. Then the women come out of the sweat bath. They are very distracted.*)

FIRST BATHING GIRL: What was it that was screaming?

SECOND BATHING GIRL: It was scary. Who knows what kind of bird it was?

FIRST BATHING GIRL: Ooh, what's this? Look at the dead animal lying on our clothes!

SECOND BATHING GIRL: Move over, Petu'! Don't you see it's a spook?

FIRST BATHING GIRL: Oh, could it really be? It must have been spying on us. Who could've killed it? Oh my god, it's holding on to our skirts!

SECOND BATHING GIRL: Oh my lord, we'll have to wash them! Come, let's pull them off so they won't stink. (*They remove them.*)

FIRST BATHING GIRL: Hurry up! Help me get rid of it so its stink won't be left here!

SECOND BATHING GIRL: It's very heavy! (*She shouts for help.*) Please come and help me! They killed a spook! Help me get rid of it! (*People enter.*)

PEOPLE: Look! They killed it! Now it can't act like a weasel eating up everyone's eggs! Now it won't steal our wives! (*They drag it right out.*)

Deadly Inheritance

(1991)

TZIAK INFORMED US that he would like a different kind of play this year, not based on myths, but on gossip. He recounted a recent case of murder in his town, Tenejapa, where two brothers, after their father died, murdered their two sisters to appropriate their land.

For those who romanticize Mayan culture and, particularly, Mayan family life, this play will be a surprise, for it revolves around one of the most feared elements in the daily life of the people who live in the rural towns of Chiapas: the discord between siblings when parents die. Anger erupts when one tries to steal away the others' inheritance. This act is condemned severely in the communities and presents the civil authorities with problems that are difficult to resolve. Descriptions of this kind of event are embellished with many details in the hope of preventing future occurrences. We decided to bring this story to the theatre not only because of the interest it stirs in Indian communities, but also because its dramatic social elements reflect real life and the desire for justice. Single women, especially, are frequently the victims of male alcoholism, greed, scorn, and abuse. A second message is the importance of solving such problems within the community rather than relying on the Mexican Ladino legal system. This social drama resonates very strongly where righteousness is frequently vindictively triumphant.

Rather than having both sisters die, we had the older sister survive to demand her rights in court. We were careful not to dress the actors in Tenejapan clothing because when we had used Zinacantec clothing in a play about male abuse, *Una mujer desesperada,* Xun, also from Zinacantán, denied that rape was a problem there and refused to perform because he said Petu's play was based on her life and discredited their community.

An underlying current in this play is the question of gender equality. The brothers are further motivated to kill their sister because she has gone to school and become what they consider to be uppity. Chavela and Petu' were lead actors in this play, which I surmise contributed to their decision, three years later, to found the women's cooperative FOMMA (Fortaleza de la Mujer Maya [The Strength of Mayan Women]). FOMMA's theatre focuses on the problems of urban Mayan women and their children living in San Cristóbal. That same year the Zapatista women demanded that traditional Mayan customs be abolished if those traditions denied women the right to choose their mate and to adopt family planning, to receive property as inheritance, and to participate in the civil government. This demand has been one of the most influential features of *Zapatismo,* especially among the Mayan women who have formed textile cooperatives, but also in every Mayan community. It has also had an impact in the other Indian communities of Mexico and even among non-Indian Mexican women.

Another concern, widely felt in all Mayan communities, has been the tendency to abandon the local justice system in favor of Ladino lawyers who show no respect for Indian culture and whose fees are extremely high. At the same time, the local judge may be barely literate and totally inept, so a clever person is apt to seek out Ladino lawyers.

When Ralph Lee saw the conclusion, in which the murderers are whipped in court, he decided it was too violent and returned to his room to write a different ending. The next day, when he presented his rewrite, the actors protested, saying that this was no longer their play. After more consultation the whipping scene remained. When *Deadly Inheritance* (*Herencia fatal*) was performed in San Cristóbal, an American anthropologist colleague declared he did not like this play because the final scene was too violent.

In another performance, for the Experiment in International Living, "the lead actor panicked and forgot his lines, but he did some quick improvisations which meant that the others had no cues, so they, too, had to improvise. It was particularly unfortunate because Cambridge PBS was making a video of the performance for us. But I believe no one in the audience realized what a disaster it seemed to all of us. From their reaction you would think we had triumphed. Let's say we did!" (Laughlin to Ziesing 1991). I commented also that "At its worst the play is a soap opera championing women's rights and justice, at its best some mention Lear" (Laughlin to Haviland 1992).

Donald Frischmann, the leading authority on Mexican popular theatre, observed a performance in Chamula.

> The audience, mainly men with some women and children, was truly fascinated with the live theatre performance. There were no

seats, and a continuous pushing match ensued throughout the performance: Everyone's goal was to earn a place at the foot of the small, elevated stage. To my initial surprise, particularly dramatic moments elicited great excitement and laughter! Several times, a physical wave of emotion swept through the entire crowd, from left to right, nearly bringing us all down on the floor!

That day at Chamula any neat dividing line between *stage drama* and *social drama* seemed to be non-existent for the indigenous audience. This was particularly striking during a scene where a confession is flogged out of two accused murderers. By this point in the play, the stage itself was full of curious and excited onlookers: children and men, surrounding the actors in an attempt to get a closer look at the stage events, which so curiously resembled episodes of *real life* out in the central plaza. That day I became fully aware, for perhaps the first time, of the power that live theatre can achieve to truly *move* an audience: emotionally as well as physically! It was wonderful to experience this rare and special moment off to one side of the dusty Chamula plaza, far from the luxuries, comforts, and conventions, which most people associate with theatre. (Frischmann 1994a, 223)

Deadly Inheritance was videotaped by Carlos Martínez in a natural setting (Martínez 1992). Carlos chose to have the victim's body hurled over the cliff. This was a second difficult starring role for Petu'!

For versions in Tzotzil and Spanish, see Montemayor 1996c.

LOXA: wearing Zinacantec clothing

FATHER: wearing Zinacantec clothing, his head wrapped in his neckerchief

TINIK: wearing Zinacantec clothing

SHAMAN: wearing Zinacantec clothing, his head wrapped in neckerchief, long pants, black robe, and staff

ELDER: wearing Zinacantec clothing, as do all other Zinacantecs

TELEX: Loxa and Tinik's brother, wearing Zinacantec clothing

CHEP: wearing Zinacantec clothing

PAXKU': wearing Zinacantec clothing

AKUXTIN: Paxku's husband

MAYOR OF ZINACANTÁN

JUDGE OF ZINACANTÁN

SHERIFF OF ZINACANTÁN: carrying whip

Act I

SCENE 1

(Inside a house in Zinacantán, the hearth is lit. Loxa and Tinik enter, supporting their groaning father.)

LOXA: We'll lay you down here, Father, next to the fire so you can warm up.

FATHER: Oh my lord, daughter, I feel very sick. I feel so cold.

TINIK: The shaman we were told is so good is free now. I'm going to bring him here. We'll see if he can cure you! *(They lay him down on a straw mat.)*

LOXA: Our father's been laid low ever since our mother died. He says he'd like to see our brothers, but now they don't want to come. They say they're very busy. I've told them over and over.

TINIK: They're probably so busy in the cantina! They've never thought about caring for their father. They never come to visit.

LOXA: Our father looks as if he's getting worse. You'd better hurry up and go get the shaman.

FATHER: Oh, daughters, you've spent a lot of your money on shamans. Don't spend more on them or afterwards you'll have no way of supporting yourselves. I realize now that there's no medicine for my sickness. It's better if you go and bring your brothers so I can see them in person. I'll tell them they shouldn't take the house away from you or the land. They haven't come to see me for a long time. Now they may not see me alive.

TINIK: Don't you say that, Father, you must keep your hopes alive. Loxa, I'll be back in a minute. I'm just going to bring the shaman. (*She exits hurriedly. Loxa makes some coffee.*)

FATHER: (*Groaning and groaning*) Ohh, mmm, oh, daughter, I've been feeling sick for months. Several shamans have come to see me, but not one of them has figured out what my sickness is. What worries me is that you'll be left behind all alone.

LOXA: Oh, Father, don't say that. You'll get better. The thing is, it's so cold. Drink some coffee to warm you up!

FATHER: (*He tries to sit up to take the gourd.*) Come and lift me, Loxa. I don't seem to be able to raise myself. (*Loxa goes to raise him up and gives him his coffee. The old man can't hold on to the gourd.*) My body has grown so weak.

(Tinik enters with the old shaman.)

TINIK: We've come, Father. I've brought your shaman.

FATHER: Thank you, daughter. I may not make it through the night. Were you so kind as to bring the boys?

TINIK: I left a message for them. The shaman should take your pulse and pray for you.

SHAMAN: Are you here, *kumpare*? What are you doing? How do you feel?

FATHER: Oh, *kumpare,* I've been sick a long time. Several shamans have seen me already, but they couldn't cure me.

SHAMAN: I guess I'll see. I'll take your pulse. We'll see what it is. (*The shaman takes the old man's pulse, but he is very weak. Then he speaks to the girls.*) You should've told me long ago. You can't feel his pulse. His soul doesn't want to return because it's been sold to the earth. If you want, I'll do what I can for you. I guess we'll see if he recovers or not. So long as you don't blame me.

LOXA: Please, sir, I beg you. What do you need?

SHAMAN: Okay, you need to get two candles, a bit of incense, and a bottle of cane liquor to pray with. That's what's needed for our Lord to stand firm so he'll recover, but I see he's very sick. He hasn't any pulse.

LOXA: (*She cries as she looks for what is needed.*) Oh my Lord, may our father not yet die. Here's what you told us is needed, sir.

SHAMAN: All right, we'll pray. We'll try our best. I guess we'll see if there's something that works.

(The shaman lines up the candles and offers incense. He prays anxiously. As he prays, he rubs an egg over his patient's body. Then he censes him again. At that point the old man begins to act strangely. He flails about. The shaman tries to do something so he'll return to normal. He sprays cane liquor

on him. When the old man recovers for a moment, he speaks to his daugh-
ters and dies. The girls cry with grief.)

SHAMAN: You see, I tried my best for you. You knew he was very sick. I'm leaving now.

LOXA: Don't leave yet, sir. Please join us.

SHAMAN: All right, I see you're all alone. Go and bring the boys. Go tell some of your neighbors. In the meantime I'll help you here.

LOXA: Thank you, sir, if you'd be so kind, since we don't know what to do now that our father has died. Thank you for helping us.

TINIK: Please, sir, he needs to be put on another bed where he'll be washed and where we'll change his clothes.

LOXA: Oh my god, Tinik, now we're all alone. Our father has gone.

TINIK: Our Lord will bear up his soul. May he be forgiven for whatever he did here on earth. I'll go bring everybody. You get together his clean clothes, his net, and the coins that our father will take with him.

LOXA: All right, sister, go and spread the word!

(Together the girls each take one of their father's legs while the shaman grabs him under the arms to lift the body of the dead man.)

SCENE 2

(The girls appear with their neighbors. Four men carry out the corpse, wrapped in a straw mat. Traditional music can be heard. Slowly they lower it, stretching it on the ground. Then they light the candles, two at his head and two at his feet. The younger son hands out cigarettes and serves the cane liquor, first to the elder in charge.)

ELDER: Sons, now that your father has died and is still lying in wake in his house, you should settle matters, so afterwards you won't start quarreling among yourselves. You know your late father divided up your things well. The house where he lived with his departed wife he left to the two girls. The land he left in equal parts for the four of you. That is what your father declared. I don't know what you think.

LOXA: That's fine, sir. We agree to that.

TINIK: Yes, indeed, sir, our father measured out things very well.

ELDER: All right. Now your late father's soul has heard that. The matter is settled among you for good. But if you don't agree, you should speak up now, so that afterwards people won't say your late father made the wrong decision. As for you, sons, do you agree to carry out your father's wishes?

Carrying out Father's body wrapped in a straw mat, 2007. Photo courtesy Sna Jtz'ibajom

TELEX: Yes, probably so, sir. It's just that we never spoke about it before he died, so we don't know what his instructions were. Please tell us what he said.

ELDER: All right, see here, son. When your father was still alive, he distributed your land so that you could live on it. When he realized he had grown old, he went to the courthouse to say that he was giving the girls the house with its land. He was giving you all the remaining land. That's what your father declared. Now his body's soul hears this so that you never quarrel nor get angry with each other. Remember that you are in the same family!

CHEP: So that's the story.... Was there anyone who heard it?

ELDER: Yes, indeed! The mayor was entrusted with the papers. He signed as witness.

TELEX: If there was a witness, then fine, that's the way it should be. If our father decided that, then we'll talk with the girls, and we'll think about how to help them, since they've been left all alone.

LOXA: Thank you, brothers. Thanks to our father we have a way to support ourselves. But you, because of your children, have many expenses.

ELDER: All right, it seems as if the departed's soul has seen that you are content. Dawn is coming. Now we should go to the cemetery and bury him.

(Everyone exits. They carry out their dead father, wrapped in a straw mat, accompanied by music.)

SCENE 3

(It is the inside of the daughters' house. It's raining, and they come in cry-
ing, followed by their brothers. They give them stools to sit on, but they
sit on the ground. They poke the fire and give them some coffee. It's hard
for them to stop crying. The sons don't speak. They just seem to be lost in
thought. They remain motionless.)

LOXA: *(She tries to hold back her tears.)* Oh my lord, our father couldn't take it. Less than a year has passed since our mother's death, and then our father dies. We tried our very best, but even so the sickness didn't pass!

TINIK: He never wanted to eat. Little by little he lost all his weight from sadness.

TELEX: We have to think how it's going to be for us, and you have to think how it's going to be for you. What happened is because you took care of our father for such a long time. That's why you never married. Who's going to support you now? It's no good for the two of you girls to be living alone.

TINIK: Oh god, we're not going to be thinking about that now! Anyway, we're used to supporting ourselves. We're not going to look for a man yet. Since you guys separated from us when you married, we planted crops on the land and looked after the sheep. That sure seemed worth it when our parents were laid low by sickness.

LOXA: What's it to us to get married? We saw that nobody came near us because they were afraid they'd have to support our parents. That's why he left this land to us. It didn't matter if we were women. We had a house. Tinik had a cornfield on her land. But we couldn't ever work on it because we were caring for our father when he fell sick. Maybe that's how we can live.

TINIK: It'll be good when there's a market for our weaving. Now that we've joined together, we'll get some money. I love to work. That's how the two of us will help each other.

LOXA: If we had husbands, we'd never be free to do anything. Look at your wives, one child after another. There's no way for them to be free.

TINIK: Not even a little bit. The women who have husbands work so hard without gaining anything from it. Their husbands just come home drunk. They use up their money, and then they hit their wives and their children. I've seen loads of men like that!

LOXA: That's true. As our late mother used to say, men aren't any good anymore. It's better if we're by ourselves. It's not like when there are men, who just bother us.

TINIK: If only there were still some good men, hard workers, good-hearted like our father! But there aren't any like that anymore. It seems as if the devil has gotten into them.

TELEX: Yes, we know you don't want to get married. That's why I tell you it's a mistake to be left living alone. Who will be in the house to protect you? Who'll respect you if there's no man around?

CHEP: Before there wasn't anyone who would bother you because our father was an important man, but now that he's dead, it'd be better if you came and lived with us.

LOXA: Oh no, our Lord wouldn't want that! We should stay here to greet the souls every All Souls' Day.

TINIK: Besides, we don't want to be hangers-on. That's why we have our own home. Thanks to God, our father left it to us.

CHEP: Why do you say you'd be hangers-on? You are our sisters. That's not a good thing to say. We are your brothers. You should respect us now. Why should we be talking about the souls of the dead? It's better if you come to our homes.

TINIK: It's fine the way we are here. You don't need to worry about us. I know how to work. We'll bring in something from our land.

TELEX: Women, why don't you understand anything? Why don't you believe us? So aren't we brothers and sisters? The thing is, we don't want anything to happen to you. It's not right that you walk alone on the path when you're going to your cornfield or coming back.

CHEP: That's men's work. Women should stay at home. You can help our wives when we go to work.

TINIK: Now that there's no one who needs looking after, now that our late father's suffering has ended, you remember we're related! Now you want to have our land and have us go and be your wives' helpers. No, brothers, we're not so stupid as that. It's better if we stay as we've always been.

LOXA: That's true, brothers. Thanks for worrying about us, but I prefer us being alone. Everybody's shown us respect. We're on good terms with our neighbors.

CHEP: So what's to become of the house and all the land our father left us? You can't work the other land. That's men's work!

TELEX: We've already begun to work on it.

TINIK: Whose permission did you get to do that? That's our land. We couldn't work on it for two years because we were caring for our parents. It's different now.

TELEX: That land is ours in common. We weren't going to let it sit inactive while you abandoned it.

TINIK: We know, too, how to work hard. If you want to take our land, you won't win out. That's why our father took the matter to town hall.

LOXA: The problem was addressed when our late father was lying in wake.

TELEX: Nobody's saying that your land is to be taken away. It's just that it shouldn't be left unused. That's why we're telling you to come live in our homes. We'll support you. You'll never be hungry. It's not right that you live alone like crazy people. This is what family means!

CHEP: Everyone is gossiping about you. They say you're very haughty. That's why nobody cares about you, since you're bad-mannered.

TINIK: We know very well who started that gossip. Since you were small, you've always been that way. But we're not going to give up. Now that you've already planted on our land, you'll have to give us half the crop.

TELEX: Don't you be so difficult! Show us a bit of respect! Why don't you understand the way things are? Come to our homes, then gradually the gossip will stop. Maybe you'll be able to get a husband.

LOXA: It's better if you leave, brothers. We don't want our problems dragging on. Think of our sadness! Our father just died and here we are quarreling.

TINIK: Listen to what Loxa says! Never mind, take the whole crop you planted on our land. But, please, don't you butt in on our land!

TELEX: Be reasonable, Tinik! What we tell you is right! The house is ours, too. Don't you run us out of it! This is where we grew up. We'll take down the house, and then we'll divide up the beams. So gather up your things and we'll all go home!

TINIK: Don't make me laugh! Where did you come from, telling us what to do? Our father was right to get witnesses in the mayor's office. He knew how bad you were, that you were envious of us, that you would bother us just because we are women. That's why nobody here in Zinacantán thinks well of you.

CHEP: (*He raises his hand to hit Tinik, who dodges his blow.*) If you insult me, your brother, I'll smash you in the mouth! You need a good punishment so you'll obey what we tell you.

LOXA: (*Crying as she talks*) Please, brothers, our father just died. Please leave us alone. You can't take us away if we don't want to leave the house. Why do we make things worse? Leave us be! We've never done anything to you!

TELEX: There's no end to this. You know how I am when I get angry. It'd be better if you obey what I say. Loxa, you're to go to my house. Tinik, you're going to Chep's house. Get ready!

TINIK: (*She runs to the fireside, grabs a burning stick, and menaces Telex with it.*) If you try to take us away by force, I'll kill you for sure. Get out! Forget we're of the same family. We never want to see you again.

(*Telex backs out with Chep right behind him. They wait to see what will happen, but they don't know what to do. They exit angrily.*)

TINIK: (*She tosses down the burning stick. She and Loxa hug each other and cry.*) Oh, Loxa, Loxa, those guys didn't even wait for one day to pass. What'll we do? I know they won't give up. They may kill us so they can get our land. They're like dogs. They were just waiting for our father to die.

LOXA: Oh my lord, Tinik! Maybe it'd be better if we accepted what Telex said. We know the sort of things they do. It's said they're robbers. Everyone is really scared of them.

TINIK: Can we stand their evil ways? No, sister. Their wives are so difficult. It's they who spread the gossip about us, that we're bad and let men into our house. I know them very well. They want us to become their servants without paying us anything. They're mean. They dream up so many things about us. They're just like their husbands.

LOXA: So what can we do?

TINIK: We should go tell the judge and the mayor. They should hear our story since they have the papers for our house and our land that our late father left to us.

LOXA: Let's go then! It's better if we let them know that our brothers are causing trouble. (*They exit by the door.*)

SCENE 4

TELEX: (*On a path in Zinacantán*) Those gabbling girls don't understand anything. They want to disgrace us. I can't stand it.

CHEP: Tinik's the one who's causing the trouble. Loxa respects us.

TELEX: That's the truth! That awful woman believes she's equal to any man. She's just spoiling for a fight. We've seen how she is.

CHEP: Tinik deserves a good beating. Maybe we'll see if she keeps on giving us trouble.

TELEX: Nothing'll make her change. That's why she never got married.

CHEP: What should we do? Shall we give up our land?

TELEX: Oh no! The awful old man should have left it to us. Senile old man!

CHEP: You shouldn't say that about our father. He just died.

TELEX: It wasn't good what he did. Look at our sisters. They never found husbands. It's because of their rebelliousness. It's our parents' fault. They helped them so much they just became ornery.

CHEP: Tinik is the worst one. Because she learned to read and write, she became rebellious. And another thing: her weaving's in demand.

TELEX: She acts as if she were a man. That awful Tinik has turned into a she-devil. Now she doesn't pay any attention to anything we tell her. (*He makes a very ugly face.*) Until we kill them, the trouble won't end.

CHEP: (*He becomes very frightened.*) Our sisters?

TELEX: Do you want to get rich or not? Tinik won't let us work on the land. It should be ours. I know everybody's scared of us. We shouldn't be kind to them anymore. If we don't own anything, then we should grab what we can. You know how we frighten everyone. If we scare them even more, then we'll win out.

CHEP: How should we do it? We can't murder somebody in the open.

TELEX: Why are you so weak? We should watch and see when she's going to her cornfield. We should have our machetes ready. We'll give it to her when she arrives.

CHEP: You're too much! It's just that there's nothing else we can do. We can make a pile if we want to!

TELEX: Okay then! But remember, if you back down, even you'll get it too! I don't want no scaredy-cat.

Act II

SCENE 1

(The girls are at home. Paxku' knocks on the door.)

PAXKU': Are you there, Tinik?

TINIK: I'm here, come in! Wait just a minute! (*Paxku' enters; Tinik addresses her older sister.*) Loxa, I'm going to work. We agreed I should go to our cooperative for the women's meeting. When that's over, I'm going to our cornfield. I'll pull off several ears of corn and bring some beans, too.

LOXA: All right then, but watch out. Chep and Telex may cause trouble. Really, I'm scared of them. They're too much. Take care, Tinik! If you see one of them coming, it's better if you run away.

TINIK: I'm not scared of them. If they tell me something, I'll answer back. The mayor knows about this. He said he'd put them in jail if they accost me. That's why I'm going with Paxku'.

LOXA: Oh god, even so, take care. I don't want anything to happen to either of you.

TINIK: Okay, sister, don't you worry. I'm going now or the bus will leave me behind. (*They exit.*)

SCENE 2

(*Chep and Telex are walking on the trail, a bit drunkenly. When Tinik and Paxku' pass by, they start to approach them.*)

CHEP: Look at the troublemaker! I heard you went to the courthouse to complain. You don't respect your own brothers!

TELEX: We'll see now that you don't have a burning stick if you keep on making trouble. For the last time, I'm asking you: Are you going to live in our homes, and are you going to give us your land? If not, we'll give you a good beating so you don't go telling stories to the mayor!

TINIK: (*They hurry along.*) Hurry up, Paxku'. We've got to get to the bus fast! (*They exit, running. Their brothers are so drunk they can't catch them.*)

TELEX: (*Very angry*) She'll pay for this later. Maybe it's just as well. I told you what we could do. We should go and wait for her when she comes out by herself. One of these days she'll go look at her cornfield.

CHEP: What'll we do about Loxa?

TELEX: Loxa is scared of us. If Tinik's gone, she'll quickly obey what we tell her. We'll tell her it's no good living all alone. Then she'll believe us.

CHEP: If that's the way it is, we need to look for a hole where we can throw Tinik's body after we kill her so nobody can see. They'll think maybe she got lost or that she went off with some man.

TELEX: That's right. We'll dig a hole, there next to Hairy Hand. We won't be seen by anyone there. Bring a shovel and a pick! Stick them in a burlap bag so nobody'll suspect us. I'll wait for you by the side of the path. We'll go together.

CHEP: Okay. (*The two exit.*)

SCENE 3

(*Tinik and Paxku' return on the path.*)

TINIK: All right, Paxku', it's gotten late. I'm not going to take any more of your time. I'm going now to look at my cornfield. I'm going to pick a few ears of corn.

PAXKU': Don't you want me to accompany you? Your brothers may keep on bothering you.

TINIK: No, Paxku', many thanks, your husband and your kids are probably waiting for you. Maybe my awful brothers have fallen asleep after being so drunk. They probably won't do anything.

PAXKU': Okay, Tinik, I'm going to fix my meal. We'll talk together tomorrow.

TINIK: See you tomorrow, Paxku'. Don't worry, nothing's going to happen to me.

(Tinik exits. Paxku' returns and meets her husband.)

AKUXTIN: What took you so long? We're all starving.

PAXKU': The meeting went on and on. I'll fix your meal. There's something I want to ask you. Please go with me. I'm very worried about Tinik because this morning we met her brothers on the path, and they were really bothering her. They even chased us. We ought to go take a look and see if anything's happened to her.

AKUXTIN: Are they causing trouble so soon after their father died?

PAXKU': They're so evil. They want to take away their sisters' land. They were going to drag them to their own homes. They were stinking drunk.

AKUXTIN: What am I supposed to do? It's better if you don't interfere. It's their business if they want to quarrel. It's not your affair.

PAXKU': Oh, Akuxtin, don't be that way! The women are all alone. Tinik's going to pick some corn. There's nobody around there. Let's make sure her brothers don't kill her.

AKUXTIN: But if they start saying I'm spying on their sisters? They're so bad we shouldn't get involved in their dispute.

PAXKU': Oh, don't keep saying that! You know I'll be there with you. We'll just go and watch from a distance. Her brothers have probably gotten there already. If they're doing something bad, we'll run to the courthouse to tell on them.

AKUXTIN: Okay, we probably shouldn't take long 'cause I'm very hungry.

PAXKU': Let's go!

AKUXTIN: Let's go, but if they settle their quarrel, we can't always be on the watch. *(They exit.)*

SCENE 4

(Tinik hurries to the cornfield. From the other side her brothers appear, carrying their machetes. It is clear that they are tipsy as they whisper to each other.)

TELEX: You see, I told you already it wouldn't take long for the awful woman to come out by herself. She sure acts as if she were a man. Now we can pay her back for humiliating us. (*He brandishes his machete.*)

CHEP: Wouldn't it be better if we just give her a beating, Telex? Remember she's our sister!

TELEX: So she can go accuse us at the courthouse? I already told you that if you back down, you'll be the first to get it! (*He swings his machete at him.*)

CHEP: (*Ducking, frightened*) No, Telex. Would you kill me, too?

TELEX: Even you, and whoever else tries to take away the land! I've already told the woman she's just like a man.

CHEP: Let's go and do what it takes! She tried to kill us, too, when she poked that burning stick at us!

TELEX: That's what I want, too, so you'll obey what I tell you. We'll circle around and hide in the brush behind the cornfield. Hurry up!

(*Bending low, they hurry out, and then Akuxtin and Paxku' appear, following them.*)

AKUXTIN: My god, you're right, Paxku'. Those evil guys want to kill their sister. At least they haven't seen us yet. If they saw us, they'd kill us. God, what'll we do? It's better if we don't say a word so we don't get involved in endless problems. Let our Lord punish them. That's better than if we're mixed up in it.

PAXKU': How can we let her be killed? Let's go tell somebody so they can help us defend her.

AKUXTIN: Who would we go and tell? The town is far away.

PAXKU': We've got to think what to do. We can't just watch her being killed.

AKUXTIN: Let's go or we might be seen! It's better if we hurry off! (*Paxku' doesn't want to go, but Akuxtin covers her mouth so she can't yell. Then he pulls her along.*) Listen to me, let's go! (*They come back secretly just when Tinik appears on the other side, picking her corn.*)

TINIK: My Lord, it's gotten late. Loxa would be worried if she knew! (*Then her brothers appear, slowly, crouching, their machetes ready. Telex jumps over to his sister and swings his machete at her neck and her back.*)

TELEX: I warned you! Take this, so you'll learn to respect us! (*Telex strikes her again with his machete, and then, seeing that Chep is scared out of his wits, he screams at him.*) Hurry up! You too! Give her some machete blows!

CHEP: What's the point, if you've already killed her?

TELEX: So I'm not the only one to give it to her! Or else they'll say I killed her by myself. Hurry up!

Telex murders his sister Tinik, 2007. Photo courtesy Sna Jtz'ibajom

(*Chep doesn't know what to do. Little by little he realizes his situation and angrily strikes the body.*)

CHEP: The devil got into her! That awful woman knew very well she was acting up, behaving like a man!

TELEX: Okay, that's what I wanted. Now we're in it together. Go get the poles over there and the burlap bag so we can carry her to Hairy Hand. We need to get completely rid of the blood stains so nothing can be seen to implicate us. It's a good thing that nobody at all passed by. (*They rub the ground well where blood was spilt. Then they carry the body, wrapped in the burlap bag, on a litter that they had hidden beforehand. Then Akuxtin appears with Paxku', quarreling.*)

PAXKU': I can't believe what you're saying, Akuxtin. Why were you so scared? Why did you let the woman be killed? You didn't do anything, you who told me you were a man! I've seen now what you're like! A coward!

AKUXTIN: (*He gives her a slap.*) Don't talk like that to your husband! You've seen what those terrible guys are like! If they killed their sister, why wouldn't they do the same to us if we go and accuse them? I'm telling you, it's better that we don't, or something will happen to us. It's better if it seems we didn't see anything.

PAXKU': (*She looks angrily now at her husband.*) I saw it! You hit me just because I'm a woman. If you were a real man … Why didn't you help defend the woman? I'm going to let the mayor know!

AKUXTIN: (*He hits her again.*) Shut up! We're going home. Don't you get mixed up in this! If I learn that you went and informed them at the courthouse, you'll get another beating! Hurry up! Let's go home! (*He pulls her off.*)

Act III

SCENE 1

(In the courthouse there is a table with a thick book on top. There are some loose sheets of paper, too. The mayor appears, and then the judge. Paxku' comes in right behind them, with signs of having been beaten. Loxa comes in crying.)

MAYOR: Judge, let's see. We'll make a report. Those two guys are being issued a summons. I guess we'll see if they can be found. Write down everything the women say!

JUDGE: (*He feels very inadequate. He doesn't know what to do.*) Mr. Mayor, everything? I probably won't have enough paper for that!

MAYOR: How can you be so dim-witted? Just the important things. That's the reason for you being a judge! Jerk! You learned to read and write for nothing!

JUDGE: It's because you told me to write down everything, mayor … so that's what I thought you wanted.

MAYOR: Okay, that's enough! Start writing!

JUDGE: All right, all right, Mr. Mayor, don't get mad. I'll start … I'll start … Let's see, on this day … What day is it, today? … They came here to tell … now I know you don't want me to say aloud what I write. What else can I do? … I keep forgetting.

MAYOR: (*Addressing Loxa*) Woman, don't cry so much. Wipe away your tears! Who knows if it isn't just that someone took your sister off.

PAXKU': I saw her when she was killed by her own brothers.

MAYOR: It's still not certain. Did your husband see it? He should come, too. Why didn't he come? Besides, the body of the person you say is dead hasn't been discovered. Who knows if they didn't just scare her.

LOXA: God, if only that were the truth! But we know what they're like. They probably hid her somewhere.

MAYOR: All right, I'll send somebody to go and bring them. Besides, someone's gone to look for Paxku's husband. It probably won't be long before they bring him. See, they've brought the awful men! (*Then the girl's two brothers appear, escorted by the sheriff, who then leaves.*)

TELEX: You're here, Mr. Mayor? Why did you summon us? That's why we came when we heard tell. What's the matter?

MAYOR: So you don't know? Let's hear then. Why did you kill Tinik? What do you guys say?

CHEP: How could you believe we'd kill our sister? How do you know, Mr. Mayor? The women are lying.

TELEX: We just told them to come and live with us so there wouldn't be any gossip. But they didn't agree. It's true it made us angry, since they keep humiliating us in public. Tinik threw a burning stick at us, but we didn't do anything.

CHEP: Since our father died, all we do is work. Ask our wives if we ever leave the house.

TELEX: It's true. In the morning we went to where they sell cane liquor, and then we went straight home.

MAYOR: Don't lie to me! You were seen drunk at the cantina. Where did you take your sister?

TELEX: Which sister, Mr. Mayor? When we returned, Tinik went to get some ears of corn. We saw her this morning with that woman there. After that we never saw her again, since it got dark.

PAXKU': They're lying, Mayor. When we came back, Tinik went to get her corn. They were waiting for her next to her cornfield. Then they killed her. I told my husband to accompany me to look out for her. He saw it, too. It's just he doesn't want to say so because he's scared of those guys.

TELEX: That woman just tells lies to get us into trouble. Who knows where Tinik went with some man.

CHEP: That's the truth, Mayor. She was just the same in her childhood. That's probably why she went, to look for lots of men. That's what she's always wanted.

MAYOR: Is that true, Loxa? Is it true that your younger sister has lots of men?

LOXA: It's not true, Mayor. It's because they want to take our land. That's why they killed her. The thing is, they didn't realize that they were seen by Paxku' and her husband.

CHEP: (*At bay*) What's this? They claim they saw us there? It's a lie. We were at home. They're lying!

TELEX: (*Speaking right away*) That's true, mayor. Don't believe all those lies. We were at home. Just now we left to come here. Ask our wives!

MAYOR: We don't need to have your wives come. You don't want to tell what you did. The thing is it's still not known where Tinik is. People saw her when she returned from San Cristóbal. She went to look at her cornfield, and it was then that she didn't come back. If you killed her, you must have hidden her body somewhere. We have to do something to get the truth out, so you'll confess. If you don't talk, I'll order you to be whipped until you confess. (*Then the sheriff appears, ushering in Akuxtin, who grows very scared when he sees the two men.*)

SHERIFF: Here's the other one who saw them.

MAYOR: Let's see, come here! That's fine now that he's come, the other one who saw them! Is Paxku' your wife?

AKUXTIN: (*Very scared*) Yes, Mr. Mayor.

MAYOR: Okay then, your wife says you accompanied her to see that nothing happened to Tinik. And besides, she says both of you saw her when her brothers killed her. Is that the truth?

AKUXTIN: (*Looking with great fright at the two men*) Ey ... No, that's not so, Mr. Mayor. We never saw anything. Paxku' told me they'd been given a bad time, but I never went along. And as for her, I never let her go because I was very hungry.

PAXKU': That's not true, Mayor! He went with me and he saw what I saw! We got to see them when they raised their machetes to kill her. But he was so scared he pulled me away and covered my mouth. Then he dragged me home.

AKUXTIN: (*He speaks meekly, but we know he is lying.*) Oh god, I don't know why my wife keeps telling lies. No, Mayor! What's it for me to get involved in others' problems? We never saw anything.

PAXKU': How come we never saw anything? You're so scared of those murderers. He hit me so I wouldn't say anything. But we sure saw them. They must have hidden her somewhere.

AKUXTIN: What would I be scared of? I'm not an old woman! What I don't like is the way my wife keeps meddling in others' affairs. That's why I didn't want her to come ... that's why ... I didn't want to go looking for Tinik.

PAXKU': He's lying, Mayor. He doesn't talk like a man! He saw Tinik was killed, and he never lifted a finger. Coward! (*She begins to cry when she sees that her husband won't say anything.*)

MAYOR: We can tell your wife is telling the truth, Akuxtin. Weren't you scared of those men?

AKUXTIN: Why would I be scared of them, Mayor, if I've been on good terms with them?

MAYOR: So that's the way it is! Who knows if you aren't hiding their crime. You probably were helping them, too.

AKUXTIN: Why do you believe this, Mr. Mayor? You heard me say I never saw anything at all.

MAYOR: You're involved in this problem now even though you don't want to be. So if you won't own up, I'm ordering all of you to be flogged until you confess. Did you see anything or not?

AKUXTIN: (*He regains his courage.*) Never mind ... Let me be flogged, Mayor! It's true. I'm telling you I didn't see anything! I don't know why my wife is talking like this. I don't know where she picked up the things she's saying!

MAYOR: I guess we'll see if you're speaking the truth! Judge, I'm telling you ... Have you written down everything that was said here?

JUDGE: Everything, mayor? It isn't that I ... well ... all right. I finished writing it down. Besides, I remember it all. Some saw it, some didn't see it. They say it was like this, they say it wasn't like this ... all lies, the way it always is. So now ... do I write down that they are to be whipped?

MAYOR: Oh, don't you understand anything? I can see you're so dumb, judge. Don't you know *that* can't be recorded? Don't you know it's illegal? What else can we do to make them confess?

JUDGE: If we tickle them, Mayor, it would be doing them a favor so they'd change their ugly faces.

MAYOR: They'll be tickled with a whip, and you'll get it, too, if you didn't record things properly. Don't you realize we're settling a murder case? Look here, Sheriff, summon everybody, let them see what we're going to do so that the murderers confess. And also hear how they lie. Let's go outside. Let's go to the courtyard.

(*They grab Telex roughly and take him out. The mayor exits, followed by the judge. The sheriff shoves the criminals out.*)

SCENE 2

(*Everyone is shouting angrily that the murderers should be whipped. Then the prisoners come in, followed closely by the sheriff, the judge, the mayor, and several others ready for the event.*)

MAYOR: Now, Sheriff, lots of people are here. Start whipping them! Give each one a hundred lashes! Do it to Telex first, because he's such a troublemaker!

SHERIFF: Okay, Mayor, whatever you say. (*He pushes Telex forward to ready him for the whipping.*) Let's see ... Turn your back to me if you don't want things to turn out worse for you, because I may miss my aim and give you a blow on your ugly face too!

TELEX: Why? I'm not guilty. The awful women are just lying so we'll be punished.

PEOPLE: (*Everyone begins shouting.*) Kill them! Whip them! It was these robbers who murdered her! Now they've been arrested, make them confess!

JUDGE: Oh, Mayor, everybody's really mad! Oh god, I don't want them to turn on me!

MAYOR: It's good they learn a lesson! That's what'll happen to you if I hear you've done something wrong, if you cover things up and conceal their guilt.

JUDGE: Me, Mr. Mayor? Oh lord, why in the world would I have to bear their guilt? Our Lord wouldn't want that! I'm a decent man!

MAYOR: All right ... all right ... it just occurred to me because all the people do is lie. I don't want to hear that kind of gossip about you, too. Or to hear you've concealed someone's guilt. That you agree with the troublemakers or obey the orders of the guy in charge.

JUDGE: That's not true, Mr. Mayor! I don't agree with anybody. I'm not covering up for anyone. You know I'd tell you whatever I've heard.

MAYOR: That's the way it should be, Judge. That's fine. Did you hear, Sheriff? Ask them who's guilty. Will he talk or not? It's better if he fesses up so he doesn't have to be whipped. Let's hear if they admit it or not. We shouldn't punish them too hard.

SHERIFF: Will you speak up, or shall I give it to you now?

TELEX: What? ... What am I to say if I didn't do anything?

MAYOR: Okay, you heard what we said. If you don't want to believe it, whip him now!

(*The sheriff whips him. Telex screams loudly but won't confess. On the fifth blow he faints. When he sees what is being done to Telex, Chep is terrified.*)

JUDGE: (*Distracted by what he's witnessing, he begins to murmur.*) Oh my lord, Mr. Mayor, won't they die because of us? It wasn't me who gave the order! Please don't get me involved, too. Wouldn't it be better if the district attorney in San Cristóbal came to see about it? What if they're innocent?

MAYOR: How can you be so stupid, Judge? What'll the people say when they hear we don't know how to try cases, that we don't know how to discover who's guilty? What indeed will the town say? See here, the three of them are just being stupid. Sheriff! We'll wait for him to come to, so he understands very well what's in for him! Now you can begin whipping the others, too!

CHEP: No, Mayor. Please don't beat me! It's true. I didn't do anything. I wasn't the one who did it!

MAYOR: Ohh, so maybe, then, you had a glimpse of what he did.

CHEP: No, Mayor. Me, I was asleep. I really had a terrible hangover, so I don't know who killed my sister.

MAYOR: So how do you know she's dead! Sheriff, give a whipping to Chep until he confesses, until he says what he did, or else we'll leave him in a pool of blood! How else would he know his sister is dead? Didn't he say first that he'd fled with his friends? It must have been you who killed your sister.

CHEP: (*When he feels the whip, he squeals like a pig.*) Ow, ow, ow! Please, Sheriff, don't hit me!

SHERIFF: How about it? Will you own up to it? Will you tell us what you did?

CHEP: Oh, by God, I didn't see anything. Our Lord knows I'm innocent.

MAYOR: He doesn't want to confess yet.... For sure you'd better give him some more whip lashes, Sheriff, until his blood flows!

CHEP: No, truly, Mr. Mayor, god knows, if you beat me again, I'll die!

TELEX: (*Wanting to frighten Chep, he growls at him.*) Don't be scared, Chep, you've gotta endure it! We're innocent!

MAYOR: Oh, see how it is! The beating didn't make God's angel pass out for long! It seems like he needs to be tickled some more! Sheriff, give it to him harder!

SHERIFF: (*Whipping him fiercely*) Feel that! So you learn to steal better! That belt of yours you stole from my cousin! What good news, not only do you steal, but you also killed your sister.

MAYOR: Don't wear yourself out, Sheriff. Remember they need a good thrashing! Isn't that so, Judge?

JUDGE: (*He has been watching the brutal whipping with great fear.*) Oh, Mr. Mayor, I don't know what to say. Let's hope to god he doesn't go too far!

MAYOR: No, do you think he's gone too far? They can stand a lot. We've hardly started. The whip should skin their hides a bit. Sheriff! Give it good to Chep!

CHEP: (*Scared to death*) Don't hit me, please, Mr. Mayor! Don't hit me! The guilty one's Telex, Mayor. It was Telex who committed murder. I just wanted to beat her, but it was Telex who struck her with a machete. Please don't hit me!

TELEX: You hussy, you witch! Don't you be scared, don't you lie! You hit her with a machete!

CHEP: That's not true, Mr. Mayor. He threatened me. He told me he'd kill me if I didn't help him. He swung his machete at me!

PAXKU': (*She quickly joins in.*) Yes, that's the truth, Mayor. First Telex struck her with a machete, and then Chep did, too. Akuxtin, don't you have anything to say now? Those bad guys have admitted their crime.

AKUXTIN: (*Shaking with fear*) Ohh, Mr. Mayor, I swear to God I never saw anything. Please don't whip me!

MAYOR: Look at him! What a wretch! Where are your balls? You deserve a good whipping!

AKUXTIN: Oh, don't do that, please, Mayor. She was struck by their machetes. If I had shouted, they would have killed me and my wife.

MAYOR: See here, Mr. Judge, you should give this man a good punishment so he takes it to heart. He'll carry rocks for two months. Besides that, he'll spend the nights in jail, well locked up.

JUDGE: So be it, Mr. Mayor! It's true he should be stuck in jail even if it's for two months. That's how he'll pay for hiding the murderers' crime. When people mistreat each other, he doesn't care what they do.

MAYOR: Mr. Judge, did you record the crimes?

JUDGE: Well ... well, you talk too fast, Mr. Mayor. After you calm down, please repeat it for me.

MAYOR: I've listened to everything. . . . Where's the dead person's body? Sheriff, give them some more lashes until they tell where they hid the dead woman's body.

CHEP: No, Mr. Mayor! Telex went and threw it in the gully by the path to Hairy Hand. He covered it with branches.

TELEX: Now you've exposed the whole thing! You've got no balls! The only good thing is that you, too, killed her. Just wait! In prison I'll give you what you deserve! You helped me hide her! We should get the same punishment. We'll go to Hell together when we die, you back-biter, son of a devil!

MAYOR: Are you going to shut up, or do we have to silence you with a whip? Sheriff, now you can take a rest! They need to be handcuffed and taken to the jail in San Cristóbal! Make sure they're well-secured! Now everybody's seen that we settled the case here in our town. The district attorney didn't have to come. He always makes things worse.

JUDGE: All right, mayor ... we should pay attention to the law. . . . it's worth something.

MAYOR: You said it! The laws shouldn't be made by those who just maltreat everyone when they try a case, with their demands for money. Now the prisoners' arraignment is recorded as I asked. We want them to receive a good punishment! Did you hear, Judge? Hurry up, ready the papers so they arrive together with the prisoners!

JUDGE: Yes, indeed! Really? Maybe they'll be let free if somebody goes and slips money to the judge in San Cristóbal. They're so clever! Oh god, this scares me! (*He exits rapidly.*)

MAYOR: (*The women can't stop crying. The mayor tries to console them.*) All right, women, now we've settled your case.... I really feel terrible about what happened to Tinik.... She was a very brave woman.... What can we do now?... Find your strength! I'll see that the title for your land is executed properly. And because of your late older sister, you, Paxku', do you want to live alone, or are you going to join your awful coward of a husband?

PAXKU': (*Filled with anger*) No, Mayor. I don't want to ever see him again. Imagine how he'll bring up my children, the way he's behaving! He's on his own, since our Lord never gave him what it takes to be a man! I'll go to Loxa's house. Now that she's alone, I'll join her and we'll help each other.

LOXA: All right, Mr. Mayor, thank you for trying our case. If you hadn't done us the favor, who knows if he wouldn't kill me, too.

MAYOR: Okay, it's over. Thanks to Paxku' who came to let us know about it. God, if only there were others as brave as you two! Don't forget, if you have other problems, come and let me know.

LOXA AND PAXKU': Thanks so much, Mr. Mayor.

MAYOR: All right, girls, please take good care of each other. I'll see you tomorrow, friends! (*He puts on his hat and exits.*)

Jaguar Dynasty

(1992)

JAGUAR DYNASTY (*Dinastía de los jaguares*) was crafted by our translator, Palas, who after searching in the historical sources called up the Spanish conquest of Chiapa de Corzo. This town, after which the state is named in part, is situated on the Grijalva River. Dating back to before the Christian era, this non-Mayan town was the most powerful force in the Lowlands. At the time of the Conquest, it was competing with Zinacantán in the Highlands.

Next follows a dream sequence presenting the creation of the Mayas according to the *Popol Vuh* [Book of counsel] (see Christianson 2000). Events described in this sixteenth-century K'iche' Guatemalan Mayan document date back to 100 BC and are depicted in the extraordinarily beautiful murals of San Bartolo in the Petén (Santoro et al. 2005).

The play closes on the banks of the Usumacinta River, where Yaxchilán vied with Palenque for domination of what is now eastern Chiapas and western Guatemala. Here we see the struggles for succession under the seventh-century ruler Pakal Balam (Shield Jaguar). Fortified with knowledge of this historical battle (recently revealed by decipherment of the glyphs), the hero apprentice declares that unity, education, and peaceful solutions must prevail so that "We Mayas will never die!"

The jaguar (*balam* or *bolom*) has been a major symbol of Mayan supernatural power since the earliest times. It, too, is shown in the San Bartolo murals.

The actors, most of whom had been unfamiliar with this history, were attracted to the way Palas used language that was distinctly formal.

Never before had a modern Mayan audience viewed on stage historical accounts of the Classic Maya. It was presented in Cancuc to a crowd of seven hundred Tzeltal Mayas and also to a full house of three hundred people for two nights in the Teatro La Fragua in Progreso, Honduras, where the audience, of Mayan descent, knew nothing of their history and greeted the play with a chorus of "bravos." Performed the following year for archaeologists at the Pre-columbian Art Research's Mesa Redonda in Palenque, it received high praise for its authenticity and historical accuracy.

Funded by Chiapas state scholarships, two students from Cancuc were added to our cast, permitting us to increase its size to ten so that the play could be performed with a suitably impressive number of individuals.

During rehearsals Ralph Lee discovered how extraordinarily difficult it was to train our actors to dance, moving their feet in unison, as jaguar gods carried out their ritual performance in act II, scene 3.

Petu' illustrates both the personal and social importance of theatre when speaking of *Jaguar Dynasty*:

> This play has made me think, and has made me dream about our ancestors, about what they were like. There have been so many gen-erations which have since passed through this world, that we need to recover the culture of our first ancestors, and show it to people who have forgotten. I cannot go from person to person, or from house to house, explaining what our ancestors were like, how they passed through this world, how they used to live. Through *Jaguar Dynasty* we can now show people how things were, and what the Con-quest was like. This play is very important for the people of Chiapas. (Frischmann 1994a, 234)

Siena Craig (1993, 67) also recognized the importance of the group's perfor-mances, noting that "Sna Jtz'ibajom uses the theater to unify the Maya across boundaries of time, space, and geography."

In preparing this material for publication, my computer deleted half a sen-tence in the following page, leaving Pakal Balam, king of Yaxchilán, dressed only from the waist down. I could find no printed record, but by looking at a video of the play at home, I was able to redress him!

For versions in Tzotzil and Spanish, see Montemayor 1996a.

CAST OF CHARACTERS

MATAWIL: prophet, wearing white loincloth, short white cape, sandals, with conch and staff, deerskin over his shoulder while holding its head

CHIAPANEC WOMAN 1: wearing long white robe with geometric flower design

CHIAPANEC WOMAN 2: same clothing as Woman 1

CHIAPANEC MAN 1: wearing short white shoulder cloth, white loincloth, sandals

CHIAPANEC MAN 2: wearing white loincloth, sandals

TWO ZINACANTEC WARRIORS: wearing long white robes with large horizontal stripes, sandals

INQUISITOR: Franciscan priest, wearing brown hooded vestment, white belt, sandals, with cross on pole

BÁLTAZAR GUERRA: Spanish conqueror, wearing helmet, black shirt, white breastplate, black robe, black shorts, shoes, with sword and whip

SANGUIEME: Chiapanec hero, wearing white loincloth

DIEGO DE NOCAYOLA: Chiapanec traitor, wearing black hat, purple shirt, black shorts, shoes

CH'OK: apprentice, wearing feathered headdress, white cape, bracelet, white loincloth, high-backed sandals, with staff, later wearing antlers and a jaguar skin

CREATOR MOTHER: wearing quetzal-feathered headdress, long green robe with white feather trim, black slippers

XKIK: mother of the twins, Xbalamke and Junajpu, wearing long white robe with geometric flower design, barefoot

SKULL

DOG (PUPPET)

JUN KAME: death god, wearing white skull mask, black costume with white skeleton design

XBALAMKE: hero twin, wearing white mask, white loincloth, red and green shorts, high sandals

XMUKANE: grandmother goddess, wearing white robe like that of Xkik

JUNAJPU: hero twin, wearing same clothing as his brother

XOK: Lady Shark, first wife of Shield Jaguar, wearing feathered headdress, long white robe with geometric flower design, sandals

PAKAL BALAM: Shield Jaguar, king of Yaxchilán, wearing a feather headdress, jade necklace, white bib covering a green sleeveless shirt, green designed shorts, high-backed sandals, with staff

KUK BALAM: Bird Jaguar, youngest son of Pakal Balam, wearing quetzal-feathered headdress, white sleeveless shirt, white cape, white loincloth, high-backed sandals

BALAM KITZE: jaguar god, wearing quetzal-feathered jaguar mask, jade necklace, jaguar skin bracelets, jaguar shorts

BALAM AKAB: jaguar god, wearing same clothes as Balam Kitze

MAJUKUTAJ: jaguar god, wearing same clothes as Balam Kitze

IKI BALAM: jaguar god, wearing same clothes as Balam Kitze

MUK'TA K'ANAL: companion of Xok, wearing same clothes as Xok

TWO SERVANTS: wearing white sleeveless shirts, white loincloth, sandals

FOUR NOBLES: wearing white sleeveless shirts, white loincloths

FIVE MAYAN WARRIORS, ONE NAMED CHIVAN BAK: wearing white sleeveless shirts, white loincloths, holding lances with banners

Act I

SCENE 1

(In the center of the stage is a pyramid. Jungle and river sounds. Matawil appears, addressing the audience.)

MATAWIL: This must be the place ordained by the gods of Heaven. Something terrible may happen here. Something terrible will happen here in our land. I must see how to prevent it. Time is running out! I will just wait for Ch'ok to come. I guess I will quickly go and hide. (*He exits, running. Jungle sounds continue.*)

(A Chiapanec woman appears, shouting, as another woman and two men appear from the other side.)

CHIAPANEC WOMAN 1: Brothers, brothers! Now they've captured Sanguieme! Our friends who fled fell from the cliff top down into the river!

CHIAPANEC WOMAN 2: Holy Mother, lord of the holy river, see after their spirits! How were they discovered? (*The men, very distressed, draw near.*)

CHIAPANEC WOMAN 1: It was Nocayola who denounced them. He was tricked. You see, he obeyed them. Then the Spaniards took command. That's how it became known.

CHIAPANEC WOMAN 2: Sanguieme killed the governor and attacked Nocayola, who fled to San Cristóbal. So they called up murderers—Mayas, Aztecs, and Spaniards. That's why I never went to accompany our people. Now we are under the guard of the tormenters.

CHIAPANEC MAN 1: (*Angrily*) Nocayola! Didn't he say he would help us? How could they believe in that man who had become a traitor?

CHIAPANEC MAN 2: He turned against us! He disclosed where Sanguieme was hiding.

CHIAPANEC WOMAN 2: The women! The children! Were the children thrown down too?

CHIAPANEC WOMAN 1: That was witnessed! They had fled into a cave high above the river. Then a Spaniard, lowering himself with a chain, discovered them and killed them!

CHIAPANEC MAN 1: How do you know? Who saw it?

CHIAPANEC WOMAN 1: Those who escaped down below saw how they fell into the river. They were the only ones who escaped.

CHIAPANEC WOMAN 2: Báltazar Guerra ordered his soldiers to stop, not to kill everyone. So they seized Sanguieme to get him to name those who were in rebellion.

CHIAPANEC MAN 2: Who was it? Who were they?

CHIAPANEC WOMAN 1: What's it to you? You'll inform on them, too?

CHIAPANEC MAN 2: Be quiet! Could you have joined them? You probably want to trick us, too, telling us lies!

CHIAPANEC WOMAN 2: God, my Lord, holy river, my holy grandfather in Heaven, now the great Sanguieme is caught and it is we who are quarreling!

CHIAPANEC WOMAN 1: If we had joined up with Sanguieme they never would have defeated us. Many people were scared. They have forgotten our gods, and now the punishment is coming.

CHIAPANEC MAN 2: Sanguieme advised the traitor. What would be the use of speaking to him?

CHIAPANEC WOMAN 2: Who would mistrust Nocayola? Doesn't he know our language? Doesn't he have the same blood as we do? Wasn't he the priest descended from the jaguar gods?

CHIAPANEC WOMAN 1: Nocayola was here with us. He was our leader. I saw them in fierce combat. He threw himself at the feet of the Spaniards' horses.

CHIAPANEC MAN 1: But he gave up four years ago. He didn't tell the truth. He didn't defend our land, our gods. He became the Spaniards' servant.

CHIAPANEC MAN 2: He no longer respects our customs. He has obeyed the Spaniards' commands. He has become an enemy of his people. He has done what he pleased without considering his own people.

CHIAPANEC MAN 1: How was Sanguieme caught? They also discovered where everyone was in hiding. You see, many women and children died in the river's depths.

CHIAPANEC WOMAN 2: When he reveals our names, they'll come and kill us, too!

CHIAPANEC WOMAN 1: I can't believe it! Nocayola will defend us!

CHIAPANEC MAN 1: We are still useful to them serving as their slaves in the mines. You have seen how angry they get when they ask us for tribute. And besides, they urge us to believe in their gods.

CHIAPANEC MAN 2: All he wants are luxury items and the cane liquor that the Spaniards give him.

CHIAPANEC MAN 1: That's so! The ones who first came had him drink cane liquor. After he drank with Báltazar Guerra he abandoned our gods. Then he began to worship the bloody cross.

CHIAPANEC WOMAN 1: I don't know. Maybe that's why Nocayola gave in to them, since he saw how some of his people were kicked to death by horses and others killed by muskets.

CHIAPANEC WOMAN 2: I still remember that massacre, the corpses strewn everywhere, our town on fire, the men's headdresses covered with blood. Our gods lay wherever the horses left them, all broken. Can those demons be stronger than our gods?

CHIAPANEC MAN 1: (*Speaking furiously*) They are very brave. My Yaqui axe is proof of that, still stained with the blood of one of them!

CHIAPANEC MAN 2: Look at this scalp and my obsidian blade! How could one scalp a devil? Can their hearts be pulled out and offered to the gods?

CHIAPANEC MAN 1: (*Enraged*) We Chiapanec warriors have been very successful. Didn't we scare away the Tzotzils and the Aztecs?

CHIAPANEC MAN 2: For many years we have defended this land that belonged to our earliest ancestors. The Mayas and the Zoques came trembling, bringing their men and women for sacrifice.

CHIAPANEC MAN 1: If only those early people, instead of fleeing, had joined forces, then we would never have been overwhelmed by the Spaniards, their firearms and their steeds.

CHIAPANEC MAN 2: (*Very angry*) But now Nocayola attacks us again. If only we had listened to Sanguieme! Instead, we believed Nocayola, who said he would kill all the Spaniards. How could we believe that?

CHIAPANEC WOMAN 1: No longer have we any hope! Now the jaguar and the river lord have seen, have known whose blood, whose flesh would come to an end, since they believed those other gods.

CHIAPANEC WOMAN 2: (*Looking about fearfully*) Be quiet, friends, be quiet! We'll flee. The Spaniards are approaching now with their horses. Maybe they are bringing Sanguieme here! (*They run out.*)

SCENE 2

(Two Zinacantec warriors enter carrying Sanguieme, whose hands and feet are bound. Following right behind is the priest and Spanish soldiers. Then Báltazar Guerra appears with Nocayola, who is wearing bright Spanish clothing. They place Sanguieme on top of the pyramid and tighten his lashing.)

INQUISITOR: By the name of God, now he will speak up and tell the names of those who have rebelled against God and against the king of Spain! *(Sanguieme does not reply; he only looks heavenward.)*

GUERRA: *(He whips Sanguieme.)* Speak, you dog! Tell us the names of those who worship the devil!

SANGUIEME: *(He stares at Nocayola.)* That one there! *(Guerra gives him another whiplash.)*

GUERRA: Inform us, dog! *Señor* Diego Nocayola is a Christian. Thanks to God he has been baptized!

SANGUIEME: I don't believe it! Our gods are alive! They are the sun, the moon, and the jaguar lord of the river. You cannot hang them on a cross! May they live forever! Nocayola is a traitor. You stopped worshipping our gods. If only I had killed you before you switched sides! You are no man at all!

GUERRA: *(He whips him again.)* Be quiet! Now tell us the names of the leaders! And where it is that you stored the gold taken from the mine. Otherwise you will be skinned!

SANGUIEME: My hatred for you is held in the heart of every Chiapanec. Stinking pigs! Gold diggers! So you have entered our land, our shadows. God, my Lord! Open your mouth, devour them, do not let them tear down your temples!

NOCAYOLA: Sanguieme, our gods exist no longer. The cross of Christ is stronger than the devils. Your defeat is caused by the power of Jesus Christ and the king of Spain. Give in if you want to survive. Join us! I will see that things go well for you. You will be made powerful, too.

SANGUIEME: No, coward! Our god, the lord of the river, will see how to take revenge! The conspirators will die together with the invaders. Everything on the surface of the earth, every seed, will be lost.

NOCAYOLA: *(Laughing as he speaks)* Ha, ha, ha! Everyone has left their land. Now they are crouched like rabbits in the forest! Like it or not, when you are dying of hunger you will obey us! Even the wicked Chamulans, too.

INQUISITOR: It is better if you obey, too, Sanguieme. Have you seen the gallows they are building over there? The prisoners who were with you will be hung on them and burned if you do not tell where you hid the gold.

Torturing the Chiapanec traitor Diego de Nocayola, performance in Chamula, 2004.
Photo copyright © Macduff Everton

SANGUIEME: Never you mind, I will die for our gods. Mojotove, see here, they are killing me now! My Holy Father, lord of the river, holy jaguars, holy sun, may I go with honor. I will surely see how to take revenge!

GUERRA: Enough of that! He will not obey the orders! What shall we do with him, Father?

INQUISITOR: Burn him alive! Let him join the devils! We have spoken to him properly so he would agree that everyone become a Christian. He does not relinquish his belief in their gods. Burn him alive!

GUERRA: He should be tortured first so that we hear the names of those who are his companions in wickedness, and so they will give us their treasure. Speak, you mad dog! Where did you hide the gold that came from the mine?

SANGUIEME: Monkeys, stick it in your mouths! Swallow it happily in Hell!

GUERRA: So that is what you want, dog! (*Addressing the Zinacantec warriors*) Pull the ropes tighter! (*Sanguieme twists with pain. He tries to break loose, but there is nothing he can do. He never speaks a word. Tied to the stake, he just sags down as the priest prays in Latin.*)

INQUISITOR: *Mihi ... data est gratia haec, in gentibus evangelizare investigabilis divitias Christi, et illuminare omnes quae sit absconditi a saeculis in Deo, qui omnia creavit. Sed conclusit scriptura omnia sub peccatum, ut promissio ex fide Iesu Christi daretur credentibus.*

NOCAYOLA: It is useless! Better if we burn him in front of everyone! We will burn his allies, too. Some we will hang. Have everyone come forth. Let them see how justice is done!

GUERRA: Well said, Señor Diego Nocayola! Now they will witness what is to be done! That is how all our enemies will be destroyed! Ha, ha, ha! You know how to rule! Burn him, then, while the people are gathered together here!

(The Mayan warriors untie him, put him in a hammock, and tie it to two posts. The priest is praying. Nocayola and Guerra are happily quaffing down cane liquor.)

NOCAYOLA: *(He goes drunkenly to where Sanguieme lies in the hammock.)* You wanted to kill me, Sanguieme. Isn't that true? You wounded me with an arrow and you burnt down my house! Now you will warm yourself in Hell, insolent dog! We'll see if your allies come to defend you! Set fire to him!

(The Mayan warriors set fire to the hammock. Nocayola turns to look at everyone, showing off his power.)

NOCAYOLA: I want Diego Nocayola to be remembered from this night forward as the deputy of God and the Spaniards here in Chiapa. Ha, ha, ha! By this cross I will be remembered!

(Everyone exits, leaving the burning flames to die down gradually.)

Act II

SCENE 1

(The prophet, Matawil, appears next to where the hammock was burnt. He wears antlers and a dark skin suit. He is followed by the boy, Ch'ok, an apprentice, also wearing antlers, a jaguar skin loincloth, and rattles on his wrists and ankles. Matawil walks supported by a cane. Ch'ok follows him cautiously, but alertly. Matawil makes sure that no one is present before turning to speak to Ch'ok.)

MATAWIL: Hurry up, Ch'ok, hurry up! We will take the ashes here while they are still warm and toss them in the river. Gather them up quickly before they cool!

CH'OK: I feel afraid, my teacher! I'm not afraid of the Spaniards or of Nocayola. What frightens me are the spirits of the Chiapanecs. They are not on good terms with the Mayas.

MATAWIL: Ohh, Ch'ok, that has been true for a long time. There were no towns that had neighborly relations. That is why it was so easy for the Spaniards to defeat us. This must end! So when will you obey my orders?

CH'OK: But I'm scared, Matawil. They aren't my friends!

MATAWIL: Even if their blood is of fire-givers, even if our blood is not their ally, hurry up and do what I say! Stop asking questions. We are in a hurry!

CH'OK: Matawil, why have you come to defend the spirits of those who attacked our ancestors?

MATAWIL: Do you want to know the truth? Our first ancestors and those of the people who have just died were friends. All of us are descended from the original ancestors, the first creators. Now will you do what I say?

CH'OK: Matawil, Sanguieme was our enemy. He made us suffer greatly from slavery, punishment. He took the blood of many of our people. His ancestors also seized much of our land. Why do we come now to defend his soul?

MATAWIL: Won't you believe me? You are delaying us with all your questions. While the ashes are still warm, hurry up and do what I tell you!

CH'OK: I'm scared. Matawil, I'll do it. (*Fearfully he gathers up the ashes.*) They aren't my friends.

MATAWIL: Everyone descended from Our Holy Mother, the jaguar men, the mother of water, they are all our own people. That is why I brought you here, so that your ancient history would be revealed to you. So long as we are here on the earth's surface, only in this way can we aid our gods and our spirits.

CH'OK: All right then, I'll do what you say, even if I don't understand it. All right, protect the spirits of those who for many years have been our enemies!

MATAWIL: Now we cannot object. The gods have changed. Now we must unite our heads and our hearts to do what must be done in our land. Hurry up, without any more complaints. Put the ashes in their place!

CH'OK: Matawil, you are teaching me. I know that what you are telling me is right. I will do it.

MATAWIL: Hurry up! Since early on you keep asking me about this. Put the ashes in their place and go toss them in the river! Hurry up, please, before they cool!

CH'OK: (*He brushes up the ashes and sets out to toss them in the river.*) Matawil, I don't know why I'm shaking so! Matawil, help me! I no longer have the strength to throw them in the river. I can't let go of them either! I'm shaking! Who knows what has taken hold of me! What could it be?

MATAWIL: Ch'ok, it is the burnt blood of Sanguieme. That is good sustenance. He knows we are here and he wants his blood to serve as food for the gods. (*Ch'ok tries again to toss the ashes in the river. Matawil shakes his cane and begins to chant.*) Ixkik, we offer a feast, our flesh made of corn! (*He censes the ashes thoroughly.*) Take our strength, first father, first mother! Be strong, Ch'ok! Toss the ashes into the river!

CH'OK: Matawil, now I am very strong! This seems like a dream, Matawil! (*He tosses the ashes into the river. Matawil blows his conch shell.*)

MATAWIL: Good, good, very good! Now we will see how the gods appear in your dreams. (*Matawil and Ch'ok sit down on opposite sides of the stage as the lights dim and music sounds.*)

SCENE 2

MATAWIL: Be happy, my Lord! Show us your power! We will see what you know. See that we offer you here your sustenance. It is the blood of your children! Holy Mother, mother of the gods, wife of our Holy Father!

CH'OK: Look upon us, mother of the water, lightning, creator, progenitor, father and mother of the whole world!

(*New music resounds as Creator Mother appears dancing, wearing a feathered robe. From the center of the pyramid springs up a gourd tree. Xkik appears, walking towards the tree with great curiosity. She mounts the pyramid, dancing, and lifts her hand to pick one of the gourds, which is transformed into a skull from which emerges the voice of Sanguieme, personifying Junajpu.*)

XKIK: (*Addressing the tree*) Doesn't this fruit seem beautiful? It was probably the gods who gave it to us! Can I pick it? (*She extends her arm.*)

SKULL: Do you really want it?

XKIK: Yes indeed I want it. (*The skull spits on her hand.*)

SKULL: With my saliva, with my mouth I give you one of our descendants. My skull no longer is of any use. All of us will die. You will ascend to the surface of the earth. Now you will not die! Believe me, you will be the mother of the immortal spirits!

SCENE 3

(*Xkik looks at her hand, touches her belly that grows. She moans and gives birth. From beneath the pyramid emerge the twins, Junajpu and Xbalamke, as if they emerged from Xkik. They dance with her, crossing back and forth. After making a turn, they leave her to dance with the Creator Mother as they climb the pyramid. Xbalamke holds up a dog as he dances. Jun Kame appears, dressed in black with a skeleton design, dancing grotesquely, groaning. He is the lord of death.)*

JUN KAME: So you are the magicians who have come from the underworld! Let's see, show me what you know how to do.

XBALAMKE: Ladies and gentlemen, look at this little dog that is full of life and wagging its tail!

JUN KAME: Kill it, kill it! I order you to kill it!

XBALAMKE: Yes, we're going to kill it and then we will revive it because we are very powerful magicians. (*Junajpu pulls out a knife and cuts off the dog's head, which falls into Jun Kame's hand. He tosses it behind the pyramid. Everyone watching screams.*)

XKIK, CREATOR MOTHER, JUN KAME: He killed it, he killed it! Can they bring it back to life?

JUN KAME: Revive it! We'll see if you can!

XBALAMKE: Watch, we're going to revive it! (*He holds the dog up high and down low, dancing with it, showing it to the public.*) See, we've brought it back to life!

XKIK, CREATOR MOTHER: They revived it! It's true that these magicians are powerful.

JUN KAME: Bah, anybody can kill a dog. If they really are powerful. . . . Let's see, kill your brother and then revive him!

JUNAJPU: We can make him come back to life. Okay, Xbalamke. Watch, everyone! I am going to take out my brother's heart and then I am going to revive him. (*Xbalamke lies on the top of the pyramid to be sacrificed. Junajpu plunges the knife into him and pulls out his heart, which he shows to the public.*) This is my brother's heart. I am going to throw it in the fire, and then with its ashes I will revive him. (*He tosses the heart behind the pyramid and then passing his hand three times over Xbalamke's inanimate body, blows on it also three times as Xbalamke begins to show signs of life. Then they and the women shout and dance triumphantly. Jun Kame is indignant.*)

JUN KAME: Enough of that! Stop your music, stop your songs, the laughing, the chatting! We lords of Hell do not like this. We will never like it. We have seen everything you have made. I want you to kill me. Then you will bring me back to life! (*The twins kill Jun Kame.*)

JUNAJPU: Today we have defeated the lords of Hell!

XBALAMKE: Today we will found the dynasty of the jaguar men!

JUNAJPU: Today we will create music and song. We will see that whatever the gods desire comes true.

XBALAMKE: Today we will create writing, numbers. Now we can count the days, just as the world turns.

Jaguar God, 2004. Photo copyright © Macduff Everton

(Xmukane appears with two gourds full of white and yellow corn, which she holds up one after the other.)

XMUKANE: Create our flesh, our bodies, our food! Call forth the lord of corn! His flesh will be our sustenance. With this we shall grow, talk, laugh, think, work, dance, and give thanks to the gods!

XBALAMKE: Yes, indeed! We will create the jaguar men, those in command.

JUNAJPU: And also the women, the mothers of water. May our grandmother, Xmukane, grind the seeds so that the men of corn will flourish.

XBALAMKE: May they enter, the spirits of the jaguar, the coyote, the parrot, and the raven who brought forth the white corn and the yellow. May they flourish and become jaguar men, real men, here on the earth's surface! *(They dance at the four corners.)*

JUNAJPU: Balam Kitze, the joking jaguar, the laughing jaguar, care for the red sky of the East! Pay no attention to death! You are the spirit of the warriors. Your laughter mocks cruel death. Laugh, jaguar of the East!

XBALAMKE: Balam Akab, jaguar of the night, you understand the nightly sky! You are the spirit of those who are the thinkers, the writers, of those who know how to dream! Care for the West, lord of night!

JUNAJPU: Majukutaj, unruly jaguar! You are the spirit of the liberators! You are the lord of dance! White guardian of the North! You are the lord of music and the drum!

XBALAMKE: Iki Balam, lord of night! Your yellow eyes will look over the South! You are the lord of whatever grows! Jaguar, you will season the food so that we may mature happily!

MATAWIL: Ch'ok, have you seen our first ancestors? The gods created jaguar men the way they had wished.

CH'OK: Maybe that is why they had such good vision. Later, perhaps the gods thought it was not right that men be so smart.

JUNAJPU: You jaguar men will increase the seed of the Olmecs, the Toltecs, and all the other people on the earth's surface! It will be you who set each town in order.

XBALAMKE: That is how it will be! Go, then, young jaguars, flourish on the earth, love each other, and bring issue! Go! *(They exit, dancing.)*

MATAWIL: That is how our first ancestors were created on the surface of the world. It was they who fashioned the tall buildings, the pyramids. They did many things according to the wishes of the gods.

CH'OK: I understand now why you said that Sanguieme was a descendant of our first fathers. But ... how was it that they became enemies?

MATAWIL: Now you will see! I will summon the spirits of the lords of Yaxchil so you may witness how the first elders fell into disorder and ruin. (*He blows his conch.*)

Act III

SCENE 1

(*The lights dim and the music changes. From the jaws of a serpent above the pyramid appears Pakal Balam, Shield Jaguar, in his imperial robes. Then appears Xok, Shark Lady, finely dressed, but clearly annoyed. Ch'ok, astonished, sits watching them. Matawil remains standing, waiting for the king. When they descend from the pyramid, Xok begins to scold the king.*)

XOK: It is not right that you have named your son, Kuk Balam, Bird Jaguar, to inherit the dynasty. My husband, you are old now! Your mad love for your young wife, Great Star, must not blind you! I am your first wife. You have a child of mine who should receive the high office.

PAKAL BALAM: I speak to you with respect, Xok. I inform you that you do not understand the ways of the dynasty. I have decided that I shall leave as king Kuk Balam. It is he who shall become the new king when I die!

Shield Jaguar, king of Yaxchilán, 2004. Photo copyright © Macduff Everton

XOK: Pakal Balam, do not humiliate me! Remember that I have two royal lines. Though the lineage of Great Star has provided us with alliances, the dynasty should enter into the hands of my child, as the gods have said.

PAKAL BALAM: But I will be old when I die, Xok. Besides, your son is not a good leader, while Kuk Balam will act for us in a grand manner.

XOK: That is only a humiliation! My family will become enraged. Should I be satisfied with that? I, who gave you my lineage so that you would rise too!

PAKAL BALAM: (*Pakal Balam addresses Matawil with an honorific*). Land and sky, tell me what I can do. The gods have decided what should be my powers. My power cannot be learned. Chilam Balam, wise man, tell this woman what you have heard!

MATAWIL: I am at your service, Lady. Xok, we have seen the blessings of the gods that have been given also to the king that he may live a long life. For that reason the boy, Kuk Balam, has been chosen to become king.

XOK: I will have nothing to do with that decision. Remember that you respected me highly when you took me for your wife!

PAKAL BALAM: Obey what I say! Your child still does not know how to speak the words of the gods, or to wage war as is required of a king. I have seen that the boy Kuk Balam is fully capable.

XOK: How am I to report to my family that you have changed your word and are giving the government to the son of that second wife?

PAKAL BALAM: Chilam Balam, here, Matawil, please tell her what are the wishes of the gods.

XOK: I obey what you say, Matawil, but I do not like what I am being told. It is we who are to do the favor of informing my family of these orders.

MATAWIL: Wait a moment, Lady Xok, I should accompany you. Those who know how to watch the stars will obey, since they see how the world moves. They will demonstrate that they are not deceivers.

PAKAL BALAM: That is what I wish. Together we will tell them. And also, we shall summon them when the new king becomes a worthy dignitary.

XOK: Why is this happening? That woman may not be happy to be respected in this way, to be treated so highly.

PAKAL BALAM: I never said that she would be the one to give her blood for the gods!

XOK: My god! That is the duty of only the king's mother, to give her blood so the gods will come forth!

PAKAL BALAM: Today I say that once and for all your lineage and that of Great Star must assure the future of the dynasty. Become brave! Do not draw apart!

XOK: I do not understand you, Shield Jaguar. Should it not be the mother of Bird Jaguar who will care for him in this way?

PAKAL BALAM: It will be the woman who most deserves it, Xok. It is you who will be raised to the level of goddess by giving your blood as if you were his mother. In that way both families will be honored.

XOK: As if I were his mother? I do not obey! So you honor your last child. You show the town that he can receive the power because he is my child!

PAKAL BALAM: Not so. I want it to be seen that he has the same power as your son. If you accept that, then you all will be contented.

XOK: If that is what you have decided, then I must obey. I know that Pakal, my first child, will not obey what you say.

PAKAL BALAM: He will do it even if it is by force. My son, named Pakal, may die before I do. That is why I wish to leave the government in good hands. Kuk Balam will have matured by the time the position is left to him.

XOK: Perhaps you speak the truth, Shield Jaguar. I will speak calmly to my son so that he will not bear you a grudge. May I leave now?

PAKAL BALAM: You may, but first there is something for Señor Matawil to tell you. He will teach you our customs in proper form. Go now, for I am going to the temple to pray to the gods. (*The three exit.*)

SCENE 2

(King Pakal Balam enters very solemnly followed by Queen Xok, Matawil, another lady, nobles and servants. They prepare to witness the ceremony of self-sacrifice in which Kuk Balam is consecrated as prince of Yaxchilán.)

MATAWIL: King Pakal Balam, give your approval before Heaven and Earth that in true form Xok does the favor of becoming a goddess.

PAKAL BALAM: Fine. Speak beautiful words!

MATAWIL: In the East we pray to the creator gods, to the great jaguars. We pray in Yaxchilán, in Balamkan, in Chinkultik, in Kalakmul, in all the realms beneath us. (*He offers incense.*) May our Lady Xok be well received, because I have spoken of her in the four corners of the sky!

(Muk'ta K'anal and another woman lead in Xok, escorting her up the pyramid, to kneel next to a basket filled with pieces of paper and cloth.)

XOK: We prayed for sixty days to the guardians of the fertile ground. Today it will come to pass. I shall provide food for the gods, to the mother of water, that she bring forth dew so that the corn will grow. Receive the offering that I give unto you, my holy lords! (*When her prayers end, Pakal Balam ascends to give her a cord wrapped around a torch.*)

PAKAL BALAM: Three times we reach you with prayer, my lords! Do not let the fire here go out! Receive the gift that my wife offers you! Creator of Kuk Balam, today I choose my successor! (*Those standing nearby talk among themselves, whispering about what they have just heard.*)

NOBLE 1: What did he say? Could Xok be his successor?

NOBLE 2: It's not her child!

NOBLE 3: And the older brothers?

NOBLE 4: Be quiet, be quiet, it is the king who has spoken!

MATAWIL: (*He addresses everyone.*) Nobles, priests, warriors, everyone who has come here.... He desired this so that we would be united forever. (*He pauses.*) Our holy lady, Xok, is descended from Father Jaguar, creator and engenderer of our dynasty. Today the woman here gives her blood to the gods.

(*Xok takes the cord from her husband and a spine from the basket,
piercing her tongue with it, and pulling the spiny cord through her tongue.
Blood spurts forth, falling into the basket. Then she burns the offering
together with incense and remains gazing upwards.*)

PAKAL BALAM: Now our queen is looking at Yat Balam, founder of our dynasty! Her blood has been received. In exchange for this meal we shall be given water and sustenance! We give three salutes to the sun, to the gods. Xok has atoned for the sins of the mother of Kuk Balam.

MATAWIL: May our father, Pakal Balam, be pleased. Oh Sun, my Lord, you are alive with us! (*The nobles dance.*)

NOBLES: Viva Pakal Balam, priest of the sun!

MATAWIL: Viva Xok and her holy blood, food of the gods!

NOBLES: Viva Xok and her sacred blood!

MATAWIL: Viva the young Kuk Balam, our prince and future king in forty years!

(*The two women help escort Xok off the stage, followed by all the others.*)

SCENE 3

(*Matawil enters, followed by Ch'ok, who begins to change his clothes
behind the pyramid.*)

MATAWIL: That is how they made peace. The people were united until Pakal Balam died. Then war erupted here in our land, up to this day.

CH'OK: Why are they still quarreling? Do they disapprove of the peace that once reigned among them?

MATAWIL: Kuk Balam had many enemies! They wanted to kill him. But he knew how to defend himself.

(As they speak, Ch'ok begins to dress in the armor and a helmet he finds behind the pyramid. Warriors with lances rush out. Ch'ok, transformed into Kuk Balam, ascends the pyramid and addresses them and the public.)

KUK BALAM: You are fierce warriors! Depart! Go and occupy the lands that have been abandoned so that their owners will never return! War! War!

(They dance briefly, contesting each other. Kuk Balam returns, pulling a warrior, Chivan Bak, by the hair and forcing him to kneel in humiliation. Matawil observes them from a distance, then moves catlike among them.)

MATAWIL: Now you will die, Chivan Bak! We shall sacrifice you in the ballpark! *(Taking him by the hair, he throws him to the other warriors.)* Bear him away! May his blood fall on the steps of our temples! *(Shouting, they drag him off. Only Kuk Balam and Matawil remain.)*

KUK BALAM: What do you think of my rule, Matawil? Do you think the gods are content? I have given them quantities of blood!

MATAWIL: Wait for me to tell you the truth.... Too much blood has flowed because of you. Your father's government showed clemency. You may be gaining many enemies.

KUK BALAM: Oh, there is no one as mighty as we are! We are so strong! And also ... I will seek slaves to build more temples. Yaxchilán will become greater, and I shall be the ruler of all!

MATAWIL: I have seen that the world is beginning to fall apart. Everything will change. Perhaps you should make alliances for the good of all.

KUK BALAM: Who is giving up? The gods want there to be war, for blood is their sustenance!

MATAWIL: The first leaders wish to pay us back. If they ally themselves, they may be able to kill us.

KUK BALAM: They can never do so! We, the true men, are invincible!

(The conquered warriors enter, take Kuk Balam by the hair, and pull off his armor and his helmet. They humiliate him and are about to sacrifice him. When one of them raises his knife, all but Ch'ok and Matawil slowly disappear.)

CH'OK: No, do not take my blood! Help me, my Lord!

MATAWIL: Wake up, Ch'ok, wake up! It is only a dream!

CH'OK: Oh, I dreamt it then!

MATAWIL: I wished you to see the consequences of the war that was waged in our land. The gods do not want this killing.

CH'OK: But . . . how could you show me the past? Who, then, are you, Matawil? How could you have the power to show me this?

MATAWIL: It is the power of the spirits of the jaguars, because they want to show you how good it is if our land works in unity.

CH'OK: Oh, it is not easy. How can they unite if they have many different gods, languages, and customs?

MATAWIL: Only our names will change. The words of the Great Creator will not change. You must learn to live together! If you do not believe this, you will have a dark future!

CH'OK: What do you mean? What will happen to our land?

MATAWIL: You will kill each other, and others will die from sickness. You will surely lose your land. You will suffer for five hundred years or longer unless you unite.

CH'OK: Live in peace? How can we live in peace if they kill us and take our land? Must we be cowards?

MATAWIL: No, Ch'ok, we must be truly strong. We must gather together to demand justice! The day will come when everyone will unite or if not, the world will bring down punishment.

CH'OK: There will surely be great punishment! What can we do so that we do not lose?

MATAWIL: Resist, Ch'ok, so that we can unite in strength. See how this one arrow breaks! (*He breaks an arrow.*) But what if you try to break a handful of arrows? (*Ch'ok tries to do so, in vain.*) You see! The jaguar twins long ago conquered death with their ingenuity, their wisdom, not by force!

CH'OK: Now I understand, great father! What can I do so the people here in our land will unite?

MATAWIL: If you think of one year, plant corn! If you think of a hundred years, plant many trees! But if you think of many more years, educate your children well! Afterwards they, on their own, will become smart!

CH'OK: You have spoken to me very wisely, Matawil. May we accept this so we kill each other no longer!

MATAWIL: I leave this in your hands, Ch'ok. You have the spirit of resistance! I am going to other lands to tell them the same. (*He exits, shaking his rattle.*)

CH'OK: Great Jaguar, Sun! When we pass evil years, do not leave our lands in tears! (*He cries, rises up, lifts his face and shakes his bundle of arrows at the public.*) We shall not die!

Let's Go to Paradise!

A TZOTZIL TRAGICOMEDY

(1993)

THE IDEA FOR *Let's Go to Paradise!* (*¡Vámonos al paraíso!*) was born in 1992 as the theatre group was returning by bus from Honduras. As we passed by many coffee fincas in the Soconusco region of southwestern Chiapas, suddenly Maryan pointed to a sign at a finca entrance. "I worked there!" he exclaimed. As he began to recall his suffering while working as a coffee picker, I suggested that that should be the basis for our next play, especially because there were still many old Chamulan men who could provide us with material for dramatic scenes.

This play focuses on how the lowland coffee growers abuse Indian peons who suffer indentured labor, machete blows for "laziness," double hours, and filthy living conditions—and if they fall sick are even buried alive to serve as fertilizer for the young bushes.

Erasto Urbina, a Ladino of San Cristóbal, supporting the reforms of President Cárdenas, worked intrepidly and bravely to reduce the abuses of fellow Ladinos.

The scenes, it is suggested, have changed very little. They depict life in the 1930s, culminating in the establishment of a coffee laborers' union which, alas, was bought out later. Following one performance, an actor addressed the audience: "Wouldn't you like a cup of the best export-quality coffee? Mayan coffee? Really: there are no more cadavers!"

Using a Spanish play on words, the German finca owner is said to be from Animalia, rather than Alemania. The *tapaculo*, "ass-stopper," is an unidentified wormlike creature. An ensign-bearer is a high member of the religious hierarchy of Zinacantán.

Recalling past memories, and parading the outrageous tricks played by Mikulax Bolom on the Ladino foreman, this play was a great success locally.

At one performance in Chiapas both actors and audience proceeded with the show in the pouring rain.

The trick in this play was to teach someone to walk on stilts so that the German finca owner could stride about in his white suit looking down on his Indian workers. Fortunately, Palas 2 was backstage at a performance at Antioch College when he saw a group of university students playing ball on stilts. He could not resist. In a few moments he had mastered the technique and was playing with them. That evening, after Palas's first time on stilts, we went to a Vietnamese restaurant where, without hesitation and for the first time, he successfully wielded chopsticks. This was also the first play where two males put on blonde wigs and gaudy dresses to buffoon the *finquero*'s wife and daughter.

For versions in Tzotzil and Spanish, see Montemayor 1996b.

CAST OF CHARACTERS

NICOLÁS (MIKULAX) BOLOM: wearing a battered, tall-crowned sombrero and a tattered, dirty white muslin shirt and shorts. He wears sandals and carries a straw mat, a net bag, and a water gourd.

MESTIZO BANDIT: wearing a half mask with a thick black moustache. He sports a red shirt, gray pants, and black shoes. He carries a machete.

CAMPESINO 1: wearing a tall-crowned sombrero with a large hole in the top, tattered and dirty white muslin shirt and longish pants, with one leg rolled up. He is barefoot.

CAMPESINO 2: Sebastián (Xap), wearing the same as Nicolás, but carrying nothing

CAMPESINO 3: wearing the same as Campesino 2

ERASTO URBINA: wearing a white shirt open at the collar, gray vest, and pants. His eyeglasses are always pushed low on the end of his nose. When disguised as Pascual (Pax) Bolom, he wears the same as Campesino 2; when a waiter, he wears a white jacket, gray pants, and black shoes.

INSPECTOR: wearing a light brown half mask with a neat moustache, white shirt and tie, a gray suit, and black shoes

DON TACHO: recruiter, a portly man, wearing a half mask with a big red nose and moustache, a gray felt hat, white shirt open at the collar, gray pants, and black shoes

CANTINA OWNER: wearing a full face mask of an old hag with white braids. She wears a white blouse, black skirt, white shoes, and has a black shawl pulled around her face.

WIFE OF CAMPESINO 2: wearing Chamulan clothes—a white blouse and black cotton skirt fastened by a wide red wool sash. She is barefoot.

FOREMAN (CAPORAL): wearing a half mask with long nose and long moustache. He wears a tattered sombrero, a blue and white checked shirt, blue pants, knee-high black boots. He carries a net bag and a water gourd, and has a pistol in his belt and a machete in its leather scabbard.

WIFE OF CAMPESINO 1: wearing the same as the wife of Campesino 2

FLEA (PUPPET)

LOUSE (PUPPET)

MOTHER OF NICOLÁS: Maruch, wearing Chamulan clothes—a brown woolen top with large red pom-poms in the center and a black cotton skirt fastened with a wide red woolen sash. She is barefoot.

WIFE OF NICOLÁS: Mikel, wearing Chamulan clothes, the same as Maruch, but with a blue blouse

SHERIFF: wearing a clean white muslin shirt, shortish pants fastened with a belt, and sandals

WULFRANO, GERMAN COFFEE PLANTATION OWNER: Wearing a full face mask, white and with large blue eyes, a fine sombrero, and a white suit. He is on stilts and carries a walking stick. He speaks with a heavy accent, doubling *R*s and turning *W*s into *V*s.

GERTRUDE, WULFRANO'S WIFE: Wearing a full pink face mask with a large, red nose and blonde hair topped with a wide-brimmed hat with flowers. She is large-bosomed and wears a red, flowered dress, white knee-length socks, and black shoes. Same accent as Wulfrano's.

BRUNILDA, WULFRANO'S DAUGHTER: Wearing a full pink face mask with blonde hair. She wears a yellow, flowered dress and white shoes. Same accent as her parents.

(Setting: A black curtain with two red panels near the green-paneled ends. Mexican flags stand atop each end. In the middle, at the top of the curtain, is a wooden scene of Chamula, thatched roof houses and crosses, which is replaced by a plantation house scene when the action moves from Chamula to the finca.)

Act I

SCENE 1

(A path near Chamula. Nicolás Bolom walks on, dressed in the tattered, dirty clothes worn by the coffee plantation workers returning home. He stops for a moment to take a quid of tobacco and continues on. A mestizo with a machete is waiting for him, hidden behind a bush. When Nicolás gets close, he jumps in front of him.)

BANDIT: Stop, you fucking Indian! Let's see, what you've got there? Looks to me like you're the one's been robbing everyone along here!

NICOLÁS: *(Startled)* No, *patrón*, I haven't done anything. I've just got my bit of *pozol* and these old clothes.

BANDIT: Clothes, what clothes? *(He snatches away Nicolás's shoulder bag and finds just what Nicolás had said was there.)* You aren't coming from the finca? You didn't run away?

NICOLÁS: Well, well, yes, *patrón*. But I finished my job. I really didn't run away, boss.

BANDIT: It looks to me like you just skipped off and now you must be picking pockets. Let's see, drop your pants!

NICOLÁS: My pants? ¡Ay, Dios! So what do you want to do to me, *patrón?* No, for God's sake, not my pants! Oh, God, help me!

BANDIT: Take them off, you impudent Indian, if you don't want me to chop you to pieces with my machete.

NICOLÁS: No, *patrón,* I'll take 'em off right now. (*He pretends to take off his pants while he prays secretly.*) Oh, Diosito, Diosito, don't let him take my pants away! Don't you see I have all my money in my moneybag? (*He starts running off, but the Bandit catches up with him and whacks him on the head with the flat of his machete. He falls on his knees and begins to pray.*) What more do you want, *Diosito?* If you won't help me now, why do I keep on praying to you? (*The Bandit gives him another machete blow that Nicolás fends off with one hand while he makes the sign of the cross with his other.*) Well, since you paid no attention to me, I'm going to pray to the devil. (*He prays as a witch, steps back to receive a dragon-like bird mask on his head. With one jerk he pulls the machete away from the Bandit and pushes him to the ground. He has become super strong and fiercely threatens the Bandit, who is paralyzed by fear as he sees the great bird menacing him.*)

BANDIT: (*Dragging himself along the ground*) Oh shit, but ... but ... but this dummy's got a devil in him. Who have I gotten mixed up with?

NICOLÁS: (*Growing bold*) Sonofabitch, you rat, you dirty pig, get out of here if you don't want me to chop you to pieces! (*Laughing diabolically*) Ha, ha, ha ha, ha! (*The Bandit gets up and runs off panic-stricken while Nicolás laughs and the dragon-bird disappears.*) I won, I won! And now I know my soul is really strong! Now, you *cabrones,* we'll see who dares try to rob me now! (*He leaves.*)

SCENE 2

(*The town hall. Two Chamulan assistants bring in a table and some chairs. A bunch of ragged campesinos comes in, followed by Erasto Urbina and a federal inspector who sit down at the table. One of the campesinos introduces them.*)

CAMPESINO 1: *Compañeros,* they've summoned us here for you to present your case, to tell them your complaints about how the coffee finca owners mistreat and steal from the coffee workers. The delegate, don Erasto Urbina, is here with an inspector—government officials. They've come to see if it is true that they're mistreating and taking the money away from the coffee

Campesino 1 complaining before the Inspector, 1993. Photo courtesy Sna Jtz'ibajom

finca workers, because when they arrive to do the inspection, the owners make it look just fine.

CAMPESINO 2: (*Interrupting*) So why wouldn't it be true? We're fucked over all the time! We only go to work in the fincas 'cause we have to. From the very time they sign us up, they begin stealing from us!

CAMPESINO 1: And then if somebody wants to escape, they send the dogs after him! They chase him on horseback, they even shoot at him!

CAMPESINO 3: The minute you arrive, you're in debt. You get there worn out after walking several days and the very next day you have to work. If somebody complains, they slap him up and send him to work far away. And if he gets mad or tries to run away, he gets it even worse. They bind his hands and hang him from a branch.

CAMPESINO 2: And if somebody is too sick to get up early, well, he goes to the job without any breakfast.

CAMPESINO 1: As if breakfast were worth it! Cold tortillas with salt and chile, and watery coffee! How can that give you any strength to work?

CAMPESINO 3: You're just pinched with hunger. So they give you credit in the store to buy cookies or sardines, but it turns out worse.

CAMPESINO 2: They charge you double or triple if the storekeeper doesn't like you. Since we don't know how to read or write, well, they jot down for you whatever they want. Then on payday you get nothing. And of course it's robbery when they measure up the coffee.

CAMPESINO 3: That's for sure. If you don't fill one box brimful, they lower it by an eighth. Every box! They're so unfair!

CAMPESINO 1: And if you complain, they come down on you and give you the worst jobs. It's hopeless.

CAMPESINO 2: Even the food's a bad deal. Just beans and, when they give it, rotten meat. Since they don't give us rice, they must think we like maggots better! (*Everyone laughs.*) Sometimes they don't even give us tortillas, and when we do get one . . . ! Sometimes all our *compañeros* come to blows trying to snatch up a piece of tortilla!

ERASTO: It's just as I was telling you, inspector. Well, friends . . . and the *patrón*, doesn't he know about it? Doesn't he do anything to make it better? (*Now Nicolás Bolom enters, having arrived late at the meeting. He sits down next to them, chewing his tobacco, with his machete still in his hand.*)

CAMPESINO 1: How could it be, *patrón?* The rich are rich for good reason! He just goes by, watching from a distance how they rob and mistreat us! I think that's what they pay the foremen to do, so they'll be fucking us up, and now they can mark up a bunch of *muertitos*.

INSPECTOR: Look, gentlemen, these are very serious accusations you are making. Slavery was abolished in this country a long time ago. When the plantation owners came to ask permission to establish their fincas, it was granted on condition that they could only hire workers, and that they would give them a decent salary, good food, good conditions, a clean place to sleep, clean bathrooms, a clinic . . .

CAMPESINO 1: (*Interrupting sarcastically*) Well, mister, they couldn't care less! With the stink, you can hardly sleep! Our *compañeros* piss and shit right next to the bunkhouse because they're scared of the ass-stopper, and you go to bed on the chance that you will be eaten by scorpions or jaguars . . . and then we all get covered with fleas and lice, sick, ruined, bald, with bumps all over our heads that you never can get rid of!

CAMPESINO 2: If only they'd pay you for what you get. They just make one deduction after another from the company store or with fines, so when the contract is up . . . lots of us don't even have the money to go home. What can we do? The rich live off the sweat of the farmhands and that's how they get fat!

ERASTO: Well, that's why we're here, *compañeros*. The inspector here has come to swear that the petitions that we have sent to the federal government are true so this injustice will end. But we must provide proof, and we must do it quickly because the inspector is only going to be here a few days. We need a volunteer to go with me who will show me all the ill-treatment that occurs on the fincas. Who agrees to go with me? (*Everyone looks at everyone else with fear in their eyes until one of them speaks.*)

CAMPESINO 1: Well, no, *patrón,* the truth is I don't think anybody wants to go with you. They can knock you off easy. Soon as they figure out who's putting the blame on them, they'll rape your wife, beat up your family, clean you out, burn down your home, and shoot you up. Since you gentlemen won't be staying here, the minute you leave, they'll start taking revenge. You can't do anything against those *cabrones.* Let's see, *compañeros,* is there anybody who's willing to be don Erasto's guide? (*They all shake their heads, scared, except for Nicolás Bolom, who very happily brandishes his machete.*)

NICOLÁS: Well, they can be real *cabrones,* but one of them won't be wanting to go around fucking up people anymore! You see, one of those bastards wanted to steal from me the little bit of pay I saved up at the finca. He wanted me to take off my pants.... I don't know where I got the guts to do it, but I grabbed away his machete! The *cabrón* was so scared, he shit in his pants! (*Everyone bursts out laughing.*) Oh, he just left behind his stink. How that poor devil stank! Ha, ha, ha! He was scared to death! And then I found his stinking pants he'd thrown away.

(*Everybody laughs and makes remarks. Then they fall silent when they see that Erasto Urbina is looking deliberately and approvingly at Nicolás Bolom.*)

ERASTO: Well, boys, it seems that now we've seen who is the only one who can go with me. *¿Muchacho, cómo es su gracia?*

NICOLÁS: Me, *patrón? No tengo gracia, patrón.* I guess I'm just a *desgraciado.* (*Everyone laughs.*)

ERASTO: No, *muchacho,* so what's your name?

NICOLÁS: Ah, well, my name is Mikulax Bolom, please you. But I've just come back from the finca, *patrón!* I'm not the one for you to take back to that Hell, *patrón.*

ERASTO: Well, there's no other choice. No one else here is as spunky as you, who has his pants fastened so tight.

NICOLÁS: Ah, it's because I took the belt off those shitty pants. I just washed it in the stream. But if you want me to, I'll take it off.

ERASTO: No, *hombre!* What I'm telling you is that you're the only brave one. Because this little job is going to be very dangerous. I want you to take me to Paradise Plantation.

NICOLÁS: You mean to say "Hell," *patrón!* That finca is as bad as bad can be! Beginning with the master who doesn't talk like a human being. He talks like an animal. But it seems to me he's a devil, 'cause he's bright red, even his hair is red, since he comes from Animalia.

ERASTO: It's the finca of that German I'm talking about, Nicolás. That's exactly where we're going to begin to bring in the law. I need to have you take me in disguise, as a worker. I want to see with my own eyes what's going on there.

NICOLÁS: With your own eyes, *patrón?* You mean with your own ass! You'll see how they fuck you over! You won't feel the hardship, but you'll feel the hardness. Don't you see? If they figure out you're spying on them, they'll chop us up into little pieces and toss us to the jaguars.

ERASTO: We have to take the chance. Don't you see that if we can't prove our accusations, the federal government won't be able to do anything to stop the plantation owners' violations of the law? There's no choice. Let's go! It's for the good of your people.

INSPECTOR: Besides, you'll be paid very well for your services. The Revolution knows how to reward the sacrifices of its sons.

NICOLÁS: Oh, sonofa ... Of the revolution, did you say? No, *patrón,* I'm sure I'm not the one you're looking for. My mother's name is Pascuala Bolom, and the poor thing is very poor. She doesn't have any salary, and my wife doesn't either. They must be waiting for me to arrive from the finca with my pay.

INSPECTOR: No, you didn't understand me. Now, don Erasto, be so kind as to explain to them what the Revolution means.

ERASTO: (*Evasive*) That won't be necessary, inspector. I'll do it because this is something that must be done so that the people don't have to keep suffering so much. This afternoon we have to sign up, because tomorrow the staff goes to the finca. We've got to go today. What do you say? Do you all agree that Nicolás Bolom is the one who should be my guide?

CAMPESINOS: (*Raising their hands, joyfully*) Yes! Mikulax! He's the most strong hearted! It's got to be Bolom!

NICOLÁS: (*Resisting*) But ... no, *compañeros!* I've got a lot of work in the *milpa!* My woman's waiting for me!

CAMPESINO 1: Well, don Erasto will keep you warm there! (*Everyone laughs.*) Besides we'll give you a present of *trago,* a drink. Or what? Would you rather pay a fine and sleep in the town jail?

NICOLÁS: No, well, then.... ¡*Ay, Dios!* I knew I'd have to pay for going about praying to the devil! It's God's will! The only thing I ask is that you take my pay to my wife and that you give me plenty of tobacco for the trip. (*Everyone leaves, cheering Nicolás.*)

SCENE 3

(A bar, the Recruiter's office. Don Tacho, the Recruiter, and his old wife bring in a table and chair. Don Tacho takes coins from a purse and stacks them on the table. His wife brings in another chair, a Victrola (boom box), and several bottles of cane liquor. Then two drunks come in, one reeling more than the other. They greet don Tacho. The one who is drunker is holding a bottle. The two fall to the ground. Nicolás and Erasto come in, Erasto disguised as a lowly campesino.)

NICOLÁS: Are you there, don Tachito?

TACHO: Nicolás, how are you doing? Weren't you on the finca?

NICOLÁS: Well, you see, *patrón,* when I was coming back from the finca they stole my pay, and so I've come here again to see if you don't have some kind of job for me and my cousin, because I thought that if we go together, it won't be so easy for them to get our pay.

TACHO: Oh, that's pretty smart of you! *(Suspicious)* Let me see if you're not on my list. You wouldn't have run away from the finca, would you?

NICOLÁS: Oh, don Tachito, the dogs would have eaten me up by now. What's the use of trying to come home if I'm just going to be food for the buzzards? Ha, ha ha! *(Everyone, even Erasto, laughs cynically.)*

TACHO: *(A bit irritable)* Ha, ha, ha! Oh, Nicolás, you're such a joker! Don't you see, there are always some *cabrones* who run away from the finca with debts, and so those debts have got to be collected.

NICOLÁS: *(Pretending to be naive)* You think they can collect from the buzzards, don Tachito? Those loafers sure don't know how to work! *(Everyone laughs again.)*

TACHO: *(With a forced laugh)* Nicolás, I don't know if you're stupid or what. *(Changing the tone of his voice)* Well then, Nicolás, do you want to work again in Paradise, you and your cousin?

NICOLÁS: Well, it seems the pay is better there, don Tachito. I don't know what you have to say, if you'll do us the favor.

TACHO: Okay, but as you know, there's a ten percent charge on the advance. See! You told your cousin, didn't you?

NICOLÁS: Yes, *patrón.* We know about that. Look, we've brought you a little present. *(He pulls a bottle of cane liquor out of his shoulder bag.)* Please sign us up.

TACHO: Well then, that's what I like. Now, as for you, cousin, what did you say your name is?

ERASTO: Pascual Bolom, *patrón.*

TACHO: Pascual! We'll see if you're as smart as your cousin! As for you, Nicolás, what is your last name?

NICOLÁS: Nicolás Bolom, and my wife's name is Micaela Bolom.

TACHO: No, I don't need your wife's name! Here's your advance, minus the ten percent commission. But you know, Nicolás, if they ask who gave you the job, don't tell anybody. I'm just giving it to you because I like you. You hear? Now that they're sending around inspectors, those guys mess everything up.

NICOLÁS: Did you say "inspicters," *patrón?* I don't know what those guys are. (*To Erasto*) You don't know what inspicters are, do you?

TACHO: Well then, with you guys the crew's filled. Tomorrow you'll leave at dawn with the *caporal.* Let's see, you, *vieja,* put on some music to cheer this place up! Nicolás, let's see, tell your cousin to serve a drink to everybody.

ERASTO: Yes, boss!

(*The old woman puts a record on and Erasto begins to serve them, one by one. Seeing him, one of the drunks opens his eyes wide and says in a loud voice:*)

CAMPESINO 2: Don Erasto! What are you doing here?

ERASTO: (*Greatly alarmed, stuffing the shot glass in the drunk's mouth*) Ah, what do you mean? God knows who you think I am. My name is Pascual Bolom!

TACHO: Let's see, *muchacho,* come here! Serve one up for my friend Nicolás. Are you new to this? Don't you know that first you serve the bigwigs?

ERASTO: Excuse me, sir, do you want another little bit?

TACHO: Fine! But first serve yourselves and then we'll have another round, before you have your haircuts. You sure need one now, Nicolás! Your hair must be full of lice!

NICOLÁS: Well, it grew, boss, 'cause I was coming home.

TACHO: (*Pretending to be drunk*) Well, this bottle that I gave you is finished. Let's see, who's going to give the next one? Ah, well, it's your turn, Pascual, because you just joined us.

ERASTO: That's fine, *patrón.* (*He takes out some money.*) Please, *patroncita,* serve us some more liquor.

CANTINA OWNER: Okay, it's fifty cents a bottle.

ERASTO: Okay, here's the pay.

CANTINA OWNER: You dumb Indian! You just gave me a dime. Give me the whole amount! (*The Cantina Owner gives him the bottle of cane liquor and carefully counts the money he has given her. After they toast each other, don Tacho gives Nicolás an order.*)

TACHO: Now as for you, Nicolás, before you guys do anything else, you're going to have a little job. Since you know how it is, you're going to cut Pascual's *cabello*.

NICOLÁS: *¿El caballo?*

TACHO: *El cabello*, you fool, his hair. Ask your *patrona* for the scissors.

NICOLÁS: Lend me your scissors, please, *patroncita*.

CANTINA OWNER: Okay, but take good care of them, you hear?

NICOLÁS: Alright, cousin, sit down on that chair.

ERASTO: Just don't cut my ears! (*Nicolás uses the large scissors, pretending to cut his hair down to the scalp, and he pulls a stocking over his head to simulate baldness. Erasto is bothered by it and feels the top of his head.*) Oh, you left me completely bald, cousin!

NICOLÁS: That's the way the *patrón* wants it.

TACHO: Okay, now you, Pascual. It's your turn to cut your cousin's hair.

ERASTO: That's fine, don Tachito. Let's see, cousin, now you sit down. (*He pretends to cut his hair and pulls on the stocking.*)

TACHO: Good. Now pick up that drunk and cut his hair, too. (*They lift him up and he resists.*)

CAMPESINO 2: What're you trying to do to me, *cabrones*? Let me go! (*They make him sit down and begin to cut his hair.*) Who's this?

NICOLÁS: It's the scissors!

CAMPESINO 2: Let me go, you, Scissors! (*When they finish cutting his hair, pulling on the stocking, he collapses on the ground again.*)

TACHO: Now grab the other one! (*They try to do it, but he's too heavy and he fights back too hard.*)

CAMPESINO 1: No, no, what are you doing to me? Don Tachito, don Tachito!

NICOLÁS: *Patrón*, he doesn't want to. This drunk doesn't want to!

TACHO: Okay, well, it's no use, just cut his hair there where he is! (*They cut his hair and put the stocking on him.*)

NICOLÁS: That's it, don Tachito. Now it's your turn to get a haircut.

TACHO: No, man, what do you mean? Don't you know I'm your *patrón*? (*They all continue drinking, except that Tacho, Nicolás, and Erasto secretly pour their drinks on the ground. Now when they have all fallen into a drunken sleep, Tacho and his wife get up and begin to search their pockets. Tacho whispers to his wife.*) Don't take too much from him. Leave him a little, because he wasn't offering drinks. That one, yes, get plenty from him. Look for it in his money belt, the amount for the two bottles because they seem very smart. Hurry up! (*While they're emptying the pockets, Nicolás and Pascual, who seem to be asleep, open their eyes now and again. When the old woman is searching in Nicolás's pockets, he pretends to talk in his sleep. Erasto pretends to be completely asleep.*)

Didn't I tell you? Don't wake them up! (*Tacho and his wife leave. In a few minutes they all wake up. One of them touches the top of his head.*)

CAMPESINO 1: What! The rats have eaten our hair and left us all bald! (*The other campesino touches his head, too, and seeing that his pocket is sticking out, looks for his money.*)

CAMPESINO 2: The *cabrones*, they robbed me! I had fifty pesos here, and they just left me thirty-five! (*The others begin to count their money, and there's a big hubbub as they all accuse each other. Erasto and Nicolás don't accuse anyone, so they're left looking at the others as if they were guilty.*) It was you, *cabrones*! Return our money or we'll beat you up! (*Tacho comes in, pretending to be alarmed, and puts himself between Nicolás and Erasto and the others.*)

TACHO: What's going on here? Leave my friends alone, you bastards! Don't you know how to behave yourselves when you're with those who give you your jobs! What the fuck are you doing?

NICOLÁS: It's that some … devils came in the night … and they stole our money, *patrón*.

TACHO: Bastards! Here nobody steals anything from anybody! If you didn't steal from each other, then you spent the money on liquor! What, don't you remember? The whole night you were asking for one drink after another, till you emptied two jugs! Besides being a bunch of drunks, you're a bunch of dumb Indians!

CAMPESINO 2: (*Hung over and arrogant*) No, *patrón*, we're not such fools. It's that your friends came here to steal from us. They'll give me back my money!

TACHO: Uppity Indian! Don't you know you're talking to your *patrón?* Either you shut up or I'll have you bound up and taken away! (*The Foreman comes in, with a rope at the ready.*)

CAMPESINO 2: (*Still filled with pride*) Well, never mind who it was, *patrón*. It must have been these ones. Give me back my money, you devil!

TACHO: Okay, *caporal!* Tie these guys up who're trying to cause trouble! And if they act up, then beat them up. All we want is for these uppity Indians to try to mess around with us! Tie them up! (*While the Foreman tries to tie one up, the campesino's wife comes in.*)

CAMPESINO 2'S WIFE: *Por el amor de Dios*, Xap, leave me some money before you go, at least so your kids can eat!

CAMPESINO 2: And you, why are you spying on me? (*He strikes her in the face and she dodges. The Foreman grabs him by the arm, but before they tie him up, Sebastián takes some coins from his pocket and throws them at his wife.*) There are your pennies, but get out of here! (*The Foreman finishes tying him up and then his* compañero, *but not Nicolás or Erasto, and they all leave.*)

Act II

SCENE 1

(Bunkhouse on the plantation. The workers arrive at the bunkhouse. Exhausted, they fall to the ground. They rest a moment. Right afterwards a cow horn sounds the reveille. Nobody wakes up. The Foreman comes in, slapping the ground with his machete.)

FOREMAN: Get up, *cabrones!* You didn't come here to be lying around. Come on, get up! Up, you bastards! 'Cause you got up late you aren't going to get any breakfast! Line up!

(Everyone gets up angrily without saying anything. They line up, scratching themselves, and complaining about the fleas and mosquitoes. One of them is sick, wearing an old woolen tunic, and shaking terribly. He falls to the ground, close to death.)

NICOLÁS: (*Alarmed*) He's dying, *patroncito!* Bring him some medicine! He's dying from the cramps!

FOREMAN: (*Cruel and contemptuous*) He's dying because he's such a fool. He didn't want to eat because the food made him sick to his stomach. Never mind. He couldn't take it. Alright, *cabrones*, carry him off!

ERASTO: But he's dying!

FOREMAN: Get on with it! Pick him up and carry him to the woods! Let's see, Nicolás, you know what's up. Take him to where we're going to plant the new coffee groves. Bring some boards!

NICOLÁS: Okay, boss!

ERASTO: But what? You can't expect us to bury him alive?

FOREMAN: (*Laughing meanly*) Don't be a fool, man! Ha, ha, ha! You must be a dumb Indian! Dump him there till he dies and then just push him into the hole. Then plant a coffee tree on top. At least he'll be of use as fertilizer, to pay off the advance.

(They carry off the dying man. The Foreman leaves on the other side. Then they come back, push him under the curtain, shovel dirt and plant a coffee tree on top, placing a small, green-painted wooden tree next to the curtain. Erasto stands looking at him incredulously.)

ERASTO: But … You mean he meant what he said? They plant coffee on top of the bodies?

NICOLÁS: They say it's so they don't waste the space. The cemetery is the coffee groves. Where you see that the plants are bigger and greener, it's almost sure there's a *muertito* down below. Don't you want a *cafecito?* Ha, ha, ha! It's good for holding wakes!

ERASTO: You think that's funny? *Dios,* it's worse than I thought!

NICOLÁS: You haven't seen anything yet, *patroncito.* Let's get going or the foreman will be roughing us up. (*They leave in a hurry. From the other side the Foreman appears, leading a crew in which there is a woman. Erasto and Nicolás join them again.*)

FOREMAN: Hurry up, *cabrones!* Those in the first group go to the section near the meadow, those in the second to the upper section of the woods. The new guys go to the section in the ravine.

NICOLÁS: *Por el amor de Dios, patroncito,* I want to ask you a favor, now we're alone. (*He goes up to the Foreman and speaks to him on the sly, giving him a bottle and some coins.*) I'm going to ask you a little favor, that you let my cousin Pascual work with me, that you don't send him to the ravine.

FOREMAN: That's fine, that's the way I like it. Who's your cousin?

NICOLÁS: That's him over there, *patroncito,* Pascual Bolom.

FOREMAN: Okay. Let's see, you, Pascual Bolom, come over to my crew. And you, with your wife, come here too.

CAMPESINO 2: And me, too?

FOREMAN: No, you go to the ravine!

CAMPESINO 2: Just me, all by myself?

FOREMAN: Why not? Aren't you man enough?

CAMPESINO 2: No ... I mean, yes!

FOREMAN: Let's go then! Hurry up!

(*He leaves with his group, followed by the woman. They appear again from the other side as if they had walked a long way.*)

NICOLÁS: (*Talking to Erasto*) Now you see. The guys who don't give him presents get sent to the ravine, where the jaguars are!

ERASTO: *Cabrón!* I'm learning my lesson! Thanks, Nicolás! (*They leave.*)

SCENE 2

(*The coffee grove. They arrive at the rows where they are going to work, where there are a bunch of coffee trees. The Foreman assigns them their rows.*)

FOREMAN: Well, we've arrived! You, since you've come with your wife will work here in the flat part. You stay at that tree and have your wife go over to the other one. (*He softens his voice as he takes the woman by the arm.*) Come over here, *muchacha*. You guys who look strong are going to work in those two rows from here up to the top of the hill!

ERASTO: But that's too much, *patrón!*

FOREMAN: That's why finca is the name of this place!

> *(They remain harvesting the coffee while the Foreman sits down. The sound of many mosquitoes, cicadas, other insects and birds can be heard. The woman looks as if she is climbing up the tree to reach the coffee berries and breaks a branch. Her husband stares at her and pretends to hit her. Nicolás and Erasto watch the scene, and Nicolás hurries over to the damaged tree, where the husband is bawling out his wife.)*

CAMPESINO 1: How could you be so stupid? You'll see what I'll do to you if the *caporal* realizes you broke that branch. He'll rough us up and send us to the ravine. Don't be a fool! Don't you see that the foreman is always right behind us?

CAMPESINO 1'S WIFE: *(Frightened and almost in tears)* Ay, Dios, it's that I was about to fall.

NICOLÁS: Come on over to my row, *paisano.* Quick, before he notices!

CAMPESINO 1: They'll send you to the ravine!

NICOLÁS: Don't you worry, *paisano.* He likes me all right. *(They change places, and Erasto comes up to Nicolás.)* Why did you come over here, *patrón?* Get back in your row or he'll blame you too.

ERASTO: Who cares. And don't call me *patrón!* I got you into this, *muchacho,* and I'm not going to let them punish you on my account. *(The Foreman gets up and comes over to them, filled with anger.)*

FOREMAN: What the fuck are you guys doing? Having a cozy chat? You're here to work, *cabrones!* Why did you change rows? *(Nicolás leaves his tree, and the Foreman spots the broken branch.)* Oh, you fools, you've broken the branch! So you still want to make a fool of me! It must have been Pascual, isn't that right? *¡Indio pendejo!*

ERASTO: It's 'cause I was about to fall, *patroncito.*

FOREMAN: *(Imitating Erasto, mocking him.)* 'Cause I was about to fall, 'cause I was about to fall, *patroncito!* Dumb Indian! And now you wanted to trick me so I wouldn't be so hard on Nicolás, right? Alright, *cabrones,* turn around! *(The two turn around and he gives each one three slaps with the flat of his machete.)* Now get to work, *cabrones!* And if you break another branch, I'll give it to you double! *(They return to their trees to work. The Foreman goes back and sits down.)*

NICOLÁS: *(Talking in a low voice to Erasto, with a grimace)* So you see, *patrón,* what happens when you put the blame on yourself! He would have just hit me.

At least he didn't send us down to the jaguar ravine. That *cabrón, hijo de* ...! But you'll see how I pay him back! (*He takes out his tobacco and begins to chew it. Erasto watches him.*)

ERASTO: What is it you're chewing so much, Nicolás? Is it tobacco?

NICOLÁS: It's the chief, *patrón*. It's called "chief" when it's prepared right. It's the very thing.

ERASTO: The very thing? But what is it? Isn't it just tobacco? What else does it have?

NICOLÁS: The way I make it, it has thirteen secrets, *patrón*. This is the very best. It's very strong. Now you'll see how we take revenge on this *cabrón*.

ERASTO: What are you going to do, Nicolás? Witchcraft?

NICOLÁS: (*Smiling*) No, *patroncito*, I'm just going to ask the chief to help me get rid of those slaps. Ha, ha, ha! Just wait a little bit. I'm going to see that it gets mad at this fucking *caporal*.

(*He prays briefly in Tzotzil over his tobacco gourd, and then he begins to whistle contentedly. Hearing him whistle, the Foreman comes over without saying a word. He finds them harvesting the coffee as fast as they can. He stands there, looking with distrust at Nicolás, who keeps whistling, stopping only to take out more tobacco to chew.*)

FOREMAN: So what's with you, did you like the paddling? How come you're so happy?

NICOLÁS: I'm fine now, *patroncito*. With this holy tobacco, now I don't feel anything. It's even given me more strength to do the job.

FOREMAN: ... Fucking mess. Indian hogwash! I don't see how you can walk around chewing that *chingadera*. It smells like horse shit!

NICOLÁS: Don't you say that to the chief, *patroncito*. It could get mad at you!

FOREMAN: How could I believe in that Indian claptrap? Well, it's late now, let's go. Did you finish your job?

NICOLÁS: I've filled two boxes, *patrón*.

FOREMAN: Let's see 'em. (*He looks over the basket.*) But how can you be such a fool? Fucking Indians that never learn! I told you they don't accept berries that aren't ripe! Just the red ones, you fool! Okay, turn your back, so you won't forget!

NICOLÁS: Oh again, *patroncito*?

FOREMAN: So? Didn't you say your fucking horse shit's a good cure for that? Now, *cabrón!* (*He hits him.*) So you'll remember it's just the red berries. Okay, repeat after me, "The red ones, just the red ones!"

NICOLÁS: The red ones, the red ones!

(He repeats it while he is being hit. He takes his tobacco gourd out and begins to chew some tobacco. Then the Foreman checks Erasto's basket. While he is doing that, Nicolás rubs tobacco on the Foreman's back.)

FOREMAN: Well, at least this guy isn't so stupid. *(Nicolás pats the Foreman on the back.)* What the hell are you doing?

NICOLÁS: Nothing, *patroncito. (He keeps rubbing tobacco on his back, giving him friendly pats, and smiling.)* Don't be mad at me, *patrón*. I swear I won't do it again. I thought they were ripe enough.

FOREMAN: Well, don't be so stupid. You've come back worse than when you left, *carajo!* Okay, let's go! *(The other members of the crew come together and file off on one side, and then come back on the other. Suddenly the Foreman stops and puts his hands on his belly.)* Oh, God, what's happening to me? Suddenly it seems like … Oh, I've got the shits. *Carajo. (He pulls down his pants and farts loudly. The others laugh behind his back. Campesino 1 covers his face with his sombrero and peers at him through the hole in the crown. Suddenly a* tapaculo, *an "ass-stopper," jumps near him, and the Foreman shoots his gun at it, trying desperately to keep it away. The others laugh, holding their mouths. The Foreman complains.)* Oh god, I knew there'd be those bugs here, those *tapaculos.* What's happening to me, *carajo?* I've got terrible diarrhea! Pff! Pff! *Carajos!* It won't stop! Who the fuck knows what I've got! *(Nicolás comes near him.)*

NICOLÁS: I told you, *patroncito!* The holy tobacco got mad at you for saying bad things about it!

FOREMAN: *Ay, Dios,* and what can I do now? Do you know how to cure this? Ow, how my stomach hurts!

NICOLÁS: Well, there's only one way. You'll have to pray to the holy chief.

FOREMAN: Give it to me then!

NICOLÁS: First you pray, and then you have to eat it! So you won't die.

FOREMAN: How do you pray?

NICOLÁS: In Tzotzil. But if you make a mistake, I'm going to bat you on the head because that's what this cure demands.

FOREMAN: I don't care! *(He squats down.)*

NICOLÁS: On your knees! *(Pushing him down) Meltzanbon li jch'ute bankilal!* Fix my stomach, chief!

FOREMAN: *¡Metz'tao ta jch'ut bankilal!* Bewitch my stomach, chief!

NICOLÁS: *(Giving the Foreman a bat on the head)* Not like that!

FOREMAN: Ow! What was it you said? I didn't hear you.

NICOLÁS: *Makbon li jtzo'e bankilal!* Plug up my shit, chief!

FOREMAN: *Matz'o li tzo'e bankilal!* Chew shit, chief! *(Nicolás angrily bats him again.)* So what was it you said?

NICOLÁS: *Lekubtaso li jch'ute bankilal!* Fix up my stomach, chief!

FOREMAN: *Jlekom ta jch'ut bankilal!* My girlfriend's in my stomach, chief!

NICOLÁS: (*He gives the Foreman another bat on the head.*) Well, I think it heard you now. Take it, eat it! (*He gives him a handful of tobacco.*)

FOREMAN: Okay. (*The Foreman begins to choke on the tobacco.*) Oh, but it's so strong!

NICOLÁS: Well, yes, it's the real chief. Now you've tasted what you called horse shit.

FOREMAN: I never thought it was a kind of medicine. (*He feels his stomach and lifts his head, showing that now he's cured.*)

NICOLÁS: But we're dying of hunger! Can't we go and eat now?

FOREMAN: Let's go then. I felt so awful, *carajo!* And now I don't feel anything! (*They all carry their loads of coffee and leave, following the Foreman.*) Alright then, hurry up!

CAMPESINO 1: There he's fucking us up again! (*The Foreman appears on one side, while don Wulfrano on stilts, wearing a white suit, appears on the other.*)

FOREMAN: *Buenas tardes,* don Wulfrano!

WULFRANO: *¡Buenas tardes, caporal!* How is the work going?

FOREMAN: Just fine, don Wulfrano. These workers look like loafers, but they're hard workers! (*Turning to the workers behind him*) Say hello to the *patrón!* His name is don Wulfrano.

CAMPESINOS: *¡Buenas tardes!* (*Don Wulfrano doesn't even look at them.*)

NICOLÁS: That's the famous *patrón* of Paraíso!

CAMPESINO 1: Is he an animal?

FOREMAN: Haven't you ever seen an *alemán?*

CAMPESINO 1: He sure looks like an animal!

SCENE 3

(*The bunkhouse. Everyone comes in, bringing a straw mat that is tossed on the floor. They are all sweaty and very dirty. They scratch themselves and swat at gnats. You can hear thunder and rainfall.*)

ERASTO: (*Annoyed*) We're going to sleep again on the ground? Dios, there are so many mosquitoes! And gnats! And fleas! Ay, Dios, this sure is Hell!

NICOLÁS: I told you, *patroncito!* You've forgotten the scorpions, the black widow spider, the ticks, and wasps, and ants, the lice, and snakes.

ERASTO: *Por Dios,* we've got to get rid of these hellish places! How can people stand these conditions? We're treated worse than animals! And you, why did you come?

CAMPESINO 2: Because my uncle told me that it was very pleasant, that they would give you good meals with lots of meat.

ERASTO: And what did you do when you found this Hell?

CAMPESINO 2: Mm, *patrón*, I was very sad. I cried day and night! I didn't want to eat a bite! I wanted to go home, but I didn't even know which direction, and I hadn't a cent for the trip. Every day I asked my uncle if we were going to leave now.

ERASTO: And in those days did you get a good meal?

CAMPESINO 2: No, *patroncito*, hardly! You see, they gave us beans, but beans with *sapote*.

ERASTO: Beans with *zapote?* Beans with *chicozapote?* (*Everyone laughs.*)

CAMPESINO 2: Ha, ha, ha! Beans with *chicos sapotes*, big, little toads that jumped into the pots because they left them on the ground! They taste so delicious! And yes, they gave us coffee, but it was *café gracioso*.

ERASTO: *Café gracioso*, what kind of coffee was that?

CAMPESINO 2: What do you think, *patrón?* Coffee full of grease because they never washed the pots! Ha, ha, ha! From the same pots they gave us *besote!* (*Everyone laughs again.*)

ERASTO: But why are you laughing? What's a *besote?*

CAMPESINO 2: Oh, *patrón!* Well, it's a *huesote pelón*, bare bones, 'cause they don't leave a piece of meat on it! Just bones in the soup, and when it's special, it has a little bit of rotten meat with maggots!

ERASTO: *Carajo!* How horrible! That poor fellow died for good reason. So much sickness, so much poverty, *por Dios!* And they dare name it Paradise! But what made you come here?

CAMPESINO 1: Well, I came because I wanted to get married, and since my father was going to have the position of ensign-bearer in two years, well, I had to save up money to help him, *patrón*.

ERASTO: But can't you make enough with what you grow on your land?

CAMPESINO 1: How could that be enough, *patrón*, with all the land they've taken from us? And then the little that's left has to be divided among the children. There's hardly enough for the corn. That's why Xap had to come as a child. And it does us no good.

ERASTO: Well, if we can get out of this ... things will change, *muchachos*. But I'm falling asleep. Sleep well, boys!

EVERYONE: *Hasta mañana*, Pax! (*They try to sleep, but they continue scratching themselves. You can hear the rain still falling. Then there is the strange hoot of a bird. Nicolás sits up shouting:*)

NICOLÁS: A jaguar bird! Who knows what bad thing it's predicting!

ERASTO: What could it predict? It's time to sleep, *cabrón!* All of you go back to sleep, 'cause tomorrow we're in for another hell of a time!

NICOLÁS: I can't sleep now … who knows what that bird wants to tell us … or could it really have been a jaguar?

ERASTO: Even if it were the devil himself, I'm going to sleep!

(He buries his head in his arms and begins to snore. Nicolás and the others see huge tarantulas, mosquitoes, and other bugs in the dark. They don't know if it's for real or if they're dreaming. Suddenly the Flea and Louse speak to Erasto.)

FLEA, LOUSE: (*Diabolically*) Ha, ha, ha! Ha, ha, ha!

FLEA: So you think you can keep us from getting our meal?

LOUSE: You were born to be the slaves of the *patrón!*

FLEA: Blood for us, and compost for the plantations!

LOUSE: We're the *patrón*'s partners!

FLEA: And we're always going to suck your blood!

LOUSE: We're going to suck out your brains!

(There's a loud whirring of bugs as the men sit up and try to chase them off, but they are stung over and over. Erasto slaps desperately at the Flea and Louse.)

ERASTO: No! We'll fight against you! We won't let you torment us anymore! *¡Basta! Basta!* We'll get rid of you!

He flails around till he falls on his mat. The others are asleep again, but Nicolás wakes up and shakes Erasto, who still is jabbering incoherently.)

NICOLÁS: Wake up, Pascual! Wake up! Don't you see? It gave you nightmares. That's just what the jaguar bird called up!

ERASTO: *¡Carajo!* What a horrible dream! Well, it must be three o'clock already! Let's go to the patio before the caporal comes and leaves us without any breakfast again! (*They all leave hurriedly.*)

SCENE 4

(A hamlet in Chamula. Nicolás's wife, Mikel, comes in with a big bundle of laundry on her back. She begins to wash it. From the other side, Nicolás's mother, Maruch, enters, carrying firewood.)

MARUCH: *¡Ay, Dios, hija!* Mikulax has been such a long time there on the *pinka!* Do you think something happened to him? It was three months ago he left!

MIKEL: *¡No, por Dios, Mamá!* He must have loads of work. Wait and see. If he doesn't come soon, he'll certainly send money so you won't have to work so hard!

MARUCH: May God hear you, Mikel! And you, too, who has to wash and weave other people's clothes, waiting and waiting for him!

MIKEL: Well, what else can we do? At least we won't run out of corn for the kids!

MARUCH: *¡Ay, hija!* Could he have found another woman?

MIKEL: Oh, no, *señora*, if I was single, well, who knows, but your son isn't like that. He wouldn't let you starve. He told me that for sure he'd bring you wool for your shawl!

MARUCH: Yes! He told me he was going so you could weave the clothes for the baby.

MIKEL: So you see! (*Worried*) Could he have been held up on the way back? Could his *compañeros* have gotten him drunk?

MARUCH: Well, who knows, Micaela? (*She cries.*) Oh God, what could have happened to my Nicolás?

MIKEL: (*Affectionately*) Don't cry anymore, *Madre!* (*Smiling, but exhausted*) So we'll do our best. God willing, he'll come back soon. (*One of the sheriffs who attended the meeting appears.*)

SHERIFF: Are you there, Señora Maruch?

MARUCH: (*Wiping away her tears*) I'm here, *señor*. What do you want?

SHERIFF: Well, the mayor sent me to bring you a message from Mikulax, that the authorities came from Mexico City and took him back to the *pinka*.

MARUCH: Oh god! So what did my son do? You think my son is a robber? What're they going to do to him?

SHERIFF: Well, no, it's not that, *señora*. They just sent him with an official to the plantation because they want to see all the bad things they do to people on the *pinkas*.

MARUCH: *¡Ay, Dios!* So they sent him ... like a cop!

SHERIFF: Well, I don't know. That's what happened.

MARUCH: *Ay, Dios,* they'll kill him!

SHERIFF: That'd be a hard thing to do, *señora*. Your Mikulax is a very smart guy.

MARUCH: And ... Why didn't he come home first? At least I could have given him some clean clothes!

SHERIFF: It's that ... he was with the officials, and they didn't want to wait even a minute. So he sends you here a little bit that he was able to earn on the *pinka*.

MARUCH: *¡Gracias a Dios!* At least his kids will be able to eat! You see, his wife is waiting, and she has to do other people's laundry!

SHERIFF: Well, the truth is, *señora,* you better pray a little. *¡Ay Dios, kajval!* I hope Mikulax will be okay.

MIKEL: What do you mean? Are they going to want to kill him?

SHERIFF: Who knows, *señora!* They left the day before yesterday. An inspector is going to arrive there the day after tomorrow.

MIKEL: *¡Ay, Dios, Mamá! Muchas gracias, señor!* Look, *Mamá,* let's go right away to get some candles to pray to San Juan!

MARUCH: Let's go, daughter! So they won't do anything to my son Mikulax! *(They leave.)*

SCENE 5

(A coffee grove. Erasto, Nicolás, Campesino 1, and his wife appear from one side while the Foreman appears from the other. You can hear the rainfall.)

FOREMAN: Well, let's go! Hurry up! We'll have to get wet! We'll see if that cures you! *(He gives Erasto and Nicolás a few light machete slaps for no good reason. Nicolás begins to chew his tobacco while they walk.)* Well, here we are! These are your rows. You, Nicolás, you stay by the first row, and you, Pascual, at the second. And you, at the last. Get to work! Come on, it seems like you're really lazy! Come on, *cabrones,* if you don't want me to rough you up! *(They set to work while the Foreman sits down.)*

NICOLÁS: *(To Erasto)* You brought a needle, didn't you?

ERASTO: Yes, I put it here in my shoulder bag. You need it?

NICOLÁS: Yes. You'll see how I'll get even with that *caporal.* Ha, ha, ha! Wait till you see what a face he puts on, but don't you laugh!

ERASTO: Well, what are you going to do to him?

NICOLÁS: Ha, ha, ha! You'll see right away! *(He takes another little bit of tobacco and begins to whistle. The Foreman comes over, snooping, and checks his basket. Nicolás stops picking and goes over to the Foreman, keeping the needle hidden.)*

FOREMAN: So, you're real happy, aren't you? If you want, I'll slap you again so you'll whistle louder!

NICOLÁS: It's because I love to work in the rain, *patrón.* You feel cooler. *(The Foreman is engrossed in checking the coffee, and Nicolás takes the advantage of pricking his arm with the needle.)*

FOREMAN: Ow, what stung me?

NICOLÁS: A black widow! Look at it, *patrón!* There it goes!

FOREMAN: *¡Ay, Dios!* A black widow! I'm going to die! Did you see it?

NICOLÁS: I saw it very well when it bit you, *patroncito.* Suck at it, suck it quickly before the poison gets you!

FOREMAN: (*Sucking his arm*) *Ay, Dios,* the poison's not coming out anymore! What's going to happen to me, *Dios mio?* You don't know a cure, do you?

NICOLÁS: Well, yes, I know of one, *patrón* … but you won't like it. But there's nothing else if you don't want to swell up and die sweating blood.

FOREMAN: No, *por Dios!* I've seen people die from a black widow. Tell me the cure right away, *cabrón!*

NICOLÁS: So that's how it is! Well, you'll have to talk to me with respect if you want me to be your *curandero.* You have to obey me in everything I tell you.

FOREMAN: That's all right, that's all right. But hurry up, so the poison won't get me.

NICOLÁS: Well the only cure is that you have to eat … your own shit.

FOREMAN: Whaat? My own shiit? Are you crazy?

NICOLÁS: Well, it's the only cure. There's nothing else, *patrón.* And you have to do it fast, before the poison gets to your brain.

FOREMAN: *¡Ay, Dios!* I don't want to! And that really cures it?

NICOLÁS: Yes, *caporal,* and do it fast!

FOREMAN: And how am I to do it?

NICOLÁS: How what? How are you going to do it? Take your gourd bowl and use that! (*The Foreman takes out his bowl and squats down, trying hard. Nicolás quickly grabs up his shoulder bag that had been tossed near the Foreman.*) But don't get my bag dirty!

FOREMAN: Is that enough?

NICOLÁS: No, you need a little more!

FOREMAN: Like that?

NICOLÁS: That's it! But put a little water in and mix it up well, like *pozol!* (*The Foreman, feeling sick to his stomach, mixes it using just one finger.*) No, mix it up well, with all your fingers! (*He does so.*) Now drink it quickly! (*Filled with disgust, he drinks it down. Nicolás watches him very seriously, but Erasto, somewhat hidden, has a hard time not bursting out in laughter.*) Alright! That's it! But I warn you, don't tell anybody.

FOREMAN: What else do I have to do?

NICOLÁS: Well, all you have to do now is go take a bath, *caporal!* And wash your hands and your mouth out very well, so nobody will know you ate shit.

FOREMAN: Okay, it seems as if your cure worked because the poison hasn't done anything to me! It's true, I hardly feel anything! The bite doesn't even hurt! I'm going to bathe in the river. (*They all leave. Then the Foreman returns, calling for Nicolás.*) Nicolás, Nicolás! (*Nicolás enters.*) You know, Nicolás, your cures really work very well! You're a good *curandero!* The poison didn't hurt me at all! You must know of a cure for something else I've got.

NICOLÁS: What other kind of cure, *caporal?* What's wrong with you?

FOREMAN: Well, it's not really a sickness … I don't know what to call it … I don't know what's happened to me. I used to get it up a lot, but now I can't do anything.

NICOLÁS: Oh, well, there's a cure for that! The shadow of a snail is good for that.

FOREMAN: The shadow of a snail?

NICOLÁS: Yes, *caporal,* the shadow of a snail, the *yat nab,* the screwworm. Have you seen it? When you're drinking your *pozol,* you have to pass the shadow of the screwworm over it. But just a little bit, because it's really strong! And don't you tell anybody!

FOREMAN: Okay! Well, I'm going to look for a screwworm! If it works I'll give you guys twice as big a meal.

NICOLÁS: *Beno, caporal.* But see here, if you want me to cure you, you'll have to give us … to me and my cousin … a better job, *caporal.*

FOREMAN: Alright then. The *patrón* needs two servants to help when there are visitors. Take a bath, change your clothes, and then go to don Wulfrano's house. You see?

NICOLÁS: Okay, *caporal.* Well, then, I'm going to cure you. You've got to find a screwworm. Right now get your pozol ready, and when the sun is good and strong, you let the shadow fall on a little bit of it.

FOREMAN: Good, good. (*He looks all around him.*) Here's a screwworm!

NICOLÁS: No, you need a bigger one!

FOREMAN: Here's one! But it's better if you show me how. *Ay, Dios,* I'm going to be fixed up! Let's see how I should do it.

NICOLÁS: Just like this, *caporal,* you let the shadow fall on just a bit of it … because you have to do it by yourself … but just a little!

FOREMAN: And if I let it fall on the whole bowl?

NICOLÁS: Oh, you'd go crazy!

FOREMAN: Oh, I don't want to go crazy!

NICOLÁS: Alright then. I'll leave you here because you have to do it by yourself. I'm going to take a bath before I go see the *patrón!*

FOREMAN: Okay, I'll catch up with you later. We'll see, we'll see, this should give good results. Is it true that I'll be able to again, like when I was a young man? (*Nicolás leaves, and the Foreman passes the screwworm over a corner of his bowl.*) What happened? I don't feel anything! Do you think I should pass the shadow over a bit more of it? Well, maybe a bit more. (*He tries again.*) It's hardly had any effect. Once and for all I'm going to pass it over the whole bowl, and we'll see what happens! (*He puts it over the whole bowl of pozol, waits a minute, and then is transformed.*) *Caray,* it's working! *¡Dios mio!* But what's happening to me? *Ay, Dios,* it seems like I'm turning into a rooster! *¡Kikiriki!*

SCENE 6

(Don Wulfrano enters from one side very obsequiously, accompanied by the Inspector. Then he goes to the back.)

WULFRANO: *¡Caporal! ¡Caporal!* (*Returning to the Inspector*) As I vas telling you, my dear friend, vee export the best coffee in the vorld from this finca. The extraordinary quality of this coffee is only possible because our vorkers have the best possible conditions and services.

INSPECTOR: I hope it's no bother, Señor Wulfrano, but I must verify that. Our government requires that Mexican workers enjoy fair working conditions, as stipulated by law.

WULFRANO: Señor Inspector, of course you can corroborate that. Let me call my caporal to take you around. (*He goes to the back.*) Vile you vait, I vould like you to have a *cafecito.* You vil see vat the coffee from Paraíso is like! Gertrude! *¡Por favor!* Gertrude! Please serve Señor Inspector his *cafecito.*

(Gertrude appears, a male actor disguised as a woman. Erasto comes in behind her, in uniform, carrying a silver tray from which he serves coffee to the Inspector.)

GERTRUDE: Good afternoon, Señor Inspector. Allow me to ask my daughter to bring some cookies. Brunilda, Brunilda! Ver could that girl have gone? You vil see vat delicious coffee our finca produces.

INSPECTOR: That is what I have been told, *señora.* It is a shame that so few people can taste it because it is all sent abroad. Isn't that true?

GERTRUDE: Vell, it is the most important market. (*Brunilda comes in.*) But I vish to introduce you to my daughter, Brunilda. Señor Inspector has come to look over the finca, *hijita.*

BRUNILDA: (*Nicolás in disguise*) Very pleased, Señor Inspector. Velcom to Paradise. I hope you find everything in order.

INSPECTOR: I hope so too, *señorita.* The truth is, I must proceed immediately to check your installations and the conditions of the workers.

WULFRANO: Vel, sir, until my *caporal* comes, I vil show you our plant. Please come this vay. As you see, all our vorkers are in uniform. These are the bunkhouses. See how clean they are! And here are the latrines. And over there the cookhouses. As you see, everything is in perfect order.

Don Wulfrano, his wife and daughter, and the Inspector, 1996.
Photo courtesy Robert M. Laughlin

(They all follow Wulfrano. The Foreman is seen running by. From the other side appear Gertrude and Erasto. The Foreman comes in chasing Brunilda, who flees, terrified.)

BRUNILDA: Oh, let me go, you pig! Vat do you think you're doing? Let me go, I tell you! Let me go! *¡Papá!*

FOREMAN: Don't run away from me, angel! *(Brunilda escapes, and as he tries to catch her, he knocks down her mother.)* I don't know what's happened to me, *patrón!* Come here, cutie! *(He embraces her.)* *¡Kikiriki!*

WULFRANO: But vat are you doing? Let my daughter go! *(He hits the Foreman.)* Let her go, I tell you! Let her go! *(Gertrude gets up and disappears. Wulfrano turns to Erasto.)* Hey, you, do something!

(Erasto drops the curtain showing the bodies under the coffee trees. Brunilda takes off her mask and dress, and Nicolás is revealed, smiling. The Foreman, startled, steps back.)

FOREMAN: Nicolás Bolom, it's you!

NICOLÁS: What's the matter, *caporal?* Did you overdo the dose? And do you all know who the waiter is? *(Erasto removes his stocking cap and puts on his glasses.)* Don Erasto Urbina! Ha, ha, ha!

ERASTO: *¡Bueno, señores!* The curtain's fallen! As you can see, inspector, this *caporal* is a devil, and for many years he has been an accomplice in the crimes, in the mistreatment of the coffee workers!

INSPECTOR: Don Erasto! *¡Caray!* What a surprise! So, you were able to take note of all the offenses, the crimes that are being committed in this place.

ERASTO: So you can see the way it really is! It's a real Hell, Inspector! Beneath the coffee trees you can find the bodies of many people, whom they buried in the cheapest way! And look at the scars on my own body from the machete blows that the *caporal* gave for no good cause. (*He shows them.*) And next I'll show you the terrible health conditions under which these people have had to work. And you saw what the *caporal* tries to do to the women!

INSPECTOR: I congratulate you, don Erasto, and you, too, Nicolás! As for you, *señores,* you will be placed under arrest. A jail sentence would be a light punishment for the likes of you! What you deserve is Hell!

NICOLÁS: This Heaven would be better, *patrón!* Make them work as farmhands and have them beaten the way they beat us! Oh, and give the *caporal* his favorite dish! Beans with *sapote,* and his *pozol* good and sour just the way he likes it! Ha, ha, ha! (*The people come in boisterously. The crowd pushes don Wulfrano and the Foreman around.*)

CAMPESINO 1: Take this pig to the woods!

CAMPESINO 1'S WIFE: The stinker!

CAMPESINO 2: Make 'em eat in the shithouse!

EVERYONE: (*In a chorus*) Down with the exploiters! We're going to have a union! *¡Qué viva* Erasto Urbina! *¡Viva el sindicato!*

(*Everyone leaves, cheering, very happy, pushing don Wulfrano and the Foreman ahead of them. Erasto returns.*)

ERASTO: This all happened in the time of Erasto Urbina, back in the thirties. But little by little, people forgot what he had done to help the Indians. The union leaders were bought off by the owners of the coffee plantations, and they put on a false front again so that we Indians would be screwed up as badly or worse than before, just like what's happening to the poor Guatemalans who work there almost for free. This is what is happening to the Mayas today on the lands of our ancestors, who once were the most civilized people of this continent.

From All for All

A TZOTZIL-TZELTAL TRAGICOMEDY

(1994)

FOR THE FIRST TIME, not a single word had been written upon Ralph's arrival. Andrés Fábregas Puig, director of the Instituto Chiapaneco de Cultura, suggested we touch on the present situation: the overrunning of four towns, including San Cristóbal de las Casas, on New Year's Day 1994 by the EZLN, the Zapatista National Liberation Army. Protesting the disastrous effect of the North American Free Trade Agreement (NAFTA) on rural Mexico, the Zapatistas demanded that the Mayan Indians be treated as first-class citizens of Mexico.

Ralph waited impatiently while the members debated for hours. Our president, Tziak, came from Tenejapa, where the Zapatista movement was gaining popularity, and he was all for celebrating the uprising, but the Zinacantecs demurred: "Who was Subcomandante Marcos? What did he want? Why is he causing all this trouble?" Following Zinacantán's centuries of opposition to Indian rebellion, they decided that the subject of the play should be ecology—a more prudent endeavor. Tziak protested, "But Marcos said that if it weren't for the jungle, they'd all be dead, so he's an ecologist!"

Shortly after the uprising, Tziak, as president of Sna Jtz'ibajom, attended a meeting attended by 285 members of Indian and campesino organizations. Their leaders, one after the other, listed their problems and presented their demands to the new interim governor. He recorded the meeting on video, which he showed to the group. "That's the truth!" they exclaimed. "That's straight talk! All right, let's put that together with ecology!" And so the playwrights from Tenejapa, Zinacantán, and Chamula debated from morning to afternoon over each possible scene, each line, while Ralph and I tossed in occasional suggestions.

But it was not easy. The phone rang. Word had spread about Tziak's video. The governor wanted a copy. Ten minutes later it was Bishop Samuel Ruiz's office, requesting a copy for the bishop and another for Marcos. Ding-a-ling, a reporter in Italy wanted to hear the latest. There was a conflict of priorities. Ralph, with the pressure of seeing a whole production staged before he left, was faced with actors who, instead of learning their lines, were poring over the latest news in *Tiempo*. "But there's a war on!"

Afterward they confessed that it was their fault—they hadn't scared each other into having a script ready for Ralph's arrival. At least they had decided (at my suggestion) that the play would have a cast of only six, which would be easier for "poor Ralph" to finish in time and more attractive for gaining invitations to foreign tours.

Xun reported:

> Foreigners asked us, "How come in this work a woman was given an important role?" since they said that we here in Chiapas don't pay much respect for women's words—just what men say. We told them the truth, that yes, men are always a bit that way, that men's commands go a bit too far, but that now it's changed. There's been a big change in how we feel today. It didn't used to be like that! Today we pay attention to them, but not too much so! No, we can't say that it's just women's talk we're involved in. But we always ask their opinion.

Not many days passed before it was decided to choose Marcos's philosophy, *de todos para todos* (from all for all), as the play's title. But our president, despite his political concern, was glad to include ecology. "The animals are suffering. If we warm ourselves with the trees, the plants will die. That's where the animals grow up. That's where they eat. If the forest disappears, where will the animals go? The poor things will die."

The play slowly took shape:

1. Campesinos work happily in their milpa.
2. Cattleman claims the land is his and orders them off.
3. Campesino complains to government agent, who, after receiving a bribe from the cattleman, sends them to the jungle.
4. Campesinos depart unhappily but get good harvest there.
5. Animals complain about loss of jungle to the Earth Lord, who agrees to send drought and sickness.
6. Six toads give sickness to sleeping campesinos. No doctor ever appears, but a Chamulan shaman, who has dreamed of animals' complaints, cures all, urging them to organize.

7. Shamed by the campesina's resolve and inspired by a young man who has returned from studies in the city, they prepare to resist.
8. Cattleman and government agent flee to cave where they are attacked by a jaguar (added later at my suggestion).
9. Juan López appears. Battle between vigilantes and campesinos. Earth Lord urges peace; campesinos demand peace with justice.

Rather than include Subcomandante Marcos as a character in the play, Tziak chose in his place Juan López, an Indian hero of the Tzeltal Rebellion in 1712 who was hanged by the Spaniards. He was reputed to have reappeared during the Zapatista Rebellion. Lest it cause the group problems, when the campesinos in the play rebel, they do not put on the ski masks or red neckerchiefs of the Zapatistas.

The day before Ralph's departure we set off for Chamula for our dress rehearsal, to be performed in the main square, facing the church. Beneath a wall festooned with a large political slogan, *Solidaridad Unidos Para El Progreso* (Solidarity United for Progress), we fitted our metal frame that would hold aloft a brightly paneled curtain topped by a Mexican flag at each end. In the center would be attached the emblem of Chiapas, its regnant lions transformed into spotted Mayan jaguars. Chamulan women and children pressed close while we assembled the masks and the few props: a mat and blanket, a couple of tables and chairs, a typewriter, a conch, a staff, a backpack, helmets, and wooden machetes and guns.

As the big-bellied, booted, red-faced cattleman strode about bossily, the Indian audience, taken by surprise, laughed hard, but when they saw how the government "land reform" agent treated the poor campesino, some of the people got mad and crowded onto the stage, shouting, "Look at that! That's what the government agent's like. It's terrible how he treats people. It's his fault. That's how the problem began. Look at what he does to us! Look at the bastard! We ought to grab him!"

At the end of the scene, the actor portraying the government agent, now filled with fear, ducked behind the curtain and turned himself into an armadillo right fast before he was pulled off the stage. But seeing the campesina, the audience exclaimed, laughing, "That's Ramona!" And when the young man, Juan López, appeared from the city, "That's Mr. Marcos, just his name is different!" As one of the actors commented, "They figured it out right off!"

While the actors agreed that some Chamulans did not understand the play because they had never seen theatre before and because it was given in Spanish, they added, "The Chamulans were glad to learn why the problem arose, why our companions in Chiapas grabbed their guns. They learned the truth about everyone who acted, what each one's part was." When the show was over, we were all invited into the Casa de Cultura, where we were offered cokes and cane liquor. "Please come again and give it another time," they said. "It looks so good to us!" (Laughlin 1995:528–530).

But it was not so positive on the home front. Tumin, a twenty-seven-year-old Chamulan, tanked up on cane liquor after Ralph's going-away party. Apparently wishing he had been given the role of the armadillo (everyone's favorite), at three in the morning he put our blanket over his back and crawled around on the rug, producing the most extraordinary hoots and squeaks, before throwing up and departing, leaving behind his hat and coat. The armadillo's beautiful sixteen-year-old wife came by to take the rug off to launder, making Mimi madder than ever as she knew it was the armadillo's job. My promise to Mimi to never have an actors' party in the house again was not considered sufficient recompense. She decided she had had enough, that she was leaving and never coming back again, and she packed her suitcase. Fortunately, she unpacked it the next day.

Traveling through Chiapas dramatizes very clearly how mestizo rule has destroyed the relationship between man and nature—and man and the gods.

> Performing this play in Chiapas, and witnessing the audience's often passionate response, even the cautious Zinacantecs were soon espousing the demands of the Zapatistas. In the scene where the Indian woman turns to the men and cries out, "*¿A poco ustedes no son hombres?*" ("You mean you aren't men?") and pledges to unite the women in resistance to the government, the entire audience, both sexes, invariably cheers. Within the cooperative and without, attitudes are changing. (Laughlin 1999, 497)

Returning from their trip to Malpaso, they gave me a report. The importance of our theatre was brought home when from Malpaso the troupe traveled by motorboat across the giant man-made lake and walked or rode horseback for hours through the jungle to reach three colonies of Tzotzil speakers where the Theatre had been warmly received each year before, where "they are living in the woods like animals, where visitors never come, where they never see the bad things the bosses do to us." In these communities, the actors worried whether the people would object to their involving the Earth Lord in political matters, but no, "we weren't stoned, we weren't clubbed, we weren't scolded." In fact, they were fascinated with the white-faced Earth Lord, all dressed in green. "'How did you know what he looks like?' they asked" (Laughlin 1995, 532). It was a good question, but one that the actors couldn't answer as they had decided on their own, after some debate, that the Earth Lord would look good in green.

Here, especially, the Theatre's message was applauded. "*¡Viva Zapatista!* It seems it isn't the Zapatistas' fault." Here is where thousands of acres of fertile land were flooded to provide one-third of Mexico's electric power, pushing the settlers into the forest reserve, El Ocote. It was here in one of the colonies that, after the evening performance, no one could get to sleep. So, with the teacher, they held a meeting:

> Much of our land here is covered with water. There is a lot of land off which we ought to be able to eat. Our land was taken. The bosses in Mexico City, they have electricity. Sitting on their chairs, they have a good time. They have TVs and radios. We have no light. We have to buy a little kerosene, a little pine wood to see the world at night. Year after year we asked for light, but we never got it. We were told, "If you want it, it costs so much. You will have to set up light posts. You'll have to carry them. Come, carry the wires! You'll feed those who set it up."

And then they told how the soldiers arrived:

> Here the soldiers are supposed to help. The government says they're wonderful. "You've never had them before. It's the soldiers who will keep watch. What the Zapatistas are doing is bad." As for us, we've seen what the soldiers dressed in blue are like. They bother people. They want free food. If you don't give them a lot, they'll grab your chickens.

With the teacher, they discussed the need to protect the little bit of jungle left on each of their eight-hectare lots, for at least they weren't like the Zapatistas with no land at all! Unless they cared for the trees, the animals would flee and they would have nothing but desert.

As the troupe left the next morning, the people pleaded with them: "They pay attention to those with money. It's true they pay no attention to us. Please, when you talk to the government, get them to pay attention to us!" And the actors, who had just heard that all the generous state promises for financial support for our cooperative had been canceled, replied, "But how can we? We're all ignored by them!"

Contemplating the importance of their mission, the actors confessed:

At the beginning we did not know why the war started. We were left behind. So coming here, I've seen, I've heard what our work is about. It's true, the name of our work, that we want everything there is. That it be shared, that we share it. That's why our play is called *From All for All*. There shouldn't be anyone with too much, nor anyone with too little. It should be the same. If only the government remembered. It just doesn't happen. (Laughlin 1995, 531–532)

There was further confirmation across the border. At the University of Florida's Wisdom of the Maya conference, directed by Allan Burns in 1994, they heard for the first time the expression "pan-Mayan." An African student at the university, amazed at their boldness, drew his hand across his throat, saying that in his country that would be their fate. Another student, son of a Chiapas cattleman, questioned the actors in detail about land invasions, wondering why they didn't look for jobs on the big coffee fincas. They replied, "If the Indians only have a piece of land the size of a house, if the boundary markers keep being pushed in, little by little their land's gone for sure! Where can they go? We want to be rich. We don't want to die." To their surprise, the young man responded, "What you say is right. God willing you shall win!"

They were asked, "And you, what are you committed to, politics or ecology?" "We just want our companions to realize how they all are suffering," the actors answered. "Who is the war leader? Is Marcos a mestizo or an Indian?" "He's a mestizo, but he cares about helping the Indians," they replied. "Is he a foreigner?" "No, he's a Mexican." The people said that they only looked at newspapers. "Sometimes it's true, sometimes it isn't. We don't know who to believe. Since you come from there we wouldn't believe what anyone else told us" (Laughlin 1995, 531).

After presenting our play to Guatemalan Mayas in Indiantown, we went to Lake Worth where "the Guatemalan leader and *marimbero*, Gerónimo Camposeco, who, with Allan Burns, had seen us perform two years before at the Kinal Winik conference at Cleveland State University, wept as he thanked us" (ibid.).

For versions in Tzotzil and Spanish, see Montemayor 1996b and Montemayor and Frischmann 2007.

In homage to the Mayan and Zoque martyrs fallen in the wars of Chiapas

CAST OF CHARACTERS

PETUL: campesino, wearing shabby farmer's clothing

MARUCH: Petul's wife, wearing a flowered blouse, a shawl, and a beribboned skirt, as of Ocosingo

DON POMPOSO: rich landholder, a portly man, wearing a half mask with a big red nose and a moustache. He sports a cowboy hat, boots, and a pistol.

GOVERNMENT LAND REFORM AGENT: wearing an ugly half mask and informal office clothing

SOCORRO: secretary, a man in drag, wearing a full pink face mask with blonde hair, flowered dress, and high heels

CAMPESINO 1: wearing shabby farmer's clothing

CAMPESINO 2: wearing shabby farmer's clothing

JAGUAR: wearing a full jaguar face mask, yellow shirt, dark pants, tail

HOWLER MONKEY: wearing a full monkey face mask, brown clothing, tail

COYOTE: wearing a full coyote face mask, gray clothing, bushy tail

ARMADILLO: wearing a full armadillo face mask, dark clothing, a bread basket with chair attached, long *petate* tail

EARTH LORD: wearing a white-complexioned full face mask and a green velvet, hooded robe

TOADS (4): wearing full toad face masks and dark clothing

SHAMAN: wearing tattered Chamulan headcloth and woolen tunic, carrying a staff

VIGILANTES (2): wearing military helmets, dark glasses, dark clothing, carrying guns

JUAN LÓPEZ: student, wearing informal city clothes and a backpack

(Setting: A black curtain with two red panels near the green-paneled ends. Mexican flags stand at each end on the top. In the middle, at the top of the curtain, hangs the shield of Chiapas, but with the Spanish lions converted into jaguars.)

Act I

SCENE 1

(A cornfield near Ocosingo. A Tzeltal couple are working happily, he harvesting corn, and she picking greens.)

PETUL: Look, wife, what a good harvest we have! Who knows if we can finish it in a week!

MARUCH: Yes, we'll have to hurry.

PETUL: I want to go to town tomorrow to buy a pig's head.

MARUCH: Yes, and bring me a little fatback, too!

PETUL: Yes, I'll get it for you and whatever else you want! Now I feel so happy. Thanks to our Lord we have a good crop. It was worth all that work!

MARUCH: Thanks to our Lord and thanks to your father who left us this land.

PETUL: Yes, thanks to them!

(A rich landowner, don Pomposo, comes in, covetously looking over their cultivated fields.)

POMPOSO: *(Pretending friendliness)* ¡Buenos días, muchachos!

PETUL: ¡Buenos días, don Pumposio!

POMPOSO: This land certainly gave you a good crop of corn!

PETUL: *(Distrustful, but proud)* Well yes, ¡Siñor don Pumposio! Thanks to our Lord this little bit of land turned out to be really good!

POMPOSO: *(Striding about, checking the soil)* But next year this land won't produce anything!

PETUL: No *siñor*, that's not true. This land has always been good.

POMPOSO: And ... How much land do you have?

PETUL: Well, not much, *patrón*. There's about an acre.

POMPOSO: Let's see, let's see. Show me your boundary markers.

PETUL: And I'm wondering what for, *patrón?*

POMPOSO: I just want to see if the stones are in the right place. It would be a shame if you've planted in vain. Come on, show them to me!

PETUL: *(Worried, he shows him the markers.)* Here are the markers, *patrón*, where they've always been.

POMPOSO: *(Becoming very gruff)* No, *muchacho*, ... you're wrong. This land has belonged to my family since the time of the Crown. I have documents that prove it. I haven't asked for this because up to now I haven't needed it. But the time has come for you to return it to me, because I want to put my cattle here.

PETUL: (*Shocked*) But … but … this little bit of land belonged to my grandparents, don Pumposio, and you know that very well. Before that it belonged to my grandparents' grandparents.

POMPOSO: (*Angrily*) I'm telling you that the king of Spain gave us this land! I have the papers that can prove it! But as for you … Let's see, where are your papers?

PETUL: (*Humiliated, sad*) Papers? No, well, we don't harvest papers here, just corn and beans, don Pumposio. For the other thing we use corncobs.

POMPOSO: You insolent Indian! I'm telling you about the property papers, because you all invaded this land without my family's permission, and now you're going to have to move off! So you can see how kind I am, I'll give you a week's time to harvest what you can.

PETUL: (*Getting mad*) But why, don Pumposio? This is our land! We aren't going to leave it!

POMPOSO: That's all I want to hear. I told you, if you don't leave in a week, I'll get you out by force!

PETUL: Out of here, you bastard!

POMPOSO: (*Pomposo leaves angrily, speaking on the side to the public.*) These insolent Indians will see how I'll fuck them!

PETUL: (*Still furious, as he shouts at Pomposo*) Don't you screw me up! (*Maruch comes up to him, looking at him with great distress.*) That bastard don Pumposio wants to ruin our land! We were so happy. I'd like to kill him.

MARUCH: Calm down. It's better if we complain to the authorities. (*Getting angry*) Just because he's not an Indian he wants to steal our property, but we can't give up!

PETUL: Let's go then! We'll see if they pay any attention to us! (*They leave quickly.*)

SCENE 2

(*Agrarian Reform office. The government agent is sitting with his feet on his desk, looking at a girlie magazine, laughing to himself. His secretary, Socorro, is putting on lipstick.*)

AGENT: How pretty this one is, but I like this other one better. (*He turns the page and whistles.*) Get her!

PETUL: Are you here, *siñorita?* (*The Agent hurriedly puts his feet down and changes his reading material.*)

SOCORRO: Can't you see I'm here? Dumb Indian! What do you want?

PETUL: I want to talk to the official.

Department of Agrarian Reform secretary, 1996. Photo courtesy Robert M. Laughlin

SOCORRO: Sir, someone wants to talk to you.

AGENT: Tell him to wait a bit, until I finish reading this report.

SOCORRO: (*To Petul, as she begins to type away furiously*) Come in! Wait a minute, you hear? Sit down on the floor over there!

PETUL: (*Humbly*) Excuse me, *siñor*, I'll wait for you here. (*He squats while the agent continues reading as if he weren't there.*) But why am I sitting on the ground? (*He gets up and peers at what Socorro is doing, is startled as she shifts the carriage. Then he walks over to look at the Agent, who angrily tosses down his papers.*)

AGENT: Well, let's see, tell me what you want. (*Socorro sets her typewriter on end and carefully files her nails.*)

PETUL: It's just, *patrón,* that don Pumposio arrived when my wife and I were harvesting our corn, and now he says he wants to have our land to put his cattle on. He asked me if I had the papers for it. I've come to see how you can solve the problem.

AGENT: You mean you don't have your papers?!

PETUL: Well, what's this about, *siñor?* I don't know what the papers are.

AGENT: Well, it's the title for your property. If you don't have it, you're in a lot of trouble.

PETUL: And what do you have to do to get a title?

AGENT: Ah, well that's going to cost you a small sum because we have to send a topographer to measure your property.

PETUL: A topocrapper, *siñor?*

AGENT: Topographer, dummy! The guy who measures the boundaries!

PETUL: All right, sir, and how much will that cost?

AGENT: Ah, we'll see about that. (*Pomposo comes in and interrupts the conversation. He gives Petul a dirty look, who steps back and also looks at him angrily.*)

POMPOSO: *Compadre,* good morning.

AGENT: Don Pomposo! What a surprise to see you here, *compadre!*

POMPOSO: Good morning, *compadre!* I just came to see if you could settle a matter for me that I've had on my mind.

AGENT: Why of course, *compadre!* But sit down! All right, Socorrito, bring my *compadre* a chair! What would you like to drink, *compadre?* (*Socorro provides the chair.*)

POMPOSO: Well, I'd accept something strong, because there's a matter that's made me really mad.

> (*Pomposo pinches Socorro, who darts out, swinging her pocketbook at him. Pomposo turns around and gives another dirty look at Petul, at which point the agent remembers that Petul is still there and shifts to an impatient tone.*)

AGENT: Well, well, as for you, I told you that we'll consider your case later. Come back in two weeks, you hear!

PETUL: All right, *patrón*. I'll see you later. (*He leaves angrily, nearly knocking over Socorro as she brings in the drinks.*) The bastards! They didn't help me just because I haven't any money.

AGENT: (*Addressing Pomposo*) Dumb Indian! When will they ever change? You're right, *compadre,* they keep on living as they were three hundred or four hundred years ago. I don't know, the Church, the educational systems, they've all done experiments with them. They've created programs to get them out of their margination, but they are absolutely tied to their customs. Indians continue to live off firewood, charcoal, drinking *pozol,* eating corn, not speaking Spanish. They keep on dressing the same way, barefoot ... I don't understand just what it is they want. When you talk to one of them, well, I feel they are happy in their same old environment.

POMPOSO: Look, I've heard that, but now I can't remember where. But changing subjects, *compadre,* that Indian who just left is stealing property that belongs to my family. Out of charity we let them live there for a long time, but now I need that land for my cattle.

AGENT: God, that'll be difficult! They've occupied that property for many years. It belongs to them legally, even though they haven't the title for it.

POMPOSO: Well, I don't know how we can do it, but you've got to give me a hand. (*He pulls out his wallet and fingers a wad of bills.*) How much do you need?

AGENT: (*Greedily groping for an answer*) Ah, *compadre,* you make it very difficult for me. It's a serious business. Look, let me try to convince them to accept land in the jungle, okay?

POMPOSO: Well, but it has to be *pronto* because I've a little business up my sleeve and I need that land now. Take this for your expenses and get the paperwork going for me.

AGENT: (*Counting the money with great pleasure*) That's fine, then. You can leave it up to me. Don't worry. I'll send them to a piece of property in the jungle.

POMPOSO: (*Laughing vulgarly*) That's fine, then. Come on, let's go get a drink to celebrate!

AGENT: All right, many thanks, *compadre!* (*They put their arms over each other's shoulders and leave happily.*)

SCENE 3

(*A field. Maruch appears crying, calling to Petul, who enters from the other side with Campesinos 1 and 2.*)

MARUCH: Oh god! Petul, Petul, hurry up!

PETUL: What happened?

MARUCH: Those devils came by and drove in their cattle. They burned down our hut. What can we do now?

PETUL: What do you mean? It's not possible. Who were they?

MARUCH: They were don Pumposio's vigilantes who came well-armed. They treated us like dogs.

CAMPESINOS: It's true, those devils treated us like animals.

PETUL: The official told me that they would give us better land in the jungle.

CAMPESINO 2: But can't we do anything to defend our property?

PETUL: Despite everything I said, maybe because we don't know how to read and write, that was the only answer they gave me.

MARUCH: How can that be? In the jungle? We're going to leave our land? That's not possible.

CAMPESINO 1: Well, there's no alternative. They're pushing us off at gunpoint. We have to accept the fact that we have to leave.

MARUCH: But we've been living here for a long time, with our families and our animals.

CAMPESINO 2: It sounds to me like a promise they'll never keep, but in the end we have no choice. I don't want to go because I was born here, and I want to die here. But if we don't go, those bastards will keep on screwing us.

MARUCH: Well then, I guess we have to go, but I can assure you I'll never get used to that place. *¡Ay, Dios!*

SCENE 4

(A jungle clearing. The Campesinos are clearing the jungle with their machetes, whistling happily.)

PETUL: It seems like the official had a good idea for us.

CAMPESINO 1: Well, yes, the soil is really good, and you can get three crops a year!

CAMPESINO 2: And with no fertilizer! It seems like that bastard, don Pumposio, did us a favor!

PETUL: Well, that's the way it looks, but he sure got our property and more than half the crop!

CAMPESINO 1: We'll see what happens. At least we've plenty of strength for the job!

CAMPESINO 2: Enough to pass around! Since now we have property rights.

PETUL: Promises. Just promises! It's been months now since he told us he was going to give us the titles. This land doesn't belong to anybody yet, *compañeros!* See how they're taking out the lumber and digging oil wells. Didn't this land belong to our ancestors?

CAMPESINO 1: Well, yes, that's right! And what do we get from it?

CAMPESINO 2: Don't they say that everything in Chiapas is Mexican? Or could it be they think that everything in Chiapas is for Mexico?

PETUL: It's true. All that Chiapas has given to the country and nothing's been given to us in return! (*They laugh sardonically and file out.*)

SCENE 5

(The jungle. Jaguar and Howler Monkey appear from opposite sides.)

JAGUAR: Argh! This is unbearable. They've driven us out now. They've messed up everything for us! Every day men are destroying more of our forest and just leaving behind their shit. Where can we go?

HOWLER: Ugh! All us animals in the jungle have to join together. We can't keep on living this way! There's nothing left to eat. There are no more ceiba trees to give us shade. We're dying of hunger.

JAGUAR: We have to do something! We've got to look for the god of the mountains, the Earth Lord, to tell him.

HOWLER: Yes, yes, yes! We'll look for the Earth Lord. It's best if we complain to the Earth Lord.

COYOTE: I'm really mad, too, with those human beings who set fire to so many trees! (*Swishing his tail at the audience*) See how I've got a burnt ass! Let's complain, let's complain! Aaoo! (*Making a hullaballoo, they depart from one side and return at the other.*)

JAGUAR: It must be here!

HOWLER: This must be the Earth Lord's cave!

COYOTE: Let's ask his permission!

JAGUAR: Let's knock! (*Howler knocks three times at the entrance, and then the Earth Lord appears.*)

EARTH LORD: How are my children, my offspring? What's happened to you? Why are you crying? Let's see, where is my seat, where is my seat?

ARMADILLO: (*Running in, crouched over, finally stopping behind the Earth Lord so he may sit down*) Yes, yes, *patrón*, here I am, here I am, here I am.

HOWLER: Please, my Lord, help us! I don't know what we can do! Now that they've destroyed our trees, we're left without any woods.

The seat of the Earth Lord, 1994. Photo courtesy Sna Jtz'ibajom

COYOTE: (*Howling*) Those men came in without your permission and began to cut down the jungle. Then it won't rain and there'll just be desert.

JAGUAR: And you used to say that this was holy ground where we could live forever. And look at it now. They're taking it all away!

COYOTE: Yes, yes, yes! We have to get rid of those fire-bugs. (*Swishing his tail at the Earth Lord, who waves him away*) See how they've left me with a burnt ass!

JAGUAR: We're dying of hunger and thirst! Now it doesn't rain like it used to!

HOWLER: And they say they're going to build more dams, dig more oil wells, build more atomic plants. They're going to leave us with nothing to live on!

COYOTE: And everything will dry up, like at the Guatemalan border and those other places that have turned to desert.

EARTH LORD: (*Angrily*) But how could that be? Did they occupy this land without my permission? They destroyed my sacred gardens?

HOWLER: That's what those evil people did. They didn't even pray to you. They just arrived to cut down and burn everything.

EARTH LORD: We have to punish them. What do you think?

ARMADILLO: Yes, yes, yes! Think up something quickly, because I'm being squashed!

ANIMALS: (*In chorus*) Yes, they must be punished! They must be punished for mistreating us!

EARTH LORD: We're going to give them a good lesson. What should it be?

JAGUAR: Well, I think we should leave them without any water. That the rain stop!

HOWLER: Or send sickness on them?

EARTH LORD: That's it. Now we won't protect them from evil spirits, and we'll send them sickness.

JAGUAR: And we'll shut down the wells and the springs.

EARTH LORD: We agree, that's what should happen!

ANIMALS: Yes, we agree. How wonderful he accepted our request!

ARMADILLO: (*The Earth Lord stands up, and the Armadillo runs forward, stretching itself.*) Aah, what a relief! Our Lord is so heavy!

> (*The Animals form a circle, squatting, and laughing merrily before they depart, bowing to the Earth Lord, who pats them as they go.*)

Jaguar and Coyote beseeching the Earth Lord for help, 1994. Photo courtesy Sna Jtz'ibajom

Act II

SCENE 1

(Petul and Maruch's hut. Petul and Maruch enter, Petul stretches out a petate, and Maruch a blanket, before they lie down.)

MARUCH: *Dios,* it's so hot! There are so many mosquitoes! It's nothing like the land we left behind.

PETUL: And who knows if we'll get a good crop of corn and beans. What if we get sick? What would we do? We're so far from any town!

MARUCH: And besides, it's so dangerous. We've seen so many snakes.

PETUL: Yes, but I'm feeling really tired. We've got to sleep.

(Four Toads hop in and do a dance.)

TOADS: Bawk, bawk, bawk! It's scabies and plagues we bring to you. May you suffer, may you cry, may you die! *(The Toads depart, and the couple wakes up feeling sick and in pain.)*

MARUCH: *¡Ay, Dios!* I don't know what's wrong with me, I have a bad headache.

PETUL: Me, too, but I've got a stomachache. I bet I'll get diarrhea. What can we do?

MARUCH: Wouldn't it be better to go tell our *compadre,* the alderman, to see if he can send for a doctor?

PETUL: Yes, wife, you're right! I'll be back in a minute. *(Petul leaves, while Maruch sits on the petate twisting and turning with pain until he returns.)*

MARUCH: Oh, my whole body aches! Oh, I'm burning up with fever! But how could we have gotten so sick when we were fine yesterday?

PETUL: I'm back, wife. Don't you worry. I talked with the alderman and he told me he had sent for the doctor, because it's not just us who's sick. Everybody's sick!

MARUCH: *¡Ay, Dios!* Why would everyone be sick?

PETUL: Who knows? We'll have to wait for the doctor to come. *(He paces back and forth anxiously while Maruch groans.)*

MARUCH: Ay, what are we going to do? I'm feeling worse and worse!

PETUL: I'm afraid the doctor's not coming. So many of our friends have died. I told my *compadre* that if the doctor couldn't come, it would be better if he sent us a shaman. But where can one be found here in the jungle? *(They leave, groaning.)*

SCENE 2

(The jungle. A Shaman appears, walking with his staff, looking at the sky.)

SHAMAN: It's getting dark. It's better if I sleep here.

(He lies down and falls asleep. Jaguar and Armadillo appear from opposite sides.)

ARMADILLO: *(Addressing Jaguar)* Guess what! I went to the place where the people came to live and what do you think?

JAGUAR: What? They couldn't have left yet? They didn't pull out?

ARMADILLO: It's not that they pulled out, but they've gotten really sick, and now they say they're waiting for the doctor because they've all gotten diarrhea.

JAGUAR: Who'd believe anyone would pay attention to them! There's no doctor who could know what they have!

ARMADILLO: What use are doctors, they never show up! You'll see. They'll all die.

JAGUAR: We'll tell the turkey buzzards so they'll have a banquet!

ARMADILLO: And when they all die, then we'll recover our land!

JAGUAR: Thanks to the Earth Lord's toads, who aside from calling for rain also know how to send sickness!

ARMADILLO: Those people deserve it for coming to live here without permission! But let's go now. See you tomorrow!

JAGUAR: Okay, see you tomorrow! *(They disappear, and the Shaman wakes up.)*

SHAMAN: That dream meant something. I don't know what, but it must be important. Well, I guess I'll go and see if I can find a job. *(He departs.)*

SCENE 3

(Petul and Maruch's hut. Petul and Maruch are lying down, groaning. The Shaman calls from the doorway and steps in.)

SHAMAN: ¡Buenos días, buenos días!

PETUL: *(Weakly)* Buenos días.

SHAMAN: I've come to see if you don't have a few days of work I can do.

PETUL: Oh, brother, there's no work here! Everyone here in town is suffering from a terrible disease that we've never had before. My wife is very sick, and I'm almost as badly off. The worst of it is that we no longer have clean water because the springs have dried up.

SHAMAN: Ah, what sickness could your wife have? If you want, I'll take her pulse to see what you're suffering from.

PETUL: Yes, please do that.

SHAMAN: God, Jesus Christ, my Lord,
 Why are your sons, your children suffering so?
 Lord of the holy Heaven,
 Lord of the holy Earth.
 Are your heads angry,
 Are your hearts angry?
 That we are here outside your house,
 Beside your house, my Lord?
 May your head be at rest,
 May this sickness be set aside,
 May this evil be laid aside, my Lord!
 Now we have spoken to the holy father.

(*He takes both their pulses.*) Now little by little you will be improving. This cure was not only for you, but for the whole town.

MARUCH: *Muchas gracias, siñor,* I think I'm feeling a bit better.

SHAMAN: But you can't leave it at that. You will have to plant more trees and plants where you cut them down, and you will have to leave this holy place.

PETUL: But where can we go if they have taken away our land? We don't deserve the punishment we have been given. It was the fault of those who tricked us, who took away the land where we lived. We will die of hunger and thirst.

SHAMAN: The only way is to respect the sacred beings, the Earth Lord and Mother Earth. For that reason I think you must return to your old land, because there your ancestors begged permission. That land belongs to you.

PETUL: But, *siñor,* they ran us off because we don't have the papers that they demand from us, we don't know how to read and write. We don't know how to defend ourselves.

SHAMAN: Well, then, you will have to become organized. You will have to join together to demand what is yours.

PETUL: *Muchas gracias, siñor.*

MARUCH: *Gracias, siñor.* (*The Shaman departs.*) I think the shaman is right. We must get organized.

PETUL: Yes, he's right. We'll see what happens.

SCENE 4

(In town. Petul appears, blowing a conch. Maruch and the Campesinos arrive.)

CAMPESINOS: *Buenas tardes,* Petul.

PETUL: *Buenas tardes.* Look, friends, we have to do something fast. We can't stay here dying of hunger and sickness. The Earth Lord got angry and punished us for invading his gardens, the patio of his house.

CAMPESINO 2: But what can we do? There's no way of confronting the landowners because the government never pays us any attention, and favors them. The vigilantes kill us, and the soldiers kill us.

MARUCH: And why can't we face up to them? You mean you aren't real men? *(The men look at each other but don't say anything.)* Well, if you aren't brave enough to go yourselves, I'm going to meet with the women so that we will go and attack them. We don't want our children to keep dying of hunger and diarrhea! Now we women, too, will organize!

PETUL: *(Going over and placing his arm around Maruch's shoulder)* Maruch is right. How can they be braver than us?

CAMPESINO 1: We have to demand what belongs to us!

CAMPESINO 2: It's better to die struggling than letting ourselves die of hunger and diarrhea!

CAMPESINO 1: But what can we do? How can we demand our rights if we don't know how to read and write?

JUAN LÓPEZ: *(Juan López appears. Tired, he takes off his backpack to sit on. He greets them with a smile, takes out a magazine and starts to read it. They stare at him and then come near.)* ¡Buenas tardes, hermanos!

PETUL: *¡Buenas tardes!* Could you be Juan López?

JUAN LÓPEZ: That's me. I see you recognize me.

CAMPESINO 1: So you've returned from the city!

CAMPESINO 2: And now you're going to stay with us?

JUAN LÓPEZ: Well, I've just come for a visit. I wanted to see how you were, because I learned they'd taken away your land.

(The Campesinos gather together, staring at each other.)

PETUL: And why don't we ask our *compañero*'s help? He's returned now and must have done some studies.

CAMPESINOS: *(Joyfully)* Yes, that's better!

CAMPESINO 2: (*Addressing Juan López*) Son of our ancestors! Oh, holy descendant of our grandparents! Here we are, the rest of us, but our eyes and our ears are of little use, our hands and our feet are clumsy.

PETUL: You who have learned now, you who know now how to read and write the letters, do not abandon, do not scorn your people.

CAMPESINO 1: You will be the good scribe. You will be the good guide.

CAMPESINO 2: You see how we are suffering. We want you to be a barrier, an obstacle, a flash of lightning for the white landowner. We want you to have a strong heart on our behalf.

PETUL: It is true that you are very tender, that you are very young, but we, the elders, the former justices, will be at your side, will be behind you, for the good of our children.

JUAN LÓPEZ: *Hermanos,* it's right that these are your thoughts. The time has come for these deceivers to stop tormenting you, murdering you, robbing you. It's time for you to learn to unite and organize to end forever the poverty and death you have endured for 502 years. I'm very glad to help you. On with the struggle!

PETUL: (*Shouting*) Let's go take our demands to the government!

JUAN LÓPEZ: We can't just take our rightful demands. The solution must be from all for all. I've seen already that even when we march by the thousands or knock down statues of conquerors, they refuse to notice us.

CAMPESINO 1: Well then, if they don't pay us any attention, what can we do about it?

CAMPESINO 2: Now almost everyone agrees. We'll all have to rise up in arms.

EVERYONE: Yes, we all agree! Let's get ready!

SCENE 5

(*In the jungle, near a cave. The government Agent comes running in filled with fear, followed by Pomposo, barefoot and without his pistol. They find a cave.*)

AGENT: God! They're shooting to kill. They say the whole bunch of.Indians are firing, even the women! But I've got to find a place to hide! (*He runs to the cave, hides his head behind the curtain, leaving his rear end sticking out.*)

POMPOSO: Now the Indians have rebelled! I have to hide, too! *Compadre, compadre,* what are you doing here? Let me by because the Indians have risen up! (*He, too, hides his head behind the curtain and tries to push the Agent aside so he can get in.*)

AGENT: We can't fit, *compadre!*

EVERYONE: You can't fit!

AGENT: Okay, get in down below! (*Pomposo hides his head between the Agent's legs. Then Jaguar appears.*)

POMPOSO: (*He tries to push his way in farther. He and the Agent start shouting.*) *¡Ay, ay!* The tiger's come, the tiger's come!

JAGUAR: What are you doing here? Don't you know this is my cave? (*Jaguar claws at their behinds and pushes them ahead of him into the cave.*)

SCENE 6

(*In town. Maruch appears at one side, followed by Petul and Juan López, crouching low. She is carrying a wooden gunstock with a blade at the end. The others have rifles. From the other side appear two armed Vigilantes. Maruch is the first to attack.*)

MARUCH: This is a struggle by everyone for everyone! Even though our blood spills, we want our children to live with justice!

(*There is gunfire. Maruch falls and then a Vigilante. Everyone is motionless as the Earth Lord appears.*)

Battle between the Zapatistas and the army, 1994. Photo courtesy Sna Jtz'ibajom

EARTH LORD: Children of the Earth! Stop this killing! Let no more blood spill! Don't you see that you all are brothers? If you wish to live happily on earth, you must learn to respect and join with each other as brothers and to respect, too, the animals and plants of the earth. If you do this, may the great spirit of the sun shine on you!

JUAN LÓPEZ: (*Standing up, grasping his gun*) That's fine, we will keep the peace! But it must be peace with justice and democracy, because without dignity there will never be peace! Never again will we be slaves! Long live the struggle of the Indian people! *¡Viva!*

EVERYONE: *¡Qué viva!*

MARUCH: *¡Viva Chiapas!*

EVERYONE: *¡Qué viva!*

(*Then they sing the Chiapas anthem.*)

Torches for a New Dawn

(1995)

TORCHES FOR A NEW DAWN (*Antorchas para el amanecer*) focuses on the necessity of replacing the current disastrous education system with a truly bilingual model, staffed by Mayas who respect their culture. Indians make up twelve percent of Mexico's population, and they speak one or more of fifty-six languages that the general public refers to as *dialectos*. In fact, many of these Indian languages, including Tzotzil and Tzeltal, have their own dialects with differing vocabulary and grammar that distinguish one or more communities from each other. When the Instituto Nacional Indigenista (National Indian Institute) arrived in the Chiapas highlands in the 1950s, they discovered that among the 25,000 Chamulans, there were only twenty-five literate men. They began the first grades with members of the community given a minimum degree of training as teachers. But this was soon abandoned, and Indian teachers were replaced by Ladino teachers with no knowledge of or respect for Mayan culture. Indeed, with extraordinary cynicism, the Indians that had been educated in bilingual normal schools were sent, if Tzotzil-speaking, to Tzeltal towns, and the reverse for Tzeltal teachers.

State and national education departments proudly announce the publication and distribution of thousands of bilingual teacher manuals, but in Chiapas, at least, these attractively illustrated manuals present a mix of all the dialects, a sort of Mayan Esperanto, spoken by nobody and which no one wishes to learn. Recently top officials of the federal and state departments of education have acknowledged their inability to cope with the situation.

Here, by means of a play within a play, the Ladino teacher is enlisted to enact with his students the history of the Spanish domination. Reference is made to Gonzalo Guerrero, who, shipwrecked in the Yucatán, adopted Mayan customs and married a local woman. We see how in 1528, Diego de Mazariegos, having conquered San Cristóbal, demands the support of the Indians of Zinacantán. Then a friar teaches an Indian to read and write, but for doing this, he is mocked by the other Dominicans. Bishop Diego de Landa, the second bishop of Yucatán, appears and orders the friars to burn the books of the Mayas. In conclusion, we learn of the outrageous behavior of modern teachers. Conveyed with dark humor, this message is close to the hearts of the Mayan audiences that have been witnesses and victims of the system. Petu's own son, Roge, when he was in elementary school in San Cristóbal, was forced to kneel on bottle tops (a modern substitute for the corn kernels once used). It was not a surprise when the Zapatistas fired all the government teachers and sent them home.

The production of this play was particularly appropriate for Sna Jtz'ibajom since the cooperative in 1987 had founded a Tzotzil-Tzeltal native literacy program. Teachers trained by Sna, using manuals of Zinacantec and Chamulan Tzotzil and Tenejapan Tzeltal, provide in their homes a six-month course. Over 7,500 students in these three communities—men, women, and children—have received diplomas in recognition of their new ability to read and write in their maternal tongue. Many have received state government prizes in bilingual literary contests.

The government's *alfabetización* (literacy) project is described in the play as *"alfabestialización."*

Maryan deliberately misnames Chiapa de Corzo as Chiapa de Corto, and Ocozocoautla as Ucusucojta.

CAST OF CHARACTERS

MARYAN: Zinacantec salt seller, wearing traditional Zinacantec clothing, huaraches, net

PROMOTER: education promoter, wearing hat, white shirt, tie, jacket, glasses, black shoes

MAID: wearing Zinacantec clothes

TEACHER

THREE STUDENTS: all wearing Zinacantec clothes

    XALIK: Student 1

    TUTU': Student 2

    PONCHA: Student 3

FRANCISCAN FRIAR: wearing brown robe, white sash

DIEGO DE MAZARIEGOS: conqueror, wearing silvery helmet, metal breastplate, coat of mail, black cape, short brown pants, black shoes

TONIK: Zinacantec interpreter

SPANISH SOLDIER: wearing silvery helmet, coat of mail, shoes, sword

ZINACANTEC 1: white cloth draped over right shoulder, white loincloth, high-backed sandals

ZINACANTEC 2: wearing neckerchief around head, long blue tunic

DIEGO DE LANDA: bishop, wearing miter, brown robe with white sleeves

SCRIBE: wearing feather headdress, white cape, loincloth, high sandals

FRIAR PEDRO: wearing black robe

DOMINICAN FRIAR 1: wearing black robe

NARRATOR 1: wearing brown striped cloth draped over right shoulder, white loincloth

NARRATOR 2: wearing Zinacantec white shirt and short pants

DOMINICAN FRIAR 2: wearing black robe

DOMINICAN FRIAR 3: wearing black robe

FRIAR TOMÁS: wearing black robe

ATANASIO: Zinacantec elder

Act I

SCENE 1

(San Cristóbal market in the 1950s. Indian merchants, men and women, enter selling fruits and vegetables. From the other side enters Maryan, a Zinacantec salt merchant who is greeted with great respect by the other

merchants, who bow to him. He touches the tops of their heads with the
back of his hand. A mestizo teacher enters and looks over the produce as the
merchants address him in Tzotzil and Spanish.)

MARYAN: *¡Manik atz'am! ¡Manik atz'am!* Buy some salt! Buy some salt!

PROMOTER: Hello, boy, how're things? *¡Buenos días!*

MARYAN: *¡Buenos días, siñor!*

PROMOTER: What are those white things you're selling?

MARYAN: It's just for my job, selling salt.

PROMOTER: Oh, but this salt is different. (*He picks up the cake, touches it, weighs it in his hand.*) Where does it come from?

MARYAN: It's from Ixtapa. It isn't from the ocean. But you should not paw it because it is holy! (*He takes it back.*) It's from a hole in the ground. It's taken from a hole.

PROMOTER: Is that so? And how deep is the hole?

MARYAN: Oh, you can hardly see to the bottom. They pull it up with a rope.

PROMOTER: And how did you learn to speak such good Spanish?

MARYAN: Well, by traveling to the cities.

PROMOTER: How far do you go selling your salt?

MARYAN: Oh god, as far as Chiapa de Corto, Ucusucojta. Yes, that far!

PROMOTER: Well, do you know how to read and write?

MARYAN: Yes indeed, but just a little bit, just a tiny bit.

PROMOTER: What's your name?

MARYAN: Maryan Sancho Sarate, sir.

PROMOTER: And how many years did you go to school?

MARYAN: Oh, it's that my father didn't let me go, because he had me caring for the sheep, many sheep. I just finished two years.

PROMOTER: Only two years!

MARYAN: Yes.

PROMOTER: See here, boy, I've got an idea for you. I don't know what you'd think of it. Don't you want a job? I think I can get you a job that's better than selling salt. Leave that to somebody else!

MARYAN: But . . . what kind of job, *siñor?*

PROMOTER: Look, the government, through the National Indian Institute, wants all your people to learn how to read and write. You could teach them right by your home.

MARYAN: In my home?

PROMOTER: Yes, in your home, in your town. And you can make a lot of progress that way. You can even be appointed to an important post in your town, man. And if you work hard you'll get a good salary. What do you think?

MARYAN: Well, I don't know, boss. What do I have to do?

PROMOTER: It's not anything difficult, man. You just need some training. We're looking for smart guys like you who can learn how to civilize your people. So you'll take a course in that. We'll give you some good training, boy! We'll see if you can do it!

MARYAN: Oh, so you're going to test me!

PROMOTER: Yes, we'll see if you have it in you. You'll be educated so you learn how to teach many others.

MARYAN: Well when does the job begin?

PROMOTER: Next Monday. See here, I'll give you this card. Can you read what it says on it? (*Maryan takes the card and looks at it doubtfully.*)

MARYAN: Welll, I think so, boss. (*He reads it with difficulty.*) A ... nto ... nio Go ... rdo ... ines ... *Pro ... mo ... toro de Alpa ... bestia ... li ... zación.*

PROMOTER: Ha, ha, ha. It says Antonio Godínez, *promotor de alfabetización.*

MARYAN: Okay, sir. And can I invite my friend?

PROMOTER: Does he know how to read and write?

MARYAN: Just a little, like me, boss.

PROMOTER: Well, that's fine. Let him come. We need people.

MARYAN: Okay, boss, we'll come on Monday.

PROMOTER: I'll be waiting for you, then. *¡Hasta luego, muchacho!* (*The Promoter exits.*)

MARYAN: *¡Adios, patrón!* (*The merchants come up to Maryan to ask him what the mestizo gave him. They glance at the card and exit right away.*) Oh god, I hope it's true what the boss just told me, because it's such hard work carrying this heavy load! (*He exits, murmuring.*) Oh, it's such a long trip home!

SCENE 2

(*A city office where a radio can be heard playing a popular song. A knock is heard on the door. A maid appears to open the door. Maryan enters with his hat in one hand and the promoter's card in the other.*)

MARYAN: Are you there? Are you there?

MAID: What do you want?

MARYAN: The boss told me to come. He gave me this card.

MAID: Let's see it!

MARYAN: Here it is. (*He hands her the card, which she inspects.*)

MAID: Oh, all right, come in! You wait while I call him!

(The Maid exits, and Maryan is left alone, looking at everything very curiously, especially the radio. He can't resist the temptation to draw close and try to see where the voices are coming out. He picks it up and turns it over, trying to find the people who are talking.)

MARYAN: Christ almighty! Could this be one of those little talking saints? Oh god, let's see if he performs a miracle for me! *(Then the Promoter comes in, catching Maryan with the radio in his hands as he tries to put it down immediately. The Promoter pretends not to notice.)*

PROMOTER: Good morning, boy!

MARYAN: Good morning, boss!

PROMOTER: That's good that you came. Couldn't you bring your *compadre*?

MARYAN: No, I couldn't let him know because he lives far away.

(Then the phone rings. The Promoter answers, but he starts to have to go to the bathroom, which can be seen as he continues the conversation. Maryan keeps looking at the radio as if it were something from outer space.)

PROMOTER: Hello! Who's speaking? Oh, it's you Mr. Secretary. How are you? I'm so pleased to speak to you! Of course, sir, we're working on that! Just yesterday I was able to hire two people who seem to be pretty smart ... I think in a week we can begin the training courses! ... *(He squirms around.)* Yes, yes, sir ... Well, I expect to see you when you come next week. Goodbye, Mr. Secretary ... *(He hangs up quickly and walks to the back.)* I just have to go take a piss! *(He exits, leaving Maryan alone. Maryan goes to the telephone and picks it up timidly.)*

MARYAN: What is this? Where are the people who live in this thing? *(He knocks on it as if it were a door.)* Hello, hello! Where are the people who were talking? Could they be devils?

(The Promoter enters, surprising Maryan with the phone. Maryan hangs up immediately and pretends he didn't have it.)

PROMOTER: *(Smiling)* Okay, so I caught you! You are going to learn what progress is, boy. What's your name? Let's see! Let's see! Oh yes, you're called Maryan. Is that right?

MARYAN: Well yes, boss.

PROMOTER: Well then, sit down! Here's a chair.... So what do you think, Maryan? ... Are you still going to work with us?

MARYAN: Well yes, boss. I talked about it with my wife, who says I can go to work. She'll just have to find a replacement for me.

PROMOTER: Your replacement? What do you mean?

MARYAN: Yes, the fellow who will take my place at the salt booth, boss.

PROMOTER: Oh, that's fine, boy. Because we need smart guys, hard-working, who will learn to teach your people how to read and write, to better their crops, to build latrines, to care after the health of the community. To become civilized!

MARYAN: Oh well . . . so it will be in my town, is that so? Is that the truth?

PROMOTER: Of course, boy! We're going to train you here. We're going to teach you how to go and civilize your town.

MARYAN: But . . . I don't know how to write very good. I can just sign my name, but my friends just make a thumbprint.

PROMOTER: Well, all right. Don't you worry. We'll teach you here. Look. You come here on Monday with your *compadre* so I can take you to the training center. They're going to teach you there what you need to know so that everybody in your town learns to read and write and to live respectably. (*He accompanies Maryan to the door, nearly pushing him out.*)

Act II

SCENE 1

(*A classroom set up in a hamlet in the Highlands. The students wait quietly. Then Maryan enters, properly dressed in his Zinacantec clothing. He greets his students properly, and they respond respectfully. Maryan goes to the blackboard and begins to explain to them how to write the different sounds.*)

MARYAN: Today we're going to learn to read. So here, A, B, then this sounds like TA TE TI TO TU.

STUDENTS: (*Together*) TATA, TETE, TITI, TOTO, TUTU.

MARYAN: This sounds like PA PE PI PO PU.

STUDENTS: PAPA, PEPE, PIPI, POPO, PUPU.

(*Suddenly a Ladino teacher comes in holding on to some papers. He waits a minute, shaking his head disapprovingly until Maryan realizes that he is there.*)

MARYAN: *Ta jtz'ibatik j-tosuk lo'il: Aa, ¿K'usi van lek jtz'ibatik? Li vo'e chuch' vo'.* [We'll write down a phrase. What shall we write?] (*The students laugh at Maryan's mistake as he has just said, "the water drinks water," then he corrects himself immediately.*) *Mo'oj: li voe chuch' vo.'* [No, the fly drinks water.]

TEACHER: *¡Buenos días!*

MARYAN: (*Smiling*) *¡Buenos días, profesor! ¿Cómo está usted?*

TEACHER: (*With a superior tone*) How is the teaching going?

MARYAN: Very good, very good! You see they're learning a lot.

TEACHER: Can I have a seat?

MARYAN: Yes, of course, sit down, sit down please!

TEACHER: Thanks. Now I want to see how you teach!

MARYAN: Well yes, you see this is how we're making progress. It's so that they'll learn Spanish, but we're teaching them in Tzotzil too!

TEACHER: And this ... what do these words mean?

MARYAN: *Li voe chuch' vo',* which means in Spanish "the fly is drinking water." For example *vo* is the same as ... fly in Spanish ... and in ... Tzotzil.

TEACHER: Ah, you mean in your dialect!

MARYAN: Well, it's Tzotzil, our language, so they can figure it out better.

TEACHER: No, no, no, my friend, what you're doing isn't right at all! Now we don't use your dialect! We've changed the educational system.... You aren't following the rules ... See here! ... You haven't brought your workbook! Now it doesn't say anything here in your dialect. Everything is now in Spanish. (*He shows Maryan the program.*)

MARYAN: (*Trying to explain*) Well, but how is this possible, professor?

TEACHER: (*Interrupting*) You mustn't tea ... No! You are going against the rules of this program. Besides, the teachers' union is behind this.

MARYAN: But these programs just come from there. It's not the same as teaching here. They think we live in the city!

TEACHER: That doesn't matter. You have to do what it says in the program! Do you understand? You have to follow the rules!

MARYAN: No, professor, this is no good at all.

TEACHER: No, you are the one who is wrong, because you mustn't teach this way! You're going to be teaching all your people to be stupid. They'll never progress!

MARYAN: But professor ...

TEACHER: It's better if you teach them in Spanish! So that in two or three years they'll all be civilized!

MARYAN: But that can't be so! Since they were learning so good!

TEACHER: Well, yes, my friend, that's the way it is! You can't teach that way anymore! Here is your guide. You must read it carefully, study your program well, so you don't go off on the wrong track! Do you understand?

MARYAN: (*Murmuring in Tzotzil to his students.*) *Mu onox jna' k'u yu'un ti x'elan ta spasike, toj lek xa ox ta xchanik ech'el, mi ja'uk sna' k'usi li ta spasike.* [I can't understand why they're doing this. They were teaching so well before. Now they don't know what they're doing.] (*One of the students stands up to speak to the Teacher.*)

XALIK: But why is this, sir, if he was teaching us well?

TEACHER: See here, kids, this is what it says in the program. That's the way it was written by the Department of Education. Look! Even the governor told us we had to make this change!

TUTU': But sir ... how are we going to understand it if it isn't written in Tzotzil?

TEACHER: See here! This ... doesn't come anymore in your dialect. See! Everything is in Spanish ...

PONCHA: (*Interrupting*) It's to make money. It's not to teach well!

TEACHER: ... everything in Spanish ... so you have to follow ... the teacher has to follow ...

XALIK: (*Interrupting, too*) But we don't want that, sir! We don't like it!

TUTU': We want the words first in Tzotzil and then in Spanish!

PONCHA: We want it the way it was!

TEACHER: Well, that's not possible. And besides, your teacher has to leave, and I'm going to stay in his place. This problem you've had will not please the governor. It won't please the secretary of education or the teachers' union.

MARYAN: Well that's too bad because the truth is ...

TEACHER: (*Interrupting*) They're going to ... they're going to kick you out for being so stubborn! Wait for me ... outside! Then you can speak to me if you want to get your job back. Do you hear? You can go now! (*He starts to push Maryan out, who resists him.*)

MARYAN: But, but, professor! They haven't notified me!

TEACHER: It's better for you if you wait for me outside! These are the orders of the Department of Education!

MARYAN: All right then ... But I assure you I'm going to go and speak to the governor!

TEACHER: Go wherever you want! What does it matter to me? (*Maryan exits angrily. The Teacher, red-faced, goes back to face the students.*) Well, kids, we're going to learn in the right way. Nothing you've seen here is any good. You see what I mean, it's worthless. Why am I telling you it's worthless? Because ... it's not going to help you make any progress! You'll just become stupid! It's better if you learn Spanish, which is the official language of all of Mexico. Tomorrow I'm going to teach you everything in Spanish. Well, now you can go. (*He turns to Poncha.*) Let's see, you, my little girl, you're going to stay with me. I'm inviting you. We'll go to my kitchen. I'm going to teach you many things.

PONCHA: *Mu xka'i maystro, mu xka'i.* [I don't understand, teacher, I don't understand.]

TEACHER: Let's go, let's go! Hurry up! (*He pulls Poncha out as they exit.*)

SCENE 2

(The same classroom. The Teacher enters, shivering with cold.)

TEACHER: Brr! It's so cold! I've been here so many months teaching these Indians and they can't learn! Monkeys are smarter than them! Besides, I can't get used to it here. There are so many fleas, bedbugs, lice! My whole body is covered with bites. I want to be back in the city! That's the good life! And I'd like to toss down a couple of beers! Well, it's almost vacation time! (*Tutu' enters.*)

TUTU': *¡Buenos días, maystro!*

TEACHER: *¡Buenos días!* Well, you've come a bit early. Let's see, write on the board what you've learned. (*Tutu' tries to write "coca-cola" on the blackboard as the other students come in.*)

PONCHA: *¡Buenos días, maystro!*

TEACHER: *¡Buenos días, Poncha!* (*Addressing Tutu'*) Caca cola? Look how sloppy those letters are! They look like spiders! I'm going to punish you! Kneel down here! And you're going to hold up these bricks! (*He makes Tutu' kneel down and hold out his arms with a brick in each hand. He then addresses Poncha.*) And you, did you finish your work?

PONCHA: Well, no, it's that I can hardly see in my home. We don't have electricity, just pine torches.

TEACHER: How come you can't see? No electricity? Don't you have a kerosene lamp? You deserve to be punished. Go to the board! (*Poncha, cowed, goes to the blackboard.*)

PONCHA: *¿K'usi ta jlok'ta un?* [What shall I write?]

TEACHER: Let's see . . . how do you write *todo*?

PONCHA: *¿Toro? ¿Toro, maystro?*

TEACHER: Yes, yes! Hurry up! (*Poncha tries to draw a bull.*)

PONCHA: Like that, *maystro*?

TEACHER: No, no, no! (*Angrily he grabs Poncha's hand and desperately makes her write.*) No, no, it's not written that way! *¡Todo! ¡Todo!* T . . . O . . . D . . . O. You see? It looks bad, but it's okay.

PONCHA: (*Crying*) *¡Mu jna', maystro, mu jna'!* [I don't know, teacher, I don't know.]

TEACHER: What do you mean "*¿Muná maystro, muna?*" (*He grabs Poncha by the ear, picks up a couple of boards with bottle tops nailed on them rough side up, and* *makes her kneel on them.*) Now you're going to stay here in the corner, kneeling on these bottle tops so you'll learn to do your work! Kneel here! And you're going to be that way all day ... without moving! Or I'll give you some slaps! (*As he does this, Xalik arrives carrying a load of firewood.*)

XALIK: ¡ ... días, maystro!

TEACHER: So, ¡*Buenas tardes!* But why not till now? It's very late!

XALIK: It's because ... it's because you told me to bring your firewood, *maystro!*

TEACHER: But you should have gotten up earlier to do that! As a punishment, and so you learn to arrive on time, you're going to bring me firewood every day next week! Put down the firewood here! But hurry up, you seem like a turtle! So you learn something! (*The Teacher tries to distract and enliven the other students by making them sing a little song.*) You're happy, aren't you?

STUDENTS: (*Feeling obliged to assent*) Yes! (*Tutu' and Poncha reply*) No!

TEACHER: Well now, everyone, we're going to sing "*¡Banderita tricolor, cómo alegras mi corazón!*" [Little tricolored flag, how happy you make my heart!] (*The students repeat it without being able to pronounce it correctly. Then Maryan returns carrying a folder of papers.*)

MARYAN: ¡*Que tal, profesor, buenos días!*

TEACHER: ¡*Que tal, maestro, buenos días!*

MARYAN: But ... what happened, what did these students do? Why do you have them like that?

TEACHER: Because they don't want to learn anything! I'm punishing them because it can't be that they don't learn anything! Look, I had them write the word *todo* and they couldn't do it.

MARYAN: Professor, that's not right! Look here, I talked to the governor, and they gave me permission to continue teaching them the way I did from the beginning. What you're doing is wrong. You shouldn't be punishing the students.

TEACHER: That's the only way these dumb Indians can learn!

MARYAN: Well, see here, I have the governor's order, so I'm going to ask you to pick up your things and give the class back to me.

TEACHER: I was given this program also by the president of the Republic. (*Xalik interrupts him, speaking to Maryan, complaining.*)

XALIK: (*Crying*) Look, *maystro,* this *torpesor* slapped me! Look at my back, it's covered with sores from carrying so much firewood for the *torpesor!*

MARYAN: But how terrible! This shouldn't happen! You don't have to stand this any longer! Let's see, my girl, get up, get up now! (*Poncha stands up, rubbing her knees, crying in Tzotzil.*)

PONCHA: My knees hurt so from the bottle tops! My feet have gone numb!

MARYAN: And you, boy, get up! What are we going to do, professor? The whole town is against you, and we have permission to stop you from teaching here. You have to report in at the capital, Tuxtla.

TEACHER: Okay, where is the order?

MARYAN: Here it is!

TEACHER: (*He looks it over.*) Oh, hell, but ... but ... well, professor, they can't run me out of here. You know I have a wife, I have children, don't be so mean, my friend.

MARYAN: It's not that I am mean, professor. It's that the people, the town officials, the students don't want you to continue teaching here because they have seen how badly you have acted.

TEACHER: (*Showing Maryan his program*) This is what it says, *maestro.* Look here!

MARYAN: It's that we've proven to the governor that these are just endless papers written at a desk. They don't know what is real! Now it's occurred to you! (*The students start to shout at the Teacher to leave.*)

STUDENTS: ¡*Batuk xa, batuk xa, maystro jkaxlan!* ¡*Mu xa jk'antik!* [Get out, get out, Ladino teacher, we don't want you.]

MARYAN: Professor, they don't like you. They want you to go. The kinds of things you have been doing we have endured for five hundred years. You can see it in the history. You know how we have always been left behind.

TEACHER: But ... how would you know the history?

MARYAN: It comes down to us from our grandparents, our parents, our officials! We don't want our children to suffer anymore!

STUDENTS: That's right, *maystro!* We don't want you to be mistreating us anymore. The professor has to leave!

MARYAN: That's the way it is, professor!

TEACHER: But I can't just leave like that. Please don't get me in trouble with the authorities. I won't teach anymore in your communities.

MARYAN: And what good does it do us to get you in trouble? What we want is for people to understand that we deserve more attention and better treatment. And that they respect our languages and our own culture.

TEACHER: Well then, how are you going to get civilized? How are you going to become modern?

MARYAN: It's not a question of us continuing to be backward, professor. What can I do so you'll understand? ... Ah, now I know. So you can see and feel a bit of what our people have been suffering, we'll do ... a play!

TEACHER: A play?

MARYAN: Yes! ... with the students. They should be a part of it too!

TEACHER: And . . . what role do you want to give me?

MARYAN: Well . . . since you know the history on the Spanish side . . . the students could tell you what you should act!

TEACHER: All right. Let's do it. I don't know why I pay any attention to you, but we'll do it. When do we start?

MARYAN: Well, I think right away (*He turns to the class and speaks to them in Tzotzil, which he then translates into Spanish.*) Kids, the professor needs to see what our people have been suffering. We'll do . . . a play!

STUDENTS: A play?

MARYAN: Yes! The way we do it in Carnival or at the Fiesta of San Sebastián. You are the ones who are going to decide who the teacher should be.

XALIK: We'll give him the job of being a poor guy.

TEACHER: A poor guy? Me?

STUDENTS: That's right! Let him feel what we've been feeling!

MARYAN: Okay, okay, let's get ready. What do you think, *maestro*?

TEACHER: Let it be! I agree. No matter what, it's going to be amusing. Let's get ready. (*Everyone exits, commenting on what they're going to do.*)

SCENE 3

(*The students and the teachers enter with the costumes, which they pile up on their seats. Joking in Spanish and Tzotzil, they start dressing. They all laugh when they see the Teacher dressed as an old Zinacantec with a striped tunic and an old beribboned hat. Maryan has the role of Diego de Mazariegos, dressed with a coat of mail and boots. He puts on his helmet and armor. Poncha is dressed in an ancient huipil; her hair is loose but fastened with a cord. Xalik is dressed as a friar.*)

FRIAR: (*Exclaiming to the public*) Now you will see how Captain Diego Mazariegos arrived here to conquer this land!

MARYAN: Don't you look good, professor! You even look like an . . . Indian! Isn't that true, kids? (*Everyone laughs.*) Okay, okay, let's get ready! Everybody take your place! (*They run.*) Let's begin!

(*Maryan takes the stage, dressed as Mazariegos, Xalik as a Franciscan friar. There is also a Spanish soldier. From the other side enters Poncha as Tonik, followed by the Teacher and Tutu' as old Zinacantecs.*)

FRIAR: Hear everyone! In the name of God and the king of Spain: This territory and its inhabitants are declared the property of the Spanish empire, in the service of Carlos V! You must all surrender peacefully. You must stop wor-

General Mazariegos and a Franciscan friar greet the Zinacantecs, 1995.
Photo courtesy Sna Jtz'ibajom

shipping your demons, be converted to Christianity, and give us all of your gold, or you will be put to the sword.

MAZARIEGOS: Fine! That is all! Now we will see if they understand the Spanish language!

TONIK: Wait just a moment, sir! Before you harm my people ... let me speak to them and tell them in our language what you have said!

MAZARIEGOS: But ... but ... This Indian woman speaks Spanish. At least I understand that much!

FRIAR: This is ... a miracle! ... And she's so pretty!

MAZARIEGOS: So, my girl, how did you learn Spanish?

TONIK: In Yucatán, sir ... I was a slave of don Gonzalo Guerrero. The Tlaxcaltecs freed me when they came to conquer Chamula.

MAZARIEGOS: Well, that's a small service that traitor did for us here! Girl, you must come with me on all the conquests!

FRIAR: Well said, *general*! This girl will be very useful in converting these pagans into being good Christians!

MAZARIEGOS: And she'll be much more useful if with her tongue she gets us the gold that we are looking for. That's the reason for the conquests!

SPANISH SOLDIER: Better said, *general,* and the king will take both those matters into account!

MAZARIEGOS: But . . . let's get on with it! (*Caressing Tonik's chin*) Let's see, pretty Indian. Tell them the order in your language. We have to know whether they are surrendering in good form.

TONIK: As you wish, sir! Wait a moment . . . let me see if I can remember what they said. (*She addresses her people in Tzotzil.*) *Jchi'iltaktik:* These bearded guys are like gods . . . or devils, sent by their Great Spirit or Great Lord to take all the land and all the people. They say we must surrender to them. We must stop worshipping our gods and worship their crucified god. If we don't do so, they will finish us off with their swords and their guns, just as they did to the Aztecs and the people of Chiapa and the Chamulans. Ah, and we must turn over to them all the gold that we can find!

ZINACANTEC 1: Devils? That's why they stink so badly! It seems like they never bathe!

ZINACANTEC 2: That's the truth! How they stink! They smell like buzzards! And they say they want to take away our land. And they want us to be their slaves? That's not possible! We who helped them conquer the Chiapanecs and the Chamulans?

TONIK: Well, they don't bathe and they seem to be crazy, but they are very powerful. It's better for us if we obey them, if we don't want them to kill us. It's better if we receive them with honor, as we had thought, and we should invite them to eat with us and stay with us. This way we'll make them our allies, and they will help us against our enemies.

ZINACANTEC 1: You are right! That's why we have brought the gold and silver shields, of the sun and the moon. We should give them as presents, since that's what they like best!

ZINACANTEC 2: Tell them also that we agree to worship their crucified god! How could they know that in the mountains we will continue to worship the sun and the moon?

MAZARIEGOS: What's all their talk? Are they going to surrender or not? Tell me right away, my little Indian, my patience is running out! (*The Zinacantecs exit to bring in the gold and silver shields.*)

TONIK: I beg you a bit of patience, sir. I am having difficulty in giving your order in our language. But they say that they are willing to serve under the god and king who dispatch such powerful gentlemen, so long as they can retain their offices and their property.

MAZARIEGOS: So long as it is not the gold that we are seeking, they may keep their neck pieces, their feathers, and their huts. So be it! Agreed! Where is the gold?

TONIK: As for the gold … Look! (*She urges the Zinacantecs to present the gold of the sun and the silver of the moon. The Spaniards are dazzled by it. Mazariegos accepts the offerings as the Friar and the Soldier give cheers.*) And as proof of their acceptance … they would like you to come to Zinacantán.

MAZARIEGOS: Thank you, my girl.

TONIK: Do you eat vegetables?

MAZARIEGOS: Well … we're so tired of nothing but corn, beans, chile pepper, and vegetables! What … don't you have any fat chickens?

TONIK: Chickens? No, sir, we don't know what they are. What are those chickens?

SPANISH SOLDIER: Well … they are those big, fat feathered birds … that say "kikiriki"!

TONIK: Ah, the ones that can hardly fly and that have skin like … yours when you are scared … or when you are cold?

SPANISH SOLDIER: That's what they are! Those ones. Sonofabitch, you understood very well!

TONIK: All right, *kaxlan, kaxlan,* well … there aren't any of them around here! No!

MAZARIEGOS: What we want, man, is a barbecue! Meat, meat!

TONIK: (*Addressing her Zinacantec companions*) They say they want *kaxlan,* but we don't have any. What can we give them?

ZINACANTEC 1: Ah, so do they want to eat people?

TONIK: No, man, they want to eat the flesh of any animal!

ZINACANTEC 2: Ah, well then, give them *tuluk', te'tikal chitom, te'tikal chij, xulem.*

TONIK: They say they can give you … turkey, wild pig, venison, or buzzard soup … with red or green sauce or hot chile sauce.

MAZARIEGOS: Okay then, that's making me so hungry! On to Zinacantán!

TONIK: Yes, sir, let us go! *¡Batik xa jchi'iltaktik!* (*Everyone follows Mazariegos and Tonik, who lead them out. They circle around and reenter. Tonik bows to Mazariegos.*) Step ahead, sir, we will serve you very soon.

MAZARIEGOS: Thank you, my girl.

TONIK: Sit down, feel at home! (*They sit down around the fire, Indian style. They are served, but then Mazariegos protests.*)

MAZARIEGOS: Where are the spoons, the forks, and a knife?

ZINACANTECS: *¿K'usi van chalik?* [What are they saying?]

TONIK: They want wooden spoons and forked sticks to scoop up their food.

ZINACANTECS: *¿K'usi taje? Ch'abal ku'untik, albo yech.* [What are they? We don't have any. Tell them that.]

TONIK: We don't have any, sir. We use our tortillas as spoons.

*(Noticing that the Zinacantecs were seasoning their food with chile,
the Spaniards ask for it, but it burns their mouths and they complain about
it to each other.)*

SPANISH SOLDIER: ¡Ay! These Indians' chile is so hot! (*They eat all they can. Wiping off his moustache with the back of his hand, Mazariegos speaks again.*)

MAZARIEGOS: Tell me, my little Indian, what is your name? I seem to have forgotten it.

TONIK: Tonik Tuluk', sir, at your service!

MAZARIEGOS: You are so well educated, I swear! But tell me, Tonik, where is the rest of the treasure?

TONIK: Oh, no, sir. What they have given you is all the gold and silver that we had in Zinacantán!

MAZARIEGOS: What? That's all? That cannot be. Do you think we can be satisfied with so little? Don't you lie! And where did this gold come from? Somebody must know where they brought it from! And if they don't tell me ... with this sword they'll go to Hell!

TONIK: (*Very upset, she translates his words to the Zinacantecs, who fearfully deny having any more gold. One of them mentions Chamula.*) *Ta la me xismilvanik ti mi mu'yuk buy ikak'betik li jk'ulejaltik une.* [They'll kill us if we don't give them our treasure.]

ZINACANTEC 1: *¿Buy xa ta jtabetik talel un? Ti ta Chamu'tik jtaojtik talel une.* [Where can we get it? We brought it from Chamula.]

TONIK: They say they got the gold in their war with the Chamulans, who are our enemies now! But ... we don't have any more, sir! There is no more gold in our land!

MAZARIEGOS: (*Annoyed and thinking it over, he turns to the friar.*) So it is those rebels, the Chamulans, who have the gold! They are very fierce! They have risen up against us, and now they refuse to work in the building of the city!

FRIAR: They are the wildest of them all! I have been told of the savage dances they perform for their demons!

MAZARIEGOS: Let's see, Tonik. It's true that the Chamulans are your enemies, isn't that so?

TONIK: Yes, sir, we have been at war with them for many years.

MAZARIEGOS: Well, now we are going to finish off your enemies. Ah, but all the warriors must join us. And you, women, must fix the food! But before that, all the men in the town must work as masons and construction workers to build Villa Real, which will be known as Chiapa de los Españoles!

TONIK: (*Translating rapidly*) All the men and women of Zinacantán must build the Spaniards' city! And they want it built of adobe and stone!

ZINACANTEC 1: (*Protesting*) And why should it be us if we gave them our gold? And we have already promised that we would be converted to Christianity!

ZINACANTEC 2: And why don't the Chamulans do it?

TONIK: (*Translating for Mazariegos*) Sir, they say that they are willing to help to conquer the Chamulans, but they don't want to work as *mu'nat,* as slaves. We Zinacantecs have always been merchants!

MAZARIEGOS: Well, now they are going to have to work as masons. Those Chamulan Indians are very fierce and they prefer to die before they have to work building our churches. On the other hand you are very ... civilized, and you don't want to die, do you, from the bites of our dogs?

TONIK: (*Translates for her companions*) *Ta la me xispasotik matar ti mi mu jch'unbetik li strabajoike.* [They say they'll kill us if we don't agree to work for them.] (*They all reply, terrified.*)

ZINACANTECS: *Mu jk'antik un bi'a. ¡Ta xi'abtejotik! ¡Ta xi'abtejotik!* [We certainly don't want that! We'll work! We'll work!]

TONIK: (*Translating for Mazariegos*) No, sir, we will work, we will work!

MAZARIEGOS: You know how to save your skin! Ah, Spain, Spain, how I miss you! So to work then! Now I want to see the Villa Real of Mazariegos, the first city founded by the king in this New Spain! Ha, ha, ha! (*They collect their things and exit.*)

SCENE 4

(*The Teacher, dressed now as a Mayan scribe, appears to present the next scene.*)

SCRIBE: Now we are going to see how the first bishop of Yucatán, Diego de Landa, burnt almost all the books of the Maya. Now only four of the ancient books remain!

(*He exits and Diego de Landa enters with the Franciscan Friar, followed by the Scribe, who trudges in unhappily. They are carrying turkey feathers, brushes, and paper.*)

DE LANDA: Now I want you to teach me how you write your letters. Come on, come, write on this paper a sentence, a prayer, whatever you want!

SCRIBE: But I don't want to.

DE LANDA: What do you mean that you don't want to? Why not? Aren't you a scribe?

SCRIBE: Because you haven't left anyone alive who knows how to read it. You have killed everyone who knew.

DE LANDA: Well, you have to do it. Otherwise you will be tortured like all the pagans who have not wanted to be converted. It's devilish, your stubbornness!

SCRIBE: But why do you want to know what my people write?

DE LANDA: To know what tricks the demon inspired in you people. Go ahead! I order you to write!

SCRIBE: (*Writes several signs on his fig bark paper book*) Well, here it is.

DE LANDA: Look at that! What ugly drawings! They look like the devil's children. And what does this say?

SCRIBE: It says *mu jk'an, mu jk'an.* I don't want to! I don't want to!

DE LANDA: Oh what a stubborn Indian! Go ahead, write, write! How do you write an A?

SCRIBE: Like this. (*He writes.*) This says *ak.*

DE LANDA: But this looks like the head of a turtle! Or ... the head of one of your devils! Besides, I don't want you to write *ak,* just the letter A. They told me you're a scribe and yet you don't even know how to write the alphabet!

SCRIBE: But the A is not written by itself. There are many ways to write it.

DE LANDA: But then how do you know what the A is? I don't understand! I don't understand! All right, write down B. (*The Scribe writes and shows him his drawing, the silhouette of a foot between two lines.*)

SCRIBE: That's it, that says "be." Do you see?

DE LANDA: What? Aren't you just tricking me? The drawing of a foot is a B? How can you people write with your feet? My god, look what the devil has taught you! You do everything backwards as if you were in hell! Now, write A, B, C, D, E, F, G ... until you finish the alphabet! (*The Scribe does it and shows de Landa his drawings.*)

SCRIBE: Here they are!

DE LANDA: All right, read them!

SCRIBE: ¡Ak, be, ca, ee, ke ...!

DE LANDA: I don't understand, I don't understand at all! ¡Santa María! You must be calling up the devil! (*He goes to the side and calls out.*) ¡Fray Pedro! ¡Fray Pedro! Come quickly and tell me if these drawings aren't the work of the devil!

FRIAR PEDRO: It's true that those letters don't seem to be Christian! So does your grace believe that those books are the work of the devil?

DE LANDA: There's no doubt about it! In Maní they had hundreds of them hidden away! And something must be done right away! The judges must order that all the books of these savages be confiscated. We will burn these devilish images! Tell all the Dominicans to come here!

FRIAR PEDRO: Yes, sir, I will call them . . . Dominicans, Dominicans! (*The Dominicans enter.*)

DE LANDA: Bring me those books of the Mayas. They are works of the devil! We must burn them quickly before they influence us!

DOMINICAN FRIAR 1: Yes, your grace, we will burn them now!

SCRIBE: But, sir, these books are sacred!

DE LANDA: Why didn't I think of burning them before! Bring the books and set them afire!

SCRIBE: Please do not burn them! They have our science, our calendars. These books are sacred!

DE LANDA: Burn them up!

(*The Dominicans enter and burn all the books as the Scribe, crying out, tries to save them. They push him aside violently. They exit, the Scribe very sadly. Then Narrators 1 and 2 enter.*)

NARRATOR 1: See here. I'm going to tell you a very old story. In Zinacantán they say that when San Sebastián appeared on this land, he brought a book that was going to be the torch and the mirror of our people. But it was lost on the road, and it fell into the hands of the scribes of the Ladinos, the mestizos, and that is why they became very rich, strong, powerful, just the way

Spanish soldier, 2001. Photo courtesy David Pentecost

the lawyers are today. If it had stayed in the Indians' hands, then we would be more powerful. But that did not happen, and that is why the Spaniards have dominated us. Because we lost the torch and the mirror!

NARRATOR 2: Now we are going to see when the first Dominicans arrived in Zinacantán, where they built the first monastery of America under Fray Tomás de la Torre, who was the first historian of Chiapas. But some of the friars did not want to show the writings to the Indians.

SCENE 5

(The Dominicans enter, laughing mockingly.)

DOMINICAN 1: Ha, ha, ha! Oh that Fray Tomás! He thinks these stupid Indians are going to learn religion and Latin as if they were smart Spaniards!

DOMINICAN 2: Ha, ha, ha! All those Indians seem good to him! I don't know if it's because he's a good man or ... a dumb one.

DOMINICAN 3: *(Alarmed)* But ... What if in fact they do learn? We'll be in for trouble!

DOMINICAN 1: Ha, ha, ha! How could you think an Indian would learn Latin? Not even us who study in Salamanca! Watch out, here comes Fray Tomás! *(Fray Tomás enters, speaking Latin, followed by an old Zinacantec, Atanasio, dressed cleanly, carrying a book under his arm.)*

FRAY TOMÁS: *Sanctum esse spiritum, qui, in illius alitis specie, ut solaretur, venire erat dignatus.*

ATANASIO: *Nullium est factile vas apudnos, qoud arte superet ab illis vasa formata.*

FRAY TOMÁS: *(Merrily and presumptuous, addressing the Dominicans)* Did you hear, brothers? This is my godson and student, Atanasio de la Torre, native of Zinacantán! He speaks Latin like a Roman!

DOMINICAN 2: Ha, ha, ha! A farmer's Roman Latin! That's too much, Fray Tomás!

DOMINICAN 3: *(Addressing Atanasio)* Let's see, Virgil, give us some of your Latin! Ha, ha, ha!

ATANASIO: If Fray Tomás will permit, I will tell you that a farmer is not frightened by such a difficult thing! *Agricolae qui corporibus exercitati sunt, utilissimi sunt ac potentes sub diu consistere.*

DOMINICAN 1: My god! And now it seems that this Indian is a wise one!

FRAY TOMÁS: Atanasio is no longer a stupid guy! He could very easily be a lawyer, and even offer Mass with all he's learned. He is more Christian and enlightened than many from Spain.

DOMINICAN 3: *(Furious)* I prohibit you from giving excuses to the devil!

FRAY TOMÁS: (*Disconcerted*) But … If we don't teach them so they can educate their children and grandchildren in their own languages, translating from Spanish and Latin, how are we going to give them the Holy Scripture?

DOMINICAN 1: Let them learn enough Spanish to confess their sins!

DOMINICAN 3: All Indians are prohibited from learning the Holy Scripture!

FRAY TOMÁS: This cannot be! How could that happen! Ohh!

ATANASIO: Impossible! I must think up something!

(*Fray Tomás and Atanasio exit, shamed and attacked by the three Dominicans, enemies of education for the Indians.*)

Act III

SCENE 1

(*Fray Tomás enters immediately from one side as the Dominicans enter from the other.*)

MARYAN: What good acting, kids! Applaud! That was fine! Bravo! (*The students enter with their chairs. They applaud and all of them take off their costumes, which they put on the Teacher's desk.*)

MARYAN: Where is my chair?

TEACHER: I'll be back. I'm going to change! (*The Teacher exits and then reenters as Maryan speaks.*)

MARYAN: That was what happened when the Spaniards arrived. That is what has happened for over five hundred years. In the Indian towns they weren't taught to read or write, neither in their own languages nor in Spanish, because it did not suit the colonizers or the exploiters. They wanted us to be humbled always, like slaves, like the cheapest labor.

TEACHER: But how did you endure so many years and agree to be so ignorant?

MARYAN: Oh, because knowledge is power, professor! When a people is subjected to such ignorance, they lose everything! They took away almost all our culture, our beliefs, our knowledge, our treasure and even … our land!

TEACHER: Well, you are right, *maestro*. That's why I insist that the teaching must be in Spanish, because the great discoveries that give us power come in Spanish, in English, in French …

MARYAN: How can you be such a burro again! Well, what's the matter, professor? Where do you think the great palaces and temples of Palenque, Yaxchilán, and Bonampak came from?

TEACHER: Well, I agree that in those times there were wise cultures, but now we have to enter modern times.

MARYAN: Well, let's see … Why don't the *jkaxlanes,* the mestizos, learn our languages while we learn yours? Or could it be that we Indians are smarter than you people?

TEACHER: Let's see, students, what do you think?

PONCHA: Um … Well I think they should also teach Tzotzil in the mestizo schools so they will treat us as equals and not mock us so much when we don't understand Spanish.

TUTU': And so they will know a bit about our customs, not like the majority of the mestizos who have no idea how we live or how we think.

TEACHER: It's because the teachers' union doesn't want the teachers to learn to teach in the mother tongue. And even though some of them know it, the others don't want to learn, or they think that they can't learn, and they are ashamed to speak.

MARYAN: Exactly. What we want is that they make bilingual education obligatory, but that they do it without discrimination.

TEACHER: Well, yes, it's been a bad habit.

MARYAN: We can't teach in our own language because we don't know how to write it well, much less study it, and we can't teach Spanish well because we don't understand it well either. It's true, too, that some teachers make love to the girl students.

STUDENTS: Ha, ha, ha!

XALIK: Yes, my teacher always arrived late and only two days a week.

TUTU': My teacher sent me and my father to work on his land.

PONCHA: (*Places an imaginary bottle on the table and then leans back*) He told me to bring his *pox,* his cane liquor, and then he used me as a pillow. (*Tutu' pushes Maryan towards Poncha as all the students laugh.*)

XALIK: That's why you got nothing but tens! (*The Teacher and Poncha stand up.*)

TEACHER: Now the curtain has fallen on us!

STUDENTS: Ha, ha, ha!

MARYAN: Well, that's what I was trying to show you, what has happened in our towns. But we must look for a solution to all this. What do you think?

XALIK: Well it seems that now there is a *Chanob Vun ta Batz'i K'op,* an Indian language school.

TEACHER: Yes, that's what we've needed! We must draw up a request for what we need … teaching materials, puppet and live theatre, books, magazines, radio programs in the various languages! And even a Maya Institute of Arts and Sciences!

STUDENTS: Yes!

MARYAN: What is needed before the books are made?

PONCHA: Well, first many people have to learn to read and write so they can write them and then read them, *maystro*!

XALIK: That's true. But they say that now there are groups of writers who have their own methods.

TUTU': Well, yes. Because even the old people can learn.... They can write down everything they know, and then the young people can learn from them.

MARYAN: That's just the very beginning! That's what the book of San Sebastián must have been. That's why the old people in their prayers to the scribes say that they are the torches and the mirrors of our towns! Because they are the torches for a new dawn! This is what is needed so the people will open their eyes and waken from our nightmare, which has lasted over five hundred years!

TEACHER: The ones who are needed so that our people live in peace with dignity and justice, so there will be equality, liberty, and amity.

MARYAN: All right. Now we've seen that even teachers can learn! Now we have the base for our new education! And also the name of our play!

TEACHER: That's right! Those who write and teach are ... the torches for a new dawn!

MARYAN: (*Addressing the students*) And what do we want to be?

EVERYONE: (*Joining their hands and raising their arms together*) Torches for a new dawn!

The Story of Our Roots

(1996)

THE STORY OF OUR ROOTS (*El cuento de nuestras raices*) is based on the play *Christ I Never Knew You!* which I wrote many years ago, drawing on a folktale that Xun's uncle, Matyo Tanchak, told me. This play was accepted by Luis Valdez's Teatro Campesino in California, but never performed. Year after year I suggested that it might be a good project for our theatre, but my suggestion was always ignored. Finally, after Palas translated it into Spanish from English, they stripped it down considerably and very well. But they did not want Christ's name in the title, fearing that they would be accused of carrying out the work of the Fundamentalist Christians. When I pointed out that the Fundamentalists would surely not present a drunken Christ, they laughed and said, "But they drink, too, even if it's on the sly!"

For five hundred years the Catholic Church has tried to evangelize the Mayas with little success. Christian figures, Christ, the Virgin Mary, and the saints were converted into deities who work alongside the ancestor gods and the Earth Lord in his Ladino aspect, ensuring health and good harvests, so long as they are remembered by mankind with words and food. The doctrine, learned by rote, if at all, in colonial times, is given virtually no attention now. The priest says Mass (now sometimes in Tzotzil or Tzeltal), baptizes babies, blesses the pictures of saints, takes confession from bride and groom. Under the guidance of Samuel Ruiz, Mayas who had resettled in the Lacandón jungle, many of them Zapatistas, discovered that the Book of Exodus gave them strength in their sufferings. The traditional Mayan Catholics, with their animistic worldview and devotion to the tribal-like patron saints of each town, believe they are the only true Catholics, the only true Christians. But now, many are being converted into Fundamentalists of many sects, while a few hundred have become Muslims who have sent representatives to Mecca and who are also splitting into rival sects.

We had Christ standing on a mound (at the base of the cross) rather than crucifying him because the actors joked that if they were to hang Christ on the cross, "maybe on Good Friday no one would go to church, but would come to see the play instead!" (Laughlin to Collins 1996). But they felt no worry about showing Christ on the cross to gringos.

When Palas, the Ladino member of Sna, asked, "Why don't you ever call 'Our Lord' 'Christ'?" they responded, "Oh, the Spaniards brought *him* over!" Then one of the actors added, "Well, this is the *rebel* Christ!" As you will see, he is a creator god, an all-powerful trickster, and very human, reminiscent of the *Popol Vuh* twins. The Ancestors, identified also as wandering Jews, wish to kill Christ because he has an ugly round head, like a squash, not a long, frontally depressed skull (like the ancient Mayas). But they are so totally incompetent that Our Lord has to cut the tree for the cross, make the cross, and even bury himself! After he rises to Heaven as the Sun, followed by his mother, the Moon, with the consent of San Salvador and the help of the Earth Lord, he punishes his tormenters with forty days and nights of rain. Then the Devil, dressed all in red, succeeds in getting Christ (in white) drunk so that Our Lord's children can procreate. The members of Sna, influenced by their work promoting native literacy, have Christ urging them to teach their children to read and write in their own language. Only that way can they succeed in this difficult world.

At our first performance, in Margaritas, seeing that the audience was mainly Ladino and not Indian, I worried whether our play would seem heretical, but the laughter and smiles of children and adults dispelled my fear. Here is Mayan Christianity that has survived for five hundred years without the knowledge of the pope!

NARRATOR: man from San Andrés, wearing black woolen robe, white shirt, Zinacantec tunic, long blue pants, sneakers

ANCESTORS 1, 2, AND 3: old Zinacantecs, wearing pointy-headed and large-nosed masks, white knee-length pants, red sashes

OUR HOLY MOTHER: Virgin Mary, Moon, wearing white blouse, Zinacantec white shawl with red stripes, black skirt

FARMER 1: Zinacantec farmer, head wrapped in neck cloth, wearing white shirt, white shorts, sandals

FARMER 2: dressed like Farmer 1 but wearing wool tunic

OUR LORD: Christ, Sun, wearing white robe, high-backed sandals

ROOSTER (PUPPET)

SPARROW (PUPPET)

BLIND MAN: head wrapped in neckcloth, wearing white shirt, white wool tunic, white knee-length pants, sandals, with spear

SAN SALVADOR: wearing white shirt, long black robe, sandals

EARTH LORD: wearing large *charro* hat, black shirt, pants, and shoes

HOLY MOTHER EARTH (THE EARTH LORD'S DAUGHTER): wearing long green robe, barefoot

CLOUD: holding white cloth with hole for face, wearing Tenejapa skirt, barefoot

BUZZARD (PUPPET)

DOVE (PUPPET)

FOUR LITTLE PEOPLE (PUPPETS)

TWO OR THREE MONKEYS (FORMERLY ANCESTORS): wearing ancestor clothes with long black tail

MAN: wearing white shirt, white wool tunic, white shorts

WOMAN: wearing Zinacantec clothing

SERPENT (PUPPET)

DEVIL: wearing a hooded red suit, sneakers

Act I

(Narrator appears in front of black and red curtain.)

NARRATOR: Well, it's cold here. (*Nodding*) Why don't you come in and join me next to the fire? I'm going to tell you a story. (*He takes a chair, puts it next to the fire. He turns off his boom box, which is playing* "No tengo dinero," *and pulls over another chair, placing it with its back to the audience.*) Sit down! Do you want a drink? (*He takes out of his shoulder bag a coke bottle filled with a clear liquid and stoppered with a corn cob. He picks up a shot glass that was next to the fire, fills it carefully, and then, putting the bottle on the ground and shifting the glass to his right hand, offers it to the empty chair with a gesture.*) ¡Kich'ban! (*Returning the toast*) ¡Ich'o! (*He empties the glass of cane liquor and puts it down next to the bottle.*) As I was about to tell you, once upon a time babies were born with long heads. One day something happened that greatly upset them.

(*Three old men with long noses, nearly bald conical heads with tufts of hair on the sides, enter, wearing long gray woolen tunics and carrying sturdy wooden staffs.*)

ANCESTOR 1: I don't know if you know about this.

ANCESTOR 2: Yes, I heard about it. They say that the child was born with a round head, like a squash!

ANCESTOR 3: That woman doesn't have a husband. Why don't we look for her and kill her child? He must be a child of the Devil!

ANCESTOR 1: Yes, we'll kill him! We'll cut his head off!

ANCESTORS: Let's go kill him then, right away! (*The Holy Mother, carrying her baby, appears at the side.*)

HOLY MOTHER: Oh god, they want to kill my little child. But . . . where can I go? I'll have to find a house to hide in. (*She runs offstage, pursued by the Ancestors, who circle about.*)

ANCESTORS: Where is she, where is she? I don't see her over here!

(*They leave. Two farmers appear and begin their planting. Right away Our Holy Mother reenters.*)

FARMER 1: Well, let's plant our corn, because now it's time.

FARMER 2: Well, come back for me when you return, since you have to go a long ways still.

HOLY MOTHER: What are you doing?

FARMER 2: I'm planting trees. I'm planting rocks.

HOLY MOTHER: Ah, well, so be it! (*A large rock appears.*)

FARMER 2: Holy shit! But why did that happen? (*The Ancestors appear in hot pursuit.*)

ANCESTOR 1: Say, mister, did you see a woman come by?

ANCESTOR 2: It's a woman who is carrying a child with a big round head, like a gourd!

FARMER 2: Yes, they just left!

ANCESTOR 3: Let's go after them!

(The Ancestors, pushing aside Farmer 2, hurry off to the left, while Our
Holy Mother appears from the right and meets Farmer 1.)

HOLY MOTHER: What are you doing?

FARMER 1: I'm planting our Lord's sunbeams and shadows. Who knows if they'll grow.

HOLY MOTHER: Ah, well, you are planting corn. If somebody comes asking for me, please fool them, because they are hunting after me. They want to kill me and my baby. Tell them that I passed by, but that it was when you were planting your corn.

FARMER 1: All right, I'll tell them that if they come, but . . . what did you do?

HOLY MOTHER: Nothing. This is my crime. (*Swinging her shawl around to show him her child*) My little baby, because his little head is round.

FARMER 1: Oh, don't worry, I'll tell them. (*Our Holy Mother exits.*) Great! My corn ripened in just three days! (*The corn, with many ears, appears, while the Ancestors come in from the left and address the Farmer.*)

ANCESTOR 2: Mister, mister, have you seen a woman with her baby come by?

ANCESTOR 3: The one who has a pumpkin head!

FARMER 1: Ohh, she came by, but it was when I was planting my corn. It must have been three months ago. It was long ago.

ANCESTORS: Hell, we'll keep after her! (*They hurry off to the left, following the Farmer, while Our Holy Mother appears on the right. She sets her child down and changes its diapers.*)

HOLY MOTHER: What beautiful plants, trees, flowers! Now, my child, sleep well, no one can find us here. (*Looking at her baby*) You will grow up fast, but when you are big you will suffer a lot. (*She covers them both with a blanket, and they sleep a moment. Then her son appears as a young man.*)

OUR LORD: Wake up, Mother, get up!

HOLY MOTHER: Son! Is it you?

OUR LORD: Yes, it's me, Mother.

HOLY MOTHER: How you've grown! What have you done?

OUR LORD: Mother, I planted fruit trees! See what wonderful fruit we have now! (*Noise can be heard.*)

HOLY MOTHER: What's that? Something's bumping about.

OUR LORD: Somebody's coming. Let's hide! (*The Ancestors appear on the right. Our Holy Mother and her child hide on the left.*)

ANCESTOR 1: Where can they be? Who knows. I don't know how many years it's been that we've been looking for them. They're so well hidden we can't see them through the trees.

ANCESTOR 2: Hurry up, bastards, they must be right here! See everything that's been planted here, peaches, every kind of fruit!

ANCESTOR 3: Here they are! We've found them at last!

OUR LORD: (*Solicitous*) Don't be afraid, Mother! Don't be scared! Let them come, don't worry, I'm big, I've grown up! I want to know what our friends are going to do with me. I'll stand up. (*Addressing the Ancestors*) Grab ahold of me! (*Our Lord stands up calmly.*)

ANCESTOR 3: Get the rope, hurry up!

ANCESTOR 1: (*He tries to tie up Our Lord, circling around him three times with the rope, but Our Lord, laughing brazenly, tosses it off.*) It doesn't work!

ANCESTOR 2: Oh hell, what can we do? We have to kill him!

ANCESTOR 1: No, that's wrong.

ANCESTOR 3: We'll kill him with our hands. We'll strangle him. (*He tries to choke Our Lord, who just keeps on laughing.*)

OUR LORD: (*Encouragingly*) Don't try to kill me this way. You'd better nail me up, make a cross. That's what you should have done!

HOLY MOTHER: Son, why do you say that? Please, you all, don't kill my boy! (*Sobbing*)

OUR LORD: Don't cry, Mother! Nothing's going to happen to me.

ANCESTOR 2: Well, that's what we'll do.

ANCESTOR 1: That's fine. That's more fun.

ANCESTOR 3: That'll be such a sight!

OUR LORD: Please cut down a tree!

ANCESTOR 2: Where's the tree? (*They search vainly until a tree appears on the left. Our Holy Mother sits in the background, center stage.*)

OUR LORD: (*Pointing to the tree*) Cut down this one!

ANCESTOR 1: (*His axe just rebounds.*) How come? What's wrong?

OUR LORD: (*Disturbed*) What's the matter with your axe?

ANCESTORS: (*Angrily*) Nothing!

OUR LORD: (*Steps forward and feels the blade*) It isn't sharp. I think we'll have to sharpen it! (*He files the axe with a stone and returns the axe to them.*)

ANCESTOR 1: (*Trying to chop, but first with the handle, then with the butt of the axe head, finally, correctly*) It's nearly halfway! Watch out! It's going to fall on top of us! (*The tree tilts as if it's about to fall. The Ancestors jump back, shouting, falling to the ground. Our Lord just laughs.*)

OUR LORD: (*Encouragingly*) I think you should cut it on the other side!

ANCESTORS: Really?

OUR LORD: Yes! (*Our Lord stands with his arms crossed, supervising the work. They cut on the other side. The tree tilts again and they back off again.*) Don't be scared! Let it fall!

ANCESTORS: (*Inspired*) We'll get our rope!

OUR LORD: Bring it! (*The Ancestors attach it to the tree and try to pull the tree down, but the tree tilts the opposite direction, pulling them along.*) We'll see how to do it. Wait and you'll see! Lend me the axe. (*Solicitously*) Now look! I think I'll cut it down myself. (*Our Lord fells the tree.*)

ANCESTOR 3: (*The Ancestors are perplexed, annoyed.*) How did this guy do it?

ANCESTOR 1: How could he use the axe better than us?

ANCESTOR 3: We couldn't do it and he got it down on his own, the bastard!

ANCESTOR 2: He's really evil!

ANCESTOR 1: (*Frightened*) Oh, that's what I told you! Who knows if he isn't our Lord! I think we're going to die.

ANCESTOR 2: (*Turning to Our Lord, recovering his confidence*) How long do you want it?

OUR LORD: Oh, I don't know, but I guess it should be eight meters.

ANCESTOR 2: Meters? What's a meter? How do we do it?

OUR LORD: Yes, crosses should be that size. Don't worry, I'll measure it with my hands. Give me a staff! (*The Ancestors hand him one of their staves. He measures a meter or five hand spans, and then he measures the trunk with the staff.*) *Jun, chib, oxib, chanib, vo'ob, vakib, vukub, vaxakib* [One ... eight]. It's just the right length!

ANCESTOR 3: (*Exasperated*) Oh hell, but what can we do so he'll die right off? (*Our Lord smiles to himself.*)

HOLY MOTHER: Son, but why should we die like this? We're alone with our enemies.

OUR LORD: Be still, Mother! You don't have to worry. We're not going to die. Our Father is in my heart. That's all.

HOLY MOTHER: (*Desperate*) Can that be true? Look at these people! How can we defeat them? If they grab you, I can't defend you. (*Our Holy Mother seats herself and weeps.*)

OUR LORD: (*Heartening her*) I'll defend you, since we're together. You see that I'm big now. Don't be afraid! Don't cry anymore. Stay with me, Mother. (*Our Lord leads his mother to the right. The Ancestors leave the trunk and run after them.*)

ANCESTOR 2: Eh, where are you going? You're not going to escape from us, you bastard!

OUR LORD: (*Annoyed, as if he were talking to a bunch of kids*) I wasn't running away. I was just going to leave my mother here. Wait for me, I'll join you in a minute, you'll see. Damn it, wait a bit! Well, wait for me here, Mother. I'll see what's going to happen to these people. (*Our Lord turns around and begins to walk back to the trunk.*) I'm going to get the trunk I left here. (*Turning to the Ancestors*) Don't you have a little cane liquor to warm me up?

ANCESTORS: (*Bad-tempered*) No, by god!

OUR LORD: Ah well, if there isn't any, never mind! I don't need it. No! I'll try to lift it by myself. The piece for the arms of the cross was left over there. I'll get it. (*Encouraging them*) Don't you worry!

ANCESTOR 2: (*Resigned*) All right. Let him bring it. (*Our Lord brings the beam and places it next to the trunk.*)

OUR LORD: (*Imperiously*) Dress it now, since I brought it myself. I'm going to sit down. (*Our Lord walks over to his mother and sits down while the Ancestors start trying to dovetail the pieces.*)

HOLY MOTHER: (*Imploring*) What are they going to do to you, son?

OUR LORD: (*Affectionately*) Don't cry, Mother. Don't be afraid. I know all about this. I'm grown now. But it's a shame there isn't a bit of cane liquor to warm us up. Never mind, I'll probably think of something tomorrow, since there isn't a drop to drink here!

HOLY MOTHER: Okay. Aren't you hungry?

OUR LORD: Well yes, I'm a little hungry. What do we have to eat?

HOLY MOTHER: Now we have tortillas, now we have corn, but the trouble is we still don't have beans. What do you think we can do, Son?

OUR LORD: I'll think about it right away. You'll see the beans! (*Happily*) They'll grow quickly! There'll be beans in an hour. For them (*gesturing to the Ancestors*) it'll be a year! (*Our Lord stands up, rubs the palms of his hands, takes out some lumps and buries them, then sits down again next to his mother.*) Let's eat the tortillas, mother! Our beans haven't grown yet. Ah, look, there they are! (*The bean plants appear. The Ancestors spot them and are amazed.*)

HOLY MOTHER: (*Proudly*) Now I see them. You buried something, and many kinds came up; white, red, black, striped, our beautiful beans!

OUR LORD: But how am I going to cook them if we don't have a pot? Wait a minute. (*As if by magic, a pot appears.*) Here it is!

HOLY MOTHER: Let's eat, then! (*Addressing the public*) My son invents so many things!

ANCESTOR 1: But how does he know how to invent those things?

OUR LORD: (*Pleased*) Eh, the beans are ready now, Mother! See, I was right. (*Our Lord gets up, and then his mother. He wanders over to see how the work on* *the cross is progressing, while his mother sits down again a little closer.*) Let's go, Mother! Now that we have our beans, we don't have anything to worry about. (*Sarcastically, to the Ancestors*) How's our work going? It isn't ready yet? It seems like you started it a year ago. Look, my beans have already grown up. (*Laughing, mockingly*) My lord, how funny!

ANCESTOR 2: How could it be a year?

ANCESTOR 1: It probably is. For sure!

ANCESTOR 3: What day is it today?

ANCESTOR 2: I don't know.

ANCESTOR 1: Tell us, what day do you think it is today?

HOLY MOTHER: (*Addressing the public*) The days had no names. They didn't have names for the days.

OUR LORD: I don't know. I'll think it up. You know that Monday's over, Tuesday, Wednesday, and Thursday. Today is Friday, tomorrow is Saturday, and the day after, Sunday. That day we'll rest.

ANCESTOR 3: How does he know what the days are called? Eh, something's not right. It's better if we grab him and kill him once and for all!

OUR LORD: (*Very patiently*) Calm down! I still have to fix the cross. (*The Ancestors stand around him, watching him fix his cross. They look upwards as the chips fly into the air.*)

HOLY MOTHER: (*Addressing the public*) My son was working on the seashore. Those chips turned into fish and shellfish when they fell into the water.

ANCESTORS: Fish! Shellfish!

ANCESTOR 2: (*Terrified*) How does he know how to do that?

ANCESTOR 1: What can we do? There's nothing we can do to him.

ANCESTOR 2: First he came with his corn. He made beans grow. He has things move in the water.

ANCESTOR 3: He is a devil. He's not a human being. He isn't one of our countrymen.

ANCESTOR 2: No, but then, what could he be?

ANCESTOR 1: How do you think such things come to his mind? We never work that way.

OUR LORD: (*Authoritatively, with his arms crossed*) Raise the cross!

(*The Ancestors try in vain to lift the cross.*)

ANCESTOR 2: Oh god! What can we do? Let's get together. We'll bring levers. (*They try to prop it up with poles, but they slip.*)

ANCESTOR 3: It slipped! Hell! Why can't we lift it?

ANCESTOR 2: And there are three of us. Something's wrong.

OUR LORD: (*Calmly*) What's the matter? There are three of you. I'm alone. Only my mother is with me. How could she help me?

ANCESTORS: We can't lift it.

OUR LORD: (*Disdainfully*) Okay. I'll see if I can lift it by myself. But don't help me. I never asked you to help me. Move aside, because I could hit you when I lift the cross to my shoulder!

(*Our Lord lifts the cross while the Ancestors mock him. One hits his arms, while another pokes his behind with his staff, and another stands watching. Our Lord carries his cross offstage.*)

ANCESTOR 2: We're going to crucify him!

ANCESTOR 3: Let's hang him up! That's all.

ANCESTOR 2: But what do you guys think? Could he be our Lord? Or is he the Devil?

ANCESTOR 3: There's no way of knowing. But we have to whip him.

(*They whip Our Lord severely as he sits on the base of the cross.*)

ANCESTOR 1: Let's go and take a rest. We're hungry now.

ANCESTOR 2: What should we do with his mother?

ANCESTOR 1: Let her sit there!

ANCESTOR 2: But what if somebody comes and takes him away?

ANCESTOR 1: They can't take him off, because he's fainted.

ANCESTOR 3: Do you think he's dead now?

ANCESTOR 2: We don't know. There's no way of knowing if he's dead or alive.

ANCESTOR 3: We'll see if he's telling the truth!

(*The Ancestors leave on the left. Our Lord is seated and his mother approaches him.*)

OUR LORD: (*He stands up.*) What do you think I should do, Mother? Do you think I should let myself be killed? (*A rooster appears at the top of the curtain and crows. Our Lord looks at it.*) Now call another time if you see somebody coming. Tell me if they're coming! I'll lie down again right away. First I have some work to do. (*A minute passes. The Rooster crows, "cock-a-doodle-do." Our Lord lies down quickly. Nobody comes. Our Lord gets up and looks at the Rooster doubtfully.*) Who's coming? Idiot! (*He hits it and the Rooster flies to the ground.*) You're good for nothing! You lied to me! I was working. Grab it, Mother! (*She does.*) We'll kill this chicken right now. We'll eat it! (*Our Lord takes the squawking rooster from his mother's hands.*) What are you good for? This is what! (*Our Lord pulls its neck and gives it to Our Holy Mother, who puts it in her net.*) Okay, I'll get another bird, Mother!

HOLY MOTHER: Do what you think best.

OUR LORD: I'll call a sparrow. The other wasn't any good. (*The Sparrow perches on Our Lord's hand.*) Let's see, little sparrow, if you're smart! If somebody comes, sing out so I'll know to sit down again. (*Our Lord finds a bright green stone and tosses it in the air. A blue curtain drops.*) See what a beautiful color the sky is now, Mom!

HOLY MOTHER: Yes! You are the creator of everything! (*The Sparrow calls, "chin-chon!" Our Lord lies down quickly.*)

OUR LORD: Our enemies are coming! (*Addressing the public*) That's why I tell you, young men and kids: you shouldn't kill sparrows.

(*The Sparrow exits. The Ancestors appear, leading a blind man, on the left.*)

ANCESTOR 3: (*Jubilant*) Now he's dead! Just as I said. Now he died.

ANCESTOR 1: What do you think we should do?

ANCESTOR 3: Well, this guy is blind.

ANCESTOR 2: If he can see again when he kills the man whom we've dumped here, then we'll believe he is our Lord.

ANCESTOR 1: What will he do?

ANCESTOR 3: We'll give him this spear to kill him!

ANCESTOR 2: We'll see what happens! Make the blind man take the spear!

ANCESTOR 1: Where should he stick it?

ANCESTOR 3: In his heart. Here, in his chest.

(*The Blind Man pokes the spear in every direction and then, with
help, spears Our Lord.*)

BLIND MAN: This is Our Lord! You guys brought me here so that you could kill him! That's what you thought. Just because I'm blind, a good-for-nothing. (*He kneels down.*) Forgive me, Lord, forgive me! (*He stands up.*) My eyes are fine now! Now I can see you!

(*The Blind Man runs off, leaving the Ancestors greatly upset,
overcome with fear.*)

ANCESTOR 2: Ah, how could it be? Then it must be Our Lord!

ANCESTOR 1: Don't bother him.

ANCESTOR 2: (*Stubbornly*) He's dead! He's dead!

ANCESTOR 3: He's bled a lot!

ANCESTOR 2: We'll come to look in three days to see what he does. Then we'll see if he's still lying here.

ANCESTOR 3: Let him dry in the sun! It seems as if he's dead now. His blood fell on the ground. We'll see what he does!

(*The Ancestors exit on the left, two happily, the other concerned. After they leave, Our Lord speaks.*)

OUR LORD: Mother, I can lie here for three hours, but not for three days. I'm not happy about this.

HOLY MOTHER: But you are bleeding.

OUR LORD: That's all right. I want to drink some water. Bring me a little water!

HOLY MOTHER: There's no water here.

OUR LORD: Go look over there! I'll see that it comes up. Bring it to me! I'll drink it.

HOLY MOTHER: (*She gives Our Lord a cup of water, then addresses the public.*) My son created the springs that will be here forever.

OUR LORD: This is how I'm going to die: I will bury myself in the ground, and they'll think I'm dead. But don't be scared, Mom! (*The Ancestors appear again on the left.*)

ANCESTOR 2: Let's take a look! The three days are up.

HOLY MOTHER: (*Smiling as she addresses the public*) They left my son lying there for three hours, but they thought three days had passed. They were confused.

ANCESTOR 1: Eh, let's see how he is! (*Our Lord winks at them. They are stupefied.*) He's come back to life!

ANCESTOR 3: We thought he'd dry up in three days!

ANCESTOR 2: Now he's alive!

ANCESTOR 1: (*Furious, calling on some god unknown to us*) Shut up! God, my Lord, how can I cross myself? (*He crosses himself desperately.*)

ANCESTOR 3: Oh, we'll have to kill him once and for all!

ANCESTOR 2: But how can we kill him? (*Our Lord jumps to the ground.*)

OUR LORD: Okay, don't worry now, Mother.

HOLY MOTHER: Now what are you thinking of doing?

OUR LORD: I'm going to bury myself.

ANCESTORS: Oh! (*Our Lord stands with his arms crossed.*)

OUR LORD: Please dig the hole! (*The Ancestors begin to dig.*)

HOLY MOTHER: (*Sobbing*) What are you saying? Why are you going to bury yourself? You'll die!

OUR LORD: (*Confidently*) I won't die! Wait and see. I'm going to bury myself. But Mother, my blood was spilled here. It will change to chile and grow.

The Ancestors gaze at Our Lord and the newly sprung chile plant, 1996.
Photo courtesy Sna Jtz'ibajom

HOLY MOTHER: Really?

OUR LORD: Yes!

(The Ancestors go look by the foot of the cross, where there is a chile plant.)

ANCESTOR 2: What did he do? Where did the chile come from? Why did this happen?

OUR LORD: It's nothing. It's not worth talking about. Mother, do you still have some of our tortillas?

HOLY MOTHER: There are a few left.

OUR LORD: Cook the beans! Cook the vegetables! Season them with chile. They're good that way! (*Addressing the Ancestors*) Is my grave ready now? It seems to me you've taken a long time. (*The Ancestors have been trying with their staves to dig the grave.*)

ANCESTOR 2: How can we dig it?

OUR LORD: With a stick? What good is that? Okay, wait a minute! (*He gets a hoe and gives it to them.*)

ANCESTORS: What's this?

ANCESTOR 2: Where did he get it?

ANCESTOR 3: Ah, just as I said, he's a devil!

ANCESTOR 1: No, he's Our Lord! Our time is up! We can't do anything! He invented his tool!

OUR LORD: Dig!

ANCESTORS: (*Trying reluctantly*) We can't dig it.

OUR LORD: You can't do it? So ... I'll dig it myself! (*He takes the hoe from them and digs.*) I'm tired of waiting so long.

ANCESTOR 1: It's true what he says!

OUR LORD: It's better if they bury me right away! Mother, bring me my shovel!

HOLY MOTHER: Okay, here it is. (*Our Holy Mother, crying, gives him the shovel.*)

OUR LORD: Don't cry, Mother! Don't be afraid! I know what I'm doing. (*The Ancestors crowd around him, watching.*)

ANCESTOR 2: How does he do it? It seems as if he began twenty years ago. But he doesn't grow old. He still looks like a boy.

OUR LORD: Come here, Mother! Tell me how deep you think I should bury myself!

HOLY MOTHER: I don't know, but ... won't you die if you bury yourself way down? How can you breathe?

OUR LORD: (*Consoling her*) Oh, I know how to do it! (*Addressing the Ancestors*) Okay, bury me! (*The Ancestors try in vain. Our Lord looks at them resignedly.*) I'd better bury myself! Come see me in three days! (*Our Lord lies down and covers himself with a black blanket while Our Holy Mother sobs. A mournful flute can be heard.*)

HOLY MOTHER: (*Crying*) My son has died. He's dead.

ANCESTOR 3: (*Devilishly happy*) Yes, now he's lost! We've done a good job. He'll rot there!

ANCESTOR 2: We'll come in three days to see if he's the same!

ANCESTORS 2 AND 3: We'll dig him up for sure! We'll dig him up! (*The Ancestors exit on the left.*)

HOLY MOTHER: (*Sadly*) The three days aren't up yet. (*The Ancestors return. Our Holy Mother addresses the public.*) They've come to dig him up on the second day. My son still hasn't recovered his strength. Just like when we step on a cocoon that's about to turn into a butterfly. If they hadn't awakened him, who knows if people would never die. We would be immortal! (*One of the Ancestors lifts the blanket covering Our Lord.*)

ANCESTOR 2: (*Surprised*) There's nothing we can do about this! He's still alive!

ANCESTOR 1: Beams of light are coming out of the ground. Our Lord is shining now like city lights. The sun is rising. Three days have passed. (*Only the top of Our Lord's golden crown can be seen.*)

HOLY MOTHER: (*Crying*) Oh, my son!

ANCESTOR 2: (*Desperately*) Forget it! Now there's nothing we can do. We've lost! Don't touch him!

ANCESTOR 1: (*With surprise*) He doesn't even stink!

ANCESTOR 3: (*Obstinately*) Ha! For the good of everyone we've killed him now! (*They withdraw to the left. Our Lord sits up very straight.*)

OUR LORD: Mother! Are you here, Mother?

HOLY MOTHER: I'm here, child!

OUR LORD: (*Triumphantly*) Ah, don't cry now! I've won! (*In a business-like way*) Do we still have our corn, our beans, our chiles, our vegetables?

HOLY MOTHER: (*Bewildered*) I don't know. I didn't look. I thought you were dying.

OUR LORD: (*Confidingly*) I'm not dying. Don't worry. Where did the murderers go?

HOLY MOTHER: I don't know.

OUR LORD: As for me, I see them. They're still over there, bunched up. Now they aren't going to do anything, Mother, but let's go. Let's go to Heaven! The people here are bad.

HOLY MOTHER: Very well.

OUR LORD: (*Decidedly*) We'll return. We'll come back to see which of these people are good and who are the bad ones! Because there were a lot of them who tried to kill us. Come along, Mother, we'll climb up! You shouldn't suffer here anymore! We'll see if San Salvador gives us a home in the sky! (*Our Lord and his mother exit and appear at the top of the curtain, as the Sun and the Moon. The Ancestors come in and lie down. Our Lord addresses them and the public.*) Okay. Now you have your sugarcane! You have your pigs. You will be alive for three more days. See how you treated me! How come, why? I never did anything to you. See, here is my mother, she is the Moon!

HOLY MOTHER: See, here is my son, he is the Sun!

ANCESTOR 2: (*Desperately*) Why does he do this to us?

ANCESTOR 3: (*Shaking his fists at Our Lord*) You're no good!

ANCESTOR 1: (*Fearfully*) He's going to kill us! He'll kill us!

OUR LORD: (*Serenely*) Of course. There were twelve who loved me. They will stay here.

NARRATOR: Then those sonofabitching Judases saw that Our Lord had left. Some tried to find him, but they couldn't find him anywhere. Where would those cowering guys find him? He was in the sky! Those Judases are still walking about. They are vagabonds. (*Then the Ancients exit on the left.*) That's what I heard long ago. Let's have another drink! (*He turns on his cassette player to the most popular song of the time, "No tengo dinero" [I haven't any money].*

Act II

(*In the sky. San Salvador is seated at a table. He is dressed as a bishop. He is busily making notes in a huge tome. A perfect bureaucrat! Our Lord appears, followed by his mother. He is a young man, sure of himself. His mother is a middle-aged woman in her forties.*)

SAN SALVADOR: You've come now?

OUR LORD: I've come.

SAN SALVADOR: Okay, how was it? Do you think it was a good thing, what my children, my offspring did? I have it all recorded here.

OUR LORD: (*Doubtfully*) No, we were treated very badly. They were going to kill me and my mother.

SAN SALVADOR: (*Taking interest*) Don't worry anymore. We'll think up something.

OUR LORD: (*Vehemently*) We'll see what punishment to give them!

SAN SALVADOR: (*Distracted, taking notes*) Oh, okay.

OUR LORD: (*Imploringly, turning to his mother who has been standing all the time with her hands tucked in her waist, and her head lowered.*) Don't you think so, Mother?

HOLY MOTHER: (*Doubtfully*) You're right, son, whatever you say, since we're here now in the sky with San Salvador.

OUR LORD: (*Firmly*) We'll go down and talk to the Earth Lord.

HOLY MOTHER: (*Horrified*) But it's too horrible down there. The stink! The ground stinks horribly. I don't want people eating each other. No, it's bad! While I was climbing up, I could still smell them. The smell reached halfway up. But we must punish them!

SAN SALVADOR: (*Putting down his pen and leaning back, with his thumbs stuck in his robes*) Okay, we can punish them. I've seen that they are very bad. (*Stretching himself*) What kind of punishment do you think we should request for our children?

OUR LORD: (*In command again*) Wait and we'll see. I'll go ask the Earth Lords to help us.

SAN SALVADOR: I'm very busy here with my papers. I haven't time to take a walk.

OUR LORD: So I'll go quickly. (*While he is coming down to the cave, he addresses the public.*) You know that the Earth Lords live in the mountains. You go to visit them every day on Holy Cross Day to ask them for rain, to protect you from snakes, and protect the crops from wind. They are so rich they can give you gold, but then they take away your souls. You must be their slaves until the soles of your sandals wear out! They can even give you their most beautiful daughters, but you have to be careful because when night comes, they turn into serpents.

(*Our Lord reaches the Earth Lords' cave. One of them comes in to sit at a table. He is dressed elegantly in black, like a charro, with a huge sombrero, pistol, and long spurs. With inquisitive black eyes, shining white teeth, and a big belly that hangs over his belt, he is impressive. Our Holy Mother Earth, with long, black hair, dressed in a green robe, decorated with snakes, follows him, holding a snake in her teeth. She drops it on the table and sits down next to the table, where she spins cotton thread in a gourd.*)

OUR LORD: Are you there, sir?

EARTH LORD: Yes, I'm here. What do you want?

OUR LORD: Look, sir, we've just come to an agreement with San Salvador to send down punishment on all the evil people, and we need your help because we should do it together.

EARTH LORD: (*With a loud voice, but indecisive*) But … how do you think we should punish them? The problem is that I can't do anything on my own.

OUR LORD: But would you like to have them here with you?

EARTH LORD: (*Giving himself the air of importance*) No, that certainly wouldn't be right. I've already had a lot of trouble with them.

OUR LORD: (*Serenely*) I believe we should bring rain to cover the earth with water, and if you don't help me … (*Threateningly*) Would you want your house to collapse? I know what I can do!

EARTH LORD: (*With ill-concealed alarm*) What would you do?

OUR LORD: You will feel … the earth moving suddenly. (*The curtain and the table shake violently.*)

EARTH LORD: (*Frightened*) What's that?

OUR LORD: If you want, I'll show you. It was just your house posts. Do you have a lot of posts for your house? Just four, held up by the wind. I've seen them. Your posts will collapse right away if I push them.

EARTH LORD: (*Promptly*) No, I don't want you to push them. Do us the favor! It's better if we punish our children.

OUR LORD: (*Complacently*) Okay, that's fine. We'll send the rain!

EARTH LORD: (*Confused*) The rain? Where will it come from?

OUR LORD: (*Addressing the public*) Maybe the Earth Lord said that because it hadn't rained for a long time. (*A cloud appears on the right.*)

EARTH LORD: (*Alarmed*) What's this cloud doing here?

OUR LORD: (*Authoritatively*) Wait and see! (*Our Lord turns to Our Holy Mother Earth.*) Go see where that cloud is coming from! Speak to it! It knows how to talk.

HOLY MOTHER EARTH: What should I say to it?

OUR LORD: Please ask it for rain.

HOLY MOTHER EARTH: (*Eagerly*) Okay, okay. (*She talks insistently to the cloud while Our Lord watches.*) Please, Lady Cloud, we want you to help us! We've come to ask you a big favor.

CLOUD: (*Speaking with slow, measured words*) Okay … what do you want?

HOLY MOTHER EARTH: We want some rain.

CLOUD: Oh, what kind of rain do you want?

HOLY MOTHER EARTH: We want downpours!

CLOUD: That's fine. When it stops raining, the water will make paths and drop down to make the ocean. (*The Cloud shakes; rain can be heard.*)

OUR LORD: How is the rain? Did the cloud obey?

HOLY MOTHER EARTH: She said "yes," … Don't worry, the earth will be flooded.

OUR LORD: (*Pensively*) That's fine! The rain will come from the west. Since the earth is very flat, part will be water and part will be left as mountains.

HOLY MOTHER EARTH: How will the mountains be made?

OUR LORD: (*Laughing indulgently*) Oh, wait and you'll see, but not until the rain stops. (*Everyone exits, and the narrator appears.*)

NARRATOR: (*Speaking strongly, while two characters with two puppets apiece place them in boxes and toss them into the blue curtain*) The rain came. My lord! It came and the earth was flooded. Some tried to climb up on the roofs. Others climbed trees. They tried to escape the best they could. But what could they do? Where could they go? Nowhere. Just the twelve who loved our Lord thought to make their chests, like coffins. Little by little they were lifted up as if they were canoes. The water reached halfway up the sky. All the others died. Our Lord was watching. He thought it was funny. He said, "How good!" The rain stopped. The water began to run. It formed rivers and ravines. The sea was left. That is where Our Lord disappears. Where Our Lord rises, the place is covered with water, too, they say. That is where the oceans are. Okay, the water dried up, but we couldn't walk there.

OUR LORD: (*Back in the sky*) Now I'm happy! Come here, Buzzard! Come see what the earth is like, and come tell me if it's drying up now, but don't you eat anything!

BUZZARD: That's fine, my Lord! I'll go see. (*It flies off.*)

OUR LORD: (*Waiting impatiently*) That damned buzzard never brought me news. It's fine if it keeps on eating rotten meat. Now I'll call the dove. (*Our Holy Mother, the Moon, appears near Our Lord.*)

(*Addressing the Dove*) You go! Go and see what the earth is like! If we can walk there yet, then I'll go. (*The Dove flies away, then returns. The Dove coos.*)

DOVE: Coo, coo!

OUR LORD: (*Translating*) "It's still not possible."

DOVE: Coo, coo!

OUR LORD: "I tried to land on the ground."

DOVE: Coo!

OUR LORD: "My feet got stuck in the mud."

HOLY MOTHER: Oh, that's why you came with white feet. That won't come off. You'll stay that way forever.

OUR LORD: Did you take a good sniff? How does it smell?

DOVE: Coo, coo!

OUR LORD: "It still stinks!" Oh, well, then I'll wait. Go one more time!

DOVE: Coo!

OUR LORD: You've come back. Is it dry yet?

DOVE: Coo!

OUR LORD: "Now we can go!" (*He turns to his mother, beseechingly.*) Let's go see what the earth is like!

HOLY MOTHER: But . . . I think it was ruined by the water.

OUR LORD: (*Persistently*) I don't believe it! It's there. Let's go take a look! We'll go and see!

HOLY MOTHER: Okay, but be careful. (*Our Lord appears down below and walks with care. Then he gestures triumphantly up to his mother.*)

OUR LORD: You see, I was right! It's dry now, Mother!

HOLY MOTHER: Ah, fine!

(*The Ancestors enter with messy clothes and sprawl on the ground. One of them has wrapped his neckerchief around his head like a turban. He has lost his tunic and curls up, shaking.*)

OUR LORD: (*Merrily*) How are you, guys?

ANCESTOR 1: (*Grumbling*) We're alive.

OUR LORD: (*Inquisitively*) How was it? What did you eat?

ANCESTOR 2: (*Angrily*) What do you care? We ate fruits on vines, on trees, whatever we could find!

OUR LORD: Are you alone?

ANCESTOR 2: We're alone.

OUR LORD: Oh, what did you do? How did you survive?

ANCESTOR 3: Don't tell me you don't know! It's your fault! May God punish you for doing what you did to us and to our friends that aren't here any longer!

OUR LORD: (*Hiding his anger and pretending to be very calm*) That's fine! Now don't you say anything else. Turn around and look at your behinds! (*They look behind and see that they have sprouted tails. When they look in front they have howler monkey faces.*)

(*Confidently*) You will be hairy and have long tails. That's what happened to you for not obeying, and you will go on eating the fruits of trees and vines. That's what you'll live on for the rest of your lives! (*The Animals exit. The lone man gets up, then crouches silently.*)

(*Merrily*) How are you doing?

MAN: (*Exhausted*) My Lord, I'm suffering! I'm very sad. I'm hungry.

OUR LORD: What? You didn't eat?

MAN: No. Where would I have found anything to eat in so much water?

OUR LORD: (*Sympathetically*) Okay, thanks to Our Lord you were saved. Mother, didn't you bring our tortillas?

HOLY MOTHER: (*Meekly*) Here they are!

OUR LORD: Here are our beans, Mom!

HOLY MOTHER: How do you want me to cook them for you?

OUR LORD: Okay . . . Put chile on them, and salt. (*Thinking*) Oh, but we left the salt behind. Bring it, Mother!

HOLY MOTHER: (*Unable to hide her irritation*) Do you think I know where to go?

OUR LORD: (*Animated, as always*) Okay, then I'll go. (*Our Lord exits on the right and returns in a minute with a handful of salt, which he gives his mother. Addressing his mother and the public.*) Salt was the foam that was left after the flood water evaporated. Just like now, when you make salt, it's what's left on the bottom of the pots. (*To his mother*) Now give this poor man something to eat! See how he is suffering! (*The Man eats. The Animals return and approach slowly. Our Lord turns to the man, worried.*) Are you all right?

MAN: (*Sitting quietly, trying to be brave*) I'm fine, but . . . I feel so sad! The problem is that I don't have anyone to talk to. I'm all alone. Oh, where did my friends go?

OUR LORD: (*Secretly amused*) Where did these animals come from?

MAN: I don't know. What happened to my friends?

OUR LORD: (*Implacable*) Oh, weren't you chatting together?

MAN: I was talking to them, but . . . (*Shaking his head*) That was a long time ago.

OUR LORD: (*Sympathetically*) Yes, it probably was. Okay, don't worry. Do you see those animals? They were your friends. (*Pointing at them offhandedly*) They don't talk anymore. Even so, they'll still be your friends. (*A bunch of bananas appears on the right. The Monkeys grab them, eat them, and scratch their faces and pubic areas, chuckling.*)

MAN: (*Fervently*) No, I don't like that. I'm scared of them. Because now they're hairy!

OUR LORD: (*Pretending to be unable to do anything about it*) Ah, no, but there's nothing we can do. (*Slyly*) What? You don't want to join the animals? (*Unconcerned, he pushes the Monkeys aside so they can go into the forest.*)

MAN: (*Becoming more desperate*) I didn't notice. It's horrible for me to only have animals for company. I want to have a good time with a human being. But please, my Lord, find a companion for me!

OUR LORD: (*Contemplatively*) I don't know. I'll think about it. All your friends have died, but I'll go see if I can find a companion someplace. I'll come tomorrow, but I have work to do now.

MAN: Ah, fine! But please don't leave me all alone.

OUR LORD: But don't you fall asleep. It's too early to sleep. (*Shaking his finger*) It's not right! (*Our Lord and his mother exit. The Man sleeps. Our Lord returns stealthily and removes one of the man's ribs while the man, lying on his back, shifts back and forth. Our Lord exits and then returns. He speaks to the Man with disgust.*) Wake up! What are you doing?

MAN: (*Shaking his head*) Hell, I fell asleep.

OUR LORD: (*Imperiously*) It's late, man! Why do you sleep so much?

MAN: (*Meekly*) I don't know. I fell asleep.

OUR LORD: Ah, are you still alone?

MAN: (*Lifting his head*) Yes, I'm alone now.

OUR LORD: (*Sympathetically*) Okay. I've come with my mother. See, do you want to talk to a companion? (*The Man nods affirmatively.*) Look at your side! Are you perfectly all right?

MAN: (*Confused*) I don't know.

OUR LORD: (*Emboldening him*) Feel if you're in good shape! (*Pointing to his chest*)

MAN: (*Panic-stricken*) What? Is my rib gone?

OUR LORD: Where did you put it? It wasn't that you ate it?

MAN: (*Totally confused*) I just don't know. I didn't feel anything.

OUR LORD: (*Still severely*) Ah, I was right to think you would go to sleep. That's why you've had this bad luck. (*More gently*) It's okay. (*He goes to his mother, who brings forward a girl and moves her next to the man.*)

MAN: (*Looking her up and down*) Oh, thank you, may God repay you!

OUR LORD: (*In a fatherly way*) Well, I bless you. Things will turn out well for you and your wife. But don't do anything bad. No! Behave yourselves! I don't want you to do anything bad. Do you understand?

MAN AND WOMAN: That's fine.

OUR LORD: Okay, there is fruit here. There are apples here. But don't eat them until I come again! And don't steal them!

MAN AND WOMAN: Ah, fine! (*Our Lord, followed by his mother, exits. A serpent appears through the curtain, with an apple.*)

SERPENT: Pst! Pst! Eh, look at this! I have an apple here! Eat it, it's delicious! Our Lord said you could eat it.

WOMAN: Ah, thank you very much! (*The Woman takes the apple, sniffs it, and takes a bite. Then she offers it to the Man.*) Take it, eat it! (*The Man eats it, and at this moment Our Lord and his mother return.*)

OUR LORD: (*Annoyed*) What are you doing? (*The Man is startled. The apple sticks in his throat.*)

MAN: (*Touching his Adam's apple, very confused*) I don't know what this is!

OUR LORD: (*Angrily*) Ah, isn't it the apple? I told you both not to eat them! (*Changing his mood, very pleased with himself*) What did you think of the woman? Are you satisfied with her? Talk to her. Don't be worried about her! Now you can eat apples.

HOLY MOTHER: Are they just going to eat apples?

OUR LORD: No. (*Cheering them up again*) Soon you are going to have piles of beans and corn, so you can eat! Work, but I don't want you to do anything bad with the woman! Please behave yourselves. You will eat together. It's good if you chat with her.

MAN: Ah, but what can we do if we don't have a house?

OUR LORD: Build your house! (*Our Lord and the Man fashion its form with their hands, next to the curtain.*)

MAN: We will build a house with a thatch roof and mud and wattle walls.

OUR LORD: But sleep apart! Don't sleep together! (*Showing them*) One sleeps here, and the other over there!

MAN: (*Gesturing*) So this is the border between us and women.

MAN AND WOMAN: Ah, okay! (*They lie down separately. Our Lord exits. The Devil appears on the left, dressed all in red with a red hood and tail.*)

DEVIL: (*Smiling*) Okay, okay. Where are you going?

OUR LORD: (*Merrily*) I'm going to see my children, my offspring.

DEVIL: Where are your children?

OUR LORD: Over there! (*Pointing to the left*)

DEVIL: The ones who have a house?

OUR LORD: Yes.

DEVIL: Ah, they're the ones?

OUR LORD: Yes.

DEVIL: How did they build their house?

OUR LORD: They made it themselves.

DEVIL: Okay. Let's go together and see them!

OUR LORD: (*In a good mood*) Let's go! (*Gesturing to his mother*) Come, Mother, don't go off and leave me! (*Turning to the Devil*) Where are you from?

DEVIL: (*Giving a big smile*) I don't know where I'm from. (*To the public, with a knowing wink*) That's why nobody knows where the Devil comes from. (*Our Lord looks over his shoulder to make sure that his mother is right behind.*)

OUR LORD: Hurry up, Mother! (*Our Lord arrives at the house and knocks on the door.*) Are you there?

MAN: We're here.

OUR LORD: Are you happy?

MAN: I'm happy. I can talk pretty now.

OUR LORD: Ah, do you still have some tortillas?

MAN: They're running out.

OUR LORD: Tomorrow I'll show you how to plant your corn and your beans.

MAN: Yes . . . really? It's tortillas that we're going to need.

OUR LORD: (*Explicitly*) You have to plant. I'm going to show you how.

MAN: Oh, okay.

DEVIL: (*Elbowing Our Lord*) This is where your children are?

OUR LORD: (*Proudly*) Yes!

DEVIL: (*Sidling up to Our Lord*) And how come there is a man and a woman? Are they going to multiply?

OUR LORD: (*Pulling back, alarmed*) No!

DEVIL: (*Sidling up again*) Eh, why do you think they aren't going to multiply? They are going to do a few little things. (*Winking maliciously*)

OUR LORD: (*Lowering his head, confused*) I don't know.

DEVIL: (*Putting his arm around Our Lord, holding him as tight as he can, while two Monkeys bring in a barrel apiece*) We're good friends. Do you want to drink a beer?

OUR LORD: (*Surprised*) Is there beer here?

DEVIL: (*Nodding, and leading Our Lord to a large barrel. Our Holy Mother sits down next to the house. The Devil puts his arm around Our Lord again.*) Yes, and there's another kind, too. (*Slyly he offers a cup to the public.*) Now the sugar is cooking away. Try it! (*They drink, toasting each other.*)

DEVIL: We're going to heat it up a little more! But don't you look! (*The Devil, with his back to the audience, unzips his fly. A Monkey hands him his fiddle, which he plays as he dances with his back to the audience, three times around the barrel, pissing.*) Now you can look! (*Our Lord turns around.*) Drink this! (*The Devil, with his left hand, offers Our Lord a shot. He takes it.*)

OUR LORD: *¡Kich'ban, kumpa!*

DEVIL: *¡Ich'o kumpágre!* Eh, let's have another. We'll play some of our music. (*He turns on his boom box to* "El demonio colorado" ["The Red Devil"], *and together with the Monkeys, they all dance. The Man and the Woman get up from their bed and dance discreetly, too.*) Up until now there never were fiestas, nor music. Just silence. There wasn't any *pox* until I had to bless it. Now they will sing at fiestas, because the musicians will have warmed up. Don't you see that with cane liquor you have one word, and I have the other? That's why I'll be next to the person who drinks a lot. That's how people get into trouble. Ha, ha! Ha, ha!

OUR LORD: Oh god, so I'm going to drink? My god!

DEVIL: And that's why they will say, *"Riox, kajval,"* "God, my Lord," when they drink. They'll remember Your Highness! (*Guffawing*) But I'll take another! (*The Devil drinks it down, then offers another shot to Our Lord, who turns his back as he downs it.*)

OUR LORD: (*Shaking his head*) It seems good. It seems good. But the trouble is that it does things to my head.

DEVIL: (*Merrily*) You're right. But never mind, let's go see your kids. Let's go! Let's go see them! (*They arrive at the door. Our Lord staggers a bit as he knocks on the door, opening it suddenly to discover the Man and the Woman embracing in bed.*)

OUR LORD: (*Falling back with alarm, his crown tipping and about to fall*) What … what are you doing?

MAN: (*Submissively*) Uh, uh … nothing, nothing!

OUR LORD: (*Doubtfully*) Eh, but why are you together?

MAN: But we're about two meters apart!

DEVIL: (*With a triumphant smile, tugging at Our Lord*) What did I tell you? (*Putting his arm over his shoulder again*) You said they wouldn't multiply. That's just what they're going to do!

The Devil offers Our Lord a shot of cane liquor, 2007. Photo courtesy Sna Jtz'ibajom

OUR LORD: (*Confused, supporting himself drunkenly by the door*) What is it they do to each other?

DEVIL: (*Addressing the public*) Now the gentleman is confused. Ha, ha, ha! (*Laughing insidiously*) But he'll probably get used to it, as they say. Sometimes when I pet a woman, then she thinks of all the rest. Do you understand? Ha, ha, ha! (*The Devil exits. Our Lord, recovering, speaks dubiously.*) Are you guys okay that way?

MAN AND WOMAN: (*In unison*) I don't know.

> (*The Man and the Woman sit up in bed. Our Lord stumbles to a little chair and sits down. Our Holy Mother follows him and sits on the ground in the far corner.*)

OUR LORD: (*Straightening his crown*) Okay, I'll come to see you tomorrow. Tomorrow I'll come and see you again. But I don't want you to be together like that. (*Shaking his finger, reproving them*) I want you to sleep apart. Chat, but sitting, like me.

MAN: What is this? (*Discovering a coke bottle half full of cane liquor and stoppered with a corn cob*)

OUR LORD: (*He looks at it, trying to remember where it came from.*) I don't know. (*He picks it up and passes it with a trembling hand to the man.*) Have it on me! Try it. I brought it for you.

MAN: (*Astutely*) Who gave it to you?

OUR LORD: (*Trying to compose himself*) My friend! (*Smiling openly and drunkenly*) My *compadre* brought me this gift! Try what's left! (*Handing it over again*)

MAN: (*Trying a swallow from the bottle*) Ah!

OUR LORD: Is it good?

MAN: It's good! It's good! But can you drink a lot?

OUR LORD: (*Reseating himself and shrugging his shoulders so hard that his crown nearly falls off*) As for me, I took two shots.

MAN: (*Very reasonably*) But . . . what do you think can happen with two shots?

OUR LORD: (*His head wobbling forward*) Take a couple of shots!

MAN: (*Taking a big swallow, rubbing his mouth and spitting a bit out*) Ah! It's good, but the trouble is that it feels as if it will burn our mouths. It's very hot.

OUR LORD: (*Taking the bottle and passing it insistently to the Man*) Take it, have another swallow!

MAN: (*Swallowing*) It's good, it's good. Can I give it to my wife?

OUR LORD: No, it's not for women! (*The Man furtively passes it to his wife, who drinks a shot and quickly hands it back to him before he returns it to Our Lord, who speaks to them paternalistically.*) But don't you drink any more! I'm going to leave it with you. I'm going to put the leftover here. But I don't want you to drink it. Tomorrow I want to find it at the same level, but if you polish it off . . . surely something very bad will happen to you!

MAN: That's fine.

OUR LORD: (*In the same tone of voice*) But sleep apart! I don't want you to sleep the way I found you!

MAN AND WOMAN: (*In unison*) That's fine! (*Our Lord staggers out with the help of Our Holy Mother.*)

OUR HOLY MOTHER: What's the matter with you?

OUR LORD: I don't know. (*They exit and then return, Our Lord yawning and stretching his arms over his head.*) Oh god, what a hangover! (*He arrives at the door and, entering, notices that the Man and Woman are together in bed.*) Oh, where's the leftover drink?

MAN: (*Sitting up slowly*) Don't you remember? We drank it!

OUR LORD: (*Very sarcastically*) It doesn't matter. (*Resigned*) I'm getting over my hangover. And I've found you sleeping just like yesterday. Did you just sleep?

MAN: That's all! That's all! That's all! Really!

OUR LORD: (*Turning to the Man and the Woman*) Ah, okay, okay! Well, you can stay here. It doesn't matter. I won't do anything to you. It's just that you've gotten into a little trouble. Watch out! I was going to come to see you, but now we're not going to talk together. Not anymore! Because you are sinners. You're probably going to have children!

WOMAN: (*Feeling her stomach*) That's probably true.

MAN: Oh god, what'll we do?

HOLY MOTHER: You'll see in nine days!

MAN: (*Kneeling humbly*) In the name of God, but what can we do, my Lord?

HOLY MOTHER: Get a little *pox*!

OUR LORD: (*Magnanimously*) I will bless you. You should be happy because you are two individuals. You should be blessed.

HOLY MOTHER: (*Addressing the public*) So we've had *pox* all this time. (*The Woman cries out.*)

(*Speaking to the Man*) Give me the *pox*, then give it to your wife! (*The Man serves both. She addresses the public again.*) The child is about to be born. Now the child is born. (*She tosses the blanket off the baby.*) It's fine. That's how we began. That's how we multiplied.

OUR LORD: (*He exits and returns, carrying a stack of paper.*) I will leave you something to look at. You must look at it. You will learn, because I'm going to leave it with you.

NARRATOR: (*He appears, stands next to Our Lord, and addresses the public.*) Our Lord left three boxes of paper and a pen. Like what some people use for their work. Our Lord gave it to them.

OUR LORD: You will learn!

NARRATOR: Our Lord said that. That's why it's important that you learn to read and write in our language. Don't be ashamed! Wake up! Wake up! Protect our culture, our language is our seed. That's the truth! (*Smiling with much feeling*)

NARRATOR AND OUR LORD: (*In unison*) Knowledge is power!

NARRATOR: Okay, thanks to Our Lord, now you know what I know! The next time you get a little *pox* or whatever, tell this story. It will make you as rich and wise as I am! (*Smiling, he waves good-bye, straightens his hat, and turns on his boom box to* "No tengo dinero." *Our Lord steps forward.*)

OUR LORD: So I tell you, one and all, put your mind to it. Learn to read and write in your own tongue!

Workers in the Other World

(1998)

WORKERS IN THE OTHER WORLD (*Trabajadores en el otro mundo*) is a revision of *Don Tomate y sus coyotes*, which was created the previous year in Immokalee, Florida. With raucously grim humor this play charts the travels of a pair of poor Chamulans who go to the border only to be tricked by the *coyote*. After they finally cross the border, they are driven across the country, packed in a van. Arriving in Florida, they are set to work picking tomatoes. One worker is physically abused, but they discover that there is no legal aid for undocumented workers. At a bar Don Tomate drops his wallet. It is picked up by the Chamulan, who buys flashy gringo clothes for himself and his wife. While the finale of the first play celebrated the foundation of the Coalition of Immokalee Workers, this play, directed to a Chiapas audience, ends with the Chamulan immigrant returning home to die of AIDS. So relevant is this drama to the present situation, with thousands of Chamulans having traveled to the States, that six years after its creation there have been requests from various communities anxious to see it again. An innovation in this play, whether performed in Spanish or Tzotzil, is the addition of English—"Eye luv yu!" "Wat?" For the majority of the audience who have never heard a word of English before, this invariably brings out roars of laughter. A slightly shorter version of *Workers in the Other World*, directed in 2003 by our intern, Reynaldo Pacheco, is now being shown in Chiapas.

The *coleto auténtico* immigrants are the people of San Cristóbal (*coletos*), who, witnessing with disgust and anger Samuel Ruiz's sympathy for Indians in general and the Zapatistas in particular, named themselves as being the only true members of the city. It is widely believed that the only members of those "authentic" families remaining in San Cristóbal are individuals too slow to venture to Mexico City. Most of them would not deign to lower themselves by seeking a job under gringos across the border.

There is little evidence that AIDS is commonly contracted by Mayas who seek work in the United States. Mayas assume that prostitutes are the bearers of that disease, considered particularly fearful since it cannot ever be cured by shamans.

Despite the fact that many Mayas feel compelled economically to cross the border, work for a couple of years, and return home with some cash, in wealthier towns such as Zinacantán the number is reduced to the adventurers. Two former members of Sna Jtz'ibajom, both Chamulans, are now in the States. In every town there are those who advise against abandoning their gods and their people.

PRESUMIDO: Chamulan wetback, wearing Texas hat, bright shirt and shorts, metal-tipped boots

TUMIN: poor Chamulan, wearing Chamulan clothes, then black hat and mestizo clothes at border, then bright gringo shirt and shorts, sporty shoes

XUNKA': wife of Tumin, wearing Chamulan clothes, then bright blouse, pants, and slippers

MATYO: brother of Tumin, wearing Chamulan clothes

LOXA: wife of Matyo, wearing Chamulan clothes

GRANDFATHER OF TUMIN AND MATYO: wearing Chamulan clothes

SMUGGLER 1: evil smuggler, wearing mestizo clothes

SMUGGLER 2: good Indian smuggler (Presumido), wearing hat and jacket

MIGRA: Immigration official, wearing black clothes and cap

FARMERS 1 AND 2: wearing mestizo clothes

FOREMAN: wearing mestizo clothes

WORKERS 1 AND 2: wearing mestizo clothes

WOMAN WORKER: wearing mestizo clothes

DON TOMATE: gringo rancher, wearing a large tomato mask covering his whole head

LABOR LAWYER: wearing black hat, dark glasses, a gray suit and tie

VICTIMS 1 AND 2: wearing mestizo clothes

WAITRESS: wearing a bright red blouse and skirt

WETBACKS 1 AND 2: wearing mestizo clothes

SHAMAN: a woman wearing Chamulan clothes

Act I

SCENE 1

(A street at the entrance of Chamula. A Chamulan who has been to the United States appears, dressed in bright gringo clothes, talking to himself.)

PRESUMIDO: *(Showing off)* The guy who left has come back! Hello! How are you? Good morning! Yeah, how are you? I speak good. I'm a different man. Now I'm civilized, a bit slicked up, but I can do the English, my darling. What do you think of me? *(He bumps into Tumin and Xunka' as they enter and greet him.)*

TUMIN: Hello!

PRESUMIDO: Oh, hello cousin, how y'all doin'? But what happened to you? You're so dirty, so filthy, so bad!

TUMIN: But who are you? Aren't you Joe Doe?

PRESUMIDO: O you don member me? O, you're kinda dum. O, no, no! Eyem Xapax.

TUMIN: He's the one they said was lost.

XUNKA': Could that be him? He's the one you told me taught you how to drink cane liquor. He's the one who wanted to pick me up.

TUMIN: How you doing? How've you been? Where'd you go?

PRESUMIDO: Oh, I went to the Estaros Sumidos. Look at my clothes! And I have a gold watch with five alarms. My boots have metal tips. My sombrero is Texan.

TUMIN: Do you still know how to speak our language?

PRESUMIDO: A teeny bit, a tiny bit. And what are you doing?

TUMIN: I'm going home now. I'm going to rest. We went to do some work.

PRESUMIDO: Oh, so that's why you're dressed like that. That's why you're all covered with dust. And you, how've you been?

TUMIN: Well, I just stayed here. I grow turnips and potatoes. And you, where are you going to stay since you sold your house?

PRESUMIDO: Well, I'm going to stay in my father-in-law's home while I build a two-story house.

XUNKA': But your wife married somebody else!

PRESUMIDO: (*Surprised, speaks in Tzotzil*) What do you mean? She went off with somebody else?

TUMIN: Yes, she did.

PRESUMIDO: Never mind, I've got loads of women up there. And my children?

TUMIN: Both your son and your daughter are married. She has a little boy. You're a grandfather now!

PRESUMIDO: Oh, okay, I'll bring him a green-eyed grandma.

XUNKA': I see you've grown fat. What did you eat?

PRESUMIDO: Oh, food with lots of groovy, I mean gravy. Food to fatten you up.

TUMIN: And how did you do? Is there a lot of work there?

PRESUMIDO: Yes, there's loads of work. And you can find money anywhere. They even use it in the restrooms to clean themselves!

TUMIN: (*Surprised, doubtful*) Oh, how great! And ... do you own a house there?

PRESUMIDO: Of course, a whole building and some factories! Yes, it's true. I've got a lot of money. Why don't you go up there? Life is different there. It's much better. I even own a bank! I was going to come in my plane, but the trouble is there's no place where I could land because of all the mountains around here.

TUMIN: And do the women work up there?

PRESUMIDO: Naturally! If your wife goes along with you, between the two of you, you'll be able to buy a new car.

XUNKA': Is that place far away or is it nearby? Could we walk there?

PRESUMIDO: Yes, it's kinda far, but you can make it!

TUMIN: You have a good idea. How much money do you think I should take?

PRESUMIDO: Oh, you have to spend a bunch.... Take a million pesos apiece and you won't need to worry. When you get there, right away you'll pick up enough money to keep going. You can earn a thousand pesos a day.

TUMIN: But ... is it true that the white guys eat children? Because I have a baby.

PRESUMIDO: No, that's not the case!

TUMIN: I'm gonna see how I can get the money!

PRESUMIDO: Well, if you own anything, sell all of it!

TUMIN: You're right. I still have my land that I inherited, my house, my burro, and other animals. And do I have to learn some English so I can talk with them?

PRESUMIDO: Oh, yes! What you have to learn is "Eye luv yu."

EVERYONE: Eye luv yu.

PRESUMIDO: That's the most important thing to learn. If they speak to you, then answer back that way! But you also have to say *chingado,* fuck, over and over, 'cause if five minutes pass without you saying *chingado,* they'll know you aren't from Mexico.

TUMIN: And you ... when do you think you're goin' back there?

PRESUMIDO: I'm not going yet. I came to spend all my money. And my guys are working away in my factory. You oughta go. You'll see how your life changes!

TUMIN: Okay, then. Thanks for your advice. We'll see you!

PRESUMIDO: You said it! *Hasta luego,* bye, bye! (*The couple exits and the conceited guy talks to himself.*) Ha, ha! Now they'll see you can't pick up any money up there. They'll suffer the way I did! We'll all be the same!

SCENE 2

(*In a house in Chamula, Matyo, Tumin's younger brother, is lunching with his wife. Tumin and his wife arrive to pay a visit.*)

TUMIN: (*Knocks and greets his brother*) Hello, Matyo, I came to visit. Can I sit down?

MATYO: That's fine. Come in and take a chair!

TUMIN: I came by to see if you'd join me when I go looking for work.

MATYO: Where to?

TUMIN: I heard how there's work in the States, in the white guy's land.

MATYO: So it's the truth!

TUMIN: Yes, I've thought it over, and I know I'm going.

MATYO: You thought it over, but what if something happens to you there and you die? You aren't going to leave your wife behind, are you? Because she's very pretty. She might run off with some other guy.

TUMIN: No, for sure I won't! I'm not gonna leave her. We're going together. So if you want to go with me, you have to take your wife too. It's better up there. We'll earn loads of money! We'll even be able to buy a car!

LOXA: You really mean to go, Xunka'? Wouldn't it be better if you stayed here and kept on working? You have a little land.

XUNKA': We've thought it over very carefully. We've seen that we can't make it with the tiny bit we produce.

LOXA: And you're going to take your baby, too?

XUNKA': Yes, because we haven't baptized it yet. When we earn some money, then we'll baptize it. And you will be its godmother.

MATYO: The truth is, I don't want to go because if I leave my wife behind, some-body could grab her because she's the prettiest one around. What do you think, Loxa? Do you want to go and work in the States?

LOXA: I'm not going because I don't know the way. I'm used to living here. I don't want to abandon my parents, my brothers. Think it over! If you want to go, then go! I don't need anyone to take your place!

MATYO: That's true!... No, I'm never going to leave behind this land that our ancestors handed down to us. I don't want to die in some foreign place. I want to die in my own town.

TUMIN: Well, we do want to go to some other world because we're so poor here.

MATYO: We know what we're doing. What if a bunch of men decided to rape my wife? No, it's better if we stay here once and for all!

TUMIN: Okay, too bad, I thought you'd go with us, but if you think it's a bad idea, never mind. So, I just want to ask you if you want to buy my TV, my burro and my turkeys. That will help me pay for my trip.

MATYO: Okay, but I can only pay you for half their value! (*Grandfather enters.*)

GRANDFATHER: *Buenos días,* children!

BROTHERS: *Buenos días,* Grandfather!

LOXA: (*Friendly*) So, you've come to visit us?

MATYO: Sit down, take a seat! Come next to the fire. It's cold.

GRANDFATHER: That's fine, thank you! It seems I can't bear the cold anymore. You know there's no one to keep me warm!

MATYO: Yes, but what can you do? See here, Grandfather, my brother and his wife are inviting me to look for work in the gringos' country. He says there's even work for our wives.

GRANDFATHER: And for how long do you plan to go?

TUMIN: A year, because you can't get much money in one or two months. You have to go for a long time. You've seen that you can't earn much here anymore. Everything costs more. We're terribly poor.

GRANDFATHER: What, you can't live off what you earn? If you have some pieces of land, you just need to work because that's how our ancestors survived. You shouldn't abandon San Juan.

TUMIN: I've spoken to Our Lord, and he pays no attention to me.

XUNKA': What my husband says is true, Grandfather. With the money we get here, we can't even clothe ourselves!

GRANDFATHER: And why do you think that? It's better if you don't go. They say that in that other place women get raped.

TUMIN: Don't try to scare us, Grandfather. We're not going to obey you any longer. Your ideas and your advice don't help me anymore. It's not the way it was when you were young. Your brain's wearing out!

GRANDFATHER: Well, son, there's no use talking if you aren't going to listen to me. You'll see there what happens.

TUMIN: Never mind, Xunka'. If they don't like it, they can stay. We know how to read and write a little. I can speak a few words in Spanish. We can go anywhere!

XUNKA': The old boy never went to school. They'll be surprised when we come back in a new car with lots of money!

TUMIN: That's the truth! He's so old. It's better if we leave now. Goodbye, Grandfather!

SCENE 3

(The couple travels to the border.)

TUMIN: Could this be the border?

XUNKA': I don't know. Now we'll see.

TUMIN: Where should we go? I'm tired. I'm going to take a nap.

XUNKA': I'm really tired, too! *(When they're sitting sleepily, a smuggler who takes illegal immigrants across the border appears.)*

SMUGGLER 1: Where are you going, guys? Where do you want to go?

TUMIN: *Siñor,* we want to cross over to the other side where the white guys live, where they say you earn a lot of money.

SMUGGLER 1: (*He stares at Xunka'.*) I'm one of the guys who takes people over to the other side, where the white guys live.... But what a pretty gal you've brought here. I'll take her for myself!

TUMIN: You fool, she's my wife! (*Addressing his wife*) Xunka', he says he takes people to the other side!

SMUGGLER 1: I take them over, but you'll have to pay for it. How much dough do you have?

TUMIN AND XUNKA': Dough?

SMUGGLER 1: Yes, money, you idiots! Don't you know English?

TUMIN: How much will it be, sir?

SMUGGLER 1: A thousand dollars for the two of you, but I have to have it right now!

TUMIN: Okay, sir, but do us the favor of taking us because this is all the money we have left.

SMUGGLER 1: Okay, I'll take you, but you have to be very careful because the Immigration guys can be anywhere. They're in planes, in cars, on horse-back. They have dogs.... And if they catch you, they send you back to the country you've come from.

TUMIN: Okay, let's go. (*Everybody cautiously walks across the stage.*)

SMUGGLER 1: Bend down! (*They all bend low.*) Look over there, over there where that spotted flag is!

TUMIN: Yes, that's great, we're almost there!

SMUGGLER 1: But the *migras* may be over there. I'm going on ahead to make sure they're not there. Then I'll come back for you.

TUMIN: Okay.

(*They sit down to rest. They are exhausted. They haven't any tortillas left to eat, and they are terribly thirsty. The Smuggler doesn't return.*)

XUNKA': But it's hot as the devil and we haven't any water!

TUMIN: Do we have any tortillas left? I'm so hungry!

XUNKA': They're all gone, and the guy who was going to take us hasn't come back. Could he have abandoned us?

TUMIN: I don't know. I'm going to take a nap here on the sand! (*Then the border guard (the Migra) appears, blowing on a horn.*)

XUNKA': (*Terrified*) What's that noise? What's coming?

TUMIN: I don't know. Hide!

(*The Migra discovers them. Even though they've hidden their heads, they can't hide their bodies.*)

MIGRA: Hey you, *qué chingados!* What the hell are you doing here? Where are you going? (*He kicks them to their feet.*)

TUMIN: Na, na, nothing, sir! (*They answer fearfully. Tumin hides behind his wife.*)

MIGRA: Let's see your papers!

TUMIN AND XUNKA': Papers?

TUMIN: Here they are, sir. (*He pulls out a roll of toilet paper.*)

MIGRA: No, not that … that's for … (*He rubs his butt.*) I want your identification!

TUMIN: But this is all we have!

MIGRA: So you want to come over without any papers, eh? Get out! We don't want you here! (*He pushes them off the stage.*)

Act II

SCENE 1

(At the border on the Mexican side, Tumin and Xunka' are seated on the ground.)

XUNKA': My god, why are we having so much trouble?

TUMIN: We were jailed for two days and two nights, and they treated us so badly. Why are they doing this to us? (*Presumido appears as a smuggler. He shouts to the wetbacks behind the curtain while Xunka' and Tumin remain seated.*)

SMUGGLER 2: Wait there, you guys. I'll make sure there's no *migra* around!

WETBACKS: Okay!

(They shout from behind the curtain. Smuggler 2 looks over his list and names the people he is to take across the border.)

SMUGGLER 2: Two are from Guatemala, two from El Salvador, three *coletos auténticos* from San Cristóbal, and two Chamulans. (*He notices the couple.*) Look at those donkeys! They must have just arrived, looking for a smuggler and they don't know who he is. Ha, ha, ha! They think they're among a bunch of fools. (*The couple sees Smuggler 2.*)

XUNKA': Look who's here! Isn't he that jerk who tricked us back home?

TUMIN: That looks like him. It seems like he's going to make fun of us before he takes us over the border. Let's speak to him even though he mocks us. What else can we do?

XUNKA': Go ahead!

Presumido looking at his list of migrants, 2005.
Photo courtesy Sna Jtz'ibajom

TUMIN: How you doin', buddy? Can you help us get to the other side? Look how much my wife and I have suffered! Help us, since you know the tricks of the trade, how to cross over.

SMUGGLER 2: You want to go up north? But to get up there, you've got to have the balls. You've got to have God and all the saints to help you! I'll take you to the ends of the earth. I'm not hanging around here anymore. Wait a minute. I'm going to see how many others are going with me. (*He looks over his list.*) What's your name?

TUMIN: Domingo Ratón, Domingo Mouse.

XUNKA': My name is Juana Jolote, Jenny Turkey, wife of Mr. Mouse.

SMUGGLER 2: I still don't have you on my list. Two more from Chamula. But you're equipped to make the trip, aren't you?

TUMIN: Yes, we've come equipped with our things.

XUNKA': Me, too. I've brought my baby.

SMUGGLER 2: Okay then, we'll wait for the others.

(*Then he calls to the other farmers. He begins to ask the name of each one, checking it against the list.*)

SMUGGLER 2: You're all here? Listen to me carefully! We're going to travel over the border. And now is when the danger begins! You have to be ready to hide! Because if you don't, they'll kill us! When I tell you, "Hide!" throw yourselves to the ground. Whatever I do, you should do. And if I tell you to crawl on your hands and knees, you do that! If we can get over this rough ground, all we have to do is cross a big river.

EVERYONE: A river?

SMUGGLER 2: Yes! Any more questions, you guys?

XUNKA': If a gringo speaks to me, what do I say?

SMUGGLER 2: If the *migras* are after us, say, "Wat?" Or "Eye luv yu." Or you can also say, "Yes, yes" but don't say "yech, yech." Now follow me and don't make any noise. (*They walk along cautiously. The Smuggler scratches his butt, and they all imitate him.*) Sonofabitch! Run! The *migras* are coming! (*They try to hide, but then they run.*) Hurry up, cross the river, but quickly! (*Xunka' is left behind with her baby.*)

XUNKA': My baby, my baby!

FARMER 1: Throw it to me! (*She throws it, he catches it, and they all cross over.*)

SMUGGLER 2: Okay, we've arrived.

FARMER 2: And what's the name of this place?

SMUGGLER 2: We're here in Arizona.

EVERYONE: Narizona?

SMUGGLER 2: No, it's called Arizona. This place is very different from ours. Don't worry. You can rest a bit. In a little while they're coming to pick us up in a truck. Now you won't have to walk.

EVERYONE: Oh, great!

XUNKA': Where are they going to take us?

SMUGGLER 2: It's best if you go to Florida. You can work there picking tomatoes. (*They sit or lie down. Soon the Foreman arrives to take them to Florida.*)

FOREMAN: Hey, what happened? What are you guys doing here?

SMUGGLER 2: Look, man, I brought you twenty-five workers. They're Mexicans, some Guatemalans, but they're strong. And there are some women, too.

FOREMAN: Okay, my friend, I need a lot of new people to harvest the tomatoes. (*He explains this so they will all understand because Smuggler 2 is going back to Mexico.*)

SMUGGLER 2: (*Addressing the wetbacks*) Friends, I recommended you to the boss so he'll treat you well. This is your boss! (*He introduces the boss to them.*) He's going to pay you a good wage, a fair one. I'm going back home. Take care! Bye, bye!

(*Smuggler 2 exits and the Foreman addresses the wetbacks.*)

FOREMAN: This twelve-hour trip is going to be very hard. The *migras* are running around everywhere. This truck can't stop for any reason. Now, climb up and make yourselves as comfortable as you can. But this woman is going to join me in the cabin.(*They start the trip, but they have a flat.*) Get out, you guys, help me fix this damned tire! Then we'll hit the road again. (*They all get out.*)

WORKER 1: They've fucked us! We've been riding sixteen hours and we still haven't gotten there!

WOMAN WORKER: I'm so glad we had a flat! Now we can go to the bathroom. (*The men and women step back to pee.*)

SCENE 2

(*They arrive in Florida, at the tomato fields. The Foreman roughly points to them where to go. When don Tomate enters, he addresses him obsequiously.*)

FOREMAN: Welcome to Florida! We've arrived. Get out you damned, shitty Indians! Boss, I've brought you twenty-five people. You'll see they'll be good at doing hard work!

DON TOMATE: Great! Congratulations! You've earned a whole lot of money.

FOREMAN: Let me know when you need more. I'll bring them to you in a jiffy.

DON TOMATE: Okay, that's fine! Leave everything in my hands! (*Addressing the wetbacks*) You guys know that you already owe me five hundred dollars, each one of you!

EVERYONE: Five hundred dollars?

DON TOMATE: Yes, and nobody can get away without paying every bit. For each bucket you fill, I'll give you a little more. Those who work hardest will earn more and can send some back to their families!

EVERYONE: Oh, that's great!

DON TOMATE: You see how good I am! Now I'm going to take a picture of you so if anyone runs away I'll be able to search for you and kill you! Come over here and line up! (*He takes a picture.*) Now you can go to your trailers and sleep. Early tomorrow morning you'll go to pick the tomatoes.

EVERYONE: Okay!

(*They exit and return, bouncing up and down, packed tight as sardines in a truck driven by the Foreman.*)

FOREMAN: (*He gets out of the truck and gives orders to the workers.*) Get out of the truck, we've arrived. It's time to work! Okay, you guys, get to work, get in your rows! (*Don Tomate enters.*)

DON TOMATE: (*Addressing the Foreman*) You know all these people are new. Give it to them hard so they learn how to work!

FOREMAN: Don't you worry, boss, we'll give them the hardest work!

DON TOMATE: Now that they're in their rows, give them their buckets and put them to work.

EVERYONE: Okay, boss. (*They all begin to work, giving their buckets to the Foreman, who dumps them in the truck. One of the workers comes up to speak to the Foreman.*)

FOREMAN: Hurry up, you bastards!

WORKER 2: Boss, I want to drink some water.

FOREMAN: You didn't come here to drink water. You came here to work!

WORKER 2: But ... I'm thirsty.

FOREMAN: Well then, drink the water out of the ditch! Drink that so you learn how to work! (*He hits the worker, knocking him to the ground. The others pick him up and carry him to the side. A pregnant worker gives her bucket to the Foreman, who thinks it's not full enough. He empties it and tosses it at her.*)

FOREMAN: Here's the bucket! You haven't done anything!

WOMAN WORKER: Ow! (*She doubles up in pain.*)

WORKER 1: (*Compassionate*) Let's see. Where did it hit you? Did it hurt?

WOMAN WORKER: Ow, my stomach hurts. I feel terrible! I don't know what's going to happen to me.

(They feel abused and try to figure out what to do as they look desperately at the woman. Since they are illegal, they can't go to a clinic, so they try to cure her at home. The husband of the woman addresses one of the other workers.)

WORKER 1: The boss is going to pay for this!

WORKER 2: How can you take revenge if you can't hit the boss? It's better if we go and complain to a lawyer I know!

WORKER 1: A lawyer?

WORKER 2: It's not easy being illegal. Use your head before they cut it off!

EVERYONE: Let's go, then!

SCENE 3

(All the Workers enter to go to the lawyer's office. He sits there waiting for them.)

WORKERS: Good afternoon, sir!

LAWYER: *(He indifferently greets them in Spanish with an American accent.)* Buenas tardes, muchachos.

WORKER 1: Look, sir, we've come to ask you a favor. On the ranch they beat up our friend here. It was the boss who did it. Please help us to settle this problem.

LAWYER: All right, but first I need two witnesses who actually saw it happen when she was beaten. *(The Lawyer, very attentive, takes out a piece of paper to write on.)*

WORKER 2: I'm one of the witnesses, sir, I saw it very well when this friend of mine was hit!

WOMAN WORKER: Yes, sir, I'm a witness, too. I saw it when blood flowed from her head.

LAWYER: All right, but the victim needs to have papers that will make it possible for her to accuse the guilty ones.

WOMAN WORKER: Look, sir, I've worked many years in this place, but I've never had this happen to me. It's true I don't have papers. They're still in negotiation!

LAWYER: I understand, but since you are illegal, I can't do anything for you. If they mistreated you, hit you, or whatever, too bad! You aren't citizens of this country!

WORKER 1: But sir, please help us! With a bucket they hit my wife in the stomach and she's pregnant. She may lose the baby!

LAWYER: Look, boys, the law here does not protect illegal workers. If they try to do something, it's pretty sure they'll be sent back to the country they came from.

WORKER 2: No, that can't be, sir, because we haven't done anything bad! We just came here to do some honest work!

LAWYER: Well, like I said, if you want to continue working here, you have to stand all the abuse you get.

WORKER 1: Well then, Mr. Lawyer, if you can't do anything for us, why the fuck are you here? If you don't do anything for the workers!

LAWYER: (*Upset*) Please don't come and order me around! I'm the top man here. You better leave before I call the *migra* to send you back home.

EVERYONE: No, certainly not! (*The Workers pull back, shocked. What the Lawyer says fills them with fear. Speaking among themselves in Tzotzil, discouraged, they withdraw.*)

WORKER 1: If he doesn't want to help us, then we're screwed! (*They exit.*)

SCENE 4

(*Tumin arrives at his trailer after work. Xunka' is waiting for him.*)

XUNKA': So now what are we going to do? You've seen how they treat us. Lawyers don't want to help us! There's no justice in this country!

TUMIN: I think we ought to look for another kind of work. (*One of the workers comes in to talk to them.*)

WORKER 1: ¡Buenas tardes!

XUNKA': ¡Buenas tardes, señor!

WORKER 1: Now I'm out of work! The boss said he sold his factory, and besides, he didn't pay any of us for our work.

TUMIN: We don't have any work either. We don't know what to do now. My wife has lost so much weight from hunger. She was so plump when I brought her! I was thinking of looking for work at that place where you were.

WORKER 1: You know what? He just changed the factory's name and it's the same owner.

XUNKA': I think it'd be better if we looked for work where they harvest oranges or some other thing.

TUMIN: You're right, but I'm scared. I don't have any papers. That's why I'm locked up here! If we get sick, who will treat us? Nobody can treat us.

XUNKA': We don't have a stove and nowhere to sleep, and besides the rent is so expensive.

TUMIN: Yes, we sleep with rats, lice, fleas, and cockroaches. Those bugs don't help pay the rent!

WORKER 1: Okay, you can chat about it with your wife. I'm going to drink a little whiskey.

TUMIN: Well then, why don't you invite me? . . . I'll pull a fast one on my wife.

WORKER 1: Let's go then.

TUMIN: (*To Xunka'*) I'll be right back. I'm not taking you because where I'm going is for men only.

XUNKA': Men have such bad habits! (*She remains sad and thoughtful.*)

Act III

SCENE 1

(In a bar don Tomate and the Foreman are having a drink together.
They are shouting drunkenly.)

DON TOMATE: (*Shouting imperiously*) Waitress, give us a couple of beers! Waitress, give us a couple of beers!

WAITRESS: Here they are, sir! (*She walks towards her clients in a very provocative way, with the beers on a tray.*)

FOREMAN: ¡Gracias, mamacita! Well, boss, let's give a toast to the good harvest we've had this year! *Salud, patrón!*

DON TOMATE: Yes, for my profits! Oh, this beer tastes so good!

FOREMAN: Well . . . what do you think, boss? Isn't it true that these Indians are hard workers?

DON TOMATE: Yes, it seems to me they know how to work.

FOREMAN: Yes, we're doing a good job screwing them. You're really taking advantage of them, boss!

DON TOMATE: You think so! Ha, ha, ha! Now we'll see what we can get out of them. Afterwards I'll hand you a few bucks.

FOREMAN: Really? I hope you raise my salary because I bring you the workers you need!

DON TOMATE: Don't you worry! You'll have it at your disposal! That's how I can count on you! Isn't that so?

FOREMAN: Okay, perfect. That's what I like to hear, boss! So we can keep on tricking those dumb guys more than they can imagine, but don't let anyone know. It's just between us!

DON TOMATE: You know it stops here. Keep your mouth shut!

(Tumin and his friend come into the bar and ask for beer as the Waitress waits on them attentively.)

WORKER 1: Cousin, let's ask for our beers in English. You ask her since you've learned a little.

TUMIN: Hey, cutie, *danos* three beers!

WAITRESS: Okay, boy, here they are!

TUMIN: Thank you, that's fine. We want a snack! *(They see don Tomate and the Foreman.)* There's the boss! That's who's sitting over there. Let's toss one down, man!

WORKER 1: Ah, that's why that girl's over there!

TUMIN: Yes, 'cause they've got lots of cash.

Don Tomate and the Foreman drink together at the bar, 2007.
Photo courtesy Sna Jtz'ibajom

DON TOMATE: (*Shouting with annoyance*) Listen here, waitress, why did you let those Indians in?

WAITRESS: 'Cause they came in to drink some beers.

DON TOMATE: (*Shouting furiously*) I don't want Indians coming into this place when we're here. Kick 'em out!

> (*The Waitress tries to get them to hurry up and leave, but they take their time.*)

WAITRESS: Sirs, please hurry up and drink it down!

WORKER 1: (*Drinks his beer very calmly as he continues to chat with his friend*)

TUMIN: I'm going to stay until I finish my beer. But we're out of work. What can we do? All that's left for us to do is buy a car without any dough! (*They laugh.*) Ha, ha, ha!

DON TOMATE: (*Criticizing them as the Foreman listens*) So, foreman, do you think it's okay that these Indians come into this place where we're having a drink?

FOREMAN: You can't get away from these Indians!

WORKER 1: It seems they're talking about us. Maybe they'll give us a job!

DON TOMATE: (*Annoyed*) Why don't they leave?

FOREMAN: They want a drink, but the poor guys haven't any money!

WORKER 1: What's up with them?

TUMIN: Why don't we invite them for a beer? Then they'll probably give us a job!

WORKER 1: It's better if we talk to the boss.

DON TOMATE: Waitress, for the last time I tell you, get those Indians out of here!

WAITRESS: Sirs, you'd better get out!

WORKER 1: But … why, if we want to drink some more?

TUMIN: Isn't this your business?

WAITRESS: Yes, but you have to leave because this place is for the bigwigs!

WORKER 1: But we're not causing any trouble, just drinking.

DON TOMATE: (*He approaches them, ready for a fight.*) So I'm telling you, get out of here! (*As he pulls his wallet out of his pocket to pay for their beers, it falls to the ground. Later, during the altercation, Tumin picks it up without anyone else noticing.*) How much do they owe, waitress?

WAITRESS: (*Addressing Don Tomate*) Thirty dollars for the two of them.

DON TOMATE: Here it is, *señorita*. Count it carefully so they won't say afterwards I didn't pay these Indians' bill. I don't want to see them here ever again! (*He grabs Worker 1 by the shirt and pushes him out without offering them jobs.*)

WORKER 1: But what did we do to him?

TUMIN: Let's get out of here!

DON TOMATE: Well, we've seen that the Indians are scared of us. Let's keep on exploiting them!

FOREMAN: I'm so glad they're gone. Now we can drink some more! Those poor guys without papers don't know what to do. They have no place to go. After they work for us, we can feed them to the alligators!

DON TOMATE: Let's celebrate and take another beer! Waitress, two more! (*He looks for his wallet to pay for the beers but doesn't find it.*) But ... where's my money? Could I have dropped it over there? Waitress, by any chance have you seen my money?

WAITRESS: No, I haven't seen anything, sir.

DON TOMATE: Those Indians in rags stole my money, but it was only a hundred dollars.

FOREMAN: We'd better have another in my house. I invite you!

DON TOMATE: Okay, let's go! (*They exit, holding onto each other, stumbling.*)

SCENE 2

(Tumin arrives drunk at the trailer he's rented. He speaks to his wife and tells her he saw Don Tomate in the bar and that Don Tomate's money fell out of his pocket.)

TUMIN: Are you here, Xunka'? I've come back!

XUNKA': I'm here. Why are you drunk? So you have money for whiskey? Don't you know that was the last little bit of money we had?

TUMIN: Don't bawl me out, wife! Don't you worry. I came on the boss, don Tomate, and his foreman in the bar. Those two fat guys were downing beers. God, but what a bar those bastards have! There are lots of women in miniskirts serving the people.

XUNKA': Oh, so there were lots of women? But why did you go into a place like that?

TUMIN: I don't know, but the boss kicked us out onto the street. At least he paid our bill, and when he took his money out of his pocket, he dropped his wallet and I grabbed it. But that bar stank so bad!

XUNKA': That's fine, but ... didn't he see you grab his money?

TUMIN: No, he was really drunk. But what'll we buy?

XUNKA': We ought to buy a car.

TUMIN: Oh, I know, we'll buy the kind of clothes the white guys wear, and then we can go out on the street!

XUNKA': That would be good, so the *migras* don't keep screwing us!

TUMIN: I'll buy pants for you! Here, take it and go shopping! (*Xunka' exits, leaving Tumin, who, very worried, talks to himself.*) Oh, damn, I feel so bad. That woman in the bar messed me up. But why did I go there? Oh well, with the new clothes I'm going to buy, I'll certainly feel better! (*He exits. The Migra comes in, talking to himself, before the couple returns in bright tourist clothes: Xunka' in pants and Tumin in shorts.*)

MIGRA: I hate to screw these poor Indians, but ... what can I do? It's my duty. I have to follow orders! Every year the ones without papers come in. They're filling up the country. But I'm going to hunt for them, like rabbits. The more I catch, the more I get paid! We'll see how many I catch today!

TUMIN: Now, wife, we've really done it up smart! Look at yourself! (*He gazes admiringly at Xunka'.*)

XUNKA': That's the truth, but your legs look so dark!

MIGRA: Hey, you speak English?

TUMIN: Yes!

XUNKA': Eye luv yu!

MIGRA: I love you too. Show me your papers!

TUMIN: No unnerstan!

MIGRA: Papers! Your papers!

TUMIN: Papers? I've lived here thirty years and nobody's asked me for papers!

MIGRA: Oh, you and your old woman are illegal. You don't belong here. You dumb Indians belong on the other side. Let's get going!

TUMIN: But sir, I'm not doin' nothin' bad!

MIGRA: This country is for white people. Get out! (*They exit, humiliated by the Migra.*)

SCENE 3

(Back in the house of Tumin's brother, Matyo, in Chamula. The Grandfather and Loxa enter to find Matyo.)

GRANDFATHER: Everything is fine, son, now we are harvesting the corn and the beans that we've grown.

MATYO: You're right, Grandfather. I've decided to leave the house with my wife early in the morning to see how our cornfield looks. It seems as if the dogs are ruining it. That's why we want to look at it. Is breakfast ready, Loxa?

LOXA: It's ready. You and Grandfather wash your hands, and then I will pass you the food.

GRANDFATHER: All right, children, be careful, because I had a bad dream.

MATYO: What was your dream, Grandfather?

GRANDFATHER: The whole house was full. That means something bad. We don't know what it could be. (*Then Tumin and Xunka' enter, talking wildly, pushing their baby in a stroller.*)

TUMIN: Hello, hello, hello!

GRANDFATHER: You've returned? How are you?

TUMIN: *¡Mocho very gut, lek oy!*

GRANDFATHER: What are they saying? They've come back half crazy! Your wife looks like a clown.

XUNKA': I look like a gringa. Isn't that true, Grandfather?

GRANDFATHER: Yes, you look like a clown! And do you remember our language still? It seems to me now you're talking in a very strange way!

MATYO: They're completely changed now, but sit down, we'll talk a bit. We're going to eat.

XUNKA': Me, I don't know how to sit on the ground anymore.

MATYO: Okay, take a chair. I'll sit on the ground. Never mind. That's what we'll have to do since we haven't any more chairs.

TUMIN: This is for you, brother. (*He hands him some old clothes.*)

XUNKA': I'm giving you a blanket, Grandfather. I hope you like the white guys' blankets.

GRANDFATHER: Thank you very much, daughter, for remembering me. It's true, I'm dying of the cold.

TUMIN: All right, Grandfather, sometimes I understand our language and sometimes I don't. There are different languages up there. There are lots of white guys and lots of blacks. We bought a car that we left up there.

XUNKA': Look, this is the key for our car. Now I've come with pants. I don't look like I did before, and I walk with slippers and my gold bracelet!

GRANDFATHER: What did you think of the place? Is it pretty?

TUMIN: The north is as pretty as it could be. We felt at home right away. It's just that I took sick, and that's why I'm so thin.

MATYO: It's true, your pants are falling off. Grandfather, ask my brother if they're going to stay here ... or if they're going back.

GRANDFATHER: As your brother says, are you going to stay, or do you want to go back?

TUMIN: Don't worry. The trouble is I'm sick. I'm asking you the favor of taking care of me. When I'm well, I'll go back and work, but I'm feeling really bad now.

XUNKA': Please do us the favor. I don't want my husband to die. I don't want to remain alone with my little boy. Please!

TUMIN: Well, I've gone to the doctors, and they don't care about us because we're not from there. That's why I came to see a shaman.

GRANDFATHER: I believe Mrs. Tzukum is here. She knows how to pray.

TUMIN: Please, brother, loan us your porch. Let us sleep there. We're used to that.

MATYO: This was because of your trips. We'll look for a shaman for you.

TUMIN: Please do me the favor then, since it seems as if I'm getting worse. I'm getting chills. It's hurting badly.

GRANDFATHER: You see, son, you disobeyed me, and that's why this happened to you. But they've gone to get Mrs. Tzukum. She knows how to pray in the caves. (*The Shaman arrives.*)

SHAMAN: Good afternoon.

GRANDFATHER: Good afternoon, ma'am. Come right in. My son returned from work, and he's come back sick. Please pulse him so we can learn what sickness he has.

SHAMAN: All right, I'll pulse him! (*She does so.*) Sir, this is a very serious sickness, and there's nothing we can do about it now! The pulse doesn't tell me anything, but it's certainly AIDS!

XUNKA': Look, my husband is going to die! (*She cries.*) We're going to be left behind, son! (*Grandfather addresses the public.*)

GRANDFATHER: You've seen what happened to them. It would have been better if they had stayed to do something for our people. But it's too late now!

LOXA: (*Addressing Xunka'*) Don't you worry, sister, come and be with us!

GRANDFATHER: So, friends, men, women, and children who have joined us here, I hope you have understood a few words about the life of a couple that was tricked. The poor guy died of AIDS without profiting anything from his trip. It's not a bad thing to go out looking for work—nobody, no one, can deny us the right to work—but we must always remember the advice of our ancestors.

When Corn Was Born

(2000)

WHEN CORN WAS BORN (*Cuando nació el maíz*) is a creation myth from Tene-japa, with similarities to other such myths throughout the Mayan world. The gods are unhappy that men and women happily crunching soft, edible pebbles, have forgotten them and are leading sinful lives. So with the aid of ants, they steal the Earth Lord's corn. Finally, the Earth Lord, in his rich Ladino aspect, is convinced by the gods that man should plant corn. Because corn farming is so difficult, man will remember the gods, respect them, and seek their aid.

In 2001, Ralph Lee slightly reduced the length of this play, renaming it the *The Origin of Corn* (*El orígen del maíz*), for performance by a Chicano cast in the La Jolla Playhouse and in many neighboring schools, where it was presented in both English and Chicano Spanish. The cast was astonished and initially upset when Ralph asked them to speak Spanish as they do among themselves, but later they were very pleased when they heard the loud applause of both teachers and students. The original play was still a favorite in Chiapas as of 2005.

CAST OF CHARACTERS

CHILD 1: male, wearing red sleeveless shirt, gray pants, sandals

CHILD 2: male, wearing short-sleeved blue shirt, gray pants, sandals

CHILD 3: female, wearing Tenejapan clothes, barefoot

CHILD 4: female, wearing white Chamulan blouse, red sweater, black skirt, sandals

GRANDMOTHER: wearing white blouse, black woolen shawl, black skirt

SKY GODS 1 AND 2: wearing large masks, black shirts

WOMAN 1: wearing Tzeltal clothes, sandals

WOMAN 2: wearing Zinacantec clothes, no sandals, then wearing Chamulan clothes

WOMAN 3: wearing red hat, red blouse and skirt, shoes

PEDRO: wearing Chamulan white neckerchief with red tassels wrapped around head, white shirt, white wool tunic, white pants, belt

NEIGHBOR 1 (CRISTÓBAL): wearing white shirt, white Chamulan wool tunic, black pants, shoes

NEIGHBOR 2: wearing Zinacantec tunic, black pants, sandals

NEIGHBOR 3: wearing white shirt, long white pants, sandals

TOAD: with mask, brown spotted shirt, black pants, sandals

EARTH LORD: wearing *charro* hat, white shirt, red jacket, black pants, shoes

ANTS 1, 2 AND 3 (PUPPETS)

SCORPION: wearing orange hooded suit, blue pants, sandals

(*Four children stand in the yard of a Mayan farmer's house
in Chiapas, Mexico.*)

CHILD 1: Oh, come on! Let's play ball!

CHILD 2: Yes! Let's play basketball! (*They begin to play, tossing the ball back and forth.*) Oh, throw it to me!

CHILD 1: Now it's my turn!

CHILD 3: Come on, throw it to me! I want to play, too!

(*One of them keeps the ball and the others chase him and pull him down on top of an ant nest. They pile on top of each other and then jump up, shouting.*)

CHILD 2: Ow, something's stinging me!

CHILD 1: Me, too!

CHILD 3: They must be fleas! (*They rub their arms and legs where they feel the bites.*)

CHILD 1: No, no, look, they're ants!

CHILD 2: Let's kill them by jumping on them. We'll be planes!

> (*They start dancing about and gliding like planes, stamping their feet, pretending to bomb the ants as they fly over them like bombers. Suddenly Grandmother comes out of the house and calls to the children.*)

GRANDMOTHER: Children, what are you doing here? Why are you making so much noise? Oh, you're killing the ants! Please don't kill them!

CHILD 2: But they stung us, Grandmother!

GRANDMOTHER: It was because you ruined their house, that's why they stung you! But come over here, I'm going to tell you a story that my grandfather told me! (*They sit in a circle around Grandmother.*)

CHILDREN: Oh, good!

CHILD 2: Wouldn't the story about Wolfman be better?

CHILD 1: No! Tell us about Batman!

GRANDMOTHER: No, children, I'm going to tell you about something much nicer than that. I'll tell you a tale that reminds us how corn was born for all mankind! Pay attention! Long ago, people didn't work to get their food. They ate soft stones. All they had to do was to pick them up off the ground.

CHILDREN: Stones?

GRANDMOTHER: Yes, stones, but they tasted good! People just multiplied, and the gods saw that the stones were running out. (*Sky Gods 1 and 2 appear. Grandmother shows them to the children, who look at them excitedly.*) So then they sent a kind of seed so the people could work and live well.

CHILDREN: Oh, that's how it was? And then? (*Grandmother exits with the children quietly following her.*)

SKY GOD 1: Well, brother, the time has come to change the world! We're going to figure out what to give our children to eat! We see they're just lying around. They don't do anything. They don't think of us, their Lords. They don't thank us for the food we give them. They have to work a bit. We can't give everything to them for free!

SKY GOD 2: Yes, you're right. It would be better for us to choose one of them to be in charge. And we'll send him vegetable seeds and beans so they can distribute them among themselves and begin to have more produce.

SKY GOD 1: Right you are, we have to give them food! Oh, but if we give them only vegetables and beans, they won't be able to do any kind of hard work! It's better if we give them corn. That's what has more strength!

The Sky Gods, 2000. Photo courtesy Robert M. Laughlin

SKY GOD 2: Well then, our children aren't going to continue the same way. Now they're not going to eat those soft stones! They'll have to suffer a bit working to get their food!

SKY GOD 1: That's what we'll do then! We'll look down to earth to see if there is one of them who hasn't sinned too much. But it seems they're all bad! They don't want to do anything! (*All those who had taken the roles of children appear as adults, walking by with their bundles as if they had been in the market.*) Look, that man has two women and a dozen children with each one!

WOMAN 1: Cristóbal, what are you doing with that woman? Come here!

WOMAN 2: You'll see, Cristóbal! I don't love you anymore!

WOMAN 1: Neither do I, come on, *comadre,* we don't need any men!

(*The Women exit. Cristóbal lies on the ground. Another Woman appears, looking at a magazine.*)

SKY GOD 2: Look, there's a woman who seems to be smart. We'll give a present of corn to her!

WOMAN 3: Wow, that man's really sexy! I need one like that! (*She exits.*)

SKY GOD 1: I don't think so. I see she's really loose. (*A man approaches, counting his money.*) Look at that man counting his money. All he cares about is getting rich and he doesn't help anyone else! (*A man gets up from the ground,* *scratches his head and lies down again lazily.*) Look at that loafer! He doesn't do anything but scratch and scratch his fleas. (*A woman comes running in.*) Look at that other one running about like crazy! She always arrives home late!

(*A drunk gets up and trips over the guy who is sleeping.*)

SKY GOD 2: That other one just walks around drinking! He ought to get to work so he can feed his kids! (*The two men exit. Pedro enters on the other side. He is dressed as a Chamulan and walks about dreamily, gazing at the stars.*)

SKY GOD 1: But that man looks as if he's innocent. He's just gazing at the stars! He surely knows how to dream. He's not like the others!

SKY GOD 2: Okay, let's visit him tonight. We'll chat with him in his dream, and we'll take him a present that will please everybody.

SKY GOD 1: Yes, we should greet him right now and tell him our plans!

SKY GOD 2: Hey, Pedro, come over here!

PEDRO: What do you want, sir?

SKY GOD 1: We're bringing you a message, son. Soon none of you will have anything to eat since every day your food is getting harder and harder to find. We've decided that you are the one who should give the others a new kind of food!

SKY GOD 2: In order to carry this out, we will visit you in your dreams and tell you what to do. Until then, keep on enjoying this beautiful world!

PEDRO: Alright, sir! (*The Sky Gods disappear.*) What could they be saying to me? Could I be dreaming? I can't believe the gods would talk to me. I'd better forget this. I'll have some pebbles for supper so I can sleep tonight without any worries. I'm going to eat them. That's what I'll do now! Mm, these pebbles are so delicious. They really are! Ah, now I'm going to bed and I'll get up in a little while. (*After his supper, Pedro sleeps soundly and snores. Then the Sky Gods reappear and speak to Pedro.*)

SKY GOD 1: Pedro, here we are! (*Two people enter and deposit the tools for Pedro to work with.*) What you should do first is look for a hilly place where you can work. Take your axe and your machete. Cut down the trees and burn them! Here is your hoe to dig up the ground. With a digging stick, plant three or four kernels in each hole!

SKY GOD 2: And here are your seeds! This is the holy corn that you will harvest one or two times a year! (*While the Sky Gods are speaking to him in his dream, Pedro moves his arms about and grunts. A girl comes in with the corn and leaves it next to Pedro. As she exits, she gives Pedro a tap to wake him up.*)

SKY GOD 1: Let's go, brother!

SKY GOD 2: Yes, let's go! (*They exit.*)

PEDRO: (*Stretching sleepily*) I dreamt the gods were talking to me! What could this strange dream mean? (*Suddenly he discovers the corn and the tools. He holds the corn in one hand.*) Ah, but what's this? It must be corn! So my dream was true! It seems like they left me something here. . . . I'll try to remember. It seems like they told me to take my axe to cut down the trees, my machete to cut the branches, my hoe to dig, and my planting stick to plant this corn. That's what was in my dream! I'll try it out right now! (*He begins to work in the field. He takes his axe and kneels before a tree, praying in Tzotzil before cutting it down.*) Forgive me, brother, holy tree! I must cut you down because the gods have allowed us to do this so that we can have our cornfield, the sacred place where our corn will grow! (*After a short while he sits down, sweating.*) But this work is so hard, now I have blisters! (*He continues working and sweating.*) What's happening to me now? Water's coming out of my body. I'm all wet! Could I have wet my pants? (*He looks down, but drops of sweat fall from his brow. He rubs it.*) Could I have a fever? But even if I do, I'm going to keep on working. (*He works now with his machete, cutting off the branches. Then two women appear arm in arm, their faces partly hidden by their* rebozos. *They peer at him and mock him.*)

WOMAN 1: What's this guy doing?

WOMAN 2: Who knows? He's ruining the ground and the trees!

WOMAN 1: Well, yes, who knows where he learned how to do such a thing. We've never seen anyone like that!

WOMAN 2: He's crazier than a coot! (*They exit, roaring with laughter. Pedro keeps on working. Then his neighbor appears and stares at him scornfully.*)

NEIGHBOR 1: But, man, what are you doing? You're as dirty as a pig! Now you stink like a dead dog!

PEDRO: I know you don't understand what I'm doing. It's really hard, but it makes me happy!

NEIGHBOR 1: So tell me then, what good will it do you?

PEDRO: I'm doing an experiment for everyone's sake.

NEIGHBOR 1: But you're so stupid! You're mistreating the earth!

PEDRO: No, man, even though you won't believe me . . . I'm planting . . . (*doubtfully*) . . . rocks!

NEIGHBOR 1: What good does it do to plant rocks if there are loads of them all around? Well, then, go on doing your crazy things! I'm leaving! (*The Neighbor exits angrily.*)

PEDRO: Get going! (*He keeps on working and begins to sing.*)

Bolom chon ta vinajel,	Jaguar serpent in the sky,
Bolom chon ta balumil,	Jaguar serpent on the earth,
Natik avisim, bolom chon,	Your whiskers are long, jaguar serpent,
K'oxk'ox avakan, bolom chon.	Your legs are short, jaguar serpent.

(*He sings and whistles as he makes holes with his digging stick, pulling out corn kernels from the bag the gods gave him. He plants the seeds and with his feet taps down the earth on top of them.*) Well, I think I've planted enough! I'll come back in two weeks to see what kind of plant it is, to see if my dream comes true! (*Pedro exits and two women enter, placing rocks in the rows where he had planted the corn. The women exit and Pedro returns, looking with alarm at the rocks.*) Oh, damn! Where is my crop? And where did these rocks come from? By god, all my work was for nothing! In every lump where I planted the corn, a rock came up instead! (*He begins to cry. The Neighbors come in, shocked.*)

NEIGHBOR 1: But for god's sake, what did you do? Look at our food! Now the little stones can't be eaten! They've gotten hard!

NEIGHBOR 2: Now what can we do?

NEIGHBOR 3: The children are starving to death! Soon we'll all die!

NEIGHBOR 1: It's your fault! Grab him! Lynch him! Hang him! (*Sky Gods 1 and 2 appear.*)

SKY GOD 1: What a good harvest you have, son! It seems you don't know how to follow our advice! You worked well, but you made a mistake! Do you remember what you did?

PEDRO: (*Repenting and trying to excuse himself*) I tried to do everything you told me!

SKY GOD 2: You did good work . . . but you told your friend a lie!

PEDRO: (*Remembering his lie right away*) Oh, forgive me, sirs!

SKY GOD 1: Alright, son, we will forgive your faults. In spite of everything you didn't work in vain. The corn is stored away!

SKY GOD 2: (*Speaking to the Neighbors, who stand with lowered heads*) You don't need to worry, children! You don't know what is happening. This man was chosen to give you a new kind of food.

SKY GOD 1: You can return home happily. Meanwhile, it's our job to get the corn. (*The Neighbors exit and the rocks are removed.*)

SKY GOD 2: And now what? We haven't any more corn left!

SKY GOD 1: We know that, but we know where it is! Earth Lord has it stored away! What we'll do is speak to him and ask him for some corn! (*Pedro exits and a cave appears. The Sky Gods exit. Pedro returns, stands in front of the cave, and calls to Earth Lord.*)

PEDRO: I think this must be the place! Sir, sir, I've come to pay you a visit! (*The Toad appears.*)

TOAD: What do you want, mister?

PEDRO: I want to speak to the Lord! Will you let me by?

TOAD: Oh, I don't know if he wants to come out! Who are you, so I can tell him your name?

PEDRO: My name is Pedro. I've been sent by the gods. (*The Sky Gods appear.*)

TOAD: My Lord, somebody wants to talk to you. It's a crazy guy who says he was sent by the gods!

EARTH LORD: Have him wait for me a minute. I'm very busy.

TOAD: The Lord says he's very busy. He asks you to wait a bit.

PEDRO: Alright, thank you very much. I'll wait for him. (*Toad stays next to the cave. Pedro addresses him politely.*) Would you like some water?

TOAD: (*Inattentive, impatient*) No.

PEDRO: (*Annoyed*) Okay then, drop dead!

EARTH LORD: (*Bothered*) What do you want?

PEDRO: We came to ask you for a bit of your corn.

EARTH LORD: What for?

PEDRO: It's because I want to plant it and harvest it to feed all the people!

EARTH LORD: What? Are you still hungry? But you're just a bunch of loafers! Anyway, I don't have any, just a little!

SKY GOD 2: But, sir, we can pay for it!

EARTH LORD: Even if you buy it, that won't work! I haven't got any! You'll just set out to ruin my gardens! No, no, no! This corn is only for me! That's all I have to say! (*Disgruntled, he goes back into his cave.*)

SKY GOD 1: So now what can we do?

SKY GOD 2: He's so stubborn. But if he won't give it to us willingly, we'll have to steal it!

PEDRO: But what do you mean? Isn't that a crime?

SKY GOD 1: We have no other choice! Besides, how do you dare question what we gods are doing?

PEDRO: Alright, my Lord, let me do my best!

SKY GOD 1: Okay, but hurry up! (*Pedro makes a try, but he is not successful because the opening is too small.*)

PEDRO: I can't do it! I can't get my hand in! The opening is so small that only a bug could get through!

SKY GOD 1: Oh, damn it! So what can we do then?

PEDRO: I know what to do! We'll look for some little ants! They can get through because they're so tiny!

SKY GOD 2: That's a good idea, son! You're not so stupid!

PEDRO: No, sir!

SKY GOD 2: Alright, okay, but where can we find those little ants? (*An ant appears at the side.*)

ANT 1: What do you want?

PEDRO: Sir, here's one!

SKY GOD 1: Fine! Convince her before she gets away from you!

PEDRO: (*Facing the Sky Gods*) Oh god, I'll see what I can do! (*Addressing Ant*) See here, pretty ant, you must enter Earth Lord's cave and bring out for us all the corn that's inside.

ANT 1: But why do I have to do that?

PEDRO: Because it's necessary. So that, so that ... we can all eat!

ANT 1: Okay, but it's so you human beings can eat, because we ants can get our own food.

PEDRO: You don't know what you're saying, little ant! Corn is the food of the gods. It's the best food of all! When we eat it we can laugh, sing, and praise the gods. Corn is holy! We will eat the kernels, and you can eat the stalks, the leaves, and everything else.

ANT 1: Okay, sir, I'll try.

PEDRO: Right on, little ant!

ANT 1: Oh, oh, no I can't! My belly's stuck tight!

PEDRO: Try harder! You have to be able to do it! Okay then, I'll help you!

ANT 1: Fine! (*Ant tries again, helped by Pedro.*) I'm in now! So what do I do?

PEDRO: What do you see there?

ANT 1: Nothing!

SKY GODS: (*Surprised, incredulous, they call out in chorus.*) Nothing?

ANT 1: (*Lying to Pedro*) It's completely empty! There isn't any corn!

PEDRO: Girl, I think you're telling me a lie! The thing is you want all the corn to be just for the ants! You'd better come on out! (*Ant tries to get out.*)

ANT 1: Uh oh, I can't get out! My stomach is stuck! Please help me lift this rock!

PEDRO: Why do you think you could get out after you fattened up so eating all that corn? Well, I'll help you! It's just that I'll have to pull you, okay? (*He pulls her, making a show of his strength.*)

ANT 1: Ouch, ouch, oo! (*Pedro flings her in the air and then is surprised when he picks her up and sees her skinny waist.*)

PEDRO: Look how pinched you are! Your waist is never going to fill out! You'll be like that forever!

ANT 1: Ow, ow, ow, damn, you nearly killed me! I'm leaving! (*Ant exits.*)

PEDRO: Go on, then! You didn't do me any good! What'll I do now? Who can I bring? Oh, now I know! I'll look for the ant called Seys! Of course! Where would that little ant be?

ANT 2: Here I am. What do you want? (*Pedro takes her in his hands.*)

PEDRO: Go into that cave and bring out all the corn!

ANT 2: Alright, I'll go in. (*She enters without any difficulty.*) Now I'm inside! What am I supposed to do now?

SKY GOD 2: What's inside there?

ANT 2: There are four piles of corn!

SKY GODS: Oh!

PEDRO: Ooh, the other one was lying! How could she do that? So that's the way they are! What does the corn look like?

ANT 2: There is red, black, yellow, and white. There's green, too, that grows wild and you don't have to plant it, but that's just for Earth Lord. But I can't carry it out because the holes in the cave are too small!

SKY GOD 1: If you can't do it, well, never mind, we'll look for some bugs that are even smaller than you!

ANT 2: Forgive me, sir!

SKY GOD 2: It's not a problem, but who can we bring?

PEDRO: I don't know. What if we bring the smallest ants? The ones that are called . . . that are called . . .

ANT 2: They're called *me' ba shanich!* They can surely take out the corn because they're smaller than me and they're stronger!

PEDRO: That's right! *Me' ba shanich!*

ANT 3: You called us?

PEDRO: Yes, we want you to go into that cave and bring out the corn. You can get in because you're so tiny.

ANT 3: I hope so, but I don't know if we'll be able to carry it out because we're not as strong as you think!

PEDRO: But I trust in you. (*Scorpion enters.*)

SCORPION: (*Swaggering*) I'm Scorpion. I'm stronger than you guys! What are you trying to do? Can I help you somehow?

PEDRO: Oh, Mr. Scorpion! We're trying to take out the seeds behind those rocks.

SCORPION: Me, I can do it! I'm tough enough to get into any cave! Just tell me where the opening is!

PEDRO: But you're so very big! You can't get through the holes! See what it's like!

SCORPION: Oh, wow! That's true, they're very small! I can't get in there! . . . Now I know what to do! (*He pretends with his arms to show an explosion.*) We'll dynamite it!

The Scorpion, 2000. Photo courtesy Robert M. Laughlin

PEDRO: No! . . . If we do that we'll burn up the corn! And besides, we might wake up Earth Lord!

SCORPION: Earth Lord? Is this his cave?

PEDRO: Yes, and he doesn't want to give us the corn that he's stored there!

SCORPION: Now I understand. But what's it good for?

PEDRO: To plant and to eat, you idiot! You haven't a thought in your head!

SCORPION: Yes, yes, yes, mister . . . now I understand . . . but we need to have the ants help us.

ANT 3: Oh, you're so stupid! Why do you think we're here!

SCORPION: (*Bowing*) Oh forgive me, lady ants! I didn't see you!

ANT 3: It's nothing, but let us do our work!

SCORPION: Okay! (*He squats next to the cave.*)

SKY GOD 2: As for you, tiny ants, you can bring it out little by little!

ANT 3: If that's what you want, we'll try to do it, sir! (*The Ants enter the cave.*)

SKY GOD 1: How's it going, little ants?

ANT 3: We're fine, there's lots of corn here!

PEDRO: Gather it all together and bring it out of the cave! (*They come out with the corn. Pedro exclaims happily.*) Now the first kernels are here!

ANT 3: Yes, sir! (*Earth Lord suddenly comes out and speaks angrily to Pedro.*)

EARTH LORD: What are you doing here again?

PEDRO: (*Frightened*) Nothing, nothing, sir! It's just that this is such a pretty place!

EARTH LORD: But this is private property! Get out of here!

SCORPION: Oh, what a devil! Why don't you like us? You're so awful! (*Scorpion jumps forward and stings Earth Lord's foot.*)

EARTH LORD: Ow, ow, ow! What stung me? Oh, why did you do that? You'll see, you damned pest! You'll pay for this! (*Meanwhile the Ants are carrying out the corn.*) Oh, now I see why you did that! You're stealing my corn, you bastards! (*He gets his rifle and points it in a circle, not knowing whom to shoot first.*) I'm going to kill all of you! (*He points at the Scorpion.*) Oh, you'll be the first, so you'll feel what you did to me! You dared to hurt me, just because you have so many feet!

SCORPION: No, sir, don't kill me! (*Laughing nervously*) It was a joke, ha, ha, ha! And besides, if you let me live … I can be your guard. I'll defend you and I can sting all the bad people who come to harm you!

EARTH LORD: Shut up, you little devil! I'm going to strike you! You'll feel my thunderbolt! Boom! (*He points his rifle at Scorpion and shoots him. Scorpion falls, thrashing his legs.*)

SCORPION: Ow! Ow, ow! You killed me, you bastard! This is the end of me! So what, thanks to God last night I had the chance to make a million kids to sting all the bad people. Good-bye! (*He exits, dragging himself out.*)

ANT 3: Here are the corn kernels! We've done our job. We put them in your hands, Pedro! We're all going home now!

PEDRO: That's fine! Many thanks, little ants. Now we don't have to worry. We won't die. It's time to plant and harvest the holy corn! I'm going to teach my friends so they'll get the hang of it. (*The Ants exit.*) Come on, everybody, take your seeds. You and your children do your best to raise the holy corn!

NEIGHBOR 1: That's fine, sir! Thanks to God, now we have the new kind of food! So let's go plant it! (*They exit.*)

SKY GOD 2: This is how our children will be happy, with a new present of corn that we are giving them. Now all we have to do is thank Earth Lord and ask him to forgive us for Scorpion's faults.

SKY GOD 1: We should call him right now so we can agree on what the earth should be like.

SKY GOD 2: Sir, Earth Lord, we wish to speak to you!

EARTH LORD: Yes, what do you want? Are you going to steal from me again? But you've already taken it all away!

SKY GOD 1: That's not it, sir. Haven't you noticed how the world has changed? Don't you like the green color that has come to earth and enriches human life?

EARTH LORD: Yes, sir, you are right. I see that the people are content. But that damned scorpion's sting still hurts me. I'm going to punish him with my thunderbolts wherever he is!

SKY GOD 2: You mustn't overdo it. Your thunder and lightning are the signs for rain to fall.

SKY GOD 1: Ask your servant, Toad, to sing so the rain will come.

SKY GOD 2: Tell the ants to swarm and walk eastwards to call forth the rain.

EARTH LORD: Agreed, sir.

SKY GOD 1: That's fine. We'll work together for our children's sake.

> *(Earth Lord and the Sky Gods exit. The people appear. One can hear the singing of toads and the roar of thunderbolts. The cornfield appears.)*

EVERYONE: (*Looking around for the toads and uttering their call in low tones*) Kerek, kerek!

PEDRO: (*Marveling*) Listen, friends! Now you can hear the toads singing. Today it's going to rain!

The milpa, 2000. Photo courtesy Robert M. Laughlin

EVERYONE: Yes!

WOMAN 1: Look at the ants, how they're all swarming! It's going to rain hard!

PEDRO: Yes, that's for sure! Now you can hear the thunder! It's raining already! (*At the sound of thunder and rain, everyone looks up smiling, squinting, and lifting up their arms.*)

WOMAN 2: We're going to have a good corn crop!

NEIGHBOR 2: Yes, with this rain we'll do very well!

WOMAN 3: Yes, that's true. We already have a good crop! Look, friends!

PEDRO: (*Pedro gathers the corn and shares it among everyone.*) Let's eat! See what good food it is! This is the fruit of our labor!

WOMAN 1: But this tortilla is so delicious!

PEDRO: Yes, this is wonderful! But we mustn't forget that we must respect the plants and the animals!

WOMAN 2: You're absolutely right! We can't live without them! But please give me another little tortilla!

EVERYONE: Yes! This food is our life!

PEDRO: Yes, now that we know how to work and have our own land, we must thank the Sky Gods and the Earth Lord!

EVERYONE: Yes!

WOMAN 2: Oh, now we know why we mustn't mistreat the ants!

GRANDMOTHER: Okay, kids, our story is over!

EVERYONE: Thank you very much!

Mexico with Us Forever!

(2001)

THE TITLE *Mexico with Us Forever!* (*¡Siempre México con nosotros!*) was chosen to give a positive swing to the Zapatistas' cry, *"¡Jamás México sin nosotros!"* (Never again Mexico without us!). This play, under the guidance of Michael Garcés, then producing artistic director of INTAR Hispanic American Arts Center of New York City, shows how political corruption, including the buying of votes, is a current practice that must not continue. The PRI party had been in control for more than seventy years, rewarding the *caciques* (town bosses) or someone else they selected by appointing them mayor. Once "elected," the mayor received the money distributed for public town expenses, which he pocketed for himself or divided up among his cronies. Attempts were made to replace this system with a supposedly more democratic one, where people vote for the mayor, but the bosses continued to buy votes or have the ballot boxes stuffed.

The townspeople finally, in 1996, united to demand compliance with the San Andrés Accords, granting autonomy to Indian communities and justice to both Indian men and women. Although these accords had been signed by the Mexican government, they were ignored by the Mexican legislature. The names of the individuals in this play are given in Tzeltal.

The Human Rights Commission is seen by the state government representative as a body that "supports rebels and loafers," while Jmanel, the mayor, says that "it does nothing." Each of them is denigrating this federal body.

Tuxtla is Tuxtla Gutiérrez, the state capital.

Because of local tension this play has been performed only at the headquarters of the women's cooperative (FOMMA), the Teatro Daniel Zebadua in San Cristóbal, and the Casa del Lago in Mexico City.

NOTE ON PRONUNCIATION: The letter *j* is pronounced as *h,* and *x* as *sh;* the symbol *'* is a glottal stop.

CAST OF CHARACTERS

JMANEL'S SPOKESMAN: wearing sombrero, white shirt, pants, black shoes

JPALAS: same clothes as Jmanel's Spokesman

XUNIL: wearing Tenejapan clothes

JPETUL/JNIK'S SPOKESMAN: wearing sombrero, checked shirt, long pants, brown shoes

XLOXA: wearing Chamulan clothes

JMANEL: wearing dark green shirt, blue jeans, brown shoes, and at the end wearing blonde wig

SLUS: Jmanel's secretary, wearing Zinacantec clothes

XMARUCH: Jmanel's wife, wearing Tenejapan clothes, gold shawl, high heels

REPRESENTATIVE: wearing a suit, tie, black hat, carrying a folder

MARTÍN/BODYGUARD 1: the Representative's bodyguard, wearing brown jacket, black pants, black shoes, dark glasses, carrying a pistol

BODYGUARD 2: wearing same clothes as Martín

FLOR: the Representative's companion, wearing mestiza clothes

JNIK: white T-shirt, black pants, black shoes

J'ALUX: wearing blue shirt, black pants, black shoes

JMARYAN: a shaman, his head wrapped in white Chamulan neckerchief, wearing white shirt and wool tunic, black pants, carrying water gourd

JTZIAK: wearing same clothes as J'alux

JXAW: Jpetul's spokesman, wearing same clothes as J'alux

JXUN: wearing same clothes as Jnik

SCENE 1

(In the square of an Indian town in the highlands of Chiapas a person announces the arrival of Professor Jmanel.)

JMANEL'S SPOKESMAN: *(With a loudspeaker calling to the people)* Men, women, please come to the square to discuss town matters!... *(He repeats)* Compañeros, I've just learned that our Professor Jmanel is back in town. He is very capable and knows a great deal. He's on good terms with the politicians. I think he is the best person to be our candidate for mayor. And he is disposed to take it on. I think we should give him all our support. What do you think, *compañeros?* *(Jpalas, Jpetul, and Xunil reply from the audience.)*

JPALAS: Yeees! We're going to vote for him!

XUNIL: And we women, too!

JMANEL'S SPOKESMAN: All right, wait for me in the town hall while I go get him to ask him to help us with our problems!

(Jmanel's Spokesman exits, and Jpalas, Jpetul, and Xunil climb on the stage.)

JPALAS: Yes, let's vote for Jmanel! Even though he named himself, let's hope he can solve the problems in our town!

XUNIL: Yes, if only he'll give his whole heart to it!

JPETUL: Because we've seen how the others always give promises, but they never come through! *(Xloxa rushes in enthusiastically.)*

XLOXA: Listen, *compañeros*, the candidate Jmanel is coming and he's coming with his wife!

(Jmanel enters with his wife. Jpalas puts down a chair for the candidate. Jmanel pays no attention as he greets everyone with a raised hand and is applauded. Then he sits down and his wife crouches next to him.)

JPALAS: Okay, Jmanel, we know that you agree to be mayor of our town, but we have to ask you some favors, too. *(Jmanel stands and walks rather indifferently to center stage.)*

JMANEL: *(Addressing the public)* That's why I'm here! Tell me everything you want. I'm glad to hear about it.

JPALAS: Look, Jmanel, you know we're very poor and many of us have no jobs. What I want is for you to find me a job. Can you help me somehow?

JMANEL: *(Thinking it over)* Hmm!... Let me think ... Do you know any carpentry?

JPALAS: No, not at all! The only thing I know how to do is plant my corn and my beans ... and take care of pigs!

JMANEL: Don't you worry, Jpalas ... the way things are, if you vote for me ... hmm!... I know they're looking for workers in the place they make ... coffins!

JPALAS: Okay, Jmanel, please take care of it for me!

JMANEL: No problem!

JPETUL: But that's not all, Jmanel! We also want you to do something good for our town. We want you to give us a road, drinking water, schools, clinics ... all the things we've never had here!

JMANEL: Fine, don't you worry, Jpetul! As soon as I get to be mayor, we'll answer all your demands!

XUNIL: That's just what we want, Jmanel! But we women, too, want you to help us with our artisanry, because . . . .

JMANEL: (*Interrupting her*) Yes, yes, Xunil! . . . We'll take the women into account, but we'll see about that later!

XUNIL: Oh, they never let us talk! They always treat us like this! They don't pay attention to women! (*Jmanel holds on to Jpetul and walks to his seat. He improvises a line as his secretary rushes in.*)

SLUS: Excuse me, Jmanel, but the political representative is coming and wants to talk to you.

JMANEL: (*Addressing his secretary*) Thanks, Slus. Wait for me outside. (*Addressing his followers*) *Compañeros*, please, can you leave me alone? I have to handle some important things with the party representative. Come another day!

JPALAS: But we want to talk to him, too!

JPETUL: Yes, we'll tell him what we need in this town, that we support your candidacy, but he must support us, too!

JMANEL: That's not necessary! I know now what you want, and I'll let him know! But be patient! I must speak to him alone. We have party business to discuss.

JPALAS: Okay, all right, Jmanel, we'll come another day. (*They exit, leaving Jmanel alone with his wife, Xmaruch.*)

XMARUCH: But Jmanel, why can't the *compañeros* hear what the representative has to say?

JMANEL: That's not possible. He's from the party's state committee. He told me not to have people around. And you, too, wait for me. This is men's business!

XMARUCH: All right, Jmanel, whatever you say! (*She exits.*)

SCENE 2

(*The politician enters, his arm around his girlfriend, Flor, followed by his bodyguards. Jmanel stands up and tries to greet him with a hug, but he is ignored.*)

JMANEL: Hey, hello, how are you?

REPRESENTATIVE: (*He advances a few feet, leaving the candidate behind as he speaks to the woman.*) Look, Flor, I have some matters to attend to with these ... hmm, wait for me in the plaza. I'll give you some money to buy those trinkets that Indians make. (*One of the bodyguards, Martín, pulls out some money and holds it up. The Representative addresses the public.*) We can justify this as campaign expenses. I'll see you in a while! (*He turns to the woman and kisses her. She coquettishly takes the money from Martín's hand. Then the Representative turns to Jmanel, greets him, and embraces him with repulsion.*) Hello, Jmanel, how've you been?

JMANEL: Well, I'm here, like always. Welcome to our town! (*He sits down without giving his chair to the Representative, who looks at him with annoyance.*) Well, getting on very well with my campaign. The people support me ... Don't you think I'm doing good? (*The Representative, without answering, stares at him, very annoyed. Jmanel understands what the matter is and offers his chair to the Representative.*) Oh, forgive me, lawyer, please sit down!

REPRESENTATIVE: (*Sitting down*) Well, Jmanel, you've been confirmed as the party's official candidate for being mayor of your town. Here is the advance we promised you for your campaign! (*Martín makes a show of handing a big wad to Jmanel.*) And here are the contents of the talks that you are to give to convince the people to vote for us. (*The other bodyguard hands him a folder.*) It's a matter of your handing out the money with discretion to the town authorities to make sure that the majority of people mark the emblem of our party on election day!

JMANEL: Okay, thanks a lot! But I want the party to support me because I can't carry out the campaign by myself!

REPRESENTATIVE: (*Pompously*) There's no problem! We choose the ones who are to be nominated. It's a matter of holding a meeting with those who have power, who control the people, and promise them that you will do what you can so they stay in power. That's the way things have always been!

JMANEL: That seems fine to me. You tell me what to do.

REPRESENTATIVE: Tomorrow we'll have meetings with those guys. Don't worry. Let us guide you and you'll see that we will win as always.

JMANEL: (*Picking up the money*) You're right. So, with this money I'm going to town! (*A group of townspeople enter, waiting impatiently for the candidate, who speaks to them.*) Do you want some money?

EVERYONE: Yees!

JMANEL: Do you want work?

EVERYONE: Yees!

JMANEL: Do you want public works?

EVERYONE: Yees!

JMANEL: Do you want soft drinks?

EVERYONE: Yees!

JMANEL: Do you want beer and cane liquor?

EVERYONE: Yees!

JMANEL: Dear *compañeros,* it is your candidate for the mayor of this town who is talking to you! (*The people whistle.*) It's for you! And besides, I promise to build bridges for you, many bridges!

XLOXA: But what if we don't have any rivers?

JMANEL: I promise them, too, and I promise you a lot of credits so you can plant your land, your corn, your beans, your chile!

JPETUL: But what if chile doesn't grow here?

JMANEL: We'll plant it. We'll hand out toys, too!

XMARUCH: But what if we don't even have children?

JMANEL: We'll make them, too!

XMARUCH: No, the kids are dying of hunger!

JMANEL: Well, we'll build a system for drinking water, and we'll give you housing, health care, and education. That's what I tell you. Put your faith in me! Since I had the honor of being nominated for mayor, I promised myself to dedicate my life to changing the state of this town. If you vote for me, I will obtain the necessary economic resources to end the poverty and margination that we have suffered for so many years! And who is better than me, who is your *compañero,* to be the mayor of this town? I'm the only one who knows what he's talking about!

EVERYONE: Yees! Bravo Jmanel! Jmanel for mayor!

(The candidate exits with whoops and cheers, followed by the crowd, except for Xloxa and two puppet spectators. One of them speaks to Jnik, who looks very upset.)

XLOXA: What did you think of the talk? Can he possibly fulfill all those promises?

JNIK: How could he? We've seen how he keeps on changing his speeches. Besides, we know he's one of the worst of the *caciques.*

XLOXA: I think Jnik is right. This Jmanel has always helped the other *caciques.* We'd better go, too. *(They exit. Jnik comes back immediately and addresses the public from center stage.)*

SCENE 3

JNIK: Well, *compañeros,* I've called this meeting so we can think together who is the best candidate for mayor. That's why we've thought to form an independent party. The elders have asked me, and I'm willing to head it so that we can wipe out this corruption that has damaged our town. Don't you want to have a real democracy? *(The people surround him.)*

EVERYONE: Yees!

JNIK: Don't you want women's rights to be respected?

EVERYONE: Yees!

JNIK: Do you want respect for the laws that deal with work, *compañeros? (Every question is greeted with an enthusiastic "yes.")*

Do you want the agrarian law to be respected and have the *ejido* continue to exist? Do you want real improvements in our town, health care, housing, education?

J'ALUX: Yees! Long live our town! *¡Viva!*

JNIK: Then we all have to work together! Or do we want the mayor continuing to rob, pocketing the town money?

EVERYONE: No!

JNIK: We've seen how the past mayors have offered so much in their campaigns and done nothing! Isn't that true, *compañeros?*

EVERYONE: Yees! Liars!

(The Representative of the official party enters with Martín, who begins to hand out money in the crowd. Those who receive cash one by one abandon Jnik, who is left totally alone.)

JNIK: The past mayors have gotten rich stealing from us! That's because they've changed our ancient customs! We've seen now that Professor Jmanel has received money from the official party to hand out to the town agents, *compañeros,* and then use that for his own good! That's not right, *compañeros!* That's buying the vote and making everything corrupt!... But don't leave, *compañeros, compañeros, compañeros* ... *(Disillusioned, he sees that the stage is empty except for the Representative and Martín in the corner, who stare at him scornfully. Martín cynically offers him a wad of bills.)* Damn! Now they've left me all alone! *(He looks at them angrily.)*

REPRESENTATIVE: *(Staring at Jnik furiously while he returns the gaze defiantly)* You're getting yourself into a mess of trouble, Jnik!

MARTÍN: *(Laughing cynically)* It seems like this year they're going to reward me for doing such good work! *(He exits.)*

SCENE 4

(The two spokesmen enter from opposite sides, making way for the two candidates who cross in the center and greet the voters. Simultaneously they praise their candidate to win the people's votes.)

JPETUL: *Compañeros,* my friends in this town, we want you to come and vote for Jnik so he will become our mayor! We want an honest man, no more corruption! There must be justice and democracy, and the opinions of the women must be taken into account! We have seen that the guys in the official party are very tricky and never do what they promise! But we have seen the work of our *compañero,* Jnik, who always wants to help the people, and we know he's honest! Besides, our party is made up of both men and women! The guys of the official party are very different. We've seen when they're in power, they no longer pay any attention to us.

JMANEL'S SPOKESMAN: *Compañeros,* we are joined by Professor Jmanel, our candidate for mayor of our town. He is here to prove the honesty of the elections! Remember, *compañeros,* that Professor Jmanel is known for his work, which always benefits the common man! We will not let ourselves be confused by those who want to upset the order in our town, enemies of progress who resent the system! And it's no good coming to whine about how we're going to steal from them! (*The crowd, intimidated by the body-guards, passes over to Jmanel's side.*) *Compañeros,* today it is not Professor Jmanel who has won. It is not the party that has won! Our town has won! ¡Viva Jmanel!

JMANEL: That's the truth, *compañeros!* The victory is yours! Thank you for supporting me! At last, I am the boss of the future ... the future of the world! *Compañeros,* come celebrate our victory! Come, there are soft drinks for everyone!

EVERYONE: (*Including Jmanel*) You can see it, you can feel it, the whole town is with us! (*Jmanel exits, followed by his supporters. Then Jnik and Jpetul enter, visibly upset and disillusioned.*)

JNIK: I never thought the people could be bought off! They're a bunch of cowards! They don't even know who to vote for!

JPETUL: That's right! It's easy to manipulate our *compañeros.* I've seen how the majority was for you.

JNIK: Me, too. I was sure I'd win! So that means they handed them money.

JPETUL: Of course! That way why wouldn't they win? They bought their vote!

JNIK: Now what we have to do is see that they don't steal the town's money!

(*As they are exiting, Jpalas, Xloxa, and Xunil enter to speak to the mayor. Jpetul gives a knowing glance to Jnik, and they join the others.*)

SCENE 5

XLOXA: Hey, *compañeros!* Come along! We're going to talk to the mayor to ask him for his support!

JNIK: (*Addressing Jpetul*) Go see what's happening!

JPALAS: Yes, and remember that the mayor promised me a job in the coffin factory!

XUNIL: We have to remind him of the promises he made!

XLOXA: Yes, let's go!

> (*The mayor enters dressed in a suit, wearing sunglasses, and has a "bed head," dyed blond. He sits down and begins to count money, separating it and sticking some in one pocket and the rest in the other. Then Xunil, Jpetul, Xloxa, and Jpalas enter and greet the mayor with respect. The mayor, in surprise, hides the bills and replies to them with disdain.*)

JMANEL: Hmm, hmm, what can I do for you?

JPALAS: Now that you're mayor, I want you to get me that job you promised me in your campaign!

JMANEL: Hmmm ... Well, bring me your social security card, your military card, and ...

JPALAS: (*Interrupting Jmanel*) Military card? But where would I find that if I don't even have a birth certificate? None of us has one!

JMANEL: Then you don't even exist!

JPALAS: Oh, Mayor, but ... aren't you looking at me?

JMANEL: Well, yes, I know you're alive, but without those papers I can't give you a job!

JPALAS: Okay, God bless you! (*Jpalas withdraws, crying. Xloxa advances to speak to Jmanel.*)

XLOXA: Good morning, Mr. Mayor, I don't know if you can give me work, too. I don't know if you can help me because my little boy is sick, and I haven't any money. I have five kids to raise. My husband left me and went off with another woman.

JMANEL: He probably left you because you don't know how to do anything!... And besides, what's that to me? That's not my problem or the town's problem. You'd better go home and solve your own problems.

XLOXA: All right. (*Xloxa exits, sighing.*)

XUNIL: Mr. Mayor, the words you spoke during your campaign have not been forgotten. I am the representative of a group of artisan women. I come to ask you to help us get support to buy material and sell our products, as you promised us.

JMANEL: You're right, but I can't help you now because they haven't freed the funds for me. And as for marketing your products ... I can't set myself up to sell them for you ... that can't be done! So, come see me in one or two months!

XUNIL: All right, what else can we do? (*Disappointed, she withdraws and joins Jpalas. Jpetul steps forward.*)

JPETUL: Mr. Mayor, we've come to see you about the public works that you told us would begin. We need a highway, drinking water, a clinic, a school, and other things....

JMANEL: Yes, agreed, but I can't help you now because there aren't any funds. They haven't freed them for me. Come and see me in two or three months, okay?

JPETUL: All right, that's all right, but will you have the funds by then?

JMANEL: Well, until I get the funds, I can't do anything. But I need you to leave me alone because I have to prepare some reports that the governor asked for.

JPETUL: Just as you say, sir!

(The townspeople pull aside and meet together.)

JPALAS: Look, first he promised us lots of things, and now he doesn't come through with it. And I thought that now I could have a job! They're pure lies!

EVERYONE: Yes, yes!

XUNIL: It's better if we leave. *(Jpalas, Xloxa, and Xunil exit.)*

JNIK: *(Addressing Jpetul, who approaches him)* So, what happened?

JPETUL: No, he's not going to carry out his promises because they haven't freed the funds for him yet.

JNIK: But how is that possible? I went to the Congress and they told me that a month ago they had entrusted the money to Jmanel.

JPETUL: So, then ... he's stealing it! What can we do?

JNIK: Well, we're going to denounce him before Congress, and we're going to warn them that if they don't solve the problem and there's trouble, it will be their fault, because we're tired of being tricked over and over again!

(Jnik and Jpetul exit just when the party Representative enters.)

SCENE 6

REPRESENTATIVE: Hello, Jmanel, how are you? You have some problem?

JMANEL: Well, yes, man! There's a group of rebellious people who are making trouble for me. They're headed by Jnik!

REPRESENTATIVE: Oh, I remember him! The opposition candidate, right?

JMANEL: Yes! Help me, please!... How can we solve this?

REPRESENTATIVE: Well, look ... Don't you worry ... Let my people in Tuxtla be in charge of this problem.

JMANEL: Okay, but you have to be careful because the people love him. It's true, they finally gave me the budget and I put aside this for you! *(He hands him a wad of bills.)*

REPRESENTATIVE: That's fine, Jmanel. (*He steps forward and takes the biggest bunch and gives the little one back to Jmanel, who accepts it resignedly.*) This is for you! (*Then he hands a bill to Jmanel.*) And this is for the town!

JMANEL: That's all? But … this is so little!

REPRESENTATIVE: Yes, man. With that you can have a party every weekend. You can get them drunk on cane liquor. They're satisfied with cheap liquor. They don't know about anything better! That's the truth … but … what happened to your hair?

JMANEL: (*Smiling, a bit shamefacedly*) Well, since I'm the mayor I have to look handsome! (*The Representative reproaches him with his hand.*)

REPRESENTATIVE: (*He reconsiders.*) You look so cool, you bastard!

JMANEL: Well, let's have a good chat.… Let's have a drink or two, don't you think? I've reserved some pretty gals for you!

REPRESENTATIVE: Fine, but it's your invitation!

JMANEL: Yes, of course! I'm inviting you. I've got a little money!

REPRESENTATIVE: But don't you give me any cane liquor!

JMANEL: No, no, there they have the kind of rum you like!

(*They exit, hugging each other. Then Xunil and Slus come running in.*)

SCENE 7

XUNIL: Come over here, Slus, I've something to tell you. You know, Jmanel has not wanted to support us, and we're going to have to close the artisanry cooperative. We haven't any pay for any one of us.

SLUS: But how could that be? He promised to support us! What are we going to do about our families? (*Xloxa enters, sobbing.*)

XLOXA: Hello, Xunil!

XUNIL: Hello, Xloxa, but what happened to you? Why are you crying?

XLOXA: It's because my baby died! I don't know if you can help me with a little money for my four other children!

XUNIL: But why did your baby die?

XLOXA: I don't know what kind of sickness it had! You remember, Jmanel promised us a clinic, but it was never built. If there had been a clinic, my poor baby wouldn't have died! (*Jpalas enters ready to cry and stands at the side.*)

XUNIL: It's all the mayor's fault. But we were so stupid to let him trick us! But look … What's the matter with Jpalas?

SLUS: Jpalas, why are you so unhappy?

JPALAS: It's that … Listen here, the mayor put out orders to seize my land because they were going to build the clinic, and it was pure lies! Now I have nowhere to live! You remember he was going to give me a job in the coffin factory? And now he says if I protest, they're going to give me a coffin, but for myself! So it's better if I go as a wetback to the United States before they kill me! (*Jnik enters, upset, followed by his friends.*)

JNIK: Come here, *compañeros,* we're going to tell the people what we've just been able to find out! (*Addressing everyone*) We're going to hold a meeting because something very serious is happening in our town! Jmanel, the mayor, is stealing the funds!

JPALAS: (*upset and disillusioned*) Oh, I don't believe anything's going to change, Jnik. It's better if I go to the United States as I thought.

XUNIL: But have you thought it over carefully? No, don't go!

JNIK: Yes, Jpalas, stay here! We're not the only ones, and together we can throw Jmanel out of office!

JPALAS: No, I'm going. . . . What can you do?

JNIK: Well, if he goes, we must get really strong so things really change here, because we've just discovered that Jmanel is taking the town's money, *compañeros!* It was three months ago that the funds were freed, and he hasn't carried out one of his promises! The worst thing is that he has been turning in false papers to Congress, telling them that some works are advancing well, like the clinic, the school, and drinking water! And that's not true, *compañeros.* He's been falsifying our signatures and using the town seal to account for the money that Congress approved! Jpetul's coming in a minute with copies of the false papers so you all will be aware of Jmanel's bad management!

(*Jpetul enters beaten up, groaning, and grumbling.*)

XUNIL: Jpetul's come!

SLUS: But what happened to you, Jpetul? Who beat you up?

JPETUL: (*Complaining*) Well . . . they hit me, the mayor's people. They grabbed me on the road when I was coming here. They beat me up and threw me over the cliff, but I was able to save the copies of the false vouchers!

JNIK: But look what they did to you! You were lucky they didn't kill you!

JPETUL: Well, I think that's what they meant to do. I think they left me for dead!

JNIK: But you saved the documents! Look, *compañeros,* here is the proof I was telling you about. With this we can prove that Jmanel and his party are stealing all the funds that were for our town.

JXAW: And then . . . what can we do?

JNIK: I think we have to kick out the mayor and appoint a town council!

XUNIL: Yes, we should appoint a town council!

SLUS: We'll need everyone's signature!

JXAW: I'm going to my community and get their signatures!

JTZIAK: Yes, we're going to bring more people so that all of us together can throw this mayor out! We won't let them continue violating our rights!

JNIK: Well, then, we'll see each other tomorrow in front of the town hall! (*Everyone exits except Jpetul.*) So, Jpetul, the way you are, can you go to the council of elders and show them these papers? They should store them away and invite the elders to the meeting so they can advise us what we must do, because there'll surely be problems!

JPETUL: Yes, of course! But watch out, Jnik, because they must be tailing you, too!

(Jpetul exits and one of the representatives enters, following behind Jnik, who is talking to himself worriedly.)

JNIK: Hell, things are getting very bad! They must have figured out that we are going to kick Jmanel out and accuse him before Congress! . . . But there's nothing else we can do . . . (*Turning around, he sees the menacing look of the Bodyguard, who is fingering the gun at his waist.*) But . . . what's with you? Are you threatening me?

MARTÍN: Okay now, Jnik, they warned you. Now you're in trouble. Move it, you're going to talk to the boss!

JNIK: Well, so it's good for you to be walking around armed. But they'll pay you back, you bastards!

(The Bodyguard pushes him out and they exit. You hear screams. Then Jmanel enters hurriedly, followed by his wife.)

SCENE 8

XMARUCH: Hey, Jmanel, wait! There's something I have to tell you!

JMANEL: (*Angrily*) What's the matter with you now?

XMARUCH: I'm very scared! Everybody is speaking against you, and the women don't want to speak to me, Jmanel. Be careful so nothing happens to you!

JMANEL: Don't worry, I have it all in hand. I have my people working out there. And besides, as I told you, this is a matter for men alone! Let's go then!

(As they exit, Jnik enters on the other side, beaten, dragged by the two bodyguards, who leave him in stage center, where he falls.)

MARTÍN: Boss, here's your man.

(The Representative enters, staring at Jnik with anger and scorn as Jnik lifts himself with difficulty and stands up.)

REPRESENTATIVE: You've been behaving bad, Jnik!

JNIK: Damned thieves!

REPRESENTATIVE: See here, so you see I'm willing to make a deal, I propose the following to you. Accept a position in our government and don't go looking around for trouble. How's that?

JNIK: You think everyone's like you!

REPRESENTATIVE: Look, don't get carried away. See how they left you! Your people abandoned you! That's because the people support this system. It treats them well. That's why it's easy to manipulate them. So what do you answer? Do you accept?

JNIK: Don't think you can blackmail me! The whole town knows now that you are a bunch of thieves, and they're going to accuse you of it in Congress!

REPRESENTATIVE: Well, for the last time, do you accept or not?

JNIK: No! *(The Representative gestures to the Bodyguards.)*

REPRESENTATIVE: Okay, boys, Jnik is leaving now. Take him home and be sure he doesn't cause any more problems.

MARTÍN: Yes, boss! *(The Bodyguards drag Jnik behind the curtain. A shot is heard and a groan.)*

REPRESENTATIVE: What a stupid waste of money! I hope the boys toss him into the canyon! Bullets are so expensive!

SCENE 9

(Jmaryan, a shaman, appears with the townspeople, headed by Jpetul.)

JPETUL: We have met, *compañeros,* because Jnik has not been seen in a week. We think the mayor had him killed. I'm sure that's what happened because they beat me up, too. What do you think, *compañeros?*

JTZIAK: Well, our shaman, Father Jmaryan, is here with us. I believe that he can do us the favor of finding him!

XUNIL: Please do us the favor, Father Jmaryan, sir. We must discover where Jnik's body and soul are!

JMARYAN: All right, don't worry! I'm going to call forth Jnik. *(A helper gives him candles and incense for the prayer. He carries out a ceremony and invocation.)* Children ... I have seen many bad things! They chopped up Jnik and threw his body parts in different places!

SLUS: (*Agitated, holds up a bloody shirt*) It's true, brothers! I found his bloody shirt at the bottom of the canyon!

JTZIAK: (*They make negative comments, condemning the action.*) It's not possible!

XLOXA: How horrible!

XUNIL: How could they have done that?

JXAW: Damned cowards!

JMARYAN: As for his body, he carried his blood in his hands up to Heaven, but his soul is with us, looking for justice. Now we must choose someone to guide us. (*The shaman looks at Jpetul, as do the people.*)

XLOXA: That person must be Jpetul, that's what we all think! Isn't that right, *compañeros?*

EVERYONE: Yees! It should be Jpetul!

XUNIL: He's the one with the strongest soul!

JMARYAN: So be it, if that's what you all want!

JPETUL: If that is what you desire, I will follow in Jnik's steps, so that his death won't have been in vain! (*He puts on Jnik's bloody shirt.*) This is our battle, so don't leave me alone!

JTZIAK: (*Various people hand over to Jpetul documents signed in the communities.*) But you aren't alone ... Here are the signatures demanding that the mayor be removed!

JPETUL: That's so good, *compañeros!* We are going to take these documents to Congress so they kick out Jmanel and name a council!

EVERYONE: Yees! Let's go to Congress! (*Jpetul exits, followed by the crowd, except the shaman, his helper, and Slus, who help him get to his feet.*)

SLUS: Oh, Father Jmaryan, what is going to become of our town?

JMARYAN: Oh, daughter, I will have to pray a great deal so this town becomes united and there's no more violence, the way it was when I was younger, when we all lived in peace. But let's go now, daughter, it's late. (*They exit, and the Representative and Jmanel enter.*)

SCENE 10

REPRESENTATIVE: Jmanel, I summoned you because there is a problem that bothers us very much in Congress. It seems that things are becoming very dangerous in your town.

JMANEL: Yes, I'm worried, too, because the people are getting angrier every day.

REPRESENTATIVE: Jpetul arrived at Congress with a group of protesters, presenting proof of mismanagement of funds and a document signed by the authorities and people of the communities asking that you resign from the mayor's office. But we have shown them that's not possible. We can use the laws to support you, but it seems like the matter won't end there. I believe you must see to it they don't ask for help from the Bureau of Indian Affairs or Human Rights. You've seen how those institutions only dedicate themselves to supporting those rebels and loafers!

JMANEL: But we know the Human Rights Commission never does anything! It would be better for us if the leader disappeared!

REPRESENTATIVE: Yes, I think the ideal thing would be to dispose of him as we did with Jnik. Don't worry, we'll help you (*Calling to Martín*) Martín ... (*Martín enters.*) Assemble your guys. I've got a job for you in Jmanel's town. (*Addressing Jmanel*) There's no need to worry, and please, man, try to control your people!

JMANEL: Okay! (*Jpetul enters excitedly, summoning the people.*)

JPETUL: *Compañeros,* come over here! We're going to have a meeting to tell the people what happened in Congress!

EVERYONE: What happened, Jpetul?

JXUN: What happened, Jpetul? How did they treat you in Congress?

JPETUL: Well, can you believe it, Jxun? In Congress they rejected our petition. They don't want to unseat Jmanel. What do you think we should do, *compañeros?*

JXUN: But we don't know, Jpetul! It's better if you tell us what we should do! We're behind you!

JPETUL: There's no other choice, *compañeros.* We'll have to take over the town hall. But without any violence!

EVERYONE: Yees! We'll capture the town hall! (*Xloxa turns and sees Martín behind her.*)

XLOXA: Look, *compañeros,* there's one of those bad guys!

JXUN: Yes, he's one of the murderers who wanted to kill Jpetul!

XUNIL: Let's lynch him!

EVERYONE: Yees! Robbers, assassins!

XLOXA: (*Turning to hold back the crowd*) No, *compañeros,* it's better if we lynch Jmanel. He's the one who's guilty of all the things that are happening in our town!

EVERYONE: Yees! Let's go! (*Everyone exits except Jpetul, who stays behind, calling to them.*)

JPETUL: *Compañeros!* Don't cause more problems! Don't us do what they've done! Don't fall for that!

(*The crowd enters; Xunil and Jxaw pull Jmanel in, his hands bound. They leave him kneeling in center stage as they jeer him.*)

JXAW: *Compañeros,* come here, we've got Jmanel! It's time for him to pay for all the evil things he's done, for the death of Jnik! It's time to carry out justice!

XUNIL: We should stone him to death. He should pay for his crimes!

EVERYONE: Yees! We should kill him! He should die! We'll burn him up!

JXUN: We should cut him to pieces, like they did to Jnik!

XLOXA: No, it's better if we hang him in the square!

JPETUL: Don't do that! We're not going to kill him, because we can't take justice in our own hands! We must respect Jmanel's rights, because if not, we'll be committing the same crimes as he did!

XMARUCH: No! What do we care about his rights? Do you think he respected the rights of the town? We ought to kill him once and for all!

JPETUL: That's no way to solve the problem! If we do that, we'll continue to suffer the intervention of the crooked, lying politicians in the affairs of the town! The time has come for us to learn how to solve our own problems in a reasonable way as our ancestors did!

JXAW: So what can we do? If we just jail him, it'll be an endless story, because Congress will free him and give him another position! We've got to do something! We can't stand around with our arms crossed!

XUNIL: It's time for all of us to execute him! Why muddle around if he's the worst of the killers?

EVERYONE: Yees, we'll finish him off!

JMANEL: No, no! Please don't kill me! Remember, it wasn't just me, but the party representative, too! It was he who ordered his bodyguards to kill Jnik!... If you pardon me, I promise you I'll be a good mayor from now on, and I promise you I'll return to Congress the money I stole!

XUNIL: But it's not Congress's money! It's the town's money!

JPETUL: What we have to do first is have him return it to the town! So it can be used for the public works where he supposedly spent it!

XLOXA: And who's going to maintain Jnik's family?

XUNIL: Jmanel should provide a pension for the widow and her children until they're grown up!

JMANEL: I agree! Take all my money!... And for Jnik's family, take my cars and sell my house!

XMARUCH: Then we have to take him to jail right now!

JPETUL: Yes, we have to take him to the police office and accuse him of Jnik's murder, together with the representative.

(They all exit, insulting Jmanel, taking him to jail. Jpetul remains in center stage.)

JPETUL: Now that the town has named me to be mayor, I invite all of you to participate in the construction of the future of our town, so that we achieve what our ancestors have advised us: to rule obeying the will of the people. I ask each of you to give me your ideas so that together we carry out a plan for the good of all. (*One by one, each of the actors enters carrying a poster, demanding their rights.*)

JXUN: Democracy and Justice! Democracy is the principle for the liberty, justice, and dignity of the people! By the will of all the people the public servants should be elected. By their will it should be decided what laws and customs to follow, respecting the rights of others so that one's own rights be respected.

XUNIL: Women's and Children's Rights! We women demand the same work opportunities as men. We also ask that we receive equal rights of inheritance, and the right to express our ideas and receive education. We demand an equal vote and equal opportunity to carry out public office. It is necessary to create a culture that respects the rights of boys and girls so they may grow up healthy and happy, learning by their games the knowledge and labor that will be useful to them as adults.

JPALAS: Indian Culture and Rights! It is the obligation of the state to provide education, culture, and training for all the ethnic groups in the country, respecting the ancestral ways and traditions of each people. Government support for freedom of religion should imply respect for the native culture and reduce the advance of foreign cultures.

Finale, 2000. Photo courtesy of Sna Jtz'ibajom

JPETUL: Labor Rights! Everyone should have the right to obtain a job with no discrimination. The salaries should permit workers to cover the basic necessities for survival—education, health care, decent housing, and legal services.

XLOXA: Bilingual Education! Native peoples must have the right to bilingual and multicultural education through the middle and higher levels, giving priority to the maternal tongue of the student, and providing the materials and teaching methods appropriate for each people.

REPRESENTATIVE: Individual Rights! Everyone within the country is free and protected by the Mexican Constitution. The authorities are not permitted to act with violence or physical aggression.

JMANEL: Autonomy! All the ethnic groups must have the right to administer their natural resources, define their territory, apply justice according to their habits and customs, have access to the means of communication, and the right to determine the development plans for their towns.

XMARUCH: End of Racism! To be an Indian must be considered a reason for pride and not shame. National identity, culture, and development must be based on this truth.

XLOXA: But the principal requirement so that we can become masters of the future of our people is that the federal, state, and local authorities recognize our needs and decisions.

EVERYONE: Yees! Mexico with us forever!

The World Turned on Its Head

(2003)

BY ROGELIO ROMÁN HERNÁNDEZ DE LA CRUZ
REVISED BY SNA JTZ'IBAJOM

THE WORLD TURNED ON ITS HEAD (*El planeta de cabeza*), unlike the previous plays that were written collaboratively by the members of Sna, is the work of Rogelio Román Hernández de la Cruz, Petu's son, who wrote it when he was eighteen. Because this play was to be performed on Valentine's Day 2003 at the Palacio de Bellas Artes in Mexico City to accompany the presentation of my *Diccionario del corazón/Mayan Hearts,* we were told that it must be shortened considerably, to last not longer than fifteen minutes. So, together with the members of Sna, remaining true to its original design, we were able to reduce the play to twenty-one minutes while at the same time lacing the text with the heart metaphors from my book. For this translation of the script I have not included the metaphors that sound very awkward in English.

In Roge's comedy about three married couples, the men are totally dominated by their wives, having to cook and clean and request permission to leave home. One husband invents the means to escape from their predicament. They tell their wives that they have no interest in sleeping with them because they are gay. The wives respond by dressing in their husbands' clothes and visiting the cantina where the men are happily drinking their beers. The unsuspecting husbands are attracted to their wives, whereupon their spouses reveal their identity and agree to be dutiful wives so long as their husbands give them the respect they deserve.

Against the advice of the members of Sna, but following my recommendation, Roge used the Tzotzil word for "gay" (*tutz,* pronounced "tuutz"). It was picked up immediately by the audience, whose laughter did not subside until the play's end. In an article by Janet Schwartz, it reached the whole world by Internet, much to Roge's pleasure. As noted earlier, AIDS is said to be contracted by having sexual relations with prostitutes, not with other men. While off-color jokes intimating homosexuality are a standard ingredient of the verbal duels indulged in by the religious officials when they are drinking together, it is a topic carefully avoided in everyday conversation. Anthropologists have yet to learn about its incidence in the Indian communities.

The caretakers at the Palacio declared that this evening was the most exciting event that they had seen there and the first time that an Indian-directed performance had occurred at this temple of elite Mexican culture.

CAST OF CHARACTERS

JUAN (COMPADRE 1): wearing mestizo clothing, as do all the others
TERESA (JUAN'S WIFE)
ANTONIO (COMPADRE 2)
LUIS (COMPADRE 3)
ANA (ANTONIO'S WIFE)
ROSA (LUIS'S WIFE)
WAITRESS

Act I

SCENE 1

(Juan and his wife in their home in a small town)

JUAN: I'm back, woman. (*Surprised*) Where's my old lady? I bet she went to gab with her *comadre,* like she always does!

TERESA: (*With a commanding voice*) Here I am, Juan. How was work?

JUAN: (*Trying to scold his wife*) Woman, where the hell were you? Why did you leave the place in such a mess? Eh? Answer me!

TERESA: (*Angrily*) Are you trying to scold me? Okay, sit down! First, I'm the person in charge here. And second, if you want to be the boss here, you should have been like that since the beginning! Now shut up and get me something to eat. But hurry up!

JUAN: (*Timidly*) Okay, dearest. I'll bring it right away!

TERESA: But hurry up, you dumb-ass!

JUAN: Do you want beans and turnips?

TERESA: Yes, I'll have that.

JUAN: Yes, dearest.

TERESA: You guys sure know how to piss us off! My *comadre* Ana's husband is just the same. You make us so pissed we can hardly eat. You'd better clean up this mess before I give you a kick! I'm going to my bedroom to eat, and then I'll take a nap!

JUAN: Okay, dearest, take a rest! (*Thoughtfully and laughing to himself*) Oh, my wife is so sweet, she didn't hit me!

ANTONIO: (*Entering with a black eye and looking about to make sure that Juan's wife is not around*) Juan, Juan, are you there?

JUAN: Yes, I'm here. Come on in!

ANTONIO: But . . . ? Your woman isn't here?

JUAN: Yes, she's lying down. Come in! Don't worry! (*Surprised*) But what happened to you, bro? You're all banged up! It was your old lady, right? So, what did you do?

ANTONIO: It was just because the pants I was wearing were a little dirty. I got them dirty on the job. I tried to take good care of them, but I was tired and didn't want to wash them. That's why she hit me.

JUAN: (*Sweeping*) Oh, these women treat us so bad. But what can we do if they're the ones in charge? At least my wife is better than yours. Mine only hits me once a week and sometimes two weeks go by without her hitting me. She only roughs me up a little bit!

ANTONIO: Your lady's something special!

JUAN: Help me so I can finish it up quickly and see if my wife will let me go out for a while.

ANTONIO: Okay. (*Singing, he helps Juan sweep.*)

JUAN: You know, *compadre,* sometimes I wonder what it feels like to be the boss.

ANTONIO: It must feel good.

JUAN: Now we're done, *compadre!*

TERESA: (*She comes in, yawning.*) So you finished, old man? Oh, so you're gossiping with our *compadre!*

JUAN: Yes, I'm done, *vieja!* Look! Your house looks like new!

TERESA: Yes, I see, it's clean! But what are you doing here, *compadre?*

ANTONIO: Just seeing what your husband is up to.

TERESA: Okay, now you've seen him! Get going! We've got things to do here!

ANTONIO: But . . . I want to know if you'll let him go out for a minute!

JUAN: (*Pleading*) Yes, sweetheart, please! Let me go out, okay?

TERESA: Okay, but come back soon! By seven o'clock and not a minute later!

JUAN: That's fine, my love! Thanks a lot! (*Everyone exits.*)

SCENE 2

(Juan and Antonio come back in.)

JUAN: (*Walking about happily*) I'm so glad my old lady let me come out! You see how good-hearted she is! Look at your watch, it's 6:30.

ANTONIO: Yeah, your old lady's got something going for her!

JUAN: What do you mean, *compadre?*

ANTONIO: No . . . I just mean you've got such a good wife! I fell over my words!

JUAN: Okay, to change the subject . . . When are you going shopping tomorrow?

ANTONIO: I think before I go to work, around six o'clock.

JUAN: Can you pick me up then?

ANTONIO: Okay, *compadre!*

LUIS: (*Enters, whistling*) What's up, guys?

JUAN AND ANTONIO: Not much, and you?

LUIS: I'm fine. In fact, I'm doin' great!

ANTONIO: Why are you so happy?

LUIS: Because now I don't have a wife who hits me, but I still have a wife.

JUAN: How come?

LUIS: Well, the other day I got tired of my wife hitting me so I started thinkin' what I could do so she'd cut it out. I was thinking about it all afternoon and then it came to me.

JUAN AND ANTONIO: (*Surprised*) What?

LUIS: Just like us, they need a companion. Get it? I thought of their weak point. If we don't act like men and sleep with them, they're going to miss it, and they're going to beg us to give them what they want. Try it and you'll see how good it turns out for you!

ANTONIO: What do you think of that, *compadre?*

JUAN: That seems really good to me. We've got to try it out! Let's go, *compadres!* One, two, one, two! (*They march out.*)

Luis celebrating with his companions, 2002. Photo copyright © Janet Schwartz

SCENE 3

TERESA: (*She appears from the other side, yawning.*) I feel so tired and that asshole hasn't come back.

JUAN: I'm back, dear!

TERESA: Why not until now? Don't you see what time it is? It's 7:01 and I told you to be back at seven! What held you up?

JUAN: I spent the time talking with my *compadre*. He was worried, too, because his wife only gave him fifteen minutes.

TERESA: Knowing what my *comadre*'s like, she'll surely give him another black eye. Now I want you to get real sexy.

JUAN: What for, dear?

TERESA: Don't you ask, just go ahead and do it!

JUAN: Okay. (*Juan exits.*)

TERESA: (*Shouting*) But hurry up!

JUAN: (*He appears wearing a sleeveless shirt.*) See how sexy I am, dear!

TERESA: (*Surprised*) Come over to me, honey!

JUAN: What for, dear? How come you're no longer telling me how bad I am, what a beast I am, like you usually do?

TERESA: Now you're the boss!

JUAN: (*Surprised*) What? I'm the one in charge? (*He mutters to himself.*) My *compadre* Luis was right.

TERESA: Come on, dear, hug me!

JUAN: No, Tere, not now.

TERESA: Why not?

JUAN: It's 'cause I've got a headache.

TERESA: Come on, don't do that to me!

JUAN: But don't you understand, Tere, I'm so tired. (*He yawns.*)

TERESA: (*Angrily*) Go on, go to bed, then!

JUAN: Thanks a lot, my love! (*He exits.*)

TERESA: What could've happened to my man that he doesn't want to come to bed with me? I have to talk about it with my *comadre!* (*She exits.*)

SCENE 4

TERESA: (*She enters.*) *Comadre,* I'm so glad to find you here. I want to have a good talk with you about something!

ANA: That's strange because I wanted to talk with you about something, too!

TERESA: I told your *compadre* that he should be sexy because I wanted to get laid, and you know what? He didn't want to because he had a headache and he was tired.

ANA: No kidding, *comadre?* That's just what I was going to tell you, too, because we have the very same problem.

TERESA: I think we'd better not let them go out because they must have other women, and that's why they don't want to be with us.

ANA: Yes, *comadre,* that's a good idea! (*They exit.*)

SCENE 5

TERESA: (*She enters.*) Did you take a nap?

JUAN: (*Lying on his bed*) A quick one.

TERESA: (*She comes to the bed and kisses him.*) But how do you feel about ...

JUAN: About what?

TERESA: About what we'd planned to do.

JUAN: What do you mean?

TERESA: Don't be an idiot!

JUAN: Oh! Now I know what you're talking about! But I still don't feel so good!

TERESA: How come?

JUAN: Just because. But sit down, honey. There's like something I want to tell you.

TERESA: What is it?

JUAN: Yesterday when I went out with my *compadre* Antonio, I realized that he's really cute and ...

TERESA: So?

JUAN: Well, he turned me on. I really liked him, and I felt so good!

TERESA: (*Shocked*) What do you mean to say? That you're becomin' ...

JUAN: I don't know, and that's why I don't want to be with you. (*He lowers his head.*)

TERESA: (*She begins to cry.*) Oh what a bad husband you turned out to be. (*Pleading with him*) Please don't become *tuutz!* From now on I will be waiting for you with the meal ready. I'll keep the house tidy, and it's you who will be in charge of things.

JUAN: (*He looks at Teresa with interest.*) I don't know, wife, I can't guarantee you anything.

TERESA: From now on I'll obey you! (*Drying her eyes, she gets up.*) Let me go see my *comadre!*

JUAN: (*Proudly*) Of course, but come back soon! (*They both exit.*)

ANA: (*She enters, sweeping.*) I've got to hurry so it will be clean when my Antonio comes back.

ROSA AND TERESA: (*They enter.*) Good afternoon, *comadre!*

ANA: Good afternoon! Come in!

ROSA: (*Timidly*) Thanks, *comadre*. We've come to tell you something! Who knows what's happening to our husbands!

ROSA: My *compadre* Juan and my husband want to become *tuutz*.

ANA: Oh, there must be something going on because I don't believe it's by chance that my husband is just like them!

TERESA: Now they're in the cantina we should take advantage of that to see what's going on.

ANA: We'll dress like men and go to the bar and offer them some beers. Then we'll tell them that we're going to make our wives believe that we're becoming *tuutz* if they won't let us be in charge.

ROSA: Good idea! So we'll act like men! We're going to look really cool!

TERESA: You've said it! (*They exit.*)

Act II

JUAN: (*He enters with Antonio.*) Now, *compadre*, we're going to do what we've always wanted to do, drink without them hitting us.

ANTONIO: Yeah, *compadre*, now we can drink till we get really shit-faced.

WAITRESS: (*From offstage*) What would you like?

JUAN: (*Calling to the waitress*) Give us two beers to start!

WAITRESS: (*She enters.*) Of course, anything for you. (*She wiggles her hips.*)

JUAN: You see what a babe the waitress is! (*He whistles at her.*)

LUIS: (*He enters and shakes their hands.*) What's up, guys? Enjoying yourselves?

JUAN: (*Warmly*) That's the way it is, thanks to your advice. Now we're free to do what we want. Now we're the ones who call the shots. But sit down, man. Have a beer. I'd like to thank you for your help.

LUIS: Okay!

WAITRESS: Here are your beers.

JUAN: Thanks, cutie, but bring another for my friend!

WAITRESS: Of course, hottie!

(*The women appear dressed as men.*)

TERESA: Look! There are our dirty husbands. Let's go then and sit down next to them.

ROSA: (*Interrupting the men's talk.*) Hi there, you guys! How's it going? Can we join you?

JUAN: Sure, sit down!

ANTONIO: I've never seen you. Are you new to town?

TERESA: Yes, we came to check out the sights, now that we're the ones at home who give the orders.

JUAN: Is that so? You didn't used to give the orders in your homes?

ANA: No, before it was our wives who told us what to do.

WAITRESS: Here's your beer, handsome.

JUAN: Thanks, doll, now bring me three more! (*He pats her shoulder.*)

TERESA: (*She hits Juan.*) What are you doing, man? Why are you hitting on her?

JUAN: What's the matter with you? Why are you punching me?

TERESA: Oh, I'm sorry! It made me jealous, but not over you. Eh? It was over the waitress.

JUAN: I thought it was my wife who was hitting me, and for sure wherever it was you bought those clothes, they're the same as mine.

TERESA: Seriously? I bought these clothes in a store where they sell very expensive things.

ANTONIO: Speaking of clothes, what that other guy has sure looks like mine. What's your name?

ANA: My name is Ana, Anus ... I meant Anastasio.

ANTONIO: I even thought you had the same name as my wife. For sure I love my little woman.

ANA: (*Warmly*) Really? Oh, ho, ho!

ANTONIO: So why does that move you?

ANA: Because it's great that you love your wife.

WAITRESS: Here are your three beers, guys!

JUAN: Thanks, doll!

TERESA: (*Angrily*) And you, don't you be such a flirt!

WAITRESS: Oh, aren't you something! (*She exits, swinging her hips.*)

JUAN: What's the matter? Don't you like chicks?

TERESA: Yes, but I don't like them slutting around like that.

LUIS: Now I remember ... we were talking about what they did so their wives would stop ordering them around.

ROSA: Well, it's very easy. We're real smart. We trick them by telling them that we like men better, and they don't like the idea of us becoming *tuutz*, so they agree to obey us.

LUIS: Oh how smart. That's just what we did, too. I told them what to do.

ROSA: Is that so?

ANTONIO: Yes, he gave us that good advice, and now we're free of our wives.

JUAN: (*Speaking drunkenly*) Girl, bring me six more beers!

WAITRESS: (*She enters, bringing the beers.*) Here they are, sweetie.

JUAN: Thanks, honey.

TERESA: (*Angrily*) I've heard enough of honeys!

JUAN: Get that! It's like you sure seem jealous!

TERESA: I already told you I'm jealous, but it's over that waitress.

ANTONIO: Luis, come over here, I want to talk to you. (*They get up from the table, holding on to each other, and speak facing the public, so that the others won't hear them.*) You know, Luis, I've something I want to tell you.

LUIS: Tell me!

ANTONIO: Have you noticed the one called Anastasio?

LUIS: Yes, what about him?

ANTONIO: I've been looking at him and I like him a lot. I don't know, but I think I might be *tuutz*.

LUIS: (*Surprised*) You don't say! Something strange is happening to me, too. The one who is sitting next to Anastasio turns me on, too.

ANTONIO: (*Shocked*) Do you think now that we're *tuutz*?

JUAN: (*He approaches them.*) What are you guys doing? What are you talking about?

ANTONIO: I'm telling you, Luis, I think we're becoming *tuutz*.

JUAN: Why do you say that?

ANTONIO: We like those guys so much who are sitting with us.

JUAN: What a coincidence! The same is happening to me. I like that guy who is sitting next to me, and when he looks at me, I like him better and better.

ANTONIO: Maybe it's because we're a little drunk.

JUAN: Let's hope that's the reason, because I don't want to start loving men. Can you imagine living with a man?

TERESA: You see, *comadres*, our damned husbands were tricking us, just so we'd stop bossing them around. They pretended to be *tuutz*, but they never thought we'd find them out.

ANA: Yes, but you know, my husband likes me, because he said so!

TERESA: What did you expect? They love us.

ROSA: (*Speaking a bit drunkenly*) Well, this is starting to make me dizzy.

TERESA: Me too, but we shouldn't stop because we're paying for it. Miss, bring us six more beers!

WAITRESS: Yes, handsome!

TERESA: Don't you call me "handsome"!

WAITRESS: Don't you like sexy women like me?

TERESA: Yes I do, but I don't like your calling me "handsome."

WAITRESS: But see what you're missing! (*She lifts her skirt to show off her legs and goes for the beers.*)

ANTONIO: Well, let's go and drink with our friends. (*They return to the table.*)

LUIS: Oh, I don't know. I don't like that. It's better if we leave here before we get the hots for them.

ROSA: Here they come.

JUAN: We're back.

ANA: What's the matter? Don't you think we're really hot?

LUIS: Yes, you make us happy.

JUAN: You know, there's something I want to tell you.

EVERYONE: What?

JUAN: It's that . . . now you, what's your name? Excuse me. (*He turns to Teresa.*)

TERESA: My name is Tomás!

JUAN: You know what, Tomás? I like you a lot. I think I'm falling in love with you!

TERESA: Yes? I like you, too!

JUAN: I liked you since I first saw you. You looked as if you would be like a woman for me.

TERESA: And I thought, a man for me. (*They embrace each other.*)

ANA: As for me, I like Antonio a lot!

ANTONIO: That's great because I like you a lot, too. (*They embrace each other.*)

ROSA: Before I tell you that I like Luis a lot, I want to tell you that we are your wives. (*They take off their caps.*)

THE COMPADRES: (*Surprised*) Oh, ho, ho! Now we're okay! Now we'll give the orders!

TERESA: And it's not because we don't want you to be free, but it's because we think it's the right thing. But only if we women can also give our opinions and say what we think so long as you'll still love us! Today we found out the truth. (*Everyone embraces each other.*) At last we'll live a happy life!

EVERYONE: (*To audience*) Thanks a lot!

APPENDIX 1

Individuals Referred to in the Text

NAME		ETHNICITY	COMMUNITY
Albina	Albina Gómez López	Tzeltal	Huixtán
Antun	Antonio de la Torre López	Tzotzil	Zinacantán
Antzelmo	Mariano Audelino Pérez Pérez	Tzotzil	Zinacantán
Chavela	Isabel Juárez Espinosa	Tzeltal	Aguacatenango
Chep	José Leopoldo Hernández Hernández	Tzotzil	Chamula
Ermenejildo	Hermenegildo Sánchez Guzmán	Tzeltal	Tenejapa
Kristobal	Cristóbal Guzmán Meza	Tzeltal	Tenejapa
Leti	Leticia Méndez Intzín	Tzeltal	Tenejapa
Manvel	Manuel Pérez Hernández	Tzotzil	Zinacantán
María	María Hernández Jiménez	Tzotzil	Chamula
Margarita	Margarita López Hernández	Tzotzil	Zinacantán
Markarita	Mónica Margarita de la Cruz López	Tzotzil	Zinacantán
Maruch	Maruch Sántiz Gómez	Tzotzil	Chamula
Maryan	Mariano López Méndez (Maryan Kalixto)	Tzotzil	Chamula
Maryan 2	Mariano de la Torre Sánchez	Tzotzil	Zinacantán
Matyo	Mateo Pérez Pérez	Tzotzil	Chamula
Palas	Francisco Álvarez Quiñones	Spanish	San Cristóbal
Palas 2	Francisco Javier Hernández Pérez	Tzotzil	Zinacantán
Petu'	Petrona de la Cruz Cruz	Tzotzil	Zinacantán
Petul	Pedro Sántiz Guzmán	Tzeltal	Cancuc
Roge	Rogelio Román Hernández Cruz	Tzotzil	Zinacantán
Rosa	Rosa Aguilar Ruíz	Tzeltal	Oxchuc
Rosenta	María Rósenda de la Cruz Vázquez	Tzotzil	Zinacantán
Sokoro	Socorro Gómez Hernández	Tzotzil	Chamula
Tumin	Domingo Pérez Sánchez	Tzotzil	Chamula
Tumin 2	Domingo Gómez Castellanos	Tzotzil	Chamula
Tziak	Diego Méndez Guzmán	Tzeltal	Tenejapa
Umberto	Humberto Jiménez Pérez	Tzotzil	Chamula
Viktoria	Victoria Muñoz	Tzotzil	Chamula
Xap	Sebastián Ramírez Intzín	Tzeltal	Tenejapa
Xpet	Petrona Guzmán Velasco	Tzeltal	Tenejapa
Xun	Juan Benito de la Torre López	Tzotzil	Zinacantán
Xun 2	Juan Pérez Vázquez	Tzeltal	Cancuc

Members and Former Members
of Sna Jtz'ibajom

NAME	ETHNICITY	COMMUNITY	DATES
1. Aguilar Ruíz, Rosa	Tzeltal	Cancuc	1992
2. Álvarez Quiñones, Francisco	Spanish	San Cristóbal	1987–2002
3. Coello Rodríguez, Antonio	Spanish	San Cristóbal	2002–2006
4. De la Cruz Cruz, Petrona	Tzotzil	Zinacantán	1989–1992
5. De la Cruz López, Mónica Margarita	Tzotzil	Zinacantán	1993–1994
6. De la Cruz Trinidad, Berthier	Spanish	Tabasco	1999–2002
7. De la Cruz Vázquez, María Rosenda	Tzotzil	Zinacantán	1995–2006
8. De la Torre López, Antonio	Tzotzil	Zinacantán	1987–1999
9. De la Torre López, Juan Benito	Tzotzil	Zinacantán	1983–2006
10. Girón Hernández, Pedro	Tzeltal	Tenejapa	1983
11. Gómez Castellanos, Domingo	Tzotzil	Chamula	1992–1994
12. Gómez Gómez, Diego	Tzotzil	Chamula	2000–2001
13. Gómez Hernández, Socorro	Tzotzil	Chamula	2001–2006
14. Gómez López, Albina	Tzeltal	Huixtán	1991–1992
15. Gómez Pérez, Mariano	Tzotzil	Zinacantán	1989
16. González Sánchez, María	Tzotzil	Zinacantán	2006
17. Guzmán Velasco, Petrona	Tzeltal	Tenejapa	2000–2002
18. Heredia Hernández, Domingo	Tzotzil	Chamula	1983–1984
19. Hernández Gómez, Francisco	Tzotzil	Zinacantán	1999–2000
20. Hernández Hernández, José Leopoldo	Tzotzil	Chamula	2002–2006
21. Hernández Hernández, Ramiro	Tzotzil	Chamula	1990–1999
22. Hernández Jiménez, María	Tzotzil	Chamula	1995–2000
23. Hernández Pérez, Francisco Javier	Tzotzil	Zinacantán	1992–1993
24. Jiménez Guzmán, Lilia	Tzeltal	Tenejapa	2002–2006
25. Jiménez Pérez, Humberto	Tzotzil	Chamula	1996–1997
26. Juárez Espinosa, Isabel	Tzeltal	Aguacatenango	1983–1992
27. López de la Cruz, Mariano Roberto	Tzotzil	Zinacantán	1993–1998

NAME	ETHNICITY	COMMUNITY	DATES
28. López Hérnandez, Margarita	Tzotzil	Zinacantán	1994–1995
29. López Intzín, Rosa	Tzeltal	Tenejapa	1998
30. López Jiménez, Petrona	Tzotzil	Chamula	1999–2000
31. López Méndez, Mariano	Tzotzil	Chamula	1983–1994
32. López Pérez, Catalina	Tzotzil	Pantelhó	1989
33. Luna Pérez, Juan Carlos	Tzotzil	Chamula	2002–2006
34. Melo de Rosas, Alfredo	Spanish	San Cristóbal	1987
35. Méndez Gómez, Elena	Tzeltal	Tenejapa	1992
36. Méndez Guzmán, Diego	Tzeltal	Tenejapa	1984–2006
37. Méndez Intzín, Leticia	Tzeltal	Tenejapa	1996–2004
38. Meza, Antonio	Tzeltal	Tenejapa	1987
39. Meza López, Antonia	Tzeltal	Tenejapa	1992
40. Muñoz, Victoria	Tzotzil	Chamula	1990
41. Muñoz Gómez, Juan	Tzotzil	Chamula	1998–2006
42. Pérez Hernández, Manuel	Tzotzil	Zinacantán	1987–1992
43. Pérez Patixtán, Juana	Tzotzil	Chamula	1992
44. Pérez Pérez, Manuel	Tzotzil	Zinacantán	1989
45. Pérez Pérez, Mariano Audelino	Tzotzil	Zinacantán	1983–1997
46. Pérez Pérez, Mateo	Tzotzil	Chamula	1985–1989
47. Pérez Sánchez, Domingo	Tzotzil	Chamula	1995–2001
48. Pérez Vázquez, Juan	Tzeltal	Cancuc	1992
49. Ramírez Intzín, Sebastián	Tzeltal	Tenejapa	1983–1986
50. Sánchez Gómez, Artemio	Tzeltal	Oxchuc	1988
51. Sánchez Guzmán, Hermenegildo	Tzeltal	Tenejapa	1993–1999
52. Sántiz Girón, Lucia	Tzeltal	Tenejapa	1995–1996
53. Sántiz Girón, Margarita	Tzeltal	Tenejapa	1996
54. Sántiz Gómez, Maruch	Tzotzil	Chamula	1993–1996
55. Xilón Gómez, Francisco	Tzotzil	Chamula	1989–1992

Length of Service

YEARS	INDIVIDUALS
21	1
20	1
15	1
14	1
12	1
11	2
10	1
9	2
8	1
5	3
4	3
3	5
2	5
1	10

MONTHS	INDIVIDUALS
6–9	6
2–6	7
1	5

Glossary

besote: big kiss
caballo: horse
cabello: hair
cabrón: sonofabitch
cacique: political boss
campesino: farmer
caporal: foreman
carajo: Damn it!
caray: Damn it!
Casa de Cultura: town cultural center
charro: cowboy
chingadera: fucking stuff
coleto: non-Indian inhabitant of San Cristóbal
comadre: co-godmother
compadre: co-godfather
compañero: companion
coyote: smuggler of people
curandero: shaman
finca: coffee plantation
finquero: coffee plantation owner
hasta luego: good-bye
hermano: compatriot
hijo: son
ich'o: Cheers!
kich'ban: Cheers!

kumale: comadre
kumpa: compadre
kumpare: compadre
ladino: mestizo, non-Indian
madrecita: nun
maestro: teacher
maystro: teacher
migra: immigration official
muchacha: girl
muchacho: boy
muertito: dead man
paisano: compatriot
patrón: boss
patrona: female boss
pendejo: jerk
petate: woven mat
pinka: finca (coffee plantation)
pox: cane liquor
pozol: corn gruel
premio: prize
presidente: mayor
puta: prostitute
síndico: trade union
trago: cane liquor
tuutz: gay
vieja: old woman, wife
Zapatismo: Zapatista movement

Bibliography

LETTERS

Letters from Robert Laughlin to:
Robert Adams, February 26, 1990
Patrick Breslin, February 23, 1992
Norman Collins, 1996
John B. Haviland, February 23, 1992
Alice Jaffé, July 8, 1993
Ledlie I. Laughlin Jr., February 25, 1992
Ralph Lee, July 10, 1993; September 12, 1993
Richard Lewis, February 29, 1992
Janet McAlpin, March 10, 1989
Josephine Merck, March 2, 1991
Pat Mora, April 26, 1990
Diana Negroponte, March 24, 1992
Jillian Steiner Sandrock, July 19, 1990
Evon Z. Vogt, February 23, 1992
Jack Warner, June 29, 1995
Lucinda Ziesing, February 23, 1991

PUBLICATIONS

Arzápalo Marín, Ramón
1987 *El ritual de los Bacabes.* Mexico City: Universidad Nacional Autónoma de México.

Aubry, Andrés
2004 "El templo de San Nicolás de los morenos." *Mesoamérica* 46: 135–151.

Barrera Vásquez, Alfredo
1965 *El libro de los cantares de Dzibalché.* Mexico City: Instituto Nacional de Antropología e Historia.

Blaffer, Sarah C.

> 1972 *The Black-man of Zinacantán: A Central American Legend.* Austin: University of Texas Press.

Breslin, Patrick

> 1994 "Coping with Change: The Maya Discover the Play's the Thing." *Smithsonian Magazine* (May 1994): 78–87.

Bricker, Victoria R.

> 1981 *The Indian Christ, the Indian King: The Historical Substrate of Maya Myth and Ritual.* Austin: University of Texas Press.

Channing, Teague

> 2002 "Loud and Clear: The Sna Jtz'ibajom Project." *Cultural Survival Quarterly* (Fall 2002): 60–61.

Christianson, Allen J. (trans. and ed.)

> 2000 *Popol Vuh: The Mythic Sections—Tales of First Beginnings from the Ancient K'iche'-Maya.* Provo, Utah: Brigham Young University.

Cook, Garrett W.

> 2000 *Renewing the Maya World: Expressive Culture in a Highland Town.* Austin: University of Texas Press.

Costantino, Rosalyn, and Diana Taylor

> 2003 *Holy Terrors: Latin American Women Perform.* Durham, North Carolina: Duke University Press.

Craig, Siena

> 1963 *El libro de los libros de Chilam Balam.* Mexico City: Fondo de Cultura Económica.
> 1993 "Maya Dreams: Pride and Resistance in the Highlands." *Summit*: 60–69.

Cruz, Petrona de la Cruz

> 2003 "A Desperate Woman: A Play in Two Acts." In *Holy Terrors: Latin American Women Perform,* ed. Rosalyn Costantino and Diana Taylor, 213–234. Durham, North Carolina: Duke University Press.

Currin, Brenda

> 1994 "Monkey Business in the Subjunctive: The Play of the Liminal and Liminoid in Two Rituals, Three Tragicomedies and One Revolution." Master's thesis, City College of New York.

de Landa, Diego

> 1978 *Yucatan Before and After the Conquest (Relación de las cosas de Yucatan).* Trans. and with notes by William Gates. New York: Dover.

Favre, Henri

　1971　*Changement et continuité chez les Mayas du Mexique: Contributión a l'etude de la situation coloniale en Amérique latine.* Paris: Éditions Anthropos.

Frischmann, Donald H.

　1991　"Active Ethnicity: Nativism, Otherness, and Indian Theatre in Mexico." *Gestos* (University of California, Irvine) 6(11): 113–126.

　1992　"El nuevo teatro maya de Yucatán y Chiapas: Grupos Sac Nicté y Sna Jtz'ibajom." *Tramoya Cuaderno de Teatro* (Universidad Veracruzana/Rutgers University) 33 (Oct.–Dec.): 53–78.

　1994a　"New Mayan Theatre in Chiapas: Anthropology, Literacy, and Social Drama." In *Negotiating Performance: Gender, Sexuality, and Theatricality in Latin/o America,* ed. Diana Taylor and Juan Villegas, 213–238. Durham and London: Duke University Press.

　1994b　"Social Movements, Transformations and Stage Drama." *Pacific Coast Philology* 29(1): 126–127.

　1995　"Contemporary Mayan Theatre and Ethnic Conflict: The Recovery and (Re)Interpretation of History." In *Imperialism and Theatre: Essays on World Theatre, Drama and Performance, 1795–1995,* ed. J. Ellen Gainor. London and New York: Routledge Press.

　1996　"Ecos del 'Pop Wuj': Desde Honduras hasta Nueva York." *Istmica* 2: 108–123. Heredia, Costa Rica: Universidad Nacional de Costa Rica.

　1997　"La montaña chiapaneca es el teatro: Lo'il Maxil presenta el 'De todos para todos.'" *La Escena Latinoamericana III* (Summer): 5–6, 46–51. Mexico City: Universidad Iberoamericana.

　2001　"La construcción del sujeto poscolonial en el discurso escénico maya contemporáneo de México." *Tramoya Cuaderno de Teatro* (Universidad Veracruzana/Rutgers University) 68 (July–Sept. 2001): 102–116.

Karttunen, Frances

　1998　"Indigenous Writing as a Vehicle of Continuity and Change in Mesoamerica." In *Native Traditions in the Postconquest World,* ed. Elizabeth Hill Boone and Tom Cummins, 421–447. Washington, D.C.: Dumbarton Oaks Research Library and Collection.

Laughlin, Miriam (Wolfe)

　1991　"Arts: The Drama of Mayan Women." *Ms.* 2(1): 88–89.

　1991　"Up Front." *Radcliffe in Latin America and the Caribbean* (1991): 30–31. Cambridge, Massachusetts.

　1991/1992　"Mayan Women Playwrights." *Belle Lettres* (Winter): 45, 47.

Laughlin, Robert M.

1975 *The Great Tzotzil Dictionary of San Lorenzo Zinacantán.* Smithsonian Contributions to Anthropology no. 19. Washington, D.C.: Smithsonian Institution Press.

1976 *Of Wonders Wild and New: Dreams from Zinacantán.* Smithsonian Contributions to Anthropology no. 22. Washington, D.C.: Smithsonian Institution Press.

1977 *Of Cabbages and Kings: Tales from Zinacantán.* Smithsonian Contributions to Anthropology no. 23. Washington, D.C.: Smithsonian Institution Press.

1992 "The Mayan Renaissance: Sna Jtz'Ibajom [*sic*], the House of the Writer." In *Native American Cultures: Before and After Columbus,* ed. Yvonne Singer, 8, 12. Honolulu: University of Hawaii Press.

1995 "From All for All." *American Anthropologist* 97(3): 528–542.

1999 "We Are the Real People: Tzotzil-Tzeltal Maya Storytelling on the Stage." In *Traditional Storytelling Today: An International Sourcebook,* ed. Margaret Read MacDonald. Chicago and London: Fitzroy Dearborn Publishers.

2002 *Diccionario del corazón/Mayan Hearts.* San Cristóbal de las Casas: Taller Leñateros.

2002–2003 *Unmasking the Maya: The Story of Sna Jtz'ibajom.* www.mnh.si.edu/anthro/maya/

Laughlin, Robert M., and John B. Haviland

1988 *The Great Tzotzil Dictionary of Santo Domingo Zinacantán: With Grammatical Analysis and Historical Commentary.* 3 vols. Smithsonian Contributions to Anthropology no. 31. Washington, D.C.: Smithsonian Institution Press.

Menchú, Rigoberta

1984 *I, Rigoberta Menchú, an Indian Woman in Guatemala.* Ed. and intro. by Elisabeth Burgo-Debray, trans. Ann Wright. London: Verso.

Montemayor, Carlos (ed.)

1996a "Xcha'kuxesel ak'ob elav ta slumal batz'i viniketik ta Chyapa I." *Renacimiento del teatro maya en Chiapas I. Sna Jtz'ibajom, Colección letras mayas contemporáneas: Chiapas,* 1. Mexico City: Instituto Nacional Indigenista.

1996b "Xcha'kuxesel ak'ob elav ta slumal batz'i viniketik ta Chyapa II." *Renacimiento del teatro maya en Chiapas II. Sna Jtz'ibajom, Colección letras mayas contemporáneas: Chiapas,* 2. Mexico City: Instituto Nacional Indigenista.

1996c "Xcha'kuxesel ak'ob elav ta slumal batz'i viniketik ta Chyapa III." *Renacimiento del teatro maya en Chiapas III. Sna Jtz'ibajom, Colección letras mayas contemporáneas: Chiapas,* 3. Mexico City: Instituto Nacional Indigenista.

Montemayor, Carlos, and Donald Frischmann (eds.)

2007 *Word of the True Peoples/Palabras de los Seres Verdaderos: Anthology of Contemporary Mexican Indigenous-Language Writers/Antología de Escritores Actuales in Lenguas Indígenas de México. Volume Three/Tomo Tres: Theater/Teatro.* Austin: University of Texas Press.

Ordoñez y Aguiar, Ramón

1907 "Historia de la creación del cielo y de la tierra." Mexico City.

Past, Ámbar

2005 "She of Great Writing, She of the Glyphs." In *Incantations by Mayan Women,* ed. Ámbar Past, with Xun Okotz and Xpetra Ernández. San Cristóbal de las Casas, Chis.: Taller de los Leñateros.

Payne, Alan W.

1932 "Calendar and Nagualism of the Tzeltals." *Maya Society Quarterly* 1: 56–64.

Pérez Hérnandez, Manuel

1992 "Vivencias de nuestra palabra: El resurgimiento de la cultura maya en Chiapas." In *Los escritores indígenas actuales II,* ed. Carlos Montemayor, 7–102. Mexico City: Fondo Editorial Tierra Adentro, Consejo Nacional para la Cultura y las Artes.

Rojas, Rosa

1993 "Blick zuruch nach vorn." *Geo Special, Die Welt der Maya* 5 (October): 46–55.

Santoro, William A., Karl A. Taube, and David Stuart

2005 "The Murals of San Bartolo, El Petén, Guatemala: Part 1, The North Wall." *Ancient America* 7. Barnardsville, North Carolina: Center for Ancient American Studies.

Steele, Cynthia

1993 "Indigenismo y posmodernidad: Narrativa indigenista, testimonio, teatro campesino y video en el Chiapas finisecular." *Revista de Crítica Literaria Latinoamericana* (Lima) 19(38): 249–260.

1994 "'A Woman Fell into the River': Negotiating Female Subjects in Contemporary Mayan Theatre." In *Negotiating Performance: Gender, Sexuality, and Theatricality in Latin/o America,* ed. Diana Taylor and Juan Villegas, 239–256. Durham and London: Duke University Press.

1994 "Indigenous Rights, Women's Rights, Human Rights: Mayan Politics and Theater in Chiapas." *Pacific Coast Philology* 29(1): 119–123.

Taube, Karl

1989 "Ritual Humor in Classic Maya Religion." In *Explorations in Language, Writing, and Culture,* ed. William Hanks and Donald Rice, 351–382. Salt Lake City: University of Utah Press.

Tedlock, Dennis (trans. and interp.)

2003 *Rabinal Achí: A Mayan Drama of War and Sacrifice.* Oxford, New York: Oxford University Press.

Underiner, Tamara L.

1998 "Incidents of Theatre in Chiapas, Tabasco, and Yucatán: Cultural Enactments in Mayan Mexico." *Theatre Journal* 50: 349–369.

2004 *Contemporary Theatre in Mayan Mexico: Death-defying Acts.* Austin: University of Texas Press.

Webster's

1955 *Webster's New World Dictionary of the American Language.* Cleveland and New York: World Publishing.

Ximénes, Francisco

1929–1931 *Historia de la provincia de San Vicente de Chiapa y Guatemala de la orden de nuestro glorioso padre Santo Domingo.* 3 vols. Guatemala City: [Tipografía Nacional].

NEWSPAPER ARTICLES

Acosta, Mariclaire

1997 "El camino largo hasta la 5.25." *La Jornada, Derechos Humanos y Ciudadanía,* 9.

Angulo, Gildo Gonzáles

1996 "El teatro como elemento para conocer mejor la vida: Comienzan a despuntar los talentos." *Por Esto!* (Mérida, Yucatán), September 4.

Bergen, Mark

1984 "Trio Takes Icy Potomac Plunge." *Alexandria Gazette,* April 18.

Blake, Catherine

1997 "Actors Focus on Life in Immokalee: A Mayan Troupe Finds the Humor in Local Troubles as It Performs for a Farmworkers' Group." *Naples Daily News,* January 23.

Burnham, Philip

  2003 "Monkey Business Brings Traditional Stories to Life." *Indian Country Today* (Santa Fe, New Mexico), March 19.

Cadena, Alberto Rocha

  1985 "Tradición y artesanía indígenas de 6 estados, unidos en una protesta: 'Diremos al Presidente que las companias japonesas se enriquecen mientras nosotros empobrecemos más.'" *El Universal* (Mexico City), December 16.

Derbez, Edmundo

  1990 "Indígenas llevan a los escenarios su marginación." *El Diario de Monterrey*, September 28.

Frischmann Carril, Donald

  1995 "'De Todos para Todos,' Lo'il Maxil: La Montaña Chiapaneca es el teatro." *La Semana de Fort Worth*, September 22.

Godínez, Miguel Angel

  1989 "Sna Jtz'ibajom." *Avante* (San Cristóbal de las Casas), February 3.

Hanifin, Cynthia

  1999 "Mayan Dancers Pay Tribute to Great Creator." *Milwaukee Journal Sentinel*, September 10.

Hernández, Rubén

  1997 "Act 1 for New Farmworker Theater Troupe in Immokalee: The New Group Hopes to Share Problems and Find Solutions through Artistic Expression." *Naples Daily News*, March 24.

Kleist, Trina

  1998 "Indian Cultural Revival Gains Strength in Mexico." *Austin American Statesman*, January 4.

Lazo, Carmen Hernan

  1989 "Necesario estimular la creación literaria y dramática de los indígenas ante la pérdida de sus identidades." *Ámbar Semanal* (Tuxtla Gutiérrez), August 14.

Leñero, Estela

  1990 "Teatro indígena en los altos de Chiapas." *Uno Más Uno* (Mexico City), January 25.

Loohauis, Jackie

  1999 "Crossing Cultures: Indian Summer Brings Together Nations of the New World." *Milwaukee Journal Sentinel*, September 8.

Mendieta, Ana

    1995 "Una historia indígena contada por indígenas." *¡Éxito!* (Chicago), April 20.

Monteverde, Eduardo

    1994 "El teatro indio recrea la Guerra de Chiapas." *De Par en Par,* March 21.

Pacheco, Reynaldo

    2004 "The World Paralyzed." *Wabash Magazine* (Winter).

Paul, Carlos, and Mónica Mateos

    1997 "El teatro que hacemos es para la verdadera humanidad: De la Cruz." *La Jornada* (Mexico City), June 27.

Ruta, Suzanne

    1994 "Writers and Rebels: In Southern Mexico They Are Much the Same." *New York Times Book Review,* February 13.

Sachs, Andrea

    1994 "Group Aims to Strengthen Mayan Culture." *Imperial Valley Press* (El Centro, California), October 4.

Sandstrom, Karen

    1992 "Mayan Puppets Act Out a Lesson." *Cleveland Plain Dealer,* October 27.

Schwartz Parnés, Janet

    2002 "Desenmascarando a los mayas." *Diario de Chiapas* (San Cristóbal de las Casas), January 26.

    2002 "En un imperio moderno los mayas escondidos." *La República en Chiapas* (Tuxtla Gutiérrez), January 26.

Sesín, Saide

    1988 "Escritores, artesanos y actores en defensa de la cultura maya: Sna Jtz'ibajom busca el apoyo económico del centro para frenar la desvaloración cultural en Chiapas." *Uno Más Uno* (Mexico City), March 1.

Weiss, Hedy

    1995 "Mayan Troupe Debuts." *Chicago Sun-Times,* April 20.

Williams, Albert

    1995 "Teatro Lo'il Maxil." *Chicago Reader,* April 21.

VIDEOS

Coello, Antonio

> 2003   *El rey de Zinacantán/Jk'ulej ta Sots'leb.*

Martínez, Carlos

> 1990   *A poco hay cimarrones? Comedia tzotzil.* January. 63 min.
>
> 1992   *Herencia fatal: Drama tzotzil.* April. 63 min.
>
> 1993   *El haragán y el zopilote: Farsa tzotzil.* May. 43 min.

Index

xiii, 75; Monkey Business Theatre performances in, 28, 29, 122; and support for Monkey Business Theatre, 16, 23, 41, 100; women in, 25–26, 150, 152, and Zapatista occupation, xv

Chicago, Illinois, 21–22, 30

Chichén Itzá, 14

Christians. *See* Fundamentalist Christians

Christ I Never Knew You, 11, 197

cimarrones, xxiv, 59–61, *68*, *71*

Cleveland, Ohio, 30

clothing. *See* costuming

Coalition of Immokalee Workers, 19, 33–36, 39, 225

Coello, Antonio, 16, 42

coletos auténticos, 13, 225

Cook, Garret W., xix

costuming, 23, 46, 75

Coxquihui, Mexico, festival in, 17

Craig, Siena, 100

Cruz Cruz, Petrona de la (Petu'), 10, 15, 18, 61, 62, 75, 77; as director, 28; and FOMMA, xxvi, 28, 76; on theatre, 27, 30, 100; on women in Chiapas, 25–26

Cruz López, Mónica Margarita de la (Markarita), 26

Cruz Vázquez, María Rosenda de la (Rosenta), 21, 23; on acting, 26; on labor, 38

Cuando menos burros, más elotes, 28

Cultural Survival, 3

dance, xxv, 100

Dance of the Trumpets. *See Rabinal Achí: A Mayan Drama of War and Sacrifice*

Deadly Inheritance, 24, 26

Desperate Woman, A. See Una mujer desesperada

Devil Priest, The, 7

Diccionario del corazón, 281

Don Tomate y sus coyotes, 34, 35, 225

Ejército Zapatista de Liberación Nacionál (EZLN), xv, xx, 38, 149

ejido system, xiv

El Ocote, 153

El Porvenir, Mexico, 18

English language, xiii; Monkey Business Theatre plays in, 11, 225

Ermenejildo. *See* Sánchez Guzmán, Hermenegildo

Experiment in International Living, 30, 76

EZLN. *See* Ejército Zapatista de Liberación Nacionál (EZLN)

family planning, 28

festivals, xviii–xix, 17, 30; in Coxquihui, 17; K'inal Winik festival, 7; Maya-Zoque festival, 20

fiestas. *See* festivals

Florida Legal Services, 34

FOMMA. *See* Fortaleza de la Mujer Maya

Fortaleza de la Mujer Maya (FOMMA), xxvi, 27, 76, 261; creation of, 28

Fox, Vicente, 42

Frischmann, Donald, 31, 40, 76–77

From All for All, xvi, xix, xxv, 19, 27, 33–34, 38; new version of, 42

Fundación Mexicana de Planificación Familiar (Mexfam), 28

Fundamentalist Christians, 14–15, 197

Gala Hispanic Theater, 30

Garcés, Michael, *xxviii*, 28, 261

Business Theatre, xvi, xxvi, 10–11, 61–62
Laurel Theater, 30
Lee, Ralph, *xxvii*, 3, 9–11, 61, 100, 149, 150, 247; masks of, 11, 35, 45; as writer, 10–11, 34, 76
Leti. *See* Méndez Intzín, Leticia (Leti)
Let's Go to Paradise, xiii, xvi, xxiv–xxv
libro de los cantares de Dzilbalché, El, xiii
libro de los libros de Chilam Balam, El, xiii
Long-Haired Devil, 7
López, Juan, 151
López Hernández, Margarita, 24
López Méndez, Mariano (Maryan), xxii, xxiii, 6, 20, 25, 62, 121; on impact of theatre, 23–24
Lost Kingdoms of the Maya, 15

Malpaso, Mexico, 152
Mam people, 45
Maní, Mexico, x
Manvel. *See* Pérez Hernández, Manuel
Marcos, Subcomandante, xx, 41, 149, 150, 151, 154
Margarita. *See* López Hernández, Margarita
Margaritas, Mexico, 198
María. *See* Hernández Jiménez, María
Markarita. *See* Cruz López, Mónica Margarita de la
Martínez, Carlos, 46, 62, 77
Maruch. *See* Sántiz Gómez, Maruch
Maryan. *See* López Méndez, Mariano
Maryan 2. *See* Torre Sánchez, Mariano de la (Maryan 2)
masks, xxv–xxvi, 11. *See also under* Lee, Ralph
Matyo. *See* Pérez Pérez, Mateo
max, xix
Maya literature, and the divine, xi. *See also specific works*

Mayan alphabet: development of new, xii; standardization of, 8
Mayan Hearts. See Diccionario del corazón
Mayan languages: and INI, xiv, 173–174; preservation of, xiii, xv, 28–29. *See also specific languages*
Mayan literacy, 173–174, 198; during colonial period, x; among non-elites, xi; preservation of, x, 174
Maya peoples: and AIDS, 226; family dynamics of, 75; and performance culture, xvii–xviii, 3, 23, 76–77; relationship with other ethnic groups, 11–12; and social mores, 10. *See also specific groups*
Maya religion: in art, xviii; Maya Christianity and Catholicism, 25, 197–198; and performance culture, xviii–xix
Maya-Zoque festival, 20
Mazariegos, Diego de, 173; toppling of statue of, xv
Menchú, Rigoberta, xiii
Méndez Guzmán, Diego (Tziak), xxiii, xxv, 6, 15, 16, 18, 20–21, 27, 75, 151; as director, 28; on Immokalee, 36; on Zapatista movement, 38, 149
Méndez Intzín, Leticia (Leti), 26–27, 35
Men with Guns, 15–16
Mérida, Mexico, 14, 27
Mesa Redonda, 30, 100
Mexfam. *See* Fundación Mexicana de Planificación Familiar
Mexico, xiii, 7, 40, 153, 173, 261. *See also specific states and cities*
Mexico City, 18–19, 30, 261, 281
Milwaukee, Wisconsin, 30
mimesis, xvii
Mixtec people, 45
Momostenango, Guatemala, xviii

Monkey Business Theatre: demographics of theatre members, 12; difficulties of membership in, 13; DVDs of, 16; first performances of, 4–8; and Immokalee, Florida, 33; impact of on actors, 23–24, 26–28, 36–40; impact of on community, 28–31, 34, 35, 100; and the indigenous perspective, xx; languages used by in performance, xvi, 10–11; and Ralph Lee, 9–11; length of service of theatre members, 12–13; multicultural outreach of, 30; plays of, generally, 10; political alignment of, xvi, 41–42; puppetry and, 4–8; and staging, 14, support for, 41; touring, difficulties of, 17–21; touring, in Mexico, xxiv, 6–7, 13–15, 17–19, 20–21, 30, 151–154; touring, in U.S., 7, 19–20, 21–22, 30, 33–36; writing process of, 10–11

monkeys. See *max*

Morris, Chip, xxiii

Motozintla, Mexico, 20

Muñoz, Victoria (Viktoria), 61

Muslims. See Islam

Na Bolom, xiii

NAFTA. *See* North American Free Trade Agreement

Nana María Cocorina, xix

National Endowment for the Humanities Summer Institute, 30

National Geographic, 15

New York City, New York, 9, 30

North American Free Trade Agreement (NAFTA), 30, 36, 149

Of Cabbages and Kings: Tales from Zinacantán, 59

Of Shoes and Ships and Sealing Wax, 1

orígen del maíz, El. See *When Corn Was Born*

Origin of Corn, The, 247

Oxchuc, Mexico, 60; members of Monkey Business Theatre from, 12

Oxfam International, 41

Pacheco, Reynaldo, 225

Pakal Balam, 99, 100

Palacio de Bellas Artes, 281

Palas. *See* Álvarez Quiñones, Francisco

Palas 2. *See* Hernández Pérez, Francisco Javier

Palenque, Mexico, 13, 30, 99, 100

pan-Mayanism, xv, 154

Pantelhó, Mexico, members of Monkey Business Theatre from, 12

Partido Revolucionario Democrático (PRD), 41

Partido Revolucionario Institucional (PRI), 261

Past, Ambar, xi

Payne, Alan, 60

PBS, 15, 17

Pérez Hernández, Manuel (Manvel), xxii, xxiii, 15, 20–21; on impact of theatre, 28–29; on puppetry, 4–6

Pérez Pérez, Mariano Audelino (Antzelmo), xxiii, xxiv, 1, 4, 6, 7, 8, 15, 20–21

Pérez Pérez, Mateo (Matyo), 6, 8, 23, 197

Pérez Sánchez, Tumin, 15, 35, 152; on traveling, 19

Pérez Vásquez, Juan (Xun 2), 23

Petu'. *See* Cruz Cruz, Petrona de la

Petul. *See* Sántiz Guzmán, Pedro (Petul)

Popol Vuh, xii, 59, 99, 198

Potomac River, 20

PRD. *See* Partido Revolucionario Democrático